International
Environmental
Cooperation

INTERNATIONAL
ENVIRONMENTAL
COOPERATION

Politics
and
Diplomacy
in Pacific Asia

Edited by Paul G. Harris

UNIVERSITY PRESS OF COLORADO

© 2002 by the University Press of Colorado

Published by the University Press of Colorado
5589 Arapahoe Avenue, Suite 206C
Boulder, Colorado 80303

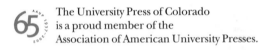

The University Press of Colorado
is a proud member of the
Association of American University Presses.

The University Press of Colorado is a cooperative publishing enterprise supported, in part, by Adams State College, Colorado State University, Fort Lewis College, Mesa State College, Metropolitan State College of Denver, University of Colorado, University of Northern Colorado, University of Southern Colorado, and Western State College of Colorado.

The paper used in this publication meets the minimum requirements of the American National Standard for Information Sciences-Permanence of Paper for Printed Library Materials. ANSI Z39.48-1992

Library of Congress Cataloging-in-Publication Data

International environmental cooperation : politics and diplomacy in Pacific Asia / edited by Paul G. Harris.
    p. cm.
Includes bibliographical references (p.).
  ISBN 0-87081-678-0 (hardcover : alk. paper)
    1. Environmental policy—Asia—International cooperation. 2. Environmental policy—Pacific Area—International cooperation. 3. Pacific Area cooperation.

  GE190.A78 I58 2002
  363.7'0526'095—dc21

                                        2002011502

Design by Daniel Pratt
Typesetting by Laura Furney

11   10   09   08   07   06   05   04   03   02   10 9 8 7 6 5 4 3 2 1

Contents

Contents

PART II: Regime Building, Interstate Cooperation, and Environmental Diplomacy

Illustrations

Contributors

JACK N. BARKENBUS is executive director of the Energy, Environment, and Resources Center at the University of Tennessee.

TODD BISSETT is an Asia specialist practicing corporate and Asian law at O'Melveny & Myers, LLP.

MORTEN BØÅS is a senior research fellow at the Centre for Development and the Environment, University of Oslo.

DONALD A. BROWN is senior counsel for sustainable development in the Pennsylvania Department of Environmental Protection and acting director of the Pennsylvania Consortium for Interdisciplinary Environmental Policy.

LORRAINE ELLIOTT is a fellow in the Department of International Relations at the Australian National University.

PAUL G. HARRIS is an associate professor of politics at Lingnan University, Hong Kong. He directs the Project on Environmental Change and Foreign Policy.

YUE CHOONG KOG is an adjunct professor at the National University of Singapore and president of East-West Engineering Consultants.

SHIN-WHA LEE is a research professor in the Ilmin International Relations Institute at Korea University, Seoul.

ANDREW B. LOEWENSTEIN is an attorney with the law firm of Foley, Hoag, & Eliot, LLP, in Boston.

SANGMIN NAM is a doctoral candidate in the School of Anthropology, Geography, and Environmental Studies at the University of Melbourne and a member of the Policy Committee of Green Korea United.

TOM NÆSS is a researcher at the Fridtjof Nansen Institute, Lysaker, Norway.

ERIC O'MALLEY works in the law firm of Dechert, Price, & Rhoads in New York.

GIOK LING OOI is a senior research fellow at the Institute of Policy Studies and adjunct associate professor at the National University of Singapore.

ALLEN L. SPRINGER is a professor of government and legal studies at Bowdoin College in Brunswick, Maine.

STEPHANIE TAI is an attorney in the Environment and Natural Resources Division of the U.S. Department of Justice.

WAKANA TAKAHASHI is a research associate at the Institute for Global Environmental Strategies in Japan.

SIMON S.C. TAY is an associate professor of international law at the National University of Singapore and chairman of the Singapore Institute of International Affairs.

Acronyms and Abbreviations

AANEA	Atmosphere Action Network East Asia
ADB	Asian Development Bank
ADF	Asian Development Fund
ADORC	Acid Deposition and Oxidant Research Center
APEC	Asia-Pacific Economic Cooperation forum
APN	Asia-Pacific Network for Global Change Research
ARF	ASEAN Regional Forum
ASEAN	Association of Southeast Asian Nations
BTU	British thermal unit
CBM	confidence-building measures
CCP	Chinese Communist Party
CFCs	chlorofluorocarbons
CIDA	Canadian International Development Agency
CITES	Convention on International Trade in Endangered Species
COBSEA	Coordinating Body on the Seas of East Asia
CSCAP	Council for Security Cooperation in the Asia Pacific
CSIS	Centre for Strategic and International Studies
DMCs	developing member countries
DOD	Department of Defense (U.S.)
EABRN	East Asian Biosphere Reserve Network
EANET	Acid Deposition Monitoring Network in East Asia
EC	European Community
ECO-ASIA	Environment Congress for Asia and Pacific
ED	executive director
EEZ	Exclusive Economic Zone
EMEP	European Monitoring and Evaluation Program
EPA	Environmental Protection Agency (U.S.)
ESCAP	United Nations Economic and Social Commission for Asia and the Pacific

EU	European Union
FCCC	Framework Convention on Climate Change
FoE Japan	Friends of the Earth Japan
FSC	Forest Stewardship Council
GAP	gray-area phenomena
GDP	gross domestic product
GEF	Global Environment Facility
GHG	greenhouse gas
IGAC	International Global Atmospheric Chemistry
IIASA	International Institute for Applied System Analysis
IMF	International Monetary Fund
IPCC	Intergovernmental Panel on Climate Change
ISIS	Institutes of Strategic and International Studies
ISO	International Standards Organization
IUCN	International Union for the Conservation of Nature
JEXIM	Japan Export-Import Bank
LRTAP	Convention on Long-Range Transboundary Air Pollution
LTP	Joint Research Project on Long-Range Air Pollutants
MCED	Ministerial Conference on Environment and Development
MEA	Multilateral Environmental Agreement
MICS-ASIA	Model Inter-Comparison Study of Long-Range Transport and Sulfur Deposition in East Asia
MOF	Ministry of Finance (Japan)
mt	metric tons
NAFTA	North American Free Trade Agreement
NATO	North Atlantic Treaty Organization
NEAC	Northeast Asian Sub-regional Program on Environmental Cooperation
NEACEC	North-East Asian Conference on Environmental Cooperation
NEASPEC	Northeast Asian Subregional Program of Environmental Cooperation
NFCP	Natural Forest Conservation Program (China)
NGO	nongovernmental organization
NIER	National Institute of Environmental Research (South Korea)
NOWPAP	Northwest Pacific Action Plan
ODA	official development assistance
OECD	Organization for Economic Cooperation and Development
OENV	Office of the Environment (Asian Development Bank)
PD	preventive diplomacy
ppm	parts per million
PPM	process and production method
PRC	People's Republic of China

RAINS-ASIA	Regional Air Pollution Information and SimulationBAsia
ROK	Republic of Korea (South Korea)
SACEP	South Asia Cooperative Environment Program
SDU	Social Dimensions Unit (Asian Development Bank)
SEAPOL	Southeast Asian Program in Ocean Law, Policy, and Management
SEI	Stockholm Environment Institute
SMEs	small and medium-sized enterprises
tC	tons of carbon equivalent
TDA	transboundary diagnostic analysis
TED	turtle excluder device
TEMM	Tripartite Environment Ministers Meeting of China, Japan, and South Korea
TRADP	Tumen River Area Development Program
TWGMSR	Technical Working Group on Marine Scientific Research
UN	United Nations
UNCED	United Nations Conference on Environment and Development
UNCLOS	United Nations Convention on the Law of the Sea
UNDESA	United Nations Department for Social and Economic Affairs
UNDP	United Nations Development Program
UNECE	United Nations Economic Committee for Europe
UNEP	United Nations Environment Program
UNESCAP	United Nations Economic and Social Commission for Asia and the Pacific
UNESCO	United Nations Educational, Scientific, and Cultural Organization
U.S.	United States
WRI	World Resources Institute
WTO	World Trade Organization
WWF	Worldwide Fund for Nature
YSLME	Yellow Sea Large Marine Ecosystem

I

Introduction:
International Environmental Cooperation
in Pacific Asia

PAUL G. HARRIS

The world is experiencing profound environmental changes and increasing scarcities of natural resources. These problems, ranging from local ones such as water pollution and urban smog to global ones like stratospheric ozone depletion and climate change, are often difficult to understand and even more difficult to solve. Pacific Asia is one region bearing the brunt of many of these environmental problems, and the countries there are also sources of many environmental problems affecting the rest of the world. About a third of the world's people live in this region—many of them very poor—and the region's economies are developing in ways harmful to the natural environment. It is therefore important to understand why the environment is being harmed in this region and how to limit and, one hopes, reverse that harm in the future. The goal of this book is to assist in developing and advancing that understanding. Toward that end, it seeks to share findings of scholarly research on international environmental cooperation in Pacific Asia.

We define Pacific Asia as the region encompassing the states and territories of East and Southeast Asia. The term *Pacific Asia* can have a normative connotation for some, who might read it as "peaceful Asia." This meaning is perhaps fitting because the ideas in this book can help foster international environmental cooperation, which in turn can spill over into other issue areas, thereby contributing to peace within the region. This region is often referred to as *Asia Pacific,* a term most often intended to include all Pacific

I

Rim countries including the Americas and Oceania, which (except for the United States) receive little attention in this volume.

Policymakers in Pacific Asia now realize that major efforts are required to address environmental decline, but their resources are often limited. International cooperation is crucial to strengthen efforts to address these problems, especially those with transboundary causes and consequences. A large body of literature on international environmental cooperation now exists (discussed later). It has helped scholars, policymakers, and stakeholders understand the factors leading to the formation and implementation of international environmental institutions. The body of work focusing on Pacific Asia, however, is rather small (especially in English), and we are only beginning to comprehend the distinctive and idiosyncratic characteristics of the region that affect when and how states there choose to work together in combating environmental pollution and resource scarcities. By bringing under one cover some of the recent work examining international environmental cooperation in Pacific Asia, this book contributes to the research that is filling this gap in our knowledge.

The book is divided into two parts. The first examines many of the issues, themes, and actors important for our understanding of international environmental cooperation among the states of Pacific Asia and between regional actors and the rest of the world. It highlights such important themes as North-South cooperation, international justice, and environmental security; and it illustrates key features of specific multilateral environmental agreements, major state actors, international organizations and financial institutions, multinational corporations, and nongovernmental organizations. Part II looks more directly at international environmental cooperation, regime building, and diplomacy in Pacific Asia—focusing on, among other issues, acid rain, nuclear waste, deforestation, and conflicts over regional seas. All of these themes, actors, and issues—and many more examined in these chapters—are important for improving our understanding of environmental problems in Pacific Asia and the essential means for dealing with them.

In this Introduction I introduce some of the environmental problems facing Pacific Asia. I then summarize some of the research on international cooperation that underlies the chapter case studies. Those familiar with this research may wish to turn directly to the detailed analyses of international environmental cooperation in Pacific Asia found in subsequent chapters.

PACIFIC ASIA'S ENVIRONMENTAL CRISIS

Subsequent chapters paint a detailed picture of environmental conditions in Pacific Asia. Here I briefly introduce some of these conditions and their context to set the stage for case studies of specific states and issues that follow (cf. Harris 2002: 141–142). To be sure, the countries of Pacific Asia are among the most ecologically diverse on earth. Their environmental resources are also among those most threatened by economic development and population pressures. The region is characterized by a diversity of political and economic systems and mostly new international environmental agreements and institutions. The most economically developed countries and regions—Japan, South Korea, Taiwan, Hong Kong, and Singapore—have the resources, if not always the political will, to deal with their own environmental problems and those of other countries in the region. But others—mainland China and most states in Southeast Asia—have limited resources and seek international assistance for environmentally sustainable development.

With few exceptions, in recent decades the populations in the region have increased while economies have been transformed from largely subsistence agriculture to major industrialization and export-driven economic growth. Despite this fast-paced growth in the final decades of the twentieth century, most countries of Pacific Asia have widespread poverty and often very poor living standards. For the most part, the countries of Pacific Asia are low and middle income compared with the most developed parts of the world, and hundreds of millions of people live in extreme poverty. The increasing pollution in the region comes from and alongside what for most countries is the more pressing struggle for economic development. The focus for all states in the region has been economic growth, which has usually come at the expense of the environment. Some of the worst environmental degradation has occurred in those countries with very high recent growth rates, notably China. In Japan, however, the government has been faced with a stagnant economy, but it has shifted toward growth less harmful to the environment.

As described in the United Nations Environment Program's (UNEP) *Global Environmental Outlook 2000* (Clarke 1999: 72–97), the predominant environmental picture of Pacific Asian countries (and indeed of nearly all of Asia) is one of degradation and decline. More specifically, in most states and territories agricultural activities have both been harmed by and exacerbated environmental decline. Forests and other areas that once provided valuable environmental services have been converted into cropland—degrading watersheds, adding to pollution, and often resulting in salinization and desertification (and thus decreased arable land). Urban areas have encroached on cropland, forcing farmers to move to new areas and starting the cycle of environmental degradation once again. In addition to conversion into cropland, the extraction of timber, construction of dams, mining, and expansion of urban areas have depleted forests throughout Pacific Asia. Deforestation leads to destruction or degradation of riparian systems and the loss of species. Biodiversity is further harmed as natural species are utilized for (often illegal) export, replaced by exotic species, and overrun by agricultural activities, tourism, urbanization, industrialization, poaching, and the fragmentation of habitats.

Freshwater is scarce in Pacific Asia, largely because of consumption by agriculture but increasingly by expanding industry and urban areas. Sewage and industrial pollution, agricultural chemicals, and urban runoff are severely degrading the region's freshwater resources. The vast marine and coastal areas are suffering from overfishing, adverse impacts of aquaculture, domestic and industrial effluents, development, land reclamation and dredging, the felling of mangrove forests, sedimentation, and oil pollution. Pacific Asia is also experiencing widespread atmospheric pollution that spreads across the region and beyond. The largest source of this pollution is increasing energy consumption by growing populations using inefficient motor transport that burns low-quality fossil fuels. Atmospheric pollution is manifested in urban smog, acid rain, and growing emissions of greenhouse gases (although in most developing countries of the region per capita greenhouse gas emissions remain far below those of the developed world). In short, much of the region suffers from significant and widespread environmental problems that demand more attention and frequently require international cooperation if they are to be dealt with effectively.

Environmental decline and economic development are not a zero-sum game; policymakers are starting to realize that pollution and overuse of natural resources can harm economic development. The economic costs of environmental destruction have been estimated at 1 to 9 percent of individual countries' economic output (ADB 1997, cited in Clark 1999: 74), and environmental damage has other direct costs. For example, in 1997 the World Bank estimated that excessive pollution caused premature deaths, sickness, and damage to productive resources and urban infrastructure in China, costing about 8 percent of the country's gross domestic product (GDP) (World Bank 1997: 24). According to a 1999 Chinese government report, the total health costs of air and water pollution in China cost the country more than $46 billion—nearly 7 percent of GDP (Pan 2001: 7). These costs are leading to new policy measures to protect the environment within Pacific Asian countries. Additionally, as countries in the region—particularly growing affluent subsections of populations—become more developed economically, there may be increasing calls for controls on pollution and harmful aspects of economic growth (cf. Inglehart 1990). So far, however, successes have been limited, and the environment continues to worsen. According to UNEP, "A 'business as usual' scenario suggests that continued rapid economic growth and industrialization may result in further environmental damage and that the region may become more degraded, less forested, more polluted and less ecologically diverse in the future" (Clarke 1999: 75).

4

Although all states in Pacific Asia are important actors in causing and addressing environmental change, several countries have central importance to regional and global environmental cooperation. For example, Japan, the second-largest economy in the world, enjoys some of the highest standards of living anywhere. It still has polluting industries, manifested in continued water pollution. Its domestic environmental movement is relatively weak—at least compared with the countries of North America and Western Europe—although environmental regulations have drastically reduced pollution. Japan also suffers from pollution of surrounding seas and from acid rain originating particularly in China. This last problem has pushed Japan to increase its international assistance for sustainable development in Pacific Asia, particularly for improved energy efficiency in China. Japan is among the countries most adamant in pushing for renewal of commercial whaling, and its demand for raw wood from Southeast Asia and increasingly in other areas (South America and Siberia) has gained it a dubious reputation in international environmental politics. Like other developed countries and regions, its high levels of consumption contribute to environmental damage farther afield. At the same time, it has taken on a greater role in global environmental diplomacy—for example, acting as a swing state among countries negotiating implementation of the Kyoto Protocol on climate change.

In contrast, Greater China—mainland China, the special administrative regions of Hong Kong and Macao, and Taiwan—is characterized by environmental and developmental diversity. China is the largest country in Pacific Asia and the most populous country in the world. It varies from densely populated, highly developed—and heavily polluted—areas in the Southeast to rural areas noteworthy for stress from decades of intense cultivation. Environmental damage is widespread and is worsening in most areas. The government is increasingly aware of environmental decline and is taking initiatives to reverse that trend, but the focus on economic growth and the sometimes incommensurable goals of the central government, local officials, industries, and the military make policy making and implementation of environmental regulations extremely difficult.

China will soon become the largest emitter of greenhouse gases; hence its path toward economic development is not merely a matter of national concern. In international environmental negotiations China has sought to increase the level of financial assistance from North to South for sustainable development. Although much of mainland China is poor and the large population is not associated with high levels of personal consumption, the same cannot be said of affluent Hong Kong and Taiwan, which draw resources from the region and have high levels of per capita consumption and pollution. The Hong Kong region's government, for its part, is aware of the impact of these factors on lifestyles and on the marketability of Hong Kong as a place to do business and as a tourist destination. Hence it is taking minimal steps to address environmental problems, as is Taiwan—albeit slowly—but in neither case has environmental protection received close to adequate attention.

As will become even clearer in the chapters that follow, environmental pollution and degradation of natural resources in Pacific Asia are having profound adverse effects on the people of the region. Some countries, such as Japan, have adapted and are witnessing improved environmental indicators in many areas. Others—the majority of areas in the region, including almost all urban areas and much of China—are experiencing accelerating adverse environmental changes. In these latter cases international cooperation is required to help governments and other actors deal with environmental problems. Where these problems are shared, as in regional seas and shared rivers, international cooperation is the only answer for successful action. But it is important to remind ourselves that the environmental problems of Pacific Asia are not restricted to that region. The area's pollution is affecting the rest of the world, meaning everyone should be concerned about controlling it. The most notable example is emissions of carbon dioxide and other so-called greenhouse gases that contribute to global warming and resulting climate change. In coming decades China *by itself* will overtake the United States as the world's largest source of greenhouse gases (in aggregate, not per capita). Other pollutants, such as industrial and transport pollution, are spreading to other continents through upper air currents, and massive amounts of pollution dumped into the region's rivers are polluting the Pacific Ocean and regional seas on which other countries depend for resources and environmental services. In short, the environmental problems of Pacific Asia are increasingly the world's problems. Therefore states outside Pacific Asia have a stake in environmental cooperation there.

INTERNATIONAL ENVIRONMENTAL COOPERATION: CASES FROM PACIFIC ASIA

International cooperation is essential to robust efforts to address local, regional, and global environmental problems. Pacific Asian states are cooperating to address many of their pressing environmental problems, but they will have to do much more in this regard. What is more, states outside the region, particularly the developed states with extensive financial and technological resources, will have to continue and even increase their involvement in international environmental cooperation in Pacific Asia. But what is needed to stimulate more international environmental cooperation in the region? More generally, why and how do states cooperate to address environmental problems? The following discussion looks briefly at these questions.

INTERNATIONAL COOPERATION

James Dougherty and Robert Pfaltzgraff (2001: 505) define international cooperation as "a set of relationships that are not based on coercion or compellence and that are legitimized by the mutual consent of members, as in international organizations [and regimes]." Lisa Martin (1993: 434) defines it as "the mutual adjustment of government policies through a process of policy coordination" in her summary of mainstream thinking on international cooperation (Martin 1993: 434–436; see also, for example, Axelrod 1984; Grieco 1990; Keohane 1984; Krasner 1985; Oye 1986; Taylor 1987). As Martin points out, a common underlying assumption is that states usually cooperate to overcome common problems. Cooperation occurs despite international anarchy (i.e., the lack of a central regional or global governing mechanism) because normally self-interested states recognize that it is often counterproductive not to cooperate and that in contrast, national self-interest can be promoted and common benefits can be derived from cooperation with other states. Thus the problem of anarchy identified by "realist" theorists is supplanted by cooperation as envisioned by "neoliberals," although the neoliberals join with realists in assuming that cooperation results from the pursuit of self-interest: "cooperation allows egoistic, rational states to better achieve their policy objectives" (Martin 1993: 435). Although governments usually cooperate in specific issue areas, this "functional" cooperation can extend to other areas (cf. Haas 1964; Mitrany 1966), leading to a growing sense of community among cooperating states (Deutsch 1957) as evidenced by the historical evolution of the European Union from a regional common market to an institution of major political integration.

International cooperation is more likely to occur when interests overlap, the number of actors is small, and actors have common characteristics conducive to cooperation (although the case of the European Union shows that substantial differences can be overcome). To be sure, barring unrelated incentives (such as payments by powerful states or hegemons or the exigencies of domestic politics), states will not cooperate unless they face a common threat or can achieve a common objective. International cooperation can be facilitated by powerful actors, as when the United States facilitated international economic cooperation in the second half of the twentieth century or (as is much more common today) when international institutions are involved in facilitating cooperation.

K. J. Holsti (1995: 362–372) has distilled several key features of international cooperation that will appear throughout this book. He identified four main sources of international cooperation: states cooperate to reduce costs, to increase efficiency, to address common threats or problems, and to lower the adverse consequences their actions have on others. According to Holsti (1995: 363), governments are "compelled to cooperate" when they face common threats or problems such as pollution "because individual action would be ineffective." They may, for example, agree to reduce their greenhouse gas emissions because combating climate change requires action by many states, not just one. Holsti (1995: 363) points out that the "threats created by modern life are, at a minimum, regional, and most have become global in recent decades. National solutions would be mostly tilting at windmills." Importantly, for states to cooperate they must usually expect joint gains and reciprocity from others. If by cooperating all parties gain from cooperation, the likelihood of it occurring and being effective is increased dramatically.

Holsti identified several stages of international cooperation, which are often highly politicized. After a problem becomes severe enough to garner public attention, it enters the domestic and eventually international agendas. Scientists and nongovernmental organizations become involved in pushing for action to address the problem. This leads to international negotiation—"an eminently political process because serious costs and sacrifices may be involved" (Holsti 1995: 364)—whereby some kind of action, including at times concrete regulation, is agreed to address the problem at hand. These actions are codified in international agreements, which in turn lead to international institutions. These institutions can be concrete organizations, such as the United Nations Environment Program, or less firmly established (although not necessarily less influential) international regimes, which have been defined as principles, norms, rules, and decision-making procedures around which actors' expectations converge in a given issue area of international relations (Krasner 1985). International regimes are, in short, accepted ideas about how states (and other relevant actors) will behave when they address a particular issue or set of common concerns. International regimes may or may not have associated organizations to facilitate actualization of their objectives.

Holsti (1995: 366–371) highlighted four common ways in which regimes regulate the actions of states—by setting standards in treaties (e.g., approved pollution levels), specifying required or prohibited actions of cooperating states (e.g., opening facilities to outside inspection or reducing trade barriers), allocating shares of scarce resources (e.g., radio spectrums or fishing grounds), or totally prohibiting certain activities (e.g., outlawing commercial whaling). These regulations are enforced through reciprocity, and depending on the regime, states that do not comply face sanctions, grassroots or official boycotts, and adverse publicity. To be sure, these types of enforcement may not work in certain issue areas, such as the security sphere, but in the environmental area they may carry greater weight with offending (or potentially offending) governments. Having said this, regimes built on a strong consensus and clear objectives are (not surprisingly) much more likely to succeed. Weak regimes—characterized by limited consensus, vague objectives, and limited provisions for punishing offenders—are much less likely to have significant impact on the shared problem for which cooperation was generated.

Much of our knowledge of how international regimes facilitate cooperation among states comes from environmental case studies (see, for example, Haas 1990; Keohane, Haas, and Levy 1993; Ostrom 1990; Young 1989, 1994, 1997, 1999). Gareth Porter, Janet Welsh Brown, and Pamela Chasek summarize major theories of how and why international regimes arise (2000: 16–20; see also Haggard and Simmons 1987). From a "structural" or "hegemonic power" perspective, regimes are formed by powerful states to facilitate their exercise of power or the provision of public goods in a given issue area. Without such powerful states, according to this view, regimes are unlikely to arise. One might argue, however, that environmental regimes have been formed even when opposed by major powers (e.g., the United States has not always supported their creation). Nevertheless, this perspective highlights the important role powerful states can play in regime formation, suggesting that the involvement of the United States and other great powers may help facilitate regime formation in Pacific Asia. Alternatively, a "utilitarian" or "game-theoretic" approach to explaining international regimes argues that they are formed when small groups of states engage in bargaining to promote their national interests. This approach may help explain difficulties encountered in Pacific Asia, where a relatively large number of states with disparate interests (and a high degree of mutual mistrust) may find it difficult to agree on where their mutual interests intersect.

Yet another theory of international regimes, the "institutional bargaining model," highlights the difficulty states have in determining their national interests in the environmental issue area. Given the complexity of those issues, it is not surprising that diplomats and policymakers cannot easily identify their states' interests. But regimes arise nevertheless. From this perspective they do so not as a result of mutual pursuit of self-interest but as an outgrowth of the diplomatic bargaining process itself. This perspective suggests that international environmental cooperation is possible when states engage in serious diplomatic dialogue on common problems, as they have often done in Pacific Asia.

Another approach to explaining international regimes focuses on the role played by "epistemic communities." An epistemic community is a group of scientists or technical experts that share a common concern about a policy problem and that, through international collaboration and connections to bureaucrats and policymakers, is able to bring a problem into domestic and international policy processes. Epistemic communities derive influence from their scientific and technical knowledge, without which policymakers and diplomats could not address international environmental problems. But the complexity of these issues means they can be politicized, raising doubts about the efficacy of science in contributing to the formation of effective international environmental regimes. As this uncertainty is replaced by better understanding of environmental problems, as well as of their consequences and effective policy measures to address them, however, cooperation can become much more likely—although even here it can be difficult. Cases of international environmental cooperation in Pacific Asia show how important epistemic communities can be, and several contributors to this volume believe they are vital elements in regime formation in the region.

Other theoretical approaches to international regime formation exist. For example, Porter, Brown, and Chasek point to the importance of domestic sociopolitical structures and processes in shaping international environmental regimes. Indeed, evidence from Pacific Asia shows that these structures and processes are crucial in explaining international regimes and the cooperation that leads to them, not to mention the degree to which they are taken seriously at the level of implementation. One upshot is that the case studies that follow will show that the earnestness with which states agree to regimes is one factor in determining their effectiveness, although many other factors are important. At the risk of upsetting the advocates of any one of these (or other) approaches to explaining international environmental regimes, we might argue that all of them help us better understand how and why international environmental regimes are formed. The case studies in the following chapters draw on these approaches and much additional research in the areas of international cooperation and international environmental cooperation in particular. They also build on that knowledge, notably with respect to Pacific Asia.

INTERNATIONAL ENVIRONMENTAL COOPERATION IN PACIFIC ASIA:
ISSUES, THEMES, AND ACTORS

Our case studies begin with two discussions of "environmental security" in the context of Pacific Asia. In Chapter 2, Lorraine Elliott proposes a framework for theorizing about the relationship between environmental scarcities and (in)security in the region. Environmental decline, resource depletion, and unsustainable development complicate the security challenges facing Pacific Asian states in a post–Cold War world. A traditional security framework, concerned primarily with territorial integrity and the potential for interstate tension and conflict, is, according to Elliott, inadequate and inappropriate as a conceptual and policy tool for understanding and defining appropriate foreign policy responses to environmental security. This is particularly true because Pacific Asian conceptions of security have always perceived economic development, political stability, and social welfare as being as important as—or even more important than—military power in securing national interests. As Elliott points out, extensive regional interest in the conceptual and policy implications of this changing security agenda has been evidenced most prominently in the Association of Southeast Asian Nations Regional Forum's attention to "comprehensive security" and in the attention paid to these issues by the Track Two Council for Security Cooperation Asia Pacific. Elliott proposes a security framework that accounts for insights offered by both liberal and human-security paradigms.

Elliott continues with an analysis of environmental change in Pacific Asia in the context of her security framework. Environmental change in the region is no longer (if it ever was) a national or subnational problem. Many of the problems are now so widespread that they are justifiably defined as common, shared, or regional concerns. In such cases the imperatives for regional cooperation as a foreign policy strategy blur the distinction between national and international environmental policy. Further, many of these problems are transboundary in either causes or consequences, thus ensuring that environmental security policy is bound up with the foreign policies of individual states in the region. With this in mind, Elliott assesses a possible repertoire of environmental security policies, premised on the proposition that a nontraditional security problem such as the environment requires nontraditional responses. Elliott argues that the conditions for stability and peace in Pacific Asia rest on preventative security responses that address the social and economic drivers of environmental decline.

As Chapter 2 highlights, environmental changes and resource scarcities in Pacific Asia pose challenges for the security of the region's states and peoples. Since at least the 1980s, governments inside and outside the region have started to view adverse environmental changes as threats to their national security. In Chapter 3, Paul G. Harris looks at environmental security in Northeast Asia, a region with some of the world's most heavily polluted areas and one in which natural resources are being placed under tremendous stress by economic growth. As we have seen, economic growth in China has led to sharp increases in emissions of pollutants that cause global warming and associated climatic changes. Whereas the effects of climate change for China and the region will likely be severe at times, they will also affect the entire world.

The United States, particularly since the early 1990s, has taken a growing interest in such problems. It came to view environmental changes as genuine threats to national security, and it particularly viewed East Asia (especially China) as a region in which environmental changes could contribute to insecurity that might affect U.S. interests. Although traditional security issues were usually considered more important, a consensus in the United States during the 1990s held that environmental issues ought to receive serious attention from the security establishment. As a consequence, the United States began to cooperate with states in the region to help them address adverse environmental changes and resource scarcities. This trend in U.S. foreign policy was important because of that country's great potential to contribute to international environmental cooperation in the region, given its economic, technological, and diplomatic resources.

With the advent of the administration of George W. Bush in 2001, however, environmental security seemed to have been downgraded as a U.S. foreign policy concern. This bodes ill for U.S. contributions to international environmental cooperation in East Asia. What is more, if the Bush administration ignores environmental issues, the incentives for states in the region to address environmental changes will likely be reduced, possibly contributing to existing tensions that threaten wider regional security and peace. Having said this, deteriorating environmental conditions in the region (not to mention career government officials and vocal environmentalists interested in these issues) may pressure the Bush administration and its security officials to give environmental security in Northeast Asia serious attention. Harris argues that the domestic and international forces that shaped the policies of the Clinton administration on environmental protection in Northeast Asia may eventually influence its successor's policies. He concludes that dire predictions of U.S. withdrawal from environmental protection efforts in the region are premature and that U.S. foreign policy over the long term is likely to continue to support international environmental cooperation there. Harris shows that politics and policy making in a powerful state actor from outside Pacific Asia can be important considerations for international environmental cooperation in the region.

In Chapter 4, Jack N. Barkenbus turns our attention to trade and economic globalization and their relationship to international environmental cooperation in East Asia and the Asia-Pacific region more broadly. As he shows, many East Asian governments and Western governmental and nongovernmental actors are at loggerheads over the incorporation of environmental conditions into future trade agreements. There is considerable pressure on East Asian states to adopt environmental standards in their trade practices, but those states reject the legitimacy of such pressures. In general, they view environmental components of trade agreements as blatant protectionism that impinges on their sovereign right to establish their own environmental standards. Barkenbus argues, however, that increasing environmental pressures are part and parcel of the process of economic globalization and that by rejecting them, East Asian states jeopardize further trade liberalization, their economic growth, and stable political relationships with other states. Moreover, East Asian states will not achieve their own trade objectives without compromising on environmental and other trade-related issues.

Given this polarization on the issue of trade and the environment, Barkenbus argues that discussions among all parties, aimed at producing common understandings, must be given much greater attention. Discussions involving all sectors of society, not just governments, are more likely to find mutually agreeable common ground that can eventually be incorporated into negotiations. Barkenbus believes an appropriate regional venue for such discussions would be a reconstituted Asia-Pacific Economic Cooperation forum (APEC). Encompassing twenty-one states around the Pacific, APEC has the right mix of members and interests to conduct productive diplomatic dialogue. For progress on the environment and trade to be achieved, however, Barkenbus recommends that APEC welcome the participation of nongovernmental organizations in its forum to fully embrace all key actors in this important debate. He thinks international environmental nongovernmental organizations are leading the effort to find a comfortable fit between further globalization and environmental protection. Globalization, according to Barkenbus, is already creating conditions for global environmental governance that includes, among other things, increasing reliance on what he calls "civil regulation" (i.e., civil society's oversight of corporate performance) to produce beneficial environmental results. Barkenbus believes all governments need to recognize the value civil society brings to environmental governance and should seek to both foster and channel this value in responsible ways. A reconstituted APEC, embracing the involvement of nongovernmental actors, would be an important step in that direction, and as such it would be an important forum for international environmental cooperation in the context of trade.

In Chapter 5, Morten Bøås discusses the role of international financial institutions, namely the Asian Development Bank (ADB), in Pacific Asian environmental diplomacy since the early 1980s. Bøås evaluates the ADB's performance in this context, analyzing its strategies when dealing with states for which environmental protection was not the main priority. In the process, he makes several policy recommendations for governments (donors and borrowers) and other stakeholders involved in ADB policy debates on environmental issues. He pays particular attention to the ADB's attempt to depoliticize the environmental agenda by defining it in a technical and functional (nonpolitical) fashion. He finds this strategy constituted a fruitful starting point for the incorporation of environmental issues into East Asian policy debates because by depoliticizing the agenda, the ADB helped achieve a reexamination of purpose within the established framework of knowledge.

Environmental issues, however, are by nature a matter of politics. This means there are strict limitations to what can be achieved by a "technocratic consensus." Many East Asian states openly questioned the weight put on environmental issues in the ADB. One important implication for international environmental cooperation in Pacific Asia is therefore that if the ADB moves too far toward a holistic developmental agenda constituted by highly politicized crosscutting issues, it will seriously annoy important constituents such as China. Likewise, if it completely retreats to become a narrow project-lending institution, it will risk a reduction in future cash flows as a result of increased criticism from nongovernmental organizations, which in turn will be followed by criticism and threats of reduced funding from donor states. This means future environmental cooperation in Pacific Asia centered on the ADB must strive to uphold a delicate balance between the positions of recipients of its aid and the extraregional donor states.

In seeking to provide policy recommendations related to this conundrum, Bøås first underlines the limitations of a "technocratic" approach to environmental issues. He acknowledges the initial success of such an approach, whereby "environmentalists" in the ADB pushed their agenda. This suggests that for actors who seek to introduce environmental issues into decisions of international financial institutions working in Pacific Asia, a deliberate technocratic approach is a good starting point. As Bøås's discussion also reveals, however, this can only be the first stage of a much broader process during which deliberate preparedness to deal with the political dimensions of these issues also occurs. The main fault with the process in the ADB was that the political dimension was suppressed for such a long time, which meant the problems and challenges for the ADB became much larger than they would have if political issues had been dealt with much earlier. Bøås argues that the main implication for international environmental cooperation in Pacific Asia is the need for a balanced approach to environmental issues, both within the ADB and in the region at large. There is little doubt that most Pacific Asian states should do more to protect the environment, but there is also little doubt that several of the arguments and concerns developing states have raised about the transformation of the ADB are also valid. Thus Chapter 6 concludes that avoiding a regional backlash on environmental questions in the context of the ADB requires a balanced approach by the bank and its donors. What is more, such an approach and its associated reforms should be followed by firm commitments from donors to fund the ADB's environmental programs.

Focusing further on the nexus between politics and environmental change issues, Chapter 6 examines the role of national economic interests in influencing international environmental cooperation in Southeast Asia, using Singapore as a case study. Regional agreements on the environment in Southeast Asia predate many broader international agreements. Yet as Giok Ling Ooi, Simon S.C. Tay, and Yue Choong Kog point out, many Southeast Asian agreements have been characterized more by good intentions and constant negotiations than by actual implementation of environmental protection measures (something that can of course be said about many other regional and global agreements). Given the state of the environment in Southeast Asia, it is not surprising that the introduction and implementation of sound environmental policies are very much bound up with regional politics, which have been fueled by political differences among national governments. Regional political rivalry, rather than cooperation, has often resulted from different approaches to governance and from intense competition for foreign investment among the economies in the region.

To illustrate this phenomenon, Chapter 6 examines the impact of various regional environmental agreements in the light of transboundary pollution problems and coping strategies adopted in resource-scarce states. More specifically, the chapter looks at the relationship between multilateral agreements, such as the Montreal Protocol for protection of the stratospheric ozone layer, and interests of businesses in the region, with particular focus on Singapore. As a small city-state reliant on imported water and other natural resources, Singapore is a good case to illustrate the strategies states with limited resources use to cope with environmental scarcities, as well as with related regional politics concerning environmental issues. In its bilateral relations with Malaysia, water resources (for which Singapore depends on Malaysia) have featured prominently. The negotiations to maintain the supply of water from Malaysia have highlighted related environmental issues, and they illustrate how Singapore's foreign policy has been one of "coping with vulnerability."

International relations and diplomacy are important dimensions of Singapore's environmental concerns, both domestic and global. International environmental cooperation remains a key strategy in its position on trade and other issues. On the international front, the importance of trade and its own economic interests has provided impetus for the tiny city-state to make its mark in global negotiations on environmental issues. Negotiations at the regional level have proven less remarkable in terms of Singapore's ability to influence environmental cooperation, but the city-state nevertheless wins points for its track record in the effort to implement measures required by the multilateral environmental agreements to which it is a signatory. The authors argue that Singapore's dependence on markets in the United States and Europe mandates its cooperation with multilateral environmental agreements. In its negotiations on the international front, continuing concern has been expressed about the impact of such agreements on Singapore's business competitiveness. Not joining in international environmental cooperation would contradict the Singapore government's wish to be increasingly integrated with global markets and the global economy.

The onset of the Asian economic crisis has stressed the urgency of such integration for Singapore. But concerns among surrounding states about economic competitiveness are limiting their willingness to seek more effective ways of cooperating on the environment. The effort to secure such cooperation has typically meant a flurry of meetings among political leaders and bureaucrats, followed by declarations of good intent. This has not been followed up with a real commitment to international or regional cooperation on major environmental issues facing individual nation-states. As such, Singapore's integration with the world economy has pushed it to implement stricter environmental controls than those in place throughout the region, but it has had very limited success in persuading its neighbors to adopt similarly strict environmental controls. Thus Chapter 6 shows the possibilities for environmental protection under willing and capable governments at the national level but also reveals the difficulties of spreading those practices more broadly.

In Chapter 7, Donald A. Brown examines the relationship between two of China's environmental problems—namely, deforestation and global warming (and resulting climate change)—in the context of emerging international norms of distributive justice. He argues that states now recognize that some of them have particular responsibilities for actualizing principles of international justice, especially when dealing with environmental problems. These principles have profound potential importance for international environmental cooperation. In particular, he says they are the basis for attributing some responsibility to other states for China's environmental problems, as well as China's potential responsibility for future environmental harm beyond its borders. Other states may be viewed to be partly responsible for the effects of global warming experienced by China, especially given China's relatively low level of greenhouse gas emissions historically compared with the developed states of the world.

China, however, may also bear some responsibility. When its emissions exceed its equitable share of greenhouse gas emissions (a level difficult to determine), it may become proportionally liable for damages from climate change felt in the rest of the world. As Brown points out, protection of national resources such as forests is usually seen as the obligation of the state in which the resources are located. Yet because global environmental problems are now affecting the quality of what were once viewed as purely national environmental resources, principles of international justice support finding some foreign responsibility for damages to those resources. Determining the amount of responsibility other states bear for damages to domestic environmental resources raises thorny questions of causation that may be difficult to unravel and will be particularly troublesome for those states that have failed to fulfill domestic responsibility to protect the resources in question.

If developed states want to shoulder some responsibility for damages to the domestic natural resources of China (and other countries), Brown suggests they could support approaches such as no-fault insurance funds to remedy damages to domestic natural resources caused by global-scale environmental problems. Even if such funds are created, however, the burden of proof to separate domestic from international responsibility will likely lie with the developing states. For this reason, it would be in their interest to devise indicators of domestic resource quality so they can prove that negative trends resulted from foreign activities. To protect domestic resources from emerging global environmental problems like climate change, developing states may need to undertake adaptation measures—such as building dykes to protect shorelines from rising oceans, establishing vector-control programs as protection against anticipated increases in vector-borne diseases, and creating alternative water supplies to substitute for anticipated reductions in existing water resources. By taking these and additional steps to deal with environmental damages as they occur, it should be easier for developing states such as China to make the case that principles of international justice entitle them to financial support for adaptation measures.

The upshot is that emerging norms of international environmental justice are important aspects of global efforts to protect the natural environment. Brown believes the international community has two clear options: it can create institutions capable of resolving conflicts over these issues, or it can allow states that will be harmed by the emerging global environmental problems to fend for themselves. The latter option will not provide the resources essential if international environmental cooperation and associated actions at the national level are to succeed.

ENVIRONMENTAL DIPLOMACY, REGIME BUILDING, AND INTERNATIONAL COOPERATION IN PACIFIC ASIA

Extending our case studies to environmental diplomacy, regime building, and the mechanisms of international cooperation, in Chapter 8 Sangmin Nam assesses the current state and process of regional environmental "governance" in Northeast Asia. Nam first describes the growing ecological interdependence in Northeast Asia, much of it stimulated by regional air and marine pollution. As a consequence of this interdependence, since the early 1990s Northeast Asia has experienced the emergence and evolution of various forms of multilateral and bilateral environmental governance. These governance mechanisms have led to different levels of institutionalization, some of which contain specific scope for action and have moved toward the establishment of organizational and financial institutions. Nam evaluates this institutionalization of international environmental cooperation, uncovering the different levels of progress, the move beyond broad policy forums to specific provisions for action, and the role of international and nongovernmental organizations and epistemic communities. Nam finds that most of the cooperative mechanisms he examined have been suffering from similar symptoms: significant gaps between national interests, lack of financial sources and consensual knowledge, and nominal roles for nonstate actors.

The ultimate purpose of institutionalization of ecological interdependence is not merely to establish institutional mechanisms for overseeing intergovernmental and regional environmental issues but also to strengthen practices that carry out effective implementation of environmental protection activities. Effective implementation implies bringing about behavioral changes of actors through governance and thus substantial amelioration of environmental harm. In the context of such objectives, however, Nam argues that regional environmental governance has fallen short. He assesses Northeast Asian efforts, pointing out that successful environmental governance in other regions has been achieved without eradicating existing heterogeneities among states, but it has involved altering their incentives. Basic provisions for the alteration of incentives in Northeast Asia could be achieved through activities targeted to address each state's domestic environmental needs that also have regional implications. The creation of "multidimensional consensual leadership" is also important for altering national interests. It mitigates existing political conflict by helping to distribute leadership to participants according to their particular environmental concerns, capacities, and enthusiasm for action. Active participation of nongovernmental organizations and epistemic communities in regional governance is also crucial, not only to urge states to implement and comply with activities defined by certain governance mechanisms but also to promote desirable norms and principles of regional governance.

In Chapter 9, Shin-wha Lee also discusses environmental regime building in Northeast Asia. Transboundary ecological issues should render strong incentives for international environmental cooperation within this region because it can help protect the natural environment. Such cooperation can also pave the way for regional confidence building as it thaws intransigent barriers of distrust, miscommunication, uncertainty, and differing views on issues that can lead to conflict. Consequently, since the late 1980s strong calls have been issued for regimes of cooperative environmental management in Northeast Asia. South Korea, Japan, and China have been engaged in bilateral and multilateral dialogues to establish or promote regional ecological cooperation to address their common environmental problems.

Despite the many incentives for cooperation, however, as Chapter 8 shows, environmental regime building in Northeast Asia has not come easily, and it remains too ineffective. In fact, according to Lee, much skepticism remains in Northeast Asia about establishing a sustained, cooperative set of institutions for regional environmental protection, largely because of preexisting differences over traditional security issues and continuing distrust from colonial periods, World War II, the Korean War, and the Cold War. A further hindrance to regional environmental cooperation lies in insufficient evidence of transfrontier environmental damage. Surprisingly, despite regional awareness of cross-border pollution, no state in the Northeast Asian region has officially claimed grave environmental damage caused by its neighbors.

According to Lee, at least five factors are required for the establishment of more effective institutional mechanisms for regional environmental cooperation: national leadership, involvement of international organizations, participation of transnational scientific networks, active involvement of nongovernmental organizations, and significant public concern. With these considerations in mind, Lee makes several recommendations: raising awareness of environmental problems among publics in the region, enhancing scientific knowledge of cross-border environmental impacts, and undertaking concerted efforts to overcome resistance to environmental cooperation stemming from national concerns about economic growth, economic competition between states, and the strong sense of sovereignty that makes imposing the standards agreed in the context of environmental regimes difficult. Unfortunately, none of these factors is realized easily in Northeast Asia. By identifying these problems, however, Lee helps frame the thinking and work necessary to facilitate greater regional environmental cooperation and regime building.

Chapter 10 supports and expands on the findings of preceding chapters with a case study of efforts to address the problem of acid rain in Northeast Asia. Wakana Takahashi points out that regional initiatives to combat acid rain in the region have been less successful than similar efforts in other regions. In fact, progress has been slow. As a basis for understanding Northeast Asian efforts, the chapter first exposes the deficiencies of the cooperative mechanisms as a whole by surveying existing and ongoing major multilateral environmental programs and plans and examining the actors involved. The chapter reviews major cooperative activities on acid rain and other environmental issues and analyzes how the weaknesses and inadequacies of environmental cooperation mechanisms have influenced and hindered the progress of cooperation on acid rain. The chapter then considers whether and how regional cooperation on the acid rain issue can be promoted in Northeast Asia. Takahashi shows that institutional and political barriers to further cooperation exist. The question is whether and how the region can escape the existing stagnation.

The key to improving the situation, according to Takahashi, lies in increased activity by international and nongovernmental organizations. Other recommendations for improving international environmental cooperation on acid rain in the region include involving scientists and their epistemic communities and ensuring that the research findings of high-quality international projects are reflected in regional policy-making processes. Although Northeast Asia needs to create a framework in which all parties in the region can participate, this cannot be easily achieved because of the political sensitivities and the security situation in the region. Only nongovernmental organizations can remedy this deficiency for the time being, according to Takahashi. At the same time, states in the region must improve their diplomatic relations and skills to handle the complex and difficult challenges of different political systems and perspectives.

This is particularly true for Japan and South Korea. Although the two countries have much in common (e.g., both are willing to promote and lead various environmental initiatives), they are presently working in different directions, resulting in parallel institutions and policy stagnation. Both states need to develop strategies for regional cooperation that incorporate their own and other states' interests, as well as the common interests of the region. To be sure, states in the region are paying more attention to, and strengthening national laws and regulations on, controlling air pollution and acid rain. And China has received substantial environmental investment toward this end through both official development assistance and foreign private investment. Considering these facts, it might be said that significant collaboration has already taken place on the issue of acid rain in Northeast Asia. Much of this collaboration, however, has been fragmented. Therefore the region needs to form links between individual initiatives and financial mechanisms, between bilateral and multilateral aid programs, among donor agencies, and between regional cooperative institutions and financial aid mechanisms.

Turning to what may be an even thornier issue, in Chapter 11 Stephanie Tai, Andrew Loewenstein, Todd Bissett, and Eric O'Malley look at concerns about Chinese and South Korean nuclear programs, particularly the waste they will increasingly create. One of the universally recognized problems with nuclear power is its generation of dangerous wastes. For states that desire to increase their use of nuclear power, the reprocessing of spent nuclear fuels is often viewed as a positive alternative to storing them, which poses significant costs and health risks. The reprocessing option comes with its own problems: the materials generated through reprocessing can be directly used in nuclear explosives, and accidents can occur during the transport of spent nuclear fuels from nuclear power plants to reprocessing facilities. Despite these dangers, South Korea and China are considering nuclear reprocessing as a means of generating power while simultaneously reducing their increasing nuclear waste stockpiles and reducing greenhouse gas emissions.

China's pilot reprocessing facility will be completed soon. This raises important issues of trade in wastes within the region, notably between South Korea and China, and the choices of South Korea and China with respect to reprocessing will likely have substantial influence on East Asia's nuclear energy choices. Both states already have well-established nuclear energy programs, and an increasing number of Asian states that do not are exploring the use of nuclear power. As this process gathers momentum, it will have important implications for security in East Asia because the countries in the region must try to reconcile and balance the risks of nuclear weapons proliferation associated with reprocessing, the pressing need to meet rising energy demands created by economic development, and the environmental impacts (both positive and negative) of nuclear power.

What explains the calculations of South Korea and China in choosing to increase use of nuclear energy despite the dangers posed by the accompanying waste? The authors have several explanations based on economic and environmental considerations. For example, from the perspective of East Asian policymakers, evidence of the ecological problems associated with nuclear energy generally, and with reprocessing specifically, may be outweighed by countervailing arguments that a better environmental balance may be struck by reprocessing spent fuels to avoid storage concerns and by looking instead to the nuclear option to satisfy swelling energy demands—thereby decreasing reliance on coal-based power (with its attendant greenhouse gas emissions). On the military side of the equation, states considering whether to engage in nuclear reprocessing and trade in reprocessed materials must evaluate the security risks of proliferation against the predicted economic and (admittedly debatable) environmental benefits. Policymakers recognize that the nuclear materials created by reprocessing can be used directly in nuclear explosives and thus that the decision to engage in reprocessing carries obvious and significant military implications. These recognized proliferation risks have not dampened enthusiasm in East Asia for trading reprocessed materials, however. This may be explained by the fact that whether proliferation is conceived as a threat to security is a matter of perception, one not necessarily perceived uniformly. Indeed, the risk of proliferation caused by trading reprocessed materials may be much more serious for those other than the immediate parties to the economic transaction because those most susceptible are more likely to be, for example, the United States and its allies. Thus fears that trading reprocessed materials could lead to new nuclear weapons threats are likely to prove ineffective in dissuading China and South Korea from reprocessing and trading nuclear materials.

In Chapter 12, Tom Næss analyzes international environmental cooperation in the South China Sea region. The South China Sea is facing an increase in severe transnational environmental problems and resource disputes. Environmental issues have long been discussed at the national political level in East Asia, but international cooperation on environmental issues in the South China Sea is rather new. Policy analysts often perceive it as an area in which China and Taiwan stand against their Southeast Asian neighbors in an unresolved sovereignty conflict over the Spratly Islands. The South China Sea, however, is not just a potential scene of military conflict; it is also a rich marine environment. Rapid economic growth, frequently coupled with depletion of natural resources, intensifies conflicts like those in the South China Sea. The environmental security aspect of this area is therefore pertinent.

Two initiatives have emerged to facilitate international cooperation on environmental issues in the South China Sea region. The first is a set of informal, multilateral meetings that have taken up issues relevant to the sea every year since 1990: the so-called South China Sea Workshops. The second is an attempt by the littoral countries of the region, in cooperation with the United Nations Environmental Program, to establish an environmental action program for the South China Sea. Næss discusses the likelihood that these regime-building efforts will succeed in making environmental questions take precedence in regional politics. He is particularly interested in highlighting the role the regional scientific community plays in diffusing knowledge and data about the current situation, thereby determining whether science and scientists are playing an important role in promoting international environmental cooperation in the South China Sea.

Næss arrives at three conclusions. First, the South China Sea Workshops and UNEP initiatives have been successful in spreading information and knowledge about environmental problems and the necessary steps for preventing them from growing. Second, an implicit maritime regime based on various arrangements and agreements among members of the Association of Southeast Asian Nations has emerged. A sort of "Asian multilateralism" experienced through the South China Sea Workshops has prevented armed conflict in the region and has even succeeded in engaging China and Taiwan in multilateral endeavors. And third, he finds obvious institutional weaknesses in the region. At the national level, the multiplicity of agencies dealing with the maritime environment and the lack of interest at the highest political levels make efficient and integrative marine policy almost impossible. This problem has accumulated at the regional level, where no agency exists that can coordinate efforts to improve the maritime environment. Næss suggests that UNEP may have the diplomatic force necessary to integrate national and regional policies more effectively.

In our final chapter, Allen Springer examines the internationalization of major Indonesian forest fires that occurred in 1997 and 1998. The fires spread through the brush, forests, and peat bogs of eastern Indonesia, destroying nearly 10 million hectares. A thick, smoky haze spread over much of Southeast Asia, affecting public health and devastating the tourist trade. The transboundary consequences of the fires transformed what was initially a national environmental problem into one of regional and even global dimensions. The resulting damage, estimated as high as US$8–$10 billion, made the Indonesian fires among the planet's most costly environmental catastrophes.

These devastating impacts focused international attention on developing practical measures to prevent or at least control a recurrence of similar fires. The nature of the international response to the fires raises important questions about the legal and institutional development of a body of international environmental practice in which states seemingly acknowledged almost thirty years ago that they were responsible for controlling environmentally degrading activities within their jurisdictions. Despite the seriousness of the problem and the early recognition that it was a disaster to which the Indonesian government had directly contributed through its land-use policies and lax enforcement of existing laws, remarkably little was said by Indonesia or other states about Indonesia's legal responsibility to control the fires and to compensate those beyond its borders who were injured. As one observer quoted by Springer described the situation, "The fires . . . challenge the adequacy of international environmental law, both in practice and in principle."

As Springer notes, recent assessments of the development of Asian environmental law describe a process whereby states look to international conventions and agreements when developing their environmental management policies and regulations rather than remaining focused internally. As Springer uses the term, this "internationalization" does not necessarily imply a conscious choice by governments whose policies and behavior might be affected by international norms. The focus is as much about the role of outside governments, organizations, and interest groups in pushing the process along as it is about a particular government. Springer's objective is to better understand some of the factors shaping attitudes, not just in Indonesia but throughout the international community, as people were forced to confront a serious environmental challenge. His chapter reviews the fires themselves, their presumed causes and effects, and the steps taken to address them on national, regional, and global levels. As he shows, many states and international organizations sought to assist Indonesia and in so doing transformed the fires into an international issue. Springer assesses the response and explains why no more was done. His central observation is that a substantial gap exists between international environmental legal principles and actual government practices. Nonetheless, he argues that internationalization is under way, a process that is acknowledging the legitimacy of the international community's interest in controlling the factors that led to the fires. He offers hope that increased public awareness and organized pressure against governments will encourage officials to accelerate this process and create stronger legal frameworks to support environmental protection efforts in Southeast Asia and beyond.

CONCLUSION

Our case studies point to the urgent need for international cooperation to address adverse environmental changes and scarcities of vital natural resources in Pacific Asia. Many environmental problems in the region are shared. Pollution passes from one country to another via rivers, ocean currents, and the atmosphere; and threatened resources are found in common areas, particularly the region's shared seas. The transboundary nature of these problems means they can rarely be solved by individual states; international cooperation is essential. What is more, many problems have adverse impacts beyond Pacific Asia, with the atmospheric pollution contributing to climate change the most prominent example. Therefore states outside Pacific Asia have a strong interest in fostering and joining international environmental cooperation in the region. But international cooperation in this issue area, like many others, is not always easy. This is especially true in Pacific Asia, where states fiercely guard their sovereignty and many seemingly incommensurable political differences, animosities, and opportunities for mistrust exist.

The scholarly research described in this book bolsters the findings of other work in the area of international environmental cooperation. It also adds to those findings by, first, looking at several issues, themes, and actors germane to environmental cooperation in Pacific Asia. We show how environmental changes in the region are increasingly perceived as threats to national security, but we also show that these changes cannot be adequately addressed until conceptions of environmental security are expanded to include social and economic issues. Furthermore, the participation of major powers from outside the region will be important for fostering the necessary international cooperation. We build on literature examining the links between trade and environment by showing that states in Pacific Asia are often opposed to incorporating environmental protection measures into trade accords. Even when they are willing to join global environmental agreements, these states must contend with their heavy reliance on global trade when implementing them. Economic as well as environmental issues are highly politicized in the region, not least in diplomatic exchanges between Pacific Asian countries on the one hand and international financial institutions and donor states on the other. We show that focusing on technical issues that avoid confronting political differences may have short-term benefits, but long-term environmental protection requires that these issues be forthrightly addressed between donor states and aid recipients in the region.

This raises the important crosscutting issue of international justice. Developing countries in the region are unlikely to take all of the necessary steps to address environmental problems with global impacts if they do not feel developed countries are treating them fairly. For their part, developed states, particularly those from outside Pacific Asia, must share more responsibility for addressing environmental problems they have helped cause. Having said this, states in the region will inevitably bear the greatest burden, and as time passes the environmental consequences of their own economic development may increase their responsibility for global environmental changes felt beyond Pacific Asia.

Our second set of contributions to the literature deals with broad issues of diplomacy and regime building to achieve international cooperation on specific environmental issues in Pacific Asia. Northeast Asia is one part of the region in which a substantial number of environmental institutions have been created through international cooperation, such as those intended to address regional acid rain. We find that making these institutions effective will require greater participation—and even leadership, insofar as possible— by civil society and international organizations (among other actors) and will also require overcoming historical differences among the region's states. Although these differences are unrelated to the region's environmental problems per se, they are so strong that they permeate environmental diplomacy. This important consideration is given relatively little attention in existing literature. Unfortunately, regional environmental institutions are generally weak. It is worth highlighting the region's political differences because although many local environmental problems become "internationalized" and thereby become subjects of regional and global environmental diplomacy, these political differences and assumptions in the region can override the best intentions of regional and outside actors seeking to foster international environmental cooperation in Pacific Asia.

To be sure, we have not analyzed all of the steps essential to reach more effective international environmental cooperation in Pacific Asia. We have sought, however, to highlight many of the problems and their key features while suggesting some possible solutions to assist policymakers and stakeholders in their efforts to address, through international cooperation, environmental changes in the region. This will benefit the billions of people in Pacific Asia—and indeed the billions more beyond—who will be increasingly affected by environmental changes there.

REFERENCES

Asian Development Bank (ADB). 1997. *Emerging Asia: Changes and Challenges.* Manila: ADB.

Axelrod, Robert. 1984. *The Evolution of Cooperation.* New York: Basic.

Clarke, Robin. 1999. *Global Environmental Outlook 2000.* London: Earthscan/United Nations Environment Program.

Deutsch, Karl W. 1957. *Political Community and the North Atlantic Area.* Princeton: Princeton University Press.

Dougherty, James E., and Robert L. Pfaltzgraff Jr. 2001. *Contending Theories of International Relations.* New York: Longman.

Grieco, Joseph. 1990. *Cooperation Among Nations.* Ithaca: Cornell University Press.

Haas, Ernst. 1964. *Beyond the Nation-State: Functionalism and International Organization.* Stanford: Stanford University Press.

Haas, Peter. 1990. *Saving the Mediterranean.* New York: Columbia University Press.

Haggard, Stephen, and Beth A. Simmons. 1987. "Theories of International Regimes." *International Organization* 41 (summer): 491–517.

Harris, Paul G. 2002. "East Asia." In John Barry and E. Gene Frankland, eds., *International Encyclopedia of Environmental Politics.* London: Routledge.

Holsti, K. J. 1995. *International Politics: A Framework for Analysis.* Englewood Cliffs: Prentice-Hall.

Inglehart, Ronald. 1990. *Culture Shift in Advanced Industrial Society.* Princeton: Princeton University Press.

Keohane, Robert O. 1984. *After Hegemony: Cooperation and Discord in the World Economy.* Princeton: Princeton University Press.

Keohane, Robert O., Peter M. Haas, and Marc A. Levy, eds. 1993. *Institutions for the Earth.* Cambridge: MIT Press.

Krasner, Stephen D., ed. 1985. *International Regimes.* Ithaca: Cornell University Press.

Martin, Lisa L. 1993. "International Cooperation." In Joel Krieger, ed., *The Oxford Companion to Politics of the World.* Oxford: Oxford University Press.

Mitrany, David. 1966. *A Working Peace System.* Chicago: Quadrangle.

Ostrom, Elinor. 1990. *Governing the Commons: The Evolution of Institutions for Collective Action.* Cambridge: Cambridge University Press.

Oye, Kenneth A., ed. 1986. *Cooperation Under Anarchy.* Princeton: Princeton University Press.

Pan, Philip P. 2001. "Plea Ignored in China's 'Cancer Village.' " *International Herald Tribune* (11 November), 7.

Porter, Gareth, Janet Welsh Brown, and Pamela S. Chasek. 2000. *Global Environmental Politics,* 3d ed. Boulder: Westview.

Taylor, Michael. 1987. *The Possibility of Cooperation.* New York: Cambridge University Press.

World Bank. 1997. *Clear Water, Blue Skies: China's Environment in the New Century.* Washington, DC: World Bank.

Young, Oran. 1989. *International Cooperation: Building Regimes for Natural Resources and the Environment.* Ithaca: Cornell University Press.

———. 1994. *International Governance.* Ithaca: Cornell University Press.

———. 1999. *Governance in World Affairs.* Ithaca: Cornell University Press.

———, ed. 1997. *Global Governance: Drawing Insights From the Environmental Experience.* Cambridge: MIT Press.

I

Issues, Themes, and Actors in International Environmental Cooperation

2

Environmental Security in East Asia: Defining a Common Agenda

LORRAINE ELLIOTT

The pursuit of security is often argued to be the central purpose of a country's foreign policy. Its dominant place on the agenda of international politics has earned it the label "high politics," concerned with the state, power, conflict, and the protection of borders. Yet the meaning and methodology of security are increasingly contested in a post–Cold War and globalized world. The way in which "security" is understood and pursued, nationally and internationally, has informed and constrained efforts to protect the environment. Theorizing security in ways that challenge an orthodox state-centric conceptualization offers the opportunity to think differently about security and environmental foreign policy goals and strategies. Although environmental and resource challenges are now most often labeled nonmilitary or nontraditional security threats, this still reveals little about the nature of those threats or who or what is made insecure by them. Nor does it provide sufficient guidance on appropriate policy responses. In the absence of a more robust exploration of this new or alternative security agenda, foreign policy initiatives to respond to the environmental security agenda lack focus and purpose and are unlikely to meet the fundamental common security challenges presented by environmental change.

This chapter examines these issues in the context of environmental change in East Asia. It begins by offering a framework for theorizing about the relationship among environmental scarcity, resource decline, and regional insecurity in East Asia. Environmental decline, resource depletion, and unsustainable development complicate the security challenges facing the East Asian region in a post–Cold War world. A traditional security framework, concerned primarily with territorial integrity and the potential for interstate tension and conflict, is argued to be inadequate and inappropriate as a conceptual and policy tool for understanding and defining appropriate foreign policy responses to environmental (in)security. This is particularly so because, as Stuart Harris and Andrew Mack observe, "regional conceptions of security" in East Asia have always perceived "economic development, political stability and social welfare" as being as important as, or even more important than, military power in "preventing violent conflict" (1997: 3). Extensive regional interest in the conceptual and policy implications of this changing security agenda has been evidenced most prominently in the attention given to comprehensive security by the Association of Southeast Asian Nations (ASEAN) Regional Forum (ARF) and the various working groups of the Track Two Council for Security Cooperation in the Asia Pacific (CSCAP).[1] The security framework is therefore broadened here to take account of the insights offered by both liberal and human-security paradigms and the consequences of so doing for foreign policy.

The second section of this chapter examines the agenda of environmental change in East Asia in the context of this security framework. Environmental change in the region is no longer (if indeed it ever was) a national or subnational problem. Many of the problems are so widespread as to be defined justifiably as common, shared, or regional concerns. In such cases the imperatives for regional cooperation as a foreign policy strategy blur the distinction between national and international environmental policy. Further, many of these problems are transboundary in either cause or consequence, thus ensuring again that environmental security policy is bound up with the foreign policy of individual countries in the region. The third section of this chapter assesses a possible repertoire of environmental security policies, based on the proposition that a nontraditional security problem such as environmental security requires nontraditional security responses.

ENVIRONMENTAL SECURITY: RETHINKING THE PARADIGM

Environmental security is usually identified as a nonmilitary or nontraditional security problem. Despite this broad label, most attention in the literature and in policy debate has focused on the potential for conflict or violence over scarce resources and environmental services. Little attention is paid to what is in fact *not* traditional about nontraditional security issues. Yet these understandings are fundamental to identifying appropriate foreign and security policy responses. One of the most important issues is whether "environmental" security is simply added to the existing list of security problems facing policymakers without changing their priorities or whether it embodies a fundamental challenge to security practices. The framework for thinking about security (traditional or otherwise) focuses on several key questions: Who or what is made secure (the referent), what core values are threatened, what are the types of threats and the nature of the problem, and (in the light of this) how should insecurity be managed and security be attained (for a summary, see Alagappa 1998: 17).

Although some diversity is found in the orthodox or traditional security literature, the general concerns are clear. The security referent is the state, defined in terms of its borders and territory. The threats to the state and its borders are assumed to be military and political, arising primarily through the potential for invasion or through conflict in the form of interstate war. Such threats come with a usually identifiable and external enemy. The values that are threatened include sovereignty, territorial integrity, political stability, and the vague notion of a unique or particular way of life caught up with the idea of nationhood and independence. The policy responses to pursue and maintain security in the face of these traditional threats focus on territorial defense through "self-help" and the maintenance of military capability, the building of military alliances, and finally, military-related diplomacy including arms control, disarmament, and conflict management strategies.

Nontraditional security, the category into which environmental security falls, deviates from this paradigm in two distinct but not always entirely discrete ways. In the first variation, what one might call the Kaplanesque variant (see Kaplan 1994), the nature of the threat changes but the referent (that is, who or what is made insecure) remains, for the most part, the state. The values under threat are still sovereignty, territorial integrity, political and legal stability, and national identity. The threats, however, come from what are increasingly referred to as gray-area phenomena, such as those associated with criminal activity and the smuggling or trafficking of people, arms, and narcotics. These challenges are still perceived as "threats to the stability of sovereign states by non-state actors and non-governmental processes and organizations" (Chalk 2000: 127). The "enemy" remains primarily external, or at least "foreign."[2] The constabulary's response, designed to protect "the state" against such phenomena and their perpetrators, becomes a key "security" response. Bilateral and multilateral initiatives acquire greater saliency and importance.

Environmental degradation does not easily meet these modified nontraditional threat criteria. It is certainly nonmilitary in scope, although the military can often be complicit in environmental change. It is, however, increasingly difficult to identify an "enemy" whose specific purpose is to transgress borders or undermine the state or political regimes through, in this case, environmental activities. Environmental challenges to national security, however defined, are as frequently sourced within states as they are outside them. Nevertheless, the orthodoxies of environmental security have most often been accommodated within the state-centric variant of nontraditional security. This focuses on an "environment-*and*-security approach" in which, as Matthias Finger notes, "the ecological crisis [is] increasingly defined as a threat to national security" (1991: 220).[3] The agenda of environmental security concerns is thus enlarged to include activities within one country that affect environmental quality in another to the extent that conflict or violence is possible. It includes the environmental (as well as political) vulnerabilities of land and maritime border regions, and it includes competition over access to resources and environmental services. As the UN Secretary-General's *Agenda for Peace* suggested, ecological damage is a new risk to stability (Boutros-Ghali 1992: 5).

Environment-related conflict or violence, in which the security of states is unsettled, can take forms other than interstate war. In adapting the orthodoxies of a traditional security paradigm to nontraditional threats such as environmental change, three areas of concern arise: (1) the potential for military activity short of war to be mobilized in the face of other kinds of threats that have an environmental component, (2) the corrosion of political and diplomatic relationships over transboundary environmental scarcities, and (3) the likelihood of subnational instabilities in which environmental scarcity is a primary or major factor.

Stability and security, however, rest on more than the absence of conflict or violence. In the second, more heterodox variation of nontraditional security, both the referent *and* the nature of the threat change. The insecurities of people, communities, economies, and the environment are acknowledged to be a valid dimension of security policy. The values under challenge include economic viability and human and community welfare and security. This insecurity agenda includes environmental degradation, pandemics such as HIV/AIDS and cholera, the impacts of criminal activity and smuggling on people and communities, and humanitarian insecurities including famine, human rights abuses, and genocide. Threats can come from within and across borders. Indeed, this variant turns on its head the usual security assumption that secure states mean secure people. It recognizes that states can sometimes be the greatest cause of insecurity for peoples within their borders. The "enemy" is also often increasingly invisible—at least some of these "threats" arise as a consequence of the everyday practices of human and corporate society and economy. Threats can arise through deliberate action by, for example, the state or competing or dominant sociopolitical groups within society. They can also arise from unintended consequences such as unsustainable development, poverty, disasters of nature, or the consequences of war—such as the dispersal of landmines and small arms. From the perspective of environmental security, this takes the agenda from one that simply adds new kinds of threats to the existing security problematic to one in which the primary focus is (or should be) threats other than those that might arise from extraterritorial military activities.

A framework that conceptualizes this second variant of nontraditional security takes into account the concerns of liberal and human security, as well as the tensions between them. In a liberal security paradigm, development or economic growth is more than a national good. Rather it has a stabilizing or security-making effect because it establishes the conditions for mutual economic engagement. This is, in effect, the economic variant of the "democratic peace" argument, and it is assumed to work most effectively with developed or so-called advanced economies. This approach is most evident in global enthusiasm for trade liberalization, although it harks back to the work of European integrationists such as David Mitrany, who anticipated peace in Europe through the enmeshment of economic sectors as a forerunner to the enmeshment of political sectors.

Without doubt, governments consider economic security to be in the national interest. The depletion of natural resources, environmental degradation, and habitat fragmentation undermine the viability of a range of economic activity and contribute to the loss of future wealth and productivity. Ecologically unsustainable development can therefore contribute to insecurities if opportunities for economic interdependence are compromised through the slowing or even reversing of economic growth. The "threat" is therefore understood to arise from the externalities associated with market failure, the economic costs of environmental scarcity within states, and the complex relationship among unsustainable development, poverty, and insecurity. Yet the kinds of neoliberal economic policies mandated by such an approach have themselves been indicted as a major cause of both environmental decline and the growing global gap between rich and poor. The assumptions that the benefits of national economic security will trickle down to ensure local economic and environmental security are vulnerable.

The concept of human security provides an antidote to this more conventional focus on states, territorial integrity, and national economic stability. This approach, favored by the United Nations Development Program (UNDP) and the Commission on Global Governance, focuses on "human life and dignity" rather than weapons and territory (UNDP 1994: 22; see also Commission on Global Governance 1995). It recognizes that "increasing stresses on the earth's life support systems and renewable natural resources have profound implications for human health and welfare that are at least as serious as traditional military threats" (Porter 1995: 218). For individuals and communities, the social, economic, and political consequences of unsustainable development and environmental change can include poverty, loss of livelihoods, cultural fragmentation, and ecological vulnerability. The web of causality that links environmental decline and human insecurity is complicated also by "differences in environmental endowment" (World Commission on Environment and Development 1987: 292). This includes differential access to resources and environmental services, disproportionate vulnerabilities to the impacts of environmental change, disproportionate contribution to environmental degradation, and unequal authority and control over resource use.

Environmental scarcity and insecurity is therefore understood to be a problem of distribution and equity rather than simply one of market failure, externalities, or zero-sum calculations about access to resources and environmental services. Human insecurity can also be a central factor in the social tensions and political instabilities and conflicts that can be features of state insecurity. If peoples and communities are insecure—in economic, social, political, and environmental terms—state security can be fragile or uncertain. Protecting individuals and communities from the consequences of environmental decline therefore becomes a national security concern in both human and state terms. In East Asia, this has become a fundamental part of how we think about and manage the environmental (in)security agenda.

SECURITIZING THE ENVIRONMENT IN EAST ASIA

Environmental insecurity in East Asia is characterized by growing environmental scarcity. This includes a continued decline in traditional living and nonliving resources (such as fish, timber, oil, and gas), as well as the degradation and depletion of what are often referred to as the new strategic resources—particularly fresh water and arable land. Environmental scarcity also encompasses a decline in the viability of environmental services, such as clean air and unpolluted water, and what the United Nations Environment Program (UNEP) defines as "habitat fragmentation" (1999: 39–41). As noted earlier, these problems are often so widespread as to be justifiably defined as regional. In many cases they are clearly transboundary. In some cases, such as air pollution or shared water resources, it is the environmental and economic impacts that cross borders. In other cases, such as illegal logging in border areas, it is the causes that are transboundary.

Ecological scarcity in East Asia is not simply a biophysical problem. Rather its causes lie in unsustainable development and the everyday practices of human economy and society. Although subsistence lifestyles in the region remain heavily dependent on natural resources, the major factors contributing to environmental decline and scarcity are environmentally unsustainable patterns of economic growth, industrialization and urbanization, increasing consumption, and growing demands for energy and resources.

ENVIRONMENTAL SCARCITY IN EAST ASIA

Deforestation, desertification, land degradation, and the loss of arable land have become enduring features of environmental decline in East Asia. Deforestation offers perhaps the most "visible evidence of the rate of environmental change" (Vervoorn 1998: 166). Primary forests have been severely depleted through logging (both commercial and illegal) and the clearance of land for commercial and subsistence agriculture. Although Asia's forest loss measured in hectares is not equal to that of Latin America or Africa, average per capita forest cover for the region is significantly lower than in other parts of the world (see UNEP 1999: 79). Asian forests also host higher levels of biodiversity than those in many other parts of the world (Japan Environment Council 1999: 137). Southeast Asia alone contains over 200 of the world's threatened mammals, almost 200 threatened bird species, close to 100 threatened fish species, and almost 30 endangered reptile and amphibian species (UNEP 1999: 76).

Some major regional consequences of deforestation and unsustainable agriculture have been land degradation and soil loss, siltation, changed water retention and runoff patterns, and food insecurity. East Asia has less cropland per capita than the world average, and over a third of the region's population lives in areas vulnerable to drought and desertification (UNEP 1999: 76). Land degradation and the expansion of urban agglomerations have forced small farmers onto marginal lands with shorter fallow periods and more chemically intensive agricultural practices. Population growth has increased pressure on food production, but at the same time the availability of freshwater resources limits the likelihood of increased agricultural yields.

Indeed, persistent overuse of water for agriculture, municipal, and industrial use is becoming a serious regional challenge, and many countries in the region face water stress.[4] Freshwater use has increased, on a gross and per capita basis, faster in East Asia than in other parts of the world. At the same time access to potable water in both urban and rural communities is often limited, and water quality is being degraded by urban and industrial pollution and by saltwater pollution of freshwater aquifers. Many of the region's rivers are biologically compromised, water is unsafe for agricultural use, and freshwater fish stocks are in decline. Water is also a regional transboundary resource. Thailand, for example, receives almost 40 percent of its water from external sources. Cambodia relies on external sources for 82 percent of its water. East Asia is also a maritime region. Few maritime areas are unclaimed, and many overlap. Coastal zones and high seas (or contested seas) are suffering from the consequences of pollution (much of it from land-based sources) and resource depletion. Most of the region's fisheries are overfished, some to the point of nonrecovery. Marine and coastal ecosystems have been further affected by the growth in aquaculture, primarily shrimp farming, and the consequent loss of economically and ecologically important mangrove ecosystems.

Economic development in East Asia has been accompanied by substantial rural-urban migration. The region now contains some of the world's major urban concentrations, including seven megacities (that is, cities with populations over 10 million).[5] Urban air quality has become a serious problem with major health and economic costs. Many major cities in the region exceed the World Health Organization's guidelines on particulates, sulfur dioxide, or both. Air pollution has increasingly taken on a transboundary dimension. In recent "haze incidents," for example, particulate-laden smoke from land-clearance fires in Indonesia spread to Singapore, Malaysia, Thailand, and Brunei—reaching health-threatening levels and affecting tourism, transport, and agriculture. Transboundary acid rain has caused increasing concern, particularly in the heavily industrialized parts of Northeast Asia.

Industrialization and urbanization, along with substantial growth in the region's use of motor vehicles, have also increased demands on energy resources. Asia's energy consumption has continued to grow at the same time global per capita consumption has declined slightly (see UNEP 1999: 89). Fossil fuels, especially coal, remain the major energy sources; and emissions of carbon dioxide—although well below global per capita averages—have increased at almost twice the world rate in the last quarter century.

THE SECURITY CHALLENGE I: WAR AND CONFLICT?

Two questions arise. First, in what ways and to what extent should these examples of environmental change and decline be taken seriously as security challenges in East Asia? Second, if they should be taken seriously (and I argue that they should), what foreign policy responses are appropriate? The matrix of cause and consequence that links this menu of environmental scarcity with regional insecurity is complex. Almost all the region's environmental and resource problems have been identified in one forum or another as a possible source of insecurity, although the nature of the causal relationship is rarely made clear. Where those relationships are explained, it is usually in the context of the possibility of conflict or confrontation between states. The most pessimistic accounts anticipate "troubling prospects" (Winnefeld and Morris 1994: 65) and "likely future conflict" (Lim and Valencia 1990: 3).[6]

Some evidence supports predictions of actual interstate conflict over resources, although this is likely in the maritime context and particularly in the South China Sea. Competing sovereignty claims there have been the main source of what to date have been small-scale clashes and standoffs, but they are bound up in part with uncertainties over the extent of energy resources, as well as concerns over access to fisheries resources. Public statements by the People's Liberation Army of China have expressed that country's determination to protect any possible reserves from what it calls the "predatory advances" of other states (cited in Dupont 1998a: 31). Sovereignty is also contested over the potentially energy-rich Diaoyu/Senkaku Islands, claimed by Japan, China, and Taiwan. Tensions and military posturing erupt periodically.

Harris notes, however, that the "historically common approach to accessing resources"—that is, military activity and conquest—has become "largely obsolete" (1995: 44). On the other hand, a number of examples exist of the mobilization of some kind of military capability, primarily low level and falling short of war, to secure or maintain access to resources or to deny others access to those resources. Thai naval vessels have accompanied fishing fleets in the face of rising concern over illegal fishing (although illegal fishing by Thailand has been a major source of tension with neighboring states). Shots have been fired on a number of occasions. In Northeast Asia, shots have also been exchanged between North Korean naval vessels and Chinese fishing trawlers and between Chinese and South Korean fishing trawlers. Russia and South Korea have at times placed their navies on alert in the face of illegal fishing activity. The Indonesian government has cited economic loss from illegal fishing as a major justification for strengthening its naval capabilities. The military is being used to protect borders and prevent cross-border logging on mainland Southeast Asia, although this has been complicated by military complicity in that logging activity and by border tensions that arise for other reasons—including refugees, insurgencies, and the narcotics trade. Despite these examples, environmental scarcity will not likely be the determining factor in major or acute conflict between states, a point Alan Dupont makes in his detailed study of possible environmental security "hot spots" in Pacific Asia (1998a: 75).

THE SECURITY CHALLENGE II: NONTRADITIONAL SECURITIES

Environmental change contributes to other kinds of regional insecurity that need to be taken seriously by strategic analysts and security policymakers. Regional security in East Asia rests on more than the absence of interstate conflict. Rather it requires good political relationships, the maintenance of dialogue, and reciprocal confidence. Environmental degradation can undermine all of these factors.

Many examples are seen of the transboundary use of resources or the transboundary environmental impact of economic activity in which diplomatic and political relationships between East Asian countries have been or could become disturbed or unsettled. These are often bound up with economic and food security. Transboundary water resources are one such example, particularly if, as the World Bank predicts, most countries in the region will be facing water shortages by 2025 (cited in Dupont 1998a: 62).

Much attention focuses on the Mekong River.[7] Despite various governance structures including the Mekong River Commission, governments there remain alert to the possibility for other countries to divert the river's waters for a range of uses (including hydropower and irrigation). This is particularly so because the 1995 agreement that presently regulates the use of the Mekong (and to which neither China nor Burma is a signatory) does not require states to obtain the approval of their Mekong neighbors for any water diversion scheme, except during the dry season. Both Cambodia and Vietnam rely heavily on the waters of the Mekong for irrigation and rice production. Laos, on the other hand, wants to use the Mekong to generate electricity for domestic consumption and for export to Thailand and Vietnam. The problems are not confined to water resources. The series of dams proposed for construction on the Mekong will not only divert water resources for other purposes but, along with the impacts of deforestation, will contribute to transboundary ecological disruption—including changes to the river's flood and siltation patterns, increase in salinity, and, potentially, serious impacts on freshwater fishing. The social and economic costs of this environmental change are also important security concerns.

Access to water remains a key feature of political tensions between Malaysia and Singapore as well. Singapore relies on Malaysia for almost half its water requirements, although this is complicated by the fact that Singapore then sells treated water back to Malaysia. The problem may become more difficult as Malaysia faces its own water shortages, particularly in Selangor and Negeri Sembilan, and as the water agreements between the two countries (some of which date to colonial times) come up for renegotiation.

Fisheries and energy resources offer other examples of environmental scarcities over which tension between states in the Asia Pacific region could erupt. Fish remains the primary source of protein for the region's peoples, as well as an important economic resource. Maritime fisheries, located primarily but not entirely in Exclusive Economic Zones (EEZs), are overfished to the point that this living and supposedly renewable resource is being severely depleted. Illegal fishing has become a serious regional problem, particularly through the encroachment of fishing vessels without licenses into EEZs and territorial seas. Dupont suggests that "inter-state confrontation over fish and other living resources . . . is emerging as a serious long-term security problem for the region" (1998b: 32).

In the case of nonliving energy resources, scarcity is likely to take two forms—growing demands for energy and a likely decline in energy self-sufficiency. Access to commercially exploitable energy resources such as hydrocarbon (oil and gas) deposits therefore becomes an important regional issue and one that could contribute to "strategic uncertainty" (Dupont 1998b: 29). As noted earlier, competition over access to energy resources (including hydropower resources) can exacerbate existing tensions, such as those in the South China Sea or the Mekong subregion.

Air pollution has become the latest transboundary issue to affect foreign relations and security concerns in the region. Perhaps the most public example of recent political and diplomatic tension over this kind of transboundary environmental impact has been the haze incidents, described earlier. Singapore, Malaysia, and Thailand have all expressed concern over the Indonesian government's inability or unwillingness to control the causes of the fires that generated the haze. In an unprecedented move, then-President Suharto was forced to apologize (twice) to his regional neighbors. In Northeast Asia the problem focuses mainly on transboundary acid rain originating primarily in China but causing anxiety in Japan and South Korea.

The relationship among environmental scarcity, interstate conflict, and political security is fairly clear in these cases. The security referent remains the state. Even if the "threat" arises from nonmilitary sources, the primary concerns are conflict and the incursion—intentional or not—into the territorial space and resource base of the state. Yet as the first section of this chapter suggested, approaches to security are limited if they concentrate only on the interstate dimension and only on the potential for extreme violence or conflict or, as developed here, the importance of mutual confidence and good political and diplomatic relationships. National and regional security can be undermined in other ways. It is important that those responsible for security and foreign policy take into account the contribution of environmental scarcities to intrastate instabilities, economic instability, and the insecurity of peoples and communities. As the discussion here demonstrates, these are not discrete policy areas. Nor are they entirely disconnected from the more obvious insecurities that arise from interstate conflict and tension or the security that arises from good political relations and cooperative impulses between states.

As suggested earlier, a liberal security model draws attention to the short- and long-term economic costs, for states and local economies, of environmental degradation and the ways in which it can undermine economic growth and regional economic interdependence that helps to establish and define regional security. The attention given in the security community to the Asian financial crisis of the late 1990s attests to this relationship. Yet enthusiasm for economic growth in East Asia has rarely taken into account the environmental costs of such growth. In other words, the environmental externalities have not been internalized. The pursuit of rapid economic growth—what Aat Vervoorn calls the "industrialization of Asia within the world economy" (1998: 157)—has contributed more to unsustainable development, environmental degradation, and resource depletion than has poverty, which is usually identified as a key factor in environmental decline.[8]

Environmental degradation imposes continuing costs on the region's economies, as well as on its peoples and communities. The Indonesian government estimates, for example, that each year the Indonesian economy loses up to $US4 billion from illegal fishing activity, twice the amount earned by the fishing industry (*Jakarta Post* 1999). The costs of the forest fire haze for 1997–1998 have been conservatively estimated at $US1.4 billion in health and lost tourism revenue and $US3 billion from losses in "timber, agriculture, non-timber forest products, hydrological and soils conservation and . . . biodiversity benefits" (Schweithelm 1998). The World Bank has estimated that air and water pollution costs the Chinese economy approximately $US54 billion annually in damage to human health and lost agricultural productivity, about 8 percent of Chinese gross domestic product (see Edwards 1997).

Sustainable economic growth that minimizes environmental costs can nevertheless be a poor measure of local and national security if distributive concerns are not taken into account. Indeed, sustainability is often defined to include a more balanced distribution of wealth. The World Commission on Environment and Development (WCED) identified "the relative neglect of economic and social justice" as a key factor in "our inability to promote the common interest in sustainable development" (WCED 1987: 47). Further, as Harris (1995: 42) observed (and this is where the more direct connection to traditional understandings of security lies), internal instability "feeds on underdevelopment," especially when it is marked by "gross inequities in the distribution of income and wealth."

Actual conflict or violence over environmental degradation, resources, and services is more likely at a subnational than the international level. Social tensions and conflict within states, however, raise concerns about national and regional political stability, as recent attention to different kinds of instabilities in Indonesia, Cambodia, the Philippines, and North Korea attests. Empirical studies on environment-induced subnational conflict bear this out. Thomas Homer-Dixon and his team at the Project on Environmental Change and Acute Conflict at the University of Toronto suggest, for example, that environmental degradation can contribute to instability and conflict through the "disruption of legitimized and authoritative social relations" (1991: 9). Norman Myers also anticipates "civil turmoil and outright violence" as a result of environmental scarcity (1989: 24). The causal links and contextual factors are varied, but inequitable access to and control over resources and environmental services are important. Economic and subsistence activity in the Asia Pacific region is increasingly characterized by "competing groups of users, includ[ing] tribal communities, peasants, fisher [people], miners, loggers and corporations" (Lim and Valencia 1990: 3). This competition is exacerbated by the kinds of pollution, ecosystem fragmentation, and scarcity outlined earlier. It is exacerbated by poverty, inadequate land tenure, and government policies that favor the privatization of common lands in predominantly corporate hands.

A few examples will give the flavor. In Thailand, conflict has erupted in Klong Tha Chin Bay and Songkhla Bay between inshore communities and commercial vessels over nocturnal anchovy fishing. The recent communal violence in Kalimantan between the Dayak peoples (a term used generally to cover most indigenous groups in both Indonesian and Malaysian Borneo) and the migrant Madurese has an environmental and resource dimension. Indigenous communities have been slowly dispossessed of their traditional access to land, forest resources, and livelihood in competition not simply with the Madurese or the transmigrated Javanese but also with corporate interests and government development imperatives. As Human Rights Watch Asia (1997) has observed, "Their sources of subsistence and cash income have been systematically depleted, and their lifestyle and culture have been treated with disdain as primitive and destructive in comparison with that of coastal Malays or immigrants from Java and Madura."

These concerns are clearly bound up with the human-security approach to environmental security. As noted earlier, the key security referent here is not the state but the individual and communities. The impact of environmental degradation undermines the health and livelihoods of the region's peoples, particularly those already economically marginalized. Security for the region in this context is defined not by the absence of conflict but in terms of measures such as those developed by the UNDP in its Human Development Index. Around 75 percent of the world's poor live in Asia (although these figures include South Asia; see UNEP 1999: 72). The loss of traditional and economically viable fisheries through pollution, ecosystem disruption, and overfishing, for example, compromises subsistence, food security, health, and income. Land degradation and deforestation have been major factors in sustained rural poverty in many countries in the region. Communities are often forced to use their land more intensively despite continued ecological impacts or to migrate to marginal lands or to the cities where environmental infrastructure is often scarce. In turn, this exacerbates the pressure on urban resources, including water and food. In many parts of the region, access to clean water is uncertain, sewage disposal facilities are rare, and the health consequences can be severe. Environmental change such as deforestation and land degradation has also been a factor in natural disasters (or disasters of nature) in the Asia-Pacific region, such as flooding in China and in the Mekong region or landslides in Thailand.

The human-security aspect of environmental change is further complicated when environmental management strategies "ignore concerns about human equity, health of ecosystems, other species and the welfare of future generations" (Postel 1996: 7). Market pricing of resources such as clean water, for example, often overlooks the ability or otherwise of the poor in urban and rural communities to pay such prices. The construction of dams on the Mekong to meet irrigation and energy demands has not only proceeded in the absence of environmental impact statements in a number of cases but has resulted (or will result) in the physical displacement and social and economic disruption of local.communities. This suggests that to enhance national and regional security and to prevent or minimize political and social instability as well as human insecurity, development must be more than environmentally sustainable; it must also be socially just.

ENVIRONMENTAL SECURITY POLICY

The complexity of the environment-security relationship discussed earlier points to the difficulties of identifying and defining response strategies. Domestic policy initiatives are clearly important. If environmental degradation poses a threat to national and regional security—whether through the potential for conflict, economic insecurity, continued inequity, and human vulnerability—policy responses need to focus on managing the causes and impacts of that environmental change at a local level. The focus here, however, is on what this means for *foreign* policy and for foreign policymakers and practitioners, including those whose focus has been "security" as more traditionally defined.

Security strategies and foreign policy responses based on traditional security modalities for protecting borders are increasingly obsolete when dealing with environmental insecurity at a national and regional level. The environment becomes "militarized" rather than "securitized" when military responses are anticipated as the strategies that will control access to resources, protect borders against environmental refugees, or take action against environmental pariah states. Focusing on environmental conflict as the main characteristic of environmental security runs the risk of narrowing policy options to those that only address symptoms. Environmental security is a common security issue in which each person or state is secure only when all are secure. The axiom for the politics of transboundary environmental change is that no one country can address environmental degradation unilaterally. Cooperation is therefore essential.

The policy challenge of a comprehensive and nontraditional approach to environmental security in the region is to respond to both cause and consequence in a way that gives priority to preventive security. This remains contentious within what is broadly understood as the security community. Scholars and practitioners of the more orthodox, realist variant of security object to the broadening of the agenda with the addition of other concerns that, although important, are considered only marginally relevant to state or national security. Mohammed Ayoob, for example, suggests that this "runs the risk of making the concept so elastic as to detract seriously from its utility as an analytical tool" (1991: 259).

The ASEAN Regional Forum and the Track Two (unofficial) process under the Council for Security Cooperation Asia Pacific have, however, acknowledged the importance and relevance of comprehensive security—including environmental security—to the definition and pursuit of regional security. ARF members inscribed the "comprehensive concept of security, including its economic and social aspects, as it pertains to the Asia-Pacific region" on the agenda at their first meeting (Chairman's Statement, reproduced in Inoguchi and Stillman 1997: 214–216). The objective of an environmental security policy should be to integrate security and environmental policies in the context of regional cooperation. Four interconnected policy initiatives underpin such an objective.

The first is the application of confidence-building measures (CBMs) and preventive diplomacy (PD) to environmental insecurities by integrating environmental scarcity into the regional security architecture. CBMs and PD have been identified as two of the region's key foreign policy strategies for pursuing regional security. ARF intersessional meetings on CBMs and seminars on PD have identified nonmilitary transnational issues, including environmental degradation, as one area in which these practices are relevant.[9]

Yet although nontraditional security issues and environmental scarcity in particular are acknowledged as part of the agenda, they have not been central to official statements or the commentary literature on confidence-building measures, preventive diplomacy, and conflict resolution. Approaches to comprehensive security remain resolutely statist and look to policy instruments more appropriate to a power politics version of security based on states, sovereignty, and the identification of deliberative military-based threats. Confidence building, for example, has focused on transparency in military operations, notification of military exercises, and exchange of military information and personnel. Studies such as those conducted by the ASEAN Institutes of Strategic and International Studies (ASEAN-ISIS) network have also focused on the military and defense components of confidence building (see Acharya 1999: 30; ASEAN-ISIS 1993). The elaboration of preventive diplomacy under ARF has been explicitly limited to severe disputes and conflicts between states to accommodate the regional principle of noninterference in the internal affairs of member states.

Yet nothing intrinsic to the definition or operating principles of either CBMs or PD prevents them from being applied to nontraditional security issues such as environmental insecurity and scarcity. Indeed, recent commentary suggests that such concerns might lend themselves more easily to such practices because they are considered less politically sensitive than traditional military issues. CBM strategies, particularly those that focus on transparency and notification, are directly relevant to the management of environmental change. They have been given expression in international environmental law through requirements for national reporting, the establishment of clearinghouse mechanisms, and the conduct of regular consultative processes under individual environmental agreements. The notion that foreign policy should be bound by a customary norm of prior informed consent (which surely falls into the category of confidence building) has been given further impetus by the 1998 Rotterdam Convention on Prior Informed Consent, even though that agreement relates only to certain hazardous chemicals and pesticides in international trade.

The modalities of preventive diplomacy as a foreign policy tool are directly applicable to nontraditional security issues, including environmental scarcities. As well as dialogue and information exchange, PD practices include fact-finding missions, a register of experts, early warning systems, intensified consultative processes, institutional building, and preventive humanitarian action—although the latter two would be controversial in East Asia.[10]

The boundaries of noninterference have imposed normative limitations on regional foreign policy on a range of issue areas. But noninterference is difficult to sustain, conceptually or practically, in the face of environmental insecurity. When it has unintended (or even intended) consequences, environmental degradation is an implicit form of interference—affecting environmental quality in another state, "violating" territorial integrity, and calling into question a government's autonomy over policy. Sovereignty means less when environmental degradation and its consequences do not respect state boundaries, and as Dupont argues, states have a "legitimate right to make their views known" (1999: 38) when their security is challenged or undermined in nontraditional ways.

The second component of a regional policy framework on environmental security is the adoption of an environmental early warning system that sets out response and monitoring strategies. The purpose of such a system is twofold. First, it can meet environmental criteria by providing policymakers with data that identify and anticipate environmental change and ecological disasters. Although the Regional Haze Action Plan adopted by the ASEAN countries has been criticized extensively, the plan has established a useful early warning precedent based on satellite monitoring coordinated by Singapore. Second, an early warning system can meet security criteria by contributing to conflict avoidance if the information can be used to antici-pate likely violence or instability. In a more general "insecurity" sense, envi-ronmental monitoring and data collection at a regional level are essential for the development of environmental standards and guidelines, as well as enabling policymakers and their advisers to calculate other insecurities such as economic and social costs. In both cases the goal is to prevent the inci-dence and escalation of "insecurity," whether measured in environmental or conflict terms. Early warning thus merges with the broader imperatives of crisis prevention.

The third dimension therefore focuses on preventive strategies that pay greater attention to identifying and managing the *causes* of regional environmental degradation. Although conflict avoidance or prevention is important, in the final analysis this requires dealing with the causes of inse-curity rather than the symptoms. As a foreign policy strategy, this kind of preventive approach to environmental security requires strengthening the conditions for environmental cooperation. Regional efforts to address envi-ronmental degradation and ecological decline will also serve as confidence-building measures, contributing to mutual confidence between states. This is likely to involve regional actors whose primary focus is neither environ-mental protection nor security, including the Asian Development Bank, the Asia-Pacific Economic Cooperation forum, and the United Nations Economic and Social Commission for Asia Pacific.

Regional environmental cooperation is more advanced in Southeast Asia. Within ASEAN, the history of cooperation on environmental issues dates to the late 1970s, although it has only recently gone much beyond declaratory statements and information exchange. The framework now in-cludes a range of soft-law instruments, including a series of declarations arising from the regular ASEAN Ministerial Meetings on the Environment and the various associated action plans that were adopted. There is to date only one formal, legally binding agreement—the 1985 ASEAN Agreement on the Conservation of Nature and Natural Resources, which has yet to enter into force. The institutional framework for cooperative dialogue on the environment is less well developed in Northeast Asia but not entirely absent. A number of bilateral agreements on environmental cooperation or protection have been supplemented by increasingly regular meetings of senior officials, interagency conferences, and nongovernmental meetings. The most important environmental CBM in Northeast Asia is probably the Northeast Asian Subregional Program on Environmental Cooperation, es-tablished in 1993 to provide a forum for discussion among China, North Korea, South Korea, Japan, Mongolia, and Russia.

Although regional environmental cooperation in Southeast Asia now pays specific attention to ecological principles and calls for joint action and harmonization of national approaches, and sustainable development is accepted as central to cooperation in Northeast Asia, environmental outcomes in both subregions have been less than successful. As the Asian Development Bank (ADB) put it, "Taken as a whole, the policy response has failed" (ADB 2000).[11] In other words, the causes of environmental scarcity and insecurity remain. In part this arises because environmental cooperation is rarely seen in practice as a form of preventive security.

Preventive action in the long term can only work effectively if the basic and underlying social and economic drivers of regional insecurities, not just regional conflicts, are addressed. This is the fourth component of a regional environmental security policy, and it expands the scope of regional environmental security responses from crisis prevention to human security. As Simon Tay observed, policies that address "poverty, social inequality and ethnic and cultural discrimination" help to build the "conditions for stability and peace—even in those situations where there is no immediate or clear threat of violence" (1997: 121, 122). There are clear national, regional, and human-security benefits in addressing the social and economic drivers of environmental decline. As good environmental and security policy, environmental strategies need to facilitate an equitable sharing of rights to, and responsibilities for, resource and environmental management. This is a human-security challenge. Not only is this likely to improve the chances of sustainable development, it also addresses the security concerns that arise when local communities resist environmental scarcities not of their own making.

CONCLUSION

The security challenges of environmental scarcity are not simply about state securities and interstate tensions. As a comprehensive and collective security problem, environmental security in East Asia must take account of instabilities within states, as well as the environmental consequences for human security. This changes the contours of security and foreign policy responses.

Meeting the demands of nontraditional or comprehensive security requires greater cooperation between "security institutions and institutions in other policy areas," including the environment (Lietzmann and Vest 1999: 9). It also requires attention to the causes embedded in loss of human welfare, as well as insecurity consequences for communities and states. Comprehensive security, which by the very nature of its scope extends beyond traditional military issues, is also therefore the concern of actors other than states, defense forces, and strategic planners. Those other actors, including regional and international institutions and nongovernmental organizations, contribute knowledge and expertise to resolve nontraditional security challenges and have a central role "as agents of preventive diplomacy" (Acharya 1999: 21–22). As Desmond Ball suggested, "Without the inclusion of intra-State conflicts, non-governmental actors and individuals as the reference subject of security, the preventive diplomacy discourse will remain substantially incomplete" (1999: 14). The same can be said about confidence-building measures. The normative and policy difficulties of developing and implementing a regional environmental security policy based on the components outlined here should not be understated. Unless they are addressed, however, the potential for environmental scarcity to undermine regional security to the point of acute conflict runs the risk of becoming a self-fulfilling prophecy.

NOTES

1. Those working groups include transnational crime, comprehensive security, and maritime cooperation.
2. For example, in the case of people smuggling, does the alleged "threat" come from those who are smuggled or from those who orchestrate the smuggling operations?
3. For more on the distinction between an environment-and-security approach and a securing the environment approach, see Elliott (1996).
4. Water-stressed countries are those with per capita annual supplies of water of between 1,000 and 2,000 cubic meters per person. Countries become "water scarce" when that supply drops below 1,000 cubic meters.
5. The seven megacities in East Asia are Bangkok, Beijing, Jakarta, Manila, Seoul, Shanghai, and Tokyo.
6. The notion of conflict over resources in East Asia is not new. Leggett suggests, for example, that access to oil infrastructure was a major reason for Japan's invasion of Burma and what was then the Dutch East Indies in World War II (1992: 70). In a similar vein, Lipschutz and Holdren argue that access to resources was one reason for U.S. intervention in Korea, to "prevent the loss . . . of Korean tungsten, Malaysian tin and rubber, New Caledonian nickel and Indonesian oil" (1990: 121).
7. The Mekong flows through Yunan Province in China, Burma, Thailand, Laos, Cambodia, and Vietnam.
8. Estimates suggest, for example, that every $US1 billion increase in Asian gross national product generates about 100 tons of hazardous and toxic waste (cited in Arif 1995: 124).
9. The Chairs' Statements from each of the three ARF Seminars on Preventive Diplomacy are reproduced in Ball (1999) and Acharya (1999).
10. For further discussion on a range of possible PD modalities, see Ball (1999) and Acharya (1999).
11. For a more extensive discussion of regional environmental cooperation under ASEAN and the difficulties ASEAN member states face in meeting environmental challenges, see Elliott (2000, 2001).

REFERENCES

Acharya, Amitav. 1999. "Preventive Diplomacy: Background and Application to the Asia-Pacific Region." In Desmond Ball and Amitav Acharya, eds., *The Next*

Lorraine Elliott

Stage: Preventive Diplomacy and Security Cooperation in the Asia-Pacific Region. Canberra Papers on Strategy and Defence 13.1. Canberra: Strategic and Defence Studies Centre, Australian National University.

Alagappa, Muthiah. 1988. "Introduction." In Muthiah Alagappa, ed., *Asian Security Practice: Material and Ideational Influences.* Stanford: Stanford University Press.

Arif, Mohamed. 1995. "Environmental Politics of the OECD and Their Implications for ASEAN." In Kiichiro Fukasaku and Joseph Tan, eds., *OECD and ASEAN Economies: The Challenge of Policy Coherence.* Paris: Organisation for Economic Cooperation and Development.

ASEAN-ISIS. 1993. *Confidence Building Measures in Southeast Asia.* Memorandum 5, December. Kuala Lumpur: Institute of Strategic and International Studies, Malaysia.

Asian Development Bank. 2000. *Asian Environmental Outlook 2001.* Manila: Asian Development Bank [see Executive Summary at http//www.adb.org].

Ayoob, Mohammed. 1991. "The Security Problematic of the Third World." *World Politics* 43, no. 2: 257–283.

Ball, Desmond. 1999. "Introduction: Toward a Better Understanding of Preventive Diplomacy." In Desmond Ball and Amitav Acharya, eds., *The Next Stage: Preventive Diplomacy and Security Cooperation in the Asia-Pacific Region.* Canberra Papers on Strategy and Defence 131. Canberra: Strategic and Defence Studies Centre, Australian National University.

Boutros-Ghali, Boutros. 1992. *An Agenda for Peace.* Report of the Secretary-General pursuant to the Statement adopted by the Summit Meeting of the Security Council on 31 January 1992, 47th session, Security Council S/24111; General Assembly A/47/277, 17 June.

Chalk, Peter A. 2000. " 'Grey Area Phenomena' and Human Security." In William T. Tow, Ramesh Thakur, and In-Taek Hyun, eds., *Asia's Emerging Regional Order.* Tokyo: United Nations University Publications.

Commission on Global Governance. 1995. *Our Global Neighbourhood.* Oxford: Oxford University Press.

Dupont, Alan. 1998a. *The Environment and Security in Pacific Asia.* Oxford: Oxford University Press for the International Institute of Strategic Studies.

———. 1998b. "Environmental Conflict in East Asia: Some Issues for the Region." In Alan Dupont, ed., *The Environment and Security: What Are the Linkages?* Canberra Papers on Strategy and Defence 125. Canberra: Strategic and Defence Studies Centre, Australian National University.

———. 1999. "The Future of the ARF: An Australian Perspective." In Khoo How San, ed., *The Future of the ARF.* Singapore: Institute of Defence and Strategic Studies, Nanyang Technological University.

Edwards, Nick. 1997. "China's Economy Hit With $54 Billion in Losses From Pollution." Singapore: Reuters [SEA-SPAN, archived at <http://www.icsea.or.id/sea-span>].

Elliott, Lorraine. 1996. "Environmental Conflict: Reviewing the Arguments." *Journal of Environment and Development* 5, no. 2 (June): 149–167.

———. 2000. "ASEAN's Environmental Regime: Pursuing Sustainability in Southeast Asia." *Global Environmental Change* 10, no. 3: 237–240.

————. 2001. "Environmental Challenges." In Daljit Singh, ed., *Southeast Asian Affairs 2001*. Singapore: Institute of Southeast Asian Studies.

Finger, Matthias. 1991. "The Military, the Nation-State and the Environment." *Ecologist* 21, no. 5 (September-October): 220–225.

Harris, Stuart. 1995. "The Economic Aspects of Security in the Asia/Pacific Region." *Journal of Strategic Studies* 18, no. 3 (September): 32–51.

Harris, Stuart, and Andrew Mack. 1997. "Security and Economics in East Asia." In Stuart Harris and Andrew Mack, eds., *Asia-Pacific Security: The Economics-Politics Nexus*. St. Leonards, New South Wales, Australia: Allen and Unwin.

Homer-Dixon, Thomas F. 1991. "On the Threshold: Environmental Changes as Causes of Acute Conflict." *International Security* 16, no. 2 (fall): 76–116.

Human Rights Watch Asia. 1997. "The Horror in Kalimantan." *Inside Indonesia* 51 (July-September), <http://insideindonesia.org/edit51/hrw2.htm>.

Inoguchi, Takashi, and Grant B. Stillman, eds. 1997. *North-east Asian Regional Security: The Role of International Institutions*. Tokyo: United Nations University Press.

Jakarta Post. 1999. "Indonesia Loses 4 Billion in Lost Revenue Every Year." 1 November [SEA-SPAN; archived at www.icsea.or.id/sea-span].

Japan Environment Council. 1999. *The State of the Environment in Asia 1999/2000*. Singapore: Institute of Southeast Asian Studies.

Kaplan, Robert D. 1994. "The Coming Anarchy?" *Atlantic Monthly* 273, no. 2 (February): 44–76.

Leggett, Jeremy. 1992. "The Environmental Impact of War: A Scientific Analysis and Greenpeace's Reaction." In Glen Plant, ed., *Environmental Protection and the Law of War*. London: Belhaven.

Lietzmann, Kurt M., and Gary D. Vest, eds. 1999. *Environment and Security in an International Context: Final Report*. Report no. 232. Brussels: NATO, Committee on the Challenges of Modern Society.

Lim Teck Ghee and Mark Valencia. 1990. "Introduction." In Lim Teck Ghee and Mark Valencia, eds., *Conflict Over Natural Resources in Southeast Asia and the Pacific*. Singapore: Oxford University Press.

Lipschutz, Ronnie D., and John P. Holdren. 1990. "Crossing Borders: Resource Flows, the Global Environment and International Security." *Bulletin of Peace Proposals* 21, no. 2: 121–133.

Myers, Norman. 1989. "Environment and Security." *Foreign Policy* 74 (spring): 23–41.

Porter, Gareth. 1995. "Environmental Security as a National Security Issue." *Current History* 94, no. 592: 218–222.

Postel, Sandra. 1996. *Dividing the Waters: Food Security, Ecosystem Health and the New Politics of Scarcity*. New York: W. W. Norton.

Schweithelm, James. 1998. *The Fire This Time: An Overview of Indonesia's Forest Fire in 1997/98*. Jakarta: WWF Indonesia Programme.

Tay, Simon. 1997. "Preventive Diplomacy and the ASEAN Regional Forum: Principles and Possibilities." In Desmond Ball and Amitav Acharya, eds., *The Next Stage: Preventive Diplomacy and Security Cooperation in the Asia-Pacific Region*. Canberra Papers on Strategy and Defence 131. Canberra: Strategic and Defence Studies Centre.

United Nations Development Programme. 1994. *Human Development Report 1994.* Oxford: Oxford University Press.

United Nations Environment Programme. 1999. *Global Environmental Outlook 2000.* London: Earthscan.

Vervoorn, Aat. 1998. *ReOrient: Change in Asian Societies.* Oxford: Oxford University Press.

Winnefeld, James A., and Mary E. Morris. 1994. *Where Environmental Concerns and Security Strategies Meet: Green Conflict in Asia and the Middle East.* Santa Monica, CA: RAND.

World Commission on Environment and Development. 1987. *Our Common Future.* Oxford: Oxford University Press.

3

Environmental Security, International Cooperation, and U.S. Foreign Policy Toward Northeast Asia

PAUL G. HARRIS

Since the early 1980s, many governments have started to view adverse environmental changes and resource scarcities as threats to national security, as Chapter 2 highlights. Environmental changes and resource scarcities can threaten economic growth, damage human health, and contribute to domestic strife and international conflict, possibly even leading to war. Because Northeast Asia includes some of the most heavily polluted areas in the world and its natural resources are under tremendous stress from economic growth, countries and peoples of the region face threats to their environmental security. In China, economic growth has led to sharp increases in emissions of pollutants causing global warming and associated climatic changes. The effects of climate change for China and the region will likely be severe at times, but they will also affect the entire world. Among the countries concerned about environmental changes in Northeast Asia is the United States. This concern is important because the United States can be a catalyst for—or a hindrance to—environmental protection and sustainable development in the region. In recent years it has worked with

The author wishes to thank Brian Bridges, James Tang, and participants in the workshop "Old Wine in New Bottles? The Bush Administration's Security Policy and Northeast Asia," Lingnan University, Hong Kong, 7–8 May 2001, for their helpful comments on an earlier draft of this chapter.

countries there to promote international environmental cooperation. The question is, will it continue this role?

Madeleine Albright, the Clinton administration's last secretary of state, described the United States as an "indispensable" power. Although many debated the veracity and desirability of this assertion, many within the U.S. government agreed with her. As such, the United States under Clinton was active in foreign affairs—as American administrations unavoidably have been since World War II—including in the realm of environmental change. Indeed, environmental issues took on a new prominence during the Clinton years, on occasion being among the most important foreign policy items on the president's and his diplomats' agendas. During the Clinton administration the United States came to accept environmental changes as genuine threats to national security, and it viewed East Asia (especially China) as a region where such changes could contribute to insecurity that might affect U.S. interests. Although traditional security issues were usually considered more important, there was a consensus in the Clinton administration that environmental issues ought to receive serious attention from the security establishment. Thus whereas trade and traditional security concerns have always been at the forefront of thinking among U.S. policymakers dealing with Northeast Asia, environmental security was also a component of U.S. foreign policy toward this region.

In sharp contrast to its predecessor, the administration of George W. Bush began its term by declaring a lack of interest in, or opposition to, previously agreed frameworks on many foreign policy issues, including many at the top of the previous administration's priorities—such as those related to environmental change. Hence the Bush administration abandoned or stepped back from previously vital negotiations in many regions, such as those to prevent conflict in the Middle East and on the Korean Peninsula, and it radically altered U.S. policy in many security issues—as manifested by, for example, its pledge to build a ballistic missile defense system and withdraw from the Anti-Ballistic Missile Treaty. In the environmental field it forcefully asserted that the United States was no longer interested in the Kyoto Protocol, a treaty designed to start reducing greenhouse gas emissions of most industrialized countries—of which the United States is by far the largest contributor.

It therefore appeared that environmental security would be downgraded in U.S. foreign policy, and it was unclear what consensus would emerge regarding environmental security in Northeast Asia. The Bush administration's international environmental policies (and much foreign policy generally), far from showing the leadership of an indispensable power, started off being if not those of a spoiler, certainly those of almost unilateral indifference. If the Bush administration ignores environmental issues, the incentive for countries in the region to address environmental changes will likely be reduced, thereby possibly contributing to existing tensions that threaten wider regional security and peace. Having said this, environmental changes themselves (not to mention environmentalists, career government officials, and other governments interested in these issues) may pressure the Bush administration and its high-level security officials to pay serious attention to environmental security in Northeast Asia. Thus the administration's indifference may not last. Environmental changes may have an unavoidable life of their own in U.S. foreign policy.

In this chapter I begin by briefly introducing the notion of environmental security (which is given much more detailed treatment in Chapter 2) and assert that it became an important foreign policy issue during previous U.S. administrations, particularly the Clinton administration. I do not try to argue that the U.S. government has at any time thought collectively that environmental changes were (or are) as important in the short term as were (and are) other traditional security issues related to Northeast Asia (e.g., China-Taiwan relations, defense relations with Japan, or missile development on the Korean Peninsula). This is followed by a discussion of the Clinton administration's policies on environmental security and some of its concerns about East Asia because insofar as U.S. foreign policy is consistent from one administration to the next (as it always is to a great degree, despite changes in leadership), this can help us anticipate the policies of the Bush administration and subsequent U.S. administrations. I then postulate how the United States will deal with environmental issues. My conclusion may be rather provocative: I think environmental security in Northeast Asia will eventually receive nearly as much attention from Bush as it did from Clinton—and perhaps even more. This is likely to be a general trend in future U.S. foreign policy, regardless of who controls the White House. The U.S. "war on terrorism" will be a major distraction, but that should not alter the general long-term trend in policy.

Apart from scholarly curiosity about U.S. foreign security policy in Northeast Asia, the questions addressed here are important for the region. The United States needs to remain engaged and active in environmental change issues because it plays such an important, sometimes overarching role.[1] It can, if it chooses, provide diplomatic leadership and thereby coax other countries to address environmental pollution and resource scarcities, and it is an important source of funding and technology necessary for environmental protection in the region. In short, the United States can be a catalyst for international environmental cooperation in Northeast Asia. If the United States avoids these issues, they may contribute to events that are destructive to the interests of the region, possibly adversely affecting the environmental security and national interests of the United States as well.

ENVIRONMENTAL SECURITY AND NORTHEAST ASIA

The concept of environmental security has been given substantial treatment in the literature for more than a decade (see Allenby 2001; Barnett 2001b; Dalby 1992; Deudney 1990; Graeger 1996; Homer-Dixon 1999; Homer-Dixon and Blitt 1998; Litfin 1999; Lowi and Shaw 2000; Mathews 1989). In short, environmental security is about the connections between human-induced environmental changes and national and (perhaps) human security. During the Cold War, U.S. conceptions of security were decidedly narrow, focusing on anticommunism and containment of the Soviet Union and its allies. Although traditional security conceptions still have traction with respect to Northeast Asia—particularly in the cases of China and North Korea—political, economic, and environmental issues have moved onto the security agenda.

To be sure, the very notion of environmental security is contested (see Conca and Dabelko 1998: 279–316; Deudney 1990; Deudney and Matthew 1999; Elliott 1998: 219–241; Levy 1995; Lowi and Shaw 2000). I will not enter that debate here, if for no other reason than because, despite the debate among scholars, environmental issues have garnered the attention of policymakers, sometimes at the highest levels—including within security bureaus of foreign ministries, defense agencies, and even military alliances (e.g., the North Atlantic Treaty Organization [NATO]). This has occurred because environmental pollution and resource scarcities have importance from a broad security perspective for a variety of reasons, most of which interact. And preexisting problems and conflicts may be exacerbated by environmental changes. The upshot is that governments have come to view environmental changes as genuine potential threats to their security—broadly defined to include threats to human health, economic development and growth, access to natural resources, stable interstate relations, and prevention of violent conflict (particularly within states). This view was shared, even led, by the United States in the 1990s (see Allenby 2001; Barnett 2001a; Blum 2001).

We can categorize environmental threats under the rubric of "hard" security—namely, those ecological and resource changes that can lead to violent conflict between states—and "soft" security—meaning threats to security more broadly defined to include economic development, human health, and the like. With regard to hard security, environmental changes have the potential to lead to violent conflict, create political instability, and undermine national governments. Some analysts argue that resource scarcities may contribute to or even cause war. Thomas Homer-Dixon and others have shown how environmental changes and resource scarcities can contribute to violent conflict, especially domestic conflict, and how those changes and scarcities might be factors in interstate conflict (although this is much less likely) (Homer-Dixon 1999; see Barnett 2000). What is important is that U.S. policymakers came to perceive these potential threats, integrating them into the U.S. foreign policy agenda.

Much more often, environmental changes and natural resource scarcities, particularly scarcities of renewable resources, will not directly cause violent conflict. Instead they hinder economic development and growth, undermine social harmony, cause illness, and generally harm human well-being. As Lorraine Elliott points out in Chapter 2, "Regional security in East Asia rests on more than the absence of interstate conflict. Rather it requires good political relationships, the maintenance of dialogue, and reciprocal confidence. Environmental degradation can undermine all of these." There are connections between the hard and soft effects of environmental changes, of course. Environmental changes can exacerbate existing conflicts or contribute to conditions that harm economic and human security, which in turn can combine with existing domestic and international animosities that decrease overall security within and among countries.

Many environmental issues confront Northeast Asia, with potentially adverse impacts on the countries there. These problems can also have direct and (more often) indirect impacts on countries outside the region, including the United States. In one of the most pessimistic assessments of the region in this regard, researchers reported that population pressures and rapid economic development are creating increasing resource scarcities and environmental destruction, which "may threaten or compromise not only future economic development but also internal stability and regional political relations" (Nautilus Institute and GLOCOM 2000: 2). According to that assessment, "Ecological stress in Northeast Asia could exacerbate international political tensions; competition over scarce resources could fuel ethnic conflicts; large movements of environmental refugees could lead to clashes with resident populations; and massive natural disasters or hard-to-control epidemics could instigate political instability" (Nautilus Institute and GLOCOM 2000: 2).

As the case of China shows vividly, environmental changes are already having adverse impacts within the region. The Chinese government, for example, recognizes that environmental degradation, such as air and water pollution, and overuse of resources are adversely affecting China's economic development and the health of its people. An assessment of China's National Environmental Protection Agency estimated that the economic cost of these factors amounts to about 14 percent of the country's gross domestic product (WRI 1999, cited in Nanto 2000: 24). This will not be good for those countries, such as the United States, hoping to benefit from China's development by increasing exports to it.

Chapter 2 described many of the environmental problems facing Northeast Asia (see also Chapter 9; Dupont 1998; Schreurs 2000: 136–142; UNEP 1999: 72–97). They include desertification and deforestation, freshwater shortages and marine pollution, declining fisheries and concerns about whale hunting, atmospheric pollution and global warming (and the impacts of resulting climate change), energy use and other natural resource scarcities, and the security implications of environmental and resource issues. Given these sometimes severe problems, it is not surprising that the countries of Northeast Asia, like the United States, have come to view environmental changes and resource scarcities as important aspects of their domestic and foreign policies. China, Japan, and South Korea have implemented laws and policies to clean up and protect their domestic environments, and they have started to cooperate bilaterally and with countries outside the region—including the United States—to address these issues.

China has been particularly concerned recently with the effects of pollution and resource scarcities on its economic development and quality of life in affected areas. It has garnered substantial external support to clean up its industries and power generation facilities and to generally make its development more environmentally sustainable. Japan has been concerned about the effect of the quality of marine ecosystems on its fishing industries, and China and Japan have worked together to clean up China's coal emissions, thereby reducing the effects of air pollution in China and acid rain in the Koreas and Japan. Even on the Korean Peninsula—where a cold war prevails—there is increasing interest in addressing potential environmental threats to national security. South Korea has tended to view its security interests narrowly in response to dangers posed by the communist North. But the South's rapid economic and political development—the former causing substantial environmental pollution and creating demand for scarce resources—has contributed to a reevaluation of its security to include nontraditional issues, including environmental ones (Bedeski 2000). Indeed, substantial pollution spreads from North to South Korea. Cooperation between the two countries is required to address these issues, and it may be one avenue to improve their relations more generally—a situation that demonstrates the potential for cooperation on environment and regional security in Northeast Asia. Environmental changes and resource scarcities may be stimuli for conflict in the region, but they can also motivate countries to cooperate.

ENVIRONMENTAL SECURITY IN
U.S. FOREIGN POLICY AFTER THE COLD WAR

Concerns about environmental issues from a broad security perspective have risen on the U.S. policy agenda, particularly following the Cold War.[2]

The U.S. government gradually accepted the notion that environmental changes could threaten U.S. national security and that it was in America's long-term interest to aid other countries in developing in an environmentally sustainable fashion to prevent or reduce threatening environmental changes, resource scarcities, and their consequences. The Clinton administration embraced the notion of environmental security as an important factor in U.S. foreign policy and U.S. defense planning in particular (see White House 1996),[3] and there were clear signs in the first Bush administration that environmental security was an important U.S. concern. Indeed interest in this issue by the U.S. government began even earlier. For example, during the Reagan administration, Richard Benedick, deputy assistant secretary of state for environment, health, and natural resources, said the administration had recognized that U.S. national interests could be undermined by instability in other countries related to environmental degradation, population pressures, and resource scarcity (State Department 1986).

FROM THE FIRST BUSH ADMINISTRATION THROUGH THE CLINTON ADMINISTRATION

George Bush was the first president to explicitly incorporate environmental issues into U.S. national security policy (Ketter, Borick, and Cabral 1999: 235). In 1991 he said securing "the sustainability and environmental security of the planet" was among U.S. security objectives (Porter 1995: 221). His secretary of state, James Baker, said in 1990 that the important U.S. foreign policy goals of democracy, prosperity, security, and cooperation were interconnected with the environment. Baker said that for this reason, he and President Bush were "committed to ensuring that environmental issues are fully integrated into [U.S.] diplomatic efforts. This is the greening of [American] foreign policy" (State Department 1990: 2).[4]

The Bush administration had to contend with a Congress sympathetic to greater U.S. action to address international environmental threats to U.S. interests. In 1989 then Senator Al Gore called for a "sacred agenda" in international relations as part of new requirements for collective security: "policies that enable the rescue of the global environment" (Gore 1989).[5] In a 1990 speech before the Senate, Democratic Senator Sam Nunn, then chairman of the Senate Armed Services Committee, described threats to U.S. national security, including what he called a "new and different threat" to that security: "the destruction of our environment" (Nunn 1990). He called on the intelligence and defense agencies of the U.S. government to pool their resources to address environmental dangers threatening both the United States and the world: "The defense establishment has a clear stake in countering this growing threat. I believe that one of our key national security objectives must be to reverse the accelerating pace of environmental destruction around the world. . . . America must lead the way in marshaling a global response to the problem of environmental degradation, and the defense establishment should play an important role" (Nunn 1990). Similarly, Republican Representative Benjamin Gilman (later chair of the House Committee on International Relations after the Republican sweep of Congress in 1994) reminded his colleagues in early 1992 that William Gates, director of the Central Intelligence Agency, had emphasized the relationship between environment and national security in House testimony. According to Gilman, "I do not think we can emphasize enough the growing understanding of the intricate and vital relationship between the environment and our surrounding ecosystems and food supply and our security" (United States 1993: 14).

Even the West's great Cold War military alliance joined the accelerating environmental security bandwagon. In 1991 the North Atlantic Treaty Organization added economic, social, and environmental problems to its list of major threats to the alliance (NATO Press Service 1991). Like the defense ministries of its member states, NATO acknowledged the connection between environmental change and national security by establishing a bureau devoted to environmental security. It is unlikely that it could have done so without the approval, and more likely active support, of the U.S. government, in particular the Department of Defense. Subsequently, environmental issues became much more prominent considerations in NATO planning (see NATO Committee n.d.; Banks 1994).

To be sure, threats from nuclear proliferation, terrorism, drugs, industrial espionage, and the like remained highest on political and national security agendas; but by the advent of the Clinton administration U.S. officials clearly recognized that successfully combating problems caused by environmental changes required a redefinition and reprioritization of national interests. Documents describing the U.S. national security strategy during the Clinton administration were permeated with references to environmental security generally and environmental threats to U.S. interests in particular (see White House 1995 and subsequent versions). To wit: "An emerging class of transnational environmental issues are increasingly affecting international stability and consequently will present new challenges to U.S. strategy" (White House 1995: 1).

Timothy Wirth, undersecretary of state for global affairs, told an audience in 1994 that "the life support systems of the entire globe are being compromised at a rapid rate—illustrating our interdependence with nature and changing relationships to the planet. Our security as Americans is inextricably linked to these trends" (quoted in de Sherbinin 1995: 29).[6] Wirth declared that the United States and other countries "are coming to understand the close connections between poverty, the environment, the economy and security. . . . It is time to retool our approach to national security—recognizing that our economic and environmental futures are one and the same" (Wirth 1995: 55). The security of the United States, he said, "depends on more than military might [because] boundaries are porous; environmental devastation and disease do not stop at national borders" (Wirth 1994). Wirth's views were indicative of the extent to which many U.S. policymakers were concerned about the effect environmental change might have on both the U.S. and global economies.

By his own account, the Clinton administration's first secretary of state, Warren Christopher, was the first person in his position to give a full-length speech on environmental issues (Christopher 1998: 412). In that speech he said, "The environment has profound impact on [U.S.] national interests in two ways: First, environmental forces transcend borders and oceans to threaten directly the health, prosperity, and jobs of American citizens. Second, addressing natural resource issues is frequently critical to achieving political and economic stability and to pursuing our strategic goals around the world" (Christopher 1996a). Christopher continued,

> In carrying out America's foreign policy, we will of course use our diplomacy backed by strong military forces to meet traditional and continuing threats to our security, as well as to meet new threats such as terrorism, weapons proliferation, drug trafficking and international crime. But we must also contend with the vast new danger posed to our national interests by damage to the environment and resulting global and regional instability. (Christopher 1996a)

To ensure that environmental issues would become part of the U.S. diplomatic agenda, Christopher and the State Department "had to persuade the American people that a healthy environment is critical to national security . . . showing how what we considered to be a 'soft' issue had a place in U.S. diplomacy alongside the more traditional 'hard' foreign policy concerns" (Christopher 1998: 414). It seemed to work. A newspaper editorial responded to the speech by saying it showed that "all the missiles and smart bombs in the U.S. arsenal will not be able to protect Americans from rising oceans and the northward movement of mosquito-borne diseases such as malaria and dengue fever" (expected consequences of global warming) ("Ecological Diplomacy" 1996).

As vice president, Al Gore was well-known for his concern for the global environment (see Gore 1992). In 1994 he said America's enemy was "more subtle than the British fleet. Climate change is the most serious problem our civilization faces, and it has caused enormous damage before in human history" (Gore 1995: 52). A few years later he said the United States had "moved beyond Cold War definitions of the United States' strategic interests. Our foreign policy must now address a broad range of threats—

including damage to the world's environment—that transcend countries and continents and require international cooperation" (Gore 1998, cited in Doran 2000: 69).

In several speeches President Clinton described the connections he saw between environment and national security. In 1993 he said Americans

> Face the extinction of untold numbers of species that might support our livelihoods and provide medication to save our lives. Unless we act now, we face a future in which the sun may scorch us, not warm us; where the change of season may take on a dreadful new meaning; and where our children's children will inherit a planet far less hospitable than the world in which we came of age. . . . In an era of global economics, global epidemics and global environmental hazards, a central challenge of our time is to promote our national interest in the context of its connectedness with the rest of the world. We share our atmosphere, our planet, our destiny with all the peoples of this world. And the policies I outline today will protect all of us because that is the only way we can protect any of us. (Clinton 1995: 50–51)

In a speech to the National Academy of Sciences in 1994, Clinton said he was influenced by scholarly work on environmental security.[7] He went on:

> If you look at the landscape of the future and you say, we have to strengthen the families of the globe; we have to encourage equitable and strong growth; we have to provide basic health care; we have to stop AIDS from spreading; we have to develop water supplies and improve agricultural yields and stem the flow of refugees and protect the environment, and on and on and on—it gives you a headache. (Clinton 1995: 2)

A headache indeed, but he and his administration were starting to take these issues seriously.[8]

Concern that environmental changes were threatening U.S. national security was not exclusive to Democratic politicians. Echoing his earlier concerns, in 1993 Representative Gilman proposed a bill establishing a National Committee on the Environment and National Security to "study the role in United States national security of security against global environmental threats, in light of recent global political changes and the rise of new environmental threats to the earth's natural resources and life support systems" (United States 1993). Recognition of environmental threats to U.S. national security also became part of Department of Defense (DOD) strategic planning.[9] A 1994 report issued by the Army War College's Strategic Studies Institute said the DOD ought to proactively address environmental change issues because "the change in the international arena since the end of the Cold War has given rise to an entirely new approach to viewing U.S. security interests, and a recognition of environmental factors in international stability and the onset of conflict" (Hughes 1994: 1–2). According to Kent Butts, the U.S. national security system recognized environmental problems as security threats, and the "term environmental security reflects the national policymakers' view of current threats to U.S. security" (1996: 22). Beginning in 1991, all National Security Strategy documents cited environmental change issues as important components of U.S. national interests (see White House 1995, 1996, and subsequent versions).[10] Butts points out that after the Cold War these documents changed to reflect the waning of the strategic nuclear threat and the ascendance of regional, economic, and environmental threats to U.S. national interests (Butts 1996: 24).[11] The focus of U.S. national security strategy shifted toward regional conflict, protecting the economy as a vital national interest and addressing environmental issues that threaten U.S. interests.

What explains the U.S. government's evolving policies on this issue? The U.S. government's recognition of environmental changes as potential threats to U.S. national interests was in part an outgrowth of reports by scholars and scientists arguing that environmental security was a function of the connected issues of environment and development throughout the world, especially in the developing world. The United States would benefit on several fronts. It might be spared many of the indirect adverse economic consequences of environmental change (such as lost markets in the developing world), it might be less likely to have to contend with the potential violent conflict that could arise from environmental destruction in developing regions, and Americans might avoid potential direct threats to their health and well-being (see Harris 2001b).

ENVIRONMENTAL SECURITY AND THE CLINTON ADMINISTRATION: CONCERNS ABOUT NORTHEAST ASIA

The Clinton strategy on environmental security contained a regional element. Its goal was to "confront pollution and the scarcity of resources in key areas where they dramatically increase tensions within and among nations" (Christopher 1996a). The Clinton administration viewed cooperation on environmental issues broadly as a means for promoting other U.S. interests. The State Department believed bilateral environmental relationships were "critical to moving the U.S. global agenda forward as well as promoting relations that further U.S. national interests in economic and political spheres" (State Department 1998a). This in part reflected demands from other countries. Indeed they sometimes raised environmental issues in regional meetings, such as those of the Asia-Pacific Economic Cooperation forum.

In Northeast Asia, the United States showed the most interest in environmental changes resulting from China's economic growth. But the United States also had environmental concerns related to Japan and South Korea. For example, cooperation on environmental issues like climate change was part of the U.S.-Japan Common Agenda, a framework for guiding joint efforts on global issues (State Department 1996b, 1999b, 2000b). Citing acid rain in Japan and the Koreas from China's coal-burning plants, internal environmental problems, and the potential impacts of China's increasing demand for energy, the State Department's first annual report on environment and foreign policy discussed the importance of regional issues. It said in part:

> The environmental fates of nations are inextricably and intimately linked within a region. . . . The ability of countries to tackle these types of problems has significant implications for their internal political and economic stability, for the political and economic stability of their region, and by extension U.S. foreign policy. Today . . . implementing American foreign policy means working on environmental issues. (State Department 1996a)

Regarding regional energy security and access to maritime resources, during the Clinton administration the United States took a consistently strong interest in territorial disputes in the East and South China Seas (see State Department 1998b). The United States, as always, was very concerned about maintaining its rights of passage through regional seas. More specifically, U.S. worries about territorial claims to these areas and associated islands was derived from more than concerns about rights of passage. They were derived from concerns about control of sea lines of communication for energy imports and access to mineral and marine living resources. As such, these claims fell under the rubric of environmental security.

Again, the chief U.S. concern with environmental security in Northeast Asia (and beyond) has been related to China. President Clinton in particular seemed profoundly concerned about the environmental consequences of economic growth in China. China was expected to overtake the United States in coming decades as the leading source of greenhouse gases (see Marland et al. 1998).[12] At one point President Clinton told President Jiang Zemin, "The greatest threat to our security that you present is that all of your people will want to get rich in exactly the same way we got rich. . . . There are just so many more of you than there are of us, and if you behave exactly the same way we do, you will do irrevocable damage to the global environment" (quoted in Friedman 1996: A23). He reiterated such statements during subsequent speeches (see White House 1997a). In a 1998 speech, President Clinton included these remarks, which were telling about his views on U.S.-China environmental relations:

China is experiencing an environmental crisis perhaps greater than any other nation in history at a comparable stage of its development. . . . Early in the [twenty-first] century China will surpass the United States as the world's largest emitter of greenhouse gases, which are dangerously warming our planet. This matters profoundly to the American people, because what comes out of smokestacks or goes into a river in China can do grievous harm beyond its borders. It is a fool's errand to believe that we can deal with our present and future global environmental challenges without strong cooperation from China. (White House 1998: 4)

He repeated this message while visiting China shortly thereafter (see Harding 1998). In short, according to one assessment, President Clinton was "suggesting that the greatest threat China presented to American security was environmental, not military" (Frank 1997a: 1). Not surprisingly, then, during the Clinton administration the United States and China cooperated on many environmental issues (e.g., fisheries, toxic chemicals, forests, clean energy) through myriad projects.[13]

In its final budget request before handing the White House over to Bush, the Clinton administration reiterated the connection between environmental changes in East Asia and U.S. interests, declaring further: "It is in the U.S. national interest to secure a sustainable global environment in order to protect the U.S. and its citizens from environmental degradation" (State Department 2000a: 24). Hence the notion of environmental security continued to influence U.S. foreign policy thinking right through the Clinton presidency. A general consensus across agencies, notably the Defense and State Departments, held that environmental issues were important enough to warrant attention, sometimes at the highest levels.

Three broad processes shaped the Clinton administration's policies toward environmental security (see Harris 2001b). First, policymakers increasingly believed environmental changes and resource scarcities were affecting and would continue to affect U.S. interests, either directly or indirectly. This led them to integrate Northeast Asian national and regional environmental issues into the U.S. security paradigm. Second, the pluralistic policy process in the United States, which allows ready access for national and even international interest groups, pushed the administration to raise the profile of environmental security within the U.S. government and pulled it (with somewhat less tenacity) to avoid doing more. Third, people within the Clinton administration were genuinely concerned about the natural environment, and they pushed the issue throughout the foreign policy process. Hence a shift occurred toward greater consideration of environmental security (albeit with rather limited action relative to potential threats). Similar forces were at work in the new Bush administration.

ENVIRONMENTAL SECURITY AND FOREIGN POLICY
IN THE BUSH ADMINISTRATION

When George W. Bush took office as U.S. president in January 2001, he and his administration quickly adopted a confrontational stance vis-à-vis the natural environment. The president reversed many of his predecessor's last-minute executive orders geared toward protecting the U.S. environment (e.g., he called for opening the Arctic National Wildlife Refuge, protected coastal areas, and national forests to resource exploitation) and toward limiting the health effects of pollution in the United States (e.g., his statements on arsenic in drinking water and salmonella in food). He also created controversy by reversing his campaign pledge to reduce emissions of carbon dioxide (the chief greenhouse gas) from U.S. electric plants, and he reiterated his opposition to the Kyoto Protocol on climate change, suggesting that an energy "crisis" was already leading to high prices for U.S. consumers.

President Bush's reversal on reducing U.S. carbon dioxide emissions and his administration's desire to withdraw from the Kyoto Protocol were ominous. The apparent downgrading of domestic and international environmental issues generally was suggestive of the administration's views, and it could lead one to expect that Northeast Asian environmental security would move down the policy agenda. It seemed all but certain that more traditional security concerns regarding Northeast Asia would push aside concern about environmental changes there. Insofar as environmental and natural resource issues exacerbate existing tensions, however—as they have, for example, on the Korean Peninsula—environmental security becomes important even from more traditional security perspectives. Despite the warning signs, it is unclear what long-term U.S. policy will be on international environmental issues. Indeed even high-level officials are probably not sure what long-term U.S. international environmental policy will look like. Witness events surrounding the Bush administration's domestic environmental policy—in which the administrator of the Environmental Protection Agency (EPA) on several occasions stated policy, only to have her statements retracted by the White House (see Seelye 2001)—and particularly the administration's policies regarding carbon dioxide cuts in the United States and its participation in the Kyoto Protocol implementation negotiations, where the EPA administrator believed Bush's campaign pledges and ran with them to international meetings—only to have the president reverse course (see Whitman 2001; *Economist* 2001a, 2001b).

Many things were (and are) happening at once to shape U.S. policies on environmental issues. The Bush administration was pressured by an alliance of conservative and industry groups to reverse his campaign pledge to limit carbon dioxide emissions of energy plants in the United States and to not only reassert his campaign pledges against the Kyoto Protocol (Bush and Cheney n.d.: 3) but to declare it moribund from the U.S. perspective (Goldstein and Pianin 2001; Pianin and Goldstein 2001; Pianin 2001b). U.S. conservative organizations also made a more general effort to weed all environmentalists from the U.S. government. But this coalition against domestic environmental protection, particularly U.S. involvement in the Kyoto Protocol implementation process, engendered substantial opposition from within and outside the United States. For example, even local Republicans in Florida (a state vulnerable to sea-level rise from climate change and one that has always been in the forefront of presidential contenders' minds— even more so after the 2000 election) called on their governor (the president's brother) to pressure Washington to rejoin the Kyoto process and start limiting U.S. greenhouse gas emissions (BBC World, 22 April 2001). And two-thirds of Americans believed the Bush administration should develop a plan to reduce greenhouse gas emissions, which three-quarters of them thought were causing global warming (Associated Press 2001). Even some religious groups, important Bush constituencies, adopted global warming as an issue they wanted to see the administration address (Whitman 2001). And the strange logic underlying the president's position on climate change—that the United States needs to find more petroleum, not conserve energy and find sustainable alternative sources of it—is unlikely to stand up in the long term. It is opposed by the majority of Americans, it increases long-term U.S. energy insecurity, and it will reduce future U.S. competitiveness as other countries increase their use of renewable energy sources.

Bush administration officials (and many Republican lawmakers) seemed obsessed with environmental degradation caused by developing countries, as indicated by their strong opposition to the Kyoto Protocol because it does not limit greenhouse gas emissions by those countries. If the U.S. government, however, continues to insist that it will not impose mandatory limits on carbon dioxide emissions (see EPA 2001a) yet takes the global warming issue seriously (see Knowlton 2001; EPA 2001b), it seems likely that emissions cuts will have to come from some other source. Thus the Bush administration may eventually see an advantage in the general framework of the Kyoto Protocol because the United States could (especially with additional negotiations among the protocol's parties) use the Clean Development Mechanism and other provisions of the protocol to leverage China's emissions limitations as a way to reduce its own. Hence it seems likely that the United States will eventually see an opportunity in continuing and even expanding efforts begun during the Clinton administration to help China limit its carbon emissions (see Logan et al. 1999). This suggests that the Bush administration may become concerned about environmental issues especially as they relate to China (even if the administration is not concerned enough about reducing U.S. pollution that affects U.S. *and* global environmental health).

More specifically, the final position of the Bush administration with regard to environmental security will be in part a function of relations between the Defense and State Departments. As indicated earlier, during the Clinton administration a general consensus held that environmental changes were potential threats to U.S. security, broadly defined. Whether a similar consensus will emerge under Bush is unclear. There are some warning signs, to be sure, but also some likely forces in play that could make taking those warnings too seriously potentially premature.

The Department of Defense under Donald Rumsfeld was clearly focused on traditional security issues, particularly following the September 2001 terror attacks on New York and Washington, D.C. But even here there is wiggle room. Rumsfeld called for a comprehensive examination of U.S. security priorities. There was much talk of completely changing nuclear strategy and targeting, encompassing previously disregarded changes in policy such as unilateral nuclear force reduction in keeping with perceived current needs and priorities, not old ones. This at least suggested that Rumsfeld and the DOD were willing to consider new post–Cold War realities when setting priorities. The Rumsfeld DOD retained the office of deputy undersecretary of defense for environmental security, created in 1993 as a new initiative of the Clinton administration (see DOD 2000a: A1). To be sure, the post was devoted to integrating environmental concerns into defense acquisition programs, base operations, and military missions rather than to the effects of environmental changes on U.S. security more broadly (DOD 1999). But keeping the position showed that the administration recognized the need for environmental considerations at a certain level of policy. At least it was not clear that environmental security had de facto been downgraded throughout the Pentagon.

The State Department under Colin Powell showed a greater understanding of international environmental issues than did the DOD and the White House. On the Kyoto Protocol, Powell and the State Department—as well as the EPA and the Commerce and Treasury Departments—did not want to reject the treaty (instead, Bush apparently listened to his economic adviser, Larry Lindsay) (Dunne 2001). The Bush State Department retained the office of undersecretary of state for global affairs, a post created by Clinton to coordinate U.S. foreign policy on many "global" issues, particularly environmental change (see State Department 2001a, 2001c). A high-profile environmentalist was not appointed to this office under Bush and Powell (unlike the situation during most of the Clinton administration), but the infrastructure remained, likely providing further impetus to retain environmental security issues in U.S. foreign policy at the interagency and day-to-day diplomatic levels. On a more general level, Powell showed a willingness to listen to career diplomats and State Department officials when making policy. They could remind him that environmental issues ought to remain part of U.S. foreign policy, and they would know the advantages for the United States of diplomatic exchanges on environmental security in Northeast Asia.

The forces that shaped U.S. policy on environmental security in Northeast Asia during the Clinton administration—perceptions of direct and, especially, indirect threats to U.S. interests from environmental changes in the region, access to the policy process of those pushing environmentalist and new security perceptions, and concern about the environment among government personnel—are also at work in the Bush administration, although the latter factor will be less important at the highest levels of government. Insofar as environmental changes in the region genuinely threaten U.S. interests—and they do, arguably—this will be important for policymakers. The policy process is inherently pluralistic, as demonstrated by the administration's efforts to limit the political damage that ensued following announcements to downgrade or reverse Clinton's policies on national and global environmental issues. And persons at the lower levels of government are still pressuring the higher levels to take environmental change issues seriously, and even some at higher levels want to do so. They see these issues as having traction for improving relations with other countries in relatively unrelated issue areas germane to U.S. interests in the region. This suggests the array of forces at work will be similar to that active during the Clinton administration, with the likely effect that the U.S. position on climate change and other international environmental issues will be less indifferent and backward than it was at the start of the Bush administration.

ENVIRONMENTAL SECURITY, NORTHEAST ASIA, AND THE BUSH ADMINISTRATION: PRESSURES FOR CONTINUED U.S. ENGAGEMENT

Despite its distaste for environmental causes and the current tunnel vision toward fighting terrorists, the Bush administration will likely come to engage environmental security in Northeast Asia. At least four broad reasons can be given to justify this assertion.

PRESSURES FROM INSIDE THE ADMINISTRATION

Some important members of the Bush administration actually take environmental issues seriously. This was evidenced by right-wing groups' attacks on Treasury Secretary Paul O'Neill's assertions, made before he took office, that he viewed global climate change as one of the most pressing issues facing the world (CEI 2001) and by attacks on the new EPA administrator's efforts to persuade the president to engage other countries on global warming before his reversal on carbon dioxide limits and outright rejection of the Kyoto Protocol (Pianin 2001a; Whitman 2001). It is also worth noting again that environmental security was part of the U.S. foreign policy agenda even during the Reagan and the first Bush administrations. Many officials from those administrations are back, and they may want to continue what they started. Although government officials will generally follow White House policy, they will voice their opinions, and they will continue to hold those views (barring a change of thinking, of course) if that policy does not fit with their perceptions of environmental risks and associated U.S. interests. As such, those perceptions will continue to mold policy in many small ways.

What is more, officials working on environmental security issues within the EPA and the Departments of Defense and State (plus other agencies) will fight to retain and even expand their roles. They will want environmental security to remain relatively high on the foreign policy agenda. Officials working on security issues in Northeast Asia will try to keep them on the agenda and will push them higher on that agenda if they can do so while promoting their personal and bureaucratic interests and the interests of the United States as they see them. For some of those officials, environmental issues will be viewed as genuine threats to U.S. security; for some others the environment will be viewed as an instrument for promoting their respective agencies' vitality (and perhaps for keeping their jobs).

PRESSURES FROM OUTSIDE THE ADMINISTRATION

Within the United States, environmentalists and their organizations will pressure the government directly and indirectly. Americans increasingly perceive environmental changes as threats to both their personal and U.S. national interests. Environmentalists will seek to foster those perceptions. Insofar as they can mobilize public opinion and demonstrate to policymakers and legislators that taking environmental threats seriously will further those officials' interests, environmental security as a policy option will not go away. In addition, independent and quasi-governmental think tanks, along with the popular media, are incrementally increasing understanding and awareness of international environmental issues among the public and policy leaders. Government officials in the United States tend to listen to public opinion, and they inevitably turn to experts for guidance on complex environmental issues. This will impact policy. These pressures from outside the government are already shaping policy, as demonstrated by the efforts of President Bush and his advisers (around the time of Earth Day 2001) to reverse the public's view of them as antienvironment and the scaling back of many of the administration's controversial energy proposals (e.g., drilling in the Arctic and the Gulf of Mexico).

Furthermore, environmental changes affect the security (broadly defined) of the countries of Northeast Asia and beyond. These countries are unlikely to idly accept a total reversal of U.S. policy that limits their access to U.S. environmental assistance or renounces disproportionate U.S. responsibility for international environmental problems. The angry international response to Bush's statements regarding U.S. carbon dioxide emissions and involvement in the Kyoto Protocol regime is a case in point. Japan expressed concern that the U.S. move away from the Kyoto process would adversely affect climate change negotiations, and China described the new U.S. position as "irresponsible" (Dempsey et al. 2001). Europeans said such a move might affect U.S.–European Union trade relations—hardly an outcome Bush administration officials would have anticipated or wanted (Fidler et al. 2001). Probably as a result of these and other expressions of outrage, the Bush administration began to show a greater willingness to work with, or at least consult, other countries on these issues.[14]

ENVIRONMENTAL PRESSURES

Even more fundamentally, we must consider the unavoidable pressures of environmental changes themselves, which will amplify all other pressures on the United States. They will exert forces on U.S. foreign policy making as conditions worsen over time or as existing problems become more salient in the minds of policymakers and publics. Environmental changes will inevitably affect the United States directly (e.g., through the effects of climate change, say, in Florida; availability of resources, such as fish; severe storms and droughts; and similar occurrences), and here the countries of Northeast Asia are important. Japan and particularly China are important sources of greenhouse gases. The Bush administration's unjust blaming of China and other developing countries for their greenhouse gas emissions will do little to make the problem go away, whereas cooperation can. With regard to China, scholars have pointed out that cooperating with that country on environmental issue is important for the United States strategically "because in addition to projecting force, China can project other elements that can do [the United States] harm. Greenhouse gases, ozone depleting CFCs [chlorofluorocarbons] and high concentrations of particulate and sulfur dioxides that move in the upper atmosphere from the western to the eastern Pacific, all have the potential for creating deterioration in our weather, air quality and climate" (Goldstone, Montaperto, and Roth 1996: 151).

Furthermore, as conditions grow worse, they will increasingly affect the countries of the region directly—for example, hindering China's economic development—thereby decreasing the possibility of increased U.S. exports to Northeast Asia or making Korean unification far too expensive for South Korea to contemplate. Environmental changes and resource scarcities will also exacerbate existing tensions in the region and will probably create new ones. This bodes ill for U.S. interests in Northeast Asia. Insofar as these pressures are perceived and felt in Washington, environmental security of Northeast Asia will remain an important component of U.S. foreign policy toward the region.

PRESSURES FOR LINKAGE AND DIPLOMATIC ENGAGEMENT

Environmental and resource issues are important for the countries of the region, and hence the United States may have to take them seriously. But somewhat apart from environmental changes themselves, environmental security provides opportunities to engage the countries of Northeast Asia diplomatically. Indeed during the Clinton administration environmental issues commonly became linked to overall bilateral relations, and progress on environmental issues was frequently viewed within the context of promoting other foreign policy goals (Frank 1997b). More broadly, these issues provide opportunities for the United States to engage the countries of the region in diplomatic discourse (and they, particularly China, also see it this way). This may be desirable and even required to limit tensions in other issue areas. By way of example, Jack Goldstone, Ronald Montaperto, and Stanley Roth (1996) have argued that "environmental issues can be a positive element in helping integrate China into the region and the world" (151), and "cooperation on environmental issues [by the United States with China] could act as a positive catalyst in our efforts to create strategic integration" (152). Indeed Byron Daynes argues that State Department officials during the Clinton administration found that "often discussion of the state of the environment opens up areas of common concern between countries" (1999: 285). It seems reasonable to assume this will apply equally to the Bush administration and its successors.

CONCLUSION

When I began preparing this chapter, I thought all indications from Washington pointed toward a major downgrading of environmental security in the foreign policy agenda of the Bush administration, including with regard to Northeast Asia. This was worrying, given the potentially important role of the United States in helping achieve international environmental cooperation in the region. I inquired about these issues at the Nautilus Institute, a U.S. think tank focusing on security and sustainable development issues in Northeast Asia. I received a terse reply to my queries: "The short answer to your question: the Bush administration doesn't care about environmental security and it will not be a priority for them, especially in Northeast Asia" (Brottem 2001). This at first seemed to make sense to me. On closer examination and after some thought, however, I think this assessment could be premature (although in the end it may prove accurate). I now think environmental security in Northeast Asia will remain on the U.S. foreign policy agenda. By its nature—important countries with major environmental changes amid economic development and growth—Northeast Asia will remain important in U.S. calculations of its interests. I will go out on a limb and suggest that the Bush administration will eventually continue most of the Clinton administration's environmental initiatives in Northeast Asia, for the reasons outlined earlier. It is possible that the security dimensions of environmental change will garner the most serious attention from the administration. It is even possible that such policies will eventually *increase* under President Bush. If the distractions of the war on terrorism continue to preoccupy the Bush administration, subsequent administrations will eventually rekindle U.S. efforts to promote environmental security. As such, the United States may continue to engage environmental issues in its foreign policy toward Northeast Asia, with broader interests and security in the region potentially enhanced.

These issues are linked to others and as such may be viewed as important topics worthy of negotiation to engage other countries and perhaps simply to prevent upsetting them with U.S. indifference to their environmental concerns. Perhaps environmental issues will be seen as possible areas for collaboration between the United States and China to help strengthen their bilateral relationship. As Alan Dupont has observed, "soft" issues like environmental change will be the most important determinants in China's international future, inevitably evoking concern of interested governments: "China's position in the world will ultimately be determined by domestic issues like unemployment, pollution and the growing pressure for political freedom, not by its capacity to stare down the United States" (Dupont 2001: 8). Insofar as both the U.S. and Chinese governments realize this, environmental cooperation could be a catalyst for peaceful relations. This would bode well for international environmental cooperation in the region.

The Clinton administration talked a great deal about addressing international environmental problems, and it did a lot in this regard. But Clinton did not do as much as many had expected. The Bush administration came into office with ominous policy pronouncements, suggesting that the environment would be placed on the back burner of foreign policy. Admittedly, environmental issues, including related security concerns, do appear less important in the perceptions of U.S. policymakers in the Bush administration. The United States may do more in this regard than many expected initially, however. These issues—including environmental security in Northeast Asia—will not go away. The environmental changes themselves, and the tensions and problems they affect and can exacerbate, will reappear on the U.S. radar screen. As such, the question is not whether the United States will continue to take these matters seriously but rather when and how it will do so.

Furthermore, the Bush administration's positions on international environmental issues are arguably unfair and even immoral. This is important because they will be viewed as such in the region. Japan is upset that "its protocol" (the Kyoto Protocol) is being severely undermined by the United States for selfish reasons (Struck 2001), and China (like almost all developing countries) does not accept President Bush's position, which says effectively that poor countries ought to restrain their development before the United States considers limiting its profligate use of energy. Other developing countries, Russia, and European governments have expressed outrage at the Bush policy on climate change (see Reuters 2001a, 2001b; *Independent* 2001; BBC 2001). Hence even on this single issue, U.S. policy on the environment has engendered distrust that affects U.S. interests. Insofar as the administration becomes aware of this, it may provide further impetus for U.S. engagement with the region's countries on issues of environmental change. International and domestic responses to its environmental policies have already forced the administration to reevaluate them, which suggests a willingness to modify policy even if genuine environmental concern among administration leaders is low.

Again, U.S. foreign policy on environmental security in Northeast Asia is more than a matter of scholarly interest. The United States has diplomatic, financial, and technological resources that can be used to promote environmental cooperation in the region. If it chooses to deploy these resources effectively, the environmental security of countries and people of the region will likely be enhanced—as will be the related interests of the United States itself. Indeed, the United States ought to do more to promote environmental security in Northeast Asia. Doing so would help mitigate the direct and indirect consequences of environmental changes there and would bolster U.S. diplomacy and leadership in the region. It is also the right thing to do because it could help protect Northeast Asia's environment and the region's resources on which ultimately all people there depend for their livelihoods and well-being (see Harris 2001a).

NOTES

1. For several interpretations of environmental issues in U.S. foreign policy, see Harris 2001c.

2. I discuss the Bush and Clinton administrations' environmental security policies and the reasons for them in greater detail in Harris 2001b, especially pp. 121–139. See also Barnett 2001a.

3. The first Clinton administration's elevation of environment as a security concern is summarized in Porter 1996.

4. He went on to say that "together, the earth's peoples must work, so that this precious web of life shall embrace, in beauty and in peace, all the generations to come" (State Department 1990: 4). This remark is surprising, considering who said it and in which administration. If Baker really believed what he said, it may be important that he remains close to the Bush family and the administration of George W. Bush—and that he was so instrumental in the late 2000 legal efforts to win the White House for the younger Bush.

5. In his book *Earth in the Balance*, Gore described global environmental changes as "fundamentally strategic" (1992: 29).

6. The very creation of the new post of undersecretary of state for global affairs was suggestive of new thinking in the U.S. foreign policy establishment, which acknowledged that U.S. interests encompassed new "global" issues like environmental change.

7. President Clinton specifically cited Thomas Homer-Dixon (see Homer-Dixon 1993).

8. Maybe this explains why President Clinton was personally engaged in international climate change negotiations, raising the issue with every head of state he met (according to his last climate change envoy, Frank Loy) (Brown 2000). The president telephoned other leaders to discuss the topic, including during the last conference of parties to the climate change convention before he left office (Drozdiak 2000).

9. For an analysis of environmental considerations in U.S. National Security Strategy documents and within the Departments of Defense and State, see Barnett 2001a.

10. For detailed discussions of environmental security in the context of U.S. foreign policy, see Allenby 2001 and Barnett 2001a.

11. A cynic might argue that bureaucrats in the military establishment were also looking for new things to do to maintain and even increase their budgets and that they wanted to find ways to retain the anticipated post–Cold War "peace dividend." At the least, the end of the Cold War prompted them to look harder at environmental issues.

12. When this will happen is less clear because China is switching much of its energy supply from coal to petroleum and gas, which produce fewer carbon dioxide emissions (EcoEquity 2001).

13. A comprehensive listing is found in Woodrow Wilson Center 1999-2000: 78–104. See also Christopher 1996b; McGrew 1998: 177; State Department 1999a, 2001b; White House 1997b, 1999, 2001; Working Group on Environment 1999-2000; Xinhua 1998, 1999, 2000.

14. Admittedly, the initial unilateralist impulse of the Bush administration returned and even strengthened as the war on terrorism entered 2002.

REFERENCES

Allenby, Braden. 2001. "New Priorities in U.S. Foreign Policy: Defining and Implementing Environmental Security." In Paul G. Harris, ed., *The Environment, International Relations, and U.S. Foreign Policy*. Washington, DC: Georgetown University Press.

Associated Press. 2001. "Americans Want Action on Climate." *International Herald Tribune* (3 April).

Banks, Robert. 1994. "The Follow-up to the Earth Summit." Draft General Report. NATO Public Data Service (mimeo of 22 December).

Barnett, Jon. 2000. "Destabilizing the Environment-Conflict Thesis." *Review of International Studies* 26, 2 (April): 271–288.

———. 2001a. "Environmental Security and U.S. Foreign Policy: A Critical Examination." In Paul G. Harris, ed., *The Environment, International Relations, and U.S. Foreign Policy*. Washington, DC: Georgetown University Press.

———. 2001b. *The Meaning of Environmental Security*. London: Zed.

BBC World. 2001. "Blair Urged to Tackle Bush Over Kyoto." BBC News (13 April) <http://news.bbc.co.uk/hi/english/uk_politics/newsid_1275000/1275244.stm>

Bedeski, Robert E. 2000. "Integration of Non-Traditional Security Issues: A Preliminary Application to South Korea." In Miriam R. Lowi and Brian R. Shaw, eds., *Environment and Security: Discourses and Practices*. New York: St. Martin's.

Blum, Douglas W. 2001. "Geopolitics, Energy, and Ecology: U.S. Foreign Policy and the Caspian Sea." In Paul G. Harris, ed., *The Environment, International Relations, and U.S. Foreign Policy*. Washington, DC: Georgetown University Press.

Brottem, Leif. 2001. E-mail message to the author (17 April).

Brown, Paul. 2000. "Forests: U.S. Concession Fails to Please Experts." *The Guardian* (21 November).

Bush, George W., and Dick Cheney. n.d. "Environment and Natural Resources." George W. Bush for President Official Site, <http://uselectionatlas.org/USPRESIDENT/frame2000issues.html>.

Butts, Kent. 1996. "National Security, the Environment and DOD." *Environmental Change and Security Project Report* 2 (spring) <http://ecsp.si.edu/default.htm>.

Christopher, Warren. 1996a. "American Diplomacy and the Global Environmental Challenges of the 21st Century." Speech to the Alumni of Stanford University, Stanford, California, 9 April.

———. 1996b. "The United States and China: Building a New Era of Cooperation for a New Century." Speech at Fudan University, Shanghai, 21 November.

———. 1998. *In the Stream of History: Shaping Foreign Policy for a New Era*. Stanford: Stanford University Press.

Clinton, William J. 1995. "President Clinton's Remarks to the National Academy of Sciences," 29 June 1994. Reproduced in *Environmental Change and Security Project Report* 1 (spring).

Competitive Enterprise Institute (CEI). 2001. "Bush Officials Favor Kyoto Policies." *Cooler Heads Newsletter* 5, 5 (7 March) <http://www.cei.org/CHNReader.asp?ID'1392>.

Conca, Ken, and Geoffrey D. Dabelko, eds. 1998. *Green Planet Blues: Environmental Politics From Stockholm to Kyoto*. Boulder: Westview.

Dalby, Simon. 1992. "Security, Modernity, Ecology: The Dilemmas of Post–Cold War Security Discourse." *Alternatives* 17: 95–134.

Daynes, Byron. 1999. "Bill Clinton: Environmental President." In Dennis L. Soden, ed., *The Environmental Presidency*. Albany: State University of New York Press.

Dempsey, Judy, et al. 2001. "US Insists It Still Backs Kyoto Treaty Aims." *Financial Times* (31 March).

Department of Defense (DOD). 1999. About Department of Defenses' (DoD) Environmental Cleanup Office, <http://www.dtic.mil/envirodod/about/html> (8 December).

———. 2000. *Annual Defense Report 2001.* Washington, DC: U.S. Department of Defense.

de Sherbinin, Alex. 1995. "World Population Growth and U.S. National Security." *Environmental Change and Security Project Report* 1 (spring).

Deudney, Daniel. 1990. "The Case Against Linking Environmental Degradation and National Security." *Millennium: Journal of International Studies* 19: 461–476.

Deudney, Daniel, and Richard A. Matthew, eds. 1999. *Contested Ground: Security and Conflict in the New Environmental Politics.* Albany: State University of New York Press.

Doran, Peter. 2000. "Upholding the 'Island of High Modernity': The Changing Climate of American Foreign Policy." In Paul G. Harris, ed., *Climate Change and American Foreign Policy.* New York: St. Martin's.

Drozdiak, William. 2000. "Sharp Disputes Snag Global-Warming Agreement at Hague Conference." *Washington Post* (25 November).

Dunne, Nancy. 2001. "White House Split as Bush Rejects Kyoto." *Financial Times* (30 March).

Dupont, Alan. 1998. *The Environment and Security in Pacific Asia.* Oxford: Oxford University Press.

———. 2001. "U.S. and China Have Drawn New Lines in the Sand." *International Herald Tribune* (14–15 April): 8.

EcoEquity. 2001. "Reality Check in China." *Climate Equity Observer* <http://wwwecoequity.org/ceo/ceo_2_6.htm>.

"Ecological Diplomacy." 1996. *Boston Globe* (14 April).

Economist. 2001a. "Rage Over Global Warming." *Economist* (7 April).

———. 2001b. "Global Warming: Oh No, Kyoto." *Economist* (7 April).

Elliott, Lorraine. 1998. *The Global Politics of the Environment.* London: Macmillan.

Environmental Protection Agency (EPA). 2001a. "Statement by EPA Administrator Christie Whitman on Climate Change." Washington, DC: U.S. EPA (16 March).

———. 2001b. "Statement by EPA Administrator Christie Whitman Meeting With Members of the European Community." Washington, DC: U.S. EPA (3 April).

Fidler, Stephen, et al. 2001. "Bush Says Kyoto Deal Would Hit Jobs and Industry." *Financial Times* (30 March).

Frank, Aaron. 1997a. "Foreword." *China Environment Series.* Washington, DC: Woodrow Wilson Center Environmental Change and Security Project: 1.

———. 1997b. "The Environment in U.S.-China Relations: Themes and Ideas From Working Group Discussion on Energy Issues." Washington, DC: Woodrow Wilson Center Environmental Change and Security Project: 33–39.

Friedman, Thomas. 1996. "Gardening With Beijing." *New York Times* (17 April).

Goldstein, Amy, and Eric Pianin. 2001. "Hill Pressure Fueled Bush's Emissions Shift." *Washington Post* (15 March).

Goldstone, Jack, Ronald Montaperto, and Stanley Roth. 1996. "Mock NSC Briefing: Environment and U.S. National Security Interests—People's Republic of China." *Environmental Change and Security Project Report* 3: 150–155.

Gore, Albert. 1989. Paper presented to the Forum on Global Change and Our Common Future, National Academy of Sciences, Washington, DC, 1 May.

———. 1992. *Earth in the Balance.* New York: Houghton Mifflin.

———. 1995. "Vice President Gore's Remarks at the White House Conference on Climate Action," 21 April 1994. Reproduced in *Environmental Change and Security Project Report* 1 (spring).

———. 1998. "Environmental Diplomacy: The Environment and United States Foreign Policy." Washington, DC: Department of State.

Graeger, N. 1996. "Environmental Security?" *Journal of Peace Research* 33, 1 (February): 109–116.

Harding, James. 1998. "Clinton Urges Environment Policies in China." *Financial Times* (2 July).

Harris, Paul G. 2001a. "Environment, Security, and Human Suffering: What Should the United States Do?" In Paul G. Harris, ed., *The Environment, International Relations, and U.S. Foreign Policy.* Washington, DC: Georgetown University Press.

———. 2001b. *International Equity and Global Environmental Politics: Power and Principles in U.S. Foreign Policy.* Aldershot: Ashgate.

———, ed. 2001c. *The Environment, International Relations, and U.S. Foreign Policy.* Washington, DC: Georgetown University Press.

Homer-Dixon, Thomas F. 1993. "Environmental Change and Violent Conflict." *Scientific American* (February): 38–45.

———. 1999. *Environment, Scarcity, and Violence.* Princeton: Princeton University Press.

Homer-Dixon, Thomas F., and Jessica Blitt, eds. 1998. *Ecoviolence: Links Among Environment, Population, and Security.* Lanham, MD: Rowman and Littlefield.

Hughes, Kent, ed. 1994. *Environmental Security: A DOD Partnership for Peace.* Washington, DC: U.S. Army War College.

Independent. 2001. "Developing Nations: U.S. Urged to Return to Global Warming Talks." *Independent* (South Africa) (12 April).

Ketter, Ronald, Chris Borick, and Michael Cabral. 1999. "The Changing Agenda of the Environment and the Commander-in-Chief." In Dennis L. Soden, ed., *The Environmental Presidency.* Albany: State University of New York Press.

Knowlton, Brian. 2001. "Bush Is Looking Greener on Environmental Issues." *International Herald Tribune* (23 April).

Levy, Marc. 1995. "Is the Environment a National Security Issue?" *International Security* 20, 2: 35–62.

Litfin, Karen T. 1999. "Constructing Environmental Security and Ecological Interdependence." *Global Governance* 5, 3 (July-September): 359–377.

Logan, Jeffrey, Aaron Frank, Jianwu Feng, and Indu John. 1999. *Climate Action in the United States and China.* Washington, DC: Battelle Memorial Institute and Woodrow Wilson International Center for Scholars.

Lowi, Miriam R., and Brian R. Shaw, eds. 2000. *Environment and Security: Discourses and Practices.* New York: St. Martin's.

Marland, G., et al. 1998. "Global, Regional, and National CO2 Emissions." In *Trends: A Compendium of Data on Global Change*. Oak Ridge, TN: Oak Ridge National Laboratory.

Mathews, Jessica Tuchman. 1989. "Redefining Security." *Foreign Affairs* 68 (spring): 162–177.

McGrew, Anthony. 1998. "Restructuring Foreign and Defense Policy: The USA." In Anthony McGrew and Christopher Brook, eds., *Asia-Pacific in the New World Order*. London: Routledge.

Nanto, Dick K. 2000. *China's Emergence as a Major Economic Power: Implications for U.S. Interests*. CRS Report for Congress. Washington, DC: Congressional Research Service.

NATO Committee on the Challenges of Modern Society. n.d. "The Challenges of Modern Society: Environmental Clearing House System" <http://www.nato.int/ccms/home.htm>.

NATO Press Service. 1991. "The Alliance's New Strategic Concept." *Press Communiqué* (7 November).

Nautilus Institute and Center for Global Communications (GLOCOM). 2000. "Energy, Environment and Security in Northeast Asia: Defining a U.S.-Japan Partnership for Regional Comprehensive Security." In *Energy, Security, Environment in Northeast Asia (ESENA) Project Final Report*. Berkeley: Nautilus Institute.

Nunn, Sam. 1990. "Strategic Environmental Research Program." Speech before the U.S. Senate. Washington, DC: U.S. Senate, 28 June.

Pianin, Eric. 2001a. "EPA Chief Lobbied on Warming Before Bush's Emissions Switch." *Washington Post* (27 March).

———. 2001b. "U.S. Aims to Pull out of Warming Treaty." *Washington Post* (28 March).

Pianin, Eric, and Amy Goldstein. 2001. "Bush Drops a Call for Emission Cuts: Energy Firms Opposed to Carbon Dioxide Pledge." *Washington Post* (14 March).

Porter, Garreth. 1995. "Environmental Security as a National Security Issue." *Current History* 94: 218–222.

———. 1996. "Advancing Environmental Security Through 'Integrated Security Resource Planning.' " *Environmental Change and Security Project Report* 2 (spring).

Reuters. 2001a. "EU: Support Rising for Climate Deal Without U.S." *New York Times* (9 April).

———. 2001b. "Chirac Tells Powell of French Concern Over Kyoto." *New York Times* (12 April).

Schreurs, Miranda A. 2000. "Environmental Security and Cooperation in Asia." In Kurt W. Radtke and Raymond Feddema, eds., *Comprehensive Security in Asia*. Boston: Brill.

Seelye, Katerine Q. 2001. "In President's Cabinet But out of Sync: White House Contradicts Whitman on Protection of Alaskan Refuge." *International Herald Tribune* (25 April): 3.

State Department. 1986. "Environment in the Foreign Policy Agenda." *Current Policy Series* 816.

———. 1990. "Diplomacy for the Environment." *Current Policy Series* 1254.

———. 1996a. *Environmental Diplomacy: The Environment and U.S. Foreign Policy.* Washington, DC: Department of State <http://www.state.gov/www/global/oes/earth.html>.

———. 1996b. "The U.S.-Japan Common Agenda: A Partnership for the 21st Century." Joint Statement by U.S. and Japanese Governments. Tokyo: Ministry of Foreign Affairs, 17 April.

———. 1998a. "Environmental Diplomacy." Fact Sheet (30 November).

———. 1998b. Testimony of Stanley O. Roth, Assistant Secretary of State for East Asian and Pacific Affairs, to the House of Representatives Committee on Foreign Relations. Washington, DC: Department of State, 7 May.

———. 1999a. "U.S.-China Water Resources Management Workshop." Washington, DC: Department of State, 4 May.

———. 1999b. "U.S.-Japan Joint Efforts on Global Issues, Such as Climate Change and Disease Control, Under the Common Agenda." Press Statement (6 April).

———. 2000a. "Congressional Budget Justification for Foreign Operations, Fiscal Year 2001." Washington, DC: Office of the Secretary of State, 15 March.

———. 2000b. "U.S.-Japan Common Agenda." Fact Sheet (26 June).

———. 2001a. Bureau of Oceans and International Environmental and Scientific Affairs <http://www.state.gov/g/oes> n.d.; accessed 20 April.

———. 2001b. "Joint Declaration on Cooperation on Environment and Development Between the United States and China." Washington, DC: Department of State, 19 May.

———. 2001c. Under Secretary for Global Affairs <http://www.state.gov/g> n.d.; accessed 1 May.

Struck, Doug. 2001. "U.S. Upsets Japan on Ecology Pact: Bid to Ignore Kyoto Accord Opens Rift With Washington." *International Herald Tribune* (29 March).

United Nations Environment Program (UNEP). 1999. *Global Environment Outlook 2000.* London: Earthscan.

United States. 1993. House Resolution 575 to Establish the National Committee on the Environment and National Security. Washington, DC: House, 103rd Cong., 26 January.

White House. 1995. *1995 National Security Strategy of Engagement and Enlargement.* Washington, DC: White House.

———. 1996. *1996 U.S. National Security Strategy of Engagement and Enlargement.* Washington, DC: White House.

———. 1997a. "Press Conference by President Clinton and President Jiang Zemin." Press Release (29 October).

———. 1997b. "Vice President Announces United States and China Advance Energy and Environment Cooperation." Press Release (29 October).

———. 1998. "Remarks by the President on U.S.-China Relations in the 21st Century." Press Release (11 June).

———. 1999. "Vice President Gore and Premier Zhu Rongji Announce Environmental Agreements at U.S.-China Policy Forum on Environment and Development." Press Release (9 April).

———. 2001. "Vice President Gore Announces Joint Statement of U.S. and China on Environment Cooperation Efforts." Press Release (19 May).

Whitman, Christine Todd. 2001. Memorandum for the President, "G-8 Meeting, Trieste." Reprinted as "Whitman to Bush: Global Warming Is a Serious Issue," in *Washington Post* online edition (memo dated 6 March).

Wirth, Timothy E. 1994. "Sustainable Development and National Security." Address before the National Press Club, Washington, DC, 12 July. *U.S. Department of State Dispatch* 5, 30 (25 July).

————. 1995. "Under Secretary Wirth's Address Before the National Press Club, 'Sustainable Development: A Progress Report,' " 12 July. Reproduced in *Environmental Change and Security Project Report* 1 (spring).

Woodrow Wilson Center. 1999/2000. "Inventory of Environmental Work in China." *China Environment Series* 3. Washington, DC: Environmental Change and Security Project: 78–188.

Working Group on Environment in U.S.-China Relations. 1999/2000. "United States Environmental Priorities in China." *China Environment Series* 3. Washington, DC: Environmental Change and Security Project: 71–73.

World Resources Institute (WRI). 1999. *China's Health and Environment: Air Pollution and Health Effects.* Washington, DC: World Resources Institute: 3 <http://www.igc.apc.org/wri/wr-98-9/prc2air.htm>.

Xinhua. 1998. "Chinese Military Chief Signs Environment Cooperation Accord, Discusses North Korea During U.S. Talks." BBC Monitoring Asia Pacific (from ProQuest) (16 September).

————. 1999. "Chinese Premier Calls for Bilateral Cooperation on Environment." BBC Monitoring Asia Pacific (from ProQuest) (11 April).

————. 2000. "China, USA Sign Environment Protection Contract." BBC Monitoring Asia Pacific (from ProQuest) (17 April).

4

Reconciling Trade and Environment in East Asia

JACK N. BARKENBUS

This chapter deals with concerns about environmental degradation in East Asia and its intersection with a particular facet of globalization, namely, trade liberalization. Considerable progress has been made since the early 1980s in eliminating barriers to free trade across state boundaries. Particular success has been achieved in reducing or eliminating costly tariffs that inhibit trade. Many nontariff barriers persist, however, and there is considerable interest in further international negotiations to remove those impediments.

Despite such sentiments, international trade talks are deadlocked. The neoliberal belief that unfettered free trade, through efficient resource allocation, works to the benefit of all is being seriously challenged by the belief that social concerns need to be accounted for in further trade liberalization and in globalization generally. The issue of how the natural environment plays into this is increasingly disputed. The U.S. government and some Western European governments are increasingly seeking to incorporate environmental issues into trade agreements, and nongovernmental initiatives to "green" the international trade regime are becoming more diverse and pervasive. For the most part, however, governments of East Asia are resisting the pressures of governmental and nongovernmental forces in the West. This interstate disagreement, if it continues, could indefinitely postpone further trade liberalization, jeopardize economic growth, and lead to broader political conflict.

Solutions to the current deadlock will require not only interstate but also intersectoral collaboration. Globalization has created a dynamic whereby the private sector and civil society are playing increasingly important roles in environmental governance (Bruehl and Rittberger 2001; O'Brien et al. 2000). Continued environmental degradation has emboldened civil society in particular to play a more forceful role. Robert Keohane and Joseph Nye (2000) have noted the "pluralization of participation" in governance decisions as a distinguishing feature of today's globalization. As will be seen, East Asian governments, so heavily invested in both current trade rules and state-centric thinking, may have difficulty dealing with a new era of heightened environmental responsibility.

TRADE LIBERALIZATION

Trade liberalization has coincided with an unprecedented period of global economic growth. The value of world trade increased from $1 trillion in 1970 to $11 trillion in 1998. At the same time, global gross domestic product (GDP) rose from $16 trillion to nearly $40 trillion (a 140 percent increase in real U.S. dollars) (CIA 1999: table 1). Export-led economies in Southeast Asia were a primary beneficiary of this growth. The East Asia/Pacific region led the world with an average GDP per capita growth of 5 percent from 1991 to 1997. Nine of the ten fastest-growing economies in the world during that period were Asian countries (Dua and Esty 1997: 1). This growth has led to dramatically rising incomes in these countries and a reduction in earnings inequality. Asian societies are being transformed at varying speeds from resource- and agriculture-based economies to industrial, service, and high-tech economies. Economic events in Asia during 1997 and 1998 demonstrated that globalization comes with risks, particularly if state-based financial institutions are not prepared or structured to appropriately handle the influx of capital from abroad. No evidence indicates, however, that major Asian societies wish to halt trade liberalization. The United States also witnessed an unprecedented decade of economic growth in the 1990s, thought to be closely related to the free trade of goods and services. Both Asian and U.S. societies therefore presume that trade liberalization can be a positive force for change. As we will see, however, this presumption is not held without considerable reservation, which is leading to powerful calls for change in the rules and practices governing trade.

Trade liberalization remains the primary focus of discussion within the Asia-Pacific Economic Cooperation (APEC) forum, a regional body currently consisting of twenty-one member economies bordering the Pacific Ocean. APEC members encompass diverse socioeconomic levels, ranging from Papua New Guinea to the United States. The so-called Bogar objectives adopted by APEC members in 1994 (although not formally negotiated or legally binding), calling for totally free trade among the developed APEC nations by 2010 and among all APEC members by 2020, remain the primary goals the regional body is seeking.

Achievement of these goals, however, appears in doubt unless existing deadlocks can be broken. At the November 2000 APEC meeting, President Clinton of the United States made a strong plea for APEC to spearhead an effort to produce a new round of talks on free trade before the World Trade Organization (WTO). The 1999 WTO meeting in Seattle was designed to kick off this new round but ended in failure, setting back rather than advancing further trade liberalization talks. Asian members of APEC, although sympathetic to President Clinton's call for a new round of trade negotiations, insisted that it had to contain the issues they were concerned with and not necessarily the issues President Clinton wished to raise. Specifically, they did not want new negotiations to cover "social" issues—that is, environmental protection and workers' rights.

Asian complaints over what trade negotiations have and have not covered in years past carry considerable legitimacy. Asian states and developing countries in general are seeking more decision-making transparency out of the WTO and more inclusiveness in decision-making forums. Industrialized country representatives, absent any input from developing countries, frequently make key decisions. Developing countries are seeking a new "development" round centering on market access for the goods they would like to export in greater quantities. This would primarily mean eliminating quotas in industrialized countries on textiles and clothing and reducing or eliminating subsidies to agricultural products. U.S. antidumping claims are often viewed as protectionist as well. Finally, developing countries would seek longer transition periods to comply with new trade impositions placed on them. All of these issues need to be addressed in a global context through the WTO or in a regional context through APEC.

Although legitimate in their complaints, the Asian aversion to also including social issues in a new trade round is shortsighted and self-defeating. A powerful constituency is building in the West to ensure that trade and social issues are, in fact, bundled in future negotiations. That constituency will only grow more powerful over time because of deteriorating environmental and social conditions globally. As one Asian observer sympathetic to the Asian argument has stated, "The writing is on the wall. . . . The relevant question for the South, therefore, is no longer whether environmental concerns should influence trade rules, or even when, but how" (Najam 2000: 405–406). This chapter will examine this "how." But first it is useful to provide the context of the trans-Pacific forces at play.

THE U.S. POSITION

The U.S. government's position on trade liberalization and the environment has evolved considerably and is instructive of policy trends in the West in general. Environmentalists complained for many years of being frozen out of trade discussions within both the Office of the U.S. Trade Representative and the U.S. Congress. The U.S. position changed during the second half of the Clinton administration. President Clinton went to the 1999 Seattle WTO meeting proclaiming that environmental and workers' rights issues should be on the WTO agenda—a message many protestors outside the WTO halls welcomed, but not one embraced by developing country delegates within the halls. Among other particulars, the U.S. position as espoused by President Clinton called for more nongovernmental organization (NGO) participation within the WTO structure, financial assistance to developing countries to help them comply with new trade rules, a formal linkage between the WTO and the United Nations Environment Program (UNEP), the inclusion of environmental reviews of future trade pacts, and the use of the WTO's Committee on Trade and the Environment as a forum to discuss broad environmental concerns (Audley 2000).

In the absence of a new round of global talks, the United States has been negotiating bilateral trade pacts with selected countries. A bilateral agreement with Jordan has been concluded that contains a provision for environmental reviews. Similar agreements are under review with Chile and Singapore.

Some have wondered whether President Bush will turn back the clock and reverse the position forged by the Clinton administration. Many in his political party would like to see such a development, and they will have increasing influence. Environmental conditions could possibly be omitted from the text of future U.S. bilateral accords and placed in accompanying side agreements. Whatever the form, to gain bipartisan approval for further trade liberalization and fast-track authority, President Bush will need to retain a social issues component within U.S. trade policy.

The current U.S. position resulted in part from recognition of the breakdown of consensus over the neoliberal position on trade. Many environmentalists have never accepted the argument that free trade would inevitably lead to a better environment. The Seattle demonstrations (as well as subsequent demonstrations in Washington, D.C., Prague, and Quebec City) added attention and urgency to the issue. Concerns in the United States go back to some of the longest-standing environment-trade conflicts coming before the international community. Noteworthy is the tuna/dolphin controversy that began in the 1970s. Through strong NGO lobbying, the U.S. Congress enacted the Marine Mammal Protection Act in 1972. Through this act and subsequent amendments, the United States embargoed imported tuna caught by foreign fleets using systems less protective of dolphins (as by-catch) than required of U.S.-based fleets. The U.S. law was protested by several nations and was argued before international trade bodies over several years. Judgment from these bodies went against the United States. This led to multilateral negotiations resulting in the International Dolphin Conservation Program.

A similar dispute arose with regard to expanded shrimp fishing and the resulting widespread death of endangered sea turtles through by-catch. In the late 1980s the U.S. Congress required domestic shrimp fishing fleets to use turtle excluder devices (TEDs) to ensure shrimp fishing would not inadvertently snare and kill turtles, and it further required similar protective devices on fleets wishing to sell their harvest to U.S. consumers. Those shrimp fishing fleets from other countries that had not received U.S. certification (confirming similar or identical systems for protecting turtles) were prohibited from exporting to the U.S. market. Numerous foreign fishing fleets began installing TEDs immediately to meet the new U.S. requirements. A number of Asian states (India, Malaysia, Pakistan, and Thailand), however, took the issue before the WTO, claiming the U.S. position was not in conformance with international trade law. After the WTO ruled against the United States and following an appeals court ruling, the United States agreed to alter the implementation of its law but not eliminate it altogether. Although virtually all shrimp fishing fleets have now installed relatively inexpensive TEDs, Malaysia continues to bring the issue before the WTO for final settlement. The fact that international trade bodies have ruled against marine resource conservation in each of these instances has fueled environmentalist opposition to further trade pacts that exclude the environmental dimension (Joyner and Tyler 2000).

A NEW ERA

The marine conservation examples are early manifestations of what could prove to be increasingly contentious disputes over environmental resource issues. Recent reports document a continuing and unrelenting human assault on the environmental and natural resource systems that sustain all life on this planet (UNEP 1999; World Resources Institute 2000). Despite all the rhetoric generated in the 1990s over lofty goals, trends are unmistakingly pointing toward a fundamentally unsustainable environmental future.

The unprecedented volume of greenhouse gases being released to the atmosphere threatens the functioning of natural systems and the well-being of the earth's inhabitants. Apart from the damages wrought by climate change, the stock of support-system resources is being significantly degraded in other ways. It is estimated, for example, that 70 percent of marine fisheries are either fully exploited or overfished. Over half of all wetlands have been altered or destroyed. Deforestation is taking place at the rate of 750,000 acres per year. Biodiversity is diminishing as extinction of mammal, nonmammal, and plant species is proceeding at an alarming rate. This degradation not only endangers the life systems on which all humans depend but is a primary culprit in elevating the burden of death and disease in developing countries. Poor water and air quality are endemic. Unsafe drinking conditions are estimated to take an annual death toll of over 5 million per year. Environmental disasters throughout the world take victims at an alarming rate. The challenge of reversing these trends in a world with a static population would be formidable. To do so with an estimated 3 billion additional inhabitants by 2050 is mind-boggling.

The increasingly dire environmental trends are mobilizing environmental NGOs. A segment of the environmental community has always been opposed to trade liberalization. The inability or unwillingness of the WTO to come to terms with this opposition has heightened activist resolve to derail the current international trade regime (Wallach and Sforza 1999). These activists' rhetoric, often containing stridently anticorporation sentiments, may not be the most informed. But one should not underestimate the strength of their fervor and organizational capabilities. Another component of the environmental community wants to see trade liberalization expand and succeed, but not without full accounting for environmental conditions. This position draws on sentiments expressed by UN Secretary-General Kofi Annan (2000) that globalization will succeed over the long term only if protection of fundamental human values is embedded within it. Environmental protection is one such value. From this perspective, globalization must come with a human face.

Both environmental camps draw their strength from strong public support for environmental quality. Public polls almost uniformly depict a populace frustrated with the inability and unwillingness of governments to halt environmental deterioration. And this concern is not just a Western, first-world phenomenon but one expressed around the globe (Brechin and Kempton 1994; Dunlap, Gallup, and Gallup 1993; Peritore 1999). It would be a mistake to relate environmental degradation in East Asia to the absence of environmental concern in the region. Global studies, just referenced, show otherwise, as do studies of the region specifically (Lee and So 1999; Yencken, Fien, and Sykes 2000). This discontent has simply not yet found sufficient political expression.

What is more, public support and the mobilization of NGOs are, step-by-step, creating a system of corporate legitimization transcending boundaries beyond state-centric regulation of commerce (domestic or international). Such a system is contingent upon commercial organizations meeting universal standards of acceptable practice (Newell 2000). A corporation's compliance with social norms is therefore just as important as its compliance with legal requirements. Companies that violate the social norm of effective environmental protection risk losing their most precious asset: reputational capital. Corporations that sell to the public recognize that citizens exercise their sovereign right to "vote" every day with their purchases. If such corporations are seen and portrayed as indifferent to their environmental impact, such a perception can have serious and immediate business repercussions. Monsanto's experience with genetically modified crops is a case study in how corporations ignore civil society and the values it represents at their peril.

Leading multinational companies recognize the changing nature of legitimacy, as evidenced by their policies to maintain uniformly high environmental standards in their facilities regardless of the country in which the facilities are located. Other manifestations of this new era are corporate commitments to reduce carbon emissions, absent any government, state, or international requirements; corporate efforts to "green" their supply chains (by requiring suppliers to reduce or eliminate the use of hazardous chemicals or to supply products requiring a percentage of recycled content); and corporate willingness to subscribe to private codes of conduct in the production of goods and services. Over 23,000 facilities across the globe have implemented formal environmental management systems to gain recognition for meeting international standards (as determined by the International Standards Organization [ISO]), and the number of facilities will grow by several times in the future. We know, for example, that IBM, Hewlett Packard, and others have asked their Chinese suppliers to acquire ISO certification (Chang-Xing 1999), and there is no reason to believe this requirement is limited to Chinese enterprises. No evidence indicates that these voluntary initiatives and other market-based strategies, such as eco-labels and certification, have had a significant negative impact on exporting firms (Jha, Markandya, and Vossenaar 1999), although their growth holds that potential. These and other initiatives constitute a limited but growing body of "civil regulation," based not on legal prescription but on social norms (Bendell 2000).

This new social compact, based in part on environmental stewardship, is closely associated with a firm reducing its "ecological footprint" by altering process and production methods. To the extent this stewardship can be accomplished through private-sector channels alone, interstate conflict need not arise. It is inevitable, however, that many independent small and medium-size enterprises (SMEs) will be required over time to match the new standards and that some governments will seek to move the global community in this direction.

In a multinational setting, the international community of states has concluded a treaty looking toward eventual elimination of twelve persistent organic pollutants and possibly more in the future. Growing use of the "precautionary principle" could lead to further product bans. Just as significant, Western European countries are leading efforts to identify and require new product standards—that is, establishing rigorous process, content, and production methods governing the creation of consumer products less burdensome to the environment. Life cycle analysis is assisting in identifying the stages of product production most environmentally burdensome. This may lead, for example, to imperatives covering allowable levels of toxic materials or recycled content in specific products or requiring sustainable resource-gathering processes—all irrespective of regulations found in exporting countries.

International trade law, however, is strongly disposed against discrimination between "like products" on the basis of process and production methods (PPMs) (Tussie and Vasquez 2000). The rationale from a trade perspective is clear: content requirements can serve as nontariff barriers to trade, operating as powerful protectionist mechanisms. To the extent content requirements become codified by governments in import conditions (such as the German government's ban on azo dyes in textile production or the Danish government's requirement for recycled content in beer containers), we can expect a direct conflict between environment and trade.

Existing trade law spells out the conditions under which the two can presumably be reconciled, but a high burden of proof is imposed on those arguing the environmental side. Trade law allows for a legitimate PPM distinction when it is necessary to protect human health or the environment or when the distinctions are related to the conservation of exhaustible natural resources. Until recently, however, the conditions could never be applied in an extraterritorial manner. In other words, one state could not impose its standards on another state. The WTO seems to have modified this position somewhat in the shrimp/turtle case raised previously. It maintained the right to rule against PPM distinctions, however, if they were applied "arbitrarily" or "unjustifiably." This has been precisely the WTO's ruling against the U.S. government in the shrimp/turtle case.

The PPM rule, and the heavy burden of proof required to override it, has understandably drawn the ire of environmentalists, many of whom demonstrated their unhappiness with the WTO in Seattle. Changes in process and production are at the heart of what environmentalists seek in today's commerce—at least those environmentalists who believe reconciliation can occur between environmental protection and capitalist society. The domain of world trade law will not deflect growing sentiment for discriminating on the basis of environmental characteristics. Therefore further conflict can be expected in the future.

EAST ASIAN OBJECTIONS

The new "social era" is becoming recognized and accepted in the United States and even driven by Western Europe. Little evidence indicates, however, that developing countries in general and East Asian countries in particular are picking up on the changes. Their aversion to linking trade and environment is well-known and long-standing and shows little sign of abating.

The most forceful individual Asian states arguing against a trade-environment linkage have been India, Pakistan, China, and Malaysia. A common reason given for opposing linkage is the fear of losing a competitive advantage in the export market. The fear is based on a twofold concern. First, Asian nations are suspicious of protectionist interests in the West masquerading as environmentalists or human rights advocates. The fact that Western labor unions frequently spearhead the drive for universal human rights abroad lends credence to their suspicions. Nothing so obvious exists in the environmental arena, but environmental arguments can clearly serve as a front for commercial interests. Second, Asian societies decry the double standards applied to them, forcing them to adopt environmental standards much stricter than those that applied to Western societies in their economic development process. Concurrently, it is often stated that global environmental problems are primarily the doing of the West, and the West consequently should bear the burden of cleanup (Mahathir 1999). Although the Asian concerns are not unfounded, they do not absolve Asian states from any responsibility for environmental stewardship. The principle of common but differentiated responsibility is one way these issues have been addressed satisfactorily in forging new multilateral environmental agreements. Technical assistance can be another tool for reaching consensus—witness U.S. efforts to provide for technical assistance in the use of TEDs. There need not be a fundamental or irreconcilable divide over the inclusion of the environment in trade matters.

Asian states have frequently resorted to the principle of state sovereignty to justify their defensive posture toward an environment-trade linkage. This justification goes back many years and was manifest in 1992 at the Earth Summit in Rio de Janeiro where the Association of Southeast Asian Nations (ASEAN) argued forcefully for the right of developing countries to have permanent sovereignty over their natural resources and criticized the view that the environment was a global commons to be dealt with collectively (Tay 2000). Obviously, the claim of state sovereignty can be a transparent mask for naked self-interest on the part of governing regimes, but it would be unwise to underestimate the genuine Asian allegiance to the state-based international system. For example, individual Asian states have frequently used regional bodies such as ASEAN to amplify their concerns over environmental impositions from abroad, but they are very wary of building strong regional ties that would take away from state autonomy. Asia-Pacific regional bodies more fully demonstrate the characteristics of an association than of an autonomous decision-making body. Asian states view regional organizations as institutions to enhance state capabilities, not transcend them. According to Charles Morrison and his colleagues (1997: 34), "The central purpose has been to consolidate the stability, security, and prosperity of the present states and state system, not to subsume sovereignty in larger entities." As such, binding norm creation and settlement of disputes are not components of Asia-Pacific regionalism. The so-called ASEAN way speaks to characteristics such as nonintervention in other states' affairs, the establishment of only nonbinding (voluntary) directives based exclusively on group consensus, and an aversion to institution building (Tay 1998). The state-centric approach becomes even more pronounced when dealing with forces outside the region.

The aggressively state-centric approach to the environment places East Asian states on a collision course with the growing nonstate environmental movements mentioned earlier. Clearly, these movements are seeking to diminish the role of internal state sovereignty (i.e., exclusive control or autonomy over what transpires within territorial boundaries) in the establishment and implementation of environmental standards. The global environmental movement is no longer the province of a relatively few dedicated activists. It has been mainstreamed, become part and parcel of transforming postmaterialist values and, as such, will persist in the face of obstacles erected by states. Global environmental trends, as noted previously, continue to deteriorate and, as such, will occasion vigorous response from civil society. The environmental movement's linkage with workers' rights in the globalization arena presents a powerful combination for change, transforming environmental protection from an economic concept ("externalities") to one bespeaking fundamental human rights (Zarsky and Tay 2000).

THE ASIAN ENVIRONMENTAL CRISIS

A widespread perception exists that Asia's unprecedented economic growth rates in the 1980s and 1990s, impressive though they were, were accomplished at the expense of the environment. The Asian approach to the environment, frequently characterized as "grow now, clean up later," has had devastating consequences, leading the Asian Development Bank to characterize Asia as the world's most polluted and environmentally degraded region (2000a). The Economic and Social Commission for Asia and the Pacific (2000: 1) recently claimed that "Asia continues to be the most polluted and environmentally degraded region while the Pacific region has the problem of diminishing natural resources and other sustainable development concerns."

A large number of publications produced since 1999 describe in great detail the grim statistics that illustrate the continuing assault on the natural environment in the Asia-Pacific region (Angel and Rock 2000; Asian Development Bank 2000b, 2000c; Economic and Social Commission for Asia and the Pacific 2000; Japan Environmental Council 2000; Seda and Tay 2000; UNEP 1999; World Bank 1999). Despite increasing public interest and attention to the environment in Asia and increasing rhetorical support for sustainable development among governments, environmental and ecosystem trends are moving in the wrong direction. The *Global Environmental Outlook 2000* (UNEP 1999) claims that at least one in three Asians has no access to safe drinking water and at least one in two has no access to sanitation. Many Asian cities are among the most polluted in the world, with air contamination well above levels considered acceptable in industrial nations. In eleven Chinese cities alone, air pollution is estimated to cause more than 50,000 premature deaths and 400,000 new cases of chronic bronchitis per year (UNEP 1999: chapter 2).

Significant environmental degradation is occurring as well, taking a toll on the poor in both urban slums and the countryside. Environmental degradation in Asia is a livelihood-altering and sometimes life-threatening issue as opposed to a postmaterialist (quality of life) concern so prevalent in the West (Hirsch and Warren 1998; Jha and Whalley 1999; Lee and So 1999). Western concerns over high rates of deforestation, which leads to habitat fragmentation and consequent loss of biological diversity, merge, however, with concerns in the East over large-scale population dislocations and increasing vulnerability to natural disasters, such as floods and landslides.

As daunting as current conditions are, they pale when compared with ultimate results of further exploitation of the environment. David Angel, Michael Rock, and Tubagus Feridhanusetyawan (2000) claim that most of Asia is in the midst, not at the end, of an urban-industrial–led development transition unparalleled in its scale and intensity. Urbanization and industrialization have not run their course. Urban population in Asia has been doubling in size every fifteen–twenty years and will increase another 69 percent by 2025. It is daunting to consider that roughly 80 percent of the industry that will be operating in 2020 (primarily in urban areas) has yet to be built. If trends continue, by 2010 Asia will produce more sulfur dioxide than Europe and the United States combined. Another decade beyond that, the Asia region will become the world's largest source of greenhouse gases (Douglass and Ooi 2000: 104–127).

A case can be made that all of this should be of no import to those outside the region and that only the Asian people and their governments are responsible for solutions. The case is weakened considerably, however, by the global impact of Asia's environment, most clearly demonstrated in the case of carbon emissions. The U.S. government has recognized this linkage, making its efforts to combat climate change contingent on commensurate actions in developing countries (of which India and China are the most prominent). Environmentalists are also likely to argue that we are all impoverished if global resources—such as fisheries and forests—are destroyed, resulting in declining biodiversity. An even more tangible manifestation of impact is the increasing amount of sulfur dioxide being generated in Northeast Asia and transported above the Pacific Ocean to North America.

NEW APPROACHES

It would appear that a fundamentally new approach to addressing the environment-trade nexus by the Asia-Pacific region would work to the benefit of all. It makes little sense to deny the legitimacy of environmental issues when they are so firmly embedded in world commerce today and will become ever more prevalent in the future. The existing bodies addressing the trade-environment conflict may not be the arenas in which to deal most forthrightly with concerns today. The WTO is overburdened with a host of issues and presents an adversarial setting not conducive to finding win-win solutions. More Multilateral Environmental Agreements (MEAs) may be desirable, but MEA building in a polarized atmosphere is enormously time-consuming, subject to the lowest common denominator form of consensus, and left to uncertain compliance and enforcement. In short, a new political architecture needs to be created that is devoted to taking up the legitimate concerns of all parties.

Any new gathering should include representatives from all sectors of society. This includes members of civil society at the leading edge of defining operating conditions for further globalization. International NGOs—such as World Wide Fund for Nature, the International Institute for Sustainable Development, World Resources Institute, and Friends of the Earth—are seeking to build bridges across sectors and states on environmental issues and could, if given a chance, play key mediating roles. The UN institutions have significantly encouraged participation of NGOs. Asian participation in such efforts, however, will require the removal of state-centric blinders. Defining acceptable conditions for commerce in the twenty-first century requires a collective undertaking and is not well served by relying solely on state sovereignty.

By all accounts, the NGO community has grown enormously within Southeast Asian countries since around 1980. Asia has a long history of citizen organization (Gan 2000), but only in modern times have Asian states accorded sufficient political space to allow NGOs to multiply. Environmental NGOs come in all flavors, including grassroots service providers, grassroots oppositional forces, political lobbying agents, research- and education-oriented bodies, and environmental watchdogs or oversight groups. The origins of these groups range from neighborhood assemblies to affiliates of international NGOs. It is therefore impossible to easily characterize environmental NGOs. Yok-shiu Lee and Alvin So (1999) speak of Asian NGOs as populist, corporatist, or postmaterialist and claim that each type can be found, at varying strengths, in most East Asian countries.

The NGO struggle for recognition, legitimacy, and influence is continuous in East Asia, as it is everywhere. Certainly, many grassroots battles have been won and much of the citizenry won over. The proliferation of environmental NGOs in East Asia, however, has not significantly altered fundamental government approaches to environmental protection or reduced the magnitude of environmental degradation. One can think of a spectrum of NGO involvement in governance ranging from nonparticipation to partnership. Many Asian leaders still think of NGOs as oppositional forces to be avoided at all costs. A middle position on the spectrum is to treat NGOs as stakeholders (i.e., groups that have a legitimate stake in policy outcomes) and to acknowledge and use them as "sounding boards." This is just beginning to take hold in Asia. As yet lacking in Asia (and still fairly rare even in the West) is the perception of NGOs as genuine partners in governance.

Lyuba Zarsky and Simon Tay (2000) characterized the "Asian way" as combining relatively open markets and economics with closed political structures. The Asian Development Bank (2000b) has identified the absence of inclusive governance as a primary reason for the deteriorating environment in Asia. Asian governments have been more interested in learning how to use NGOs to accomplish their purposes (co-optation) than in learning how to engage NGOs collectively in addressing real environmental problems. Again, Zarsky and Tay (2000: 138) raise the fundamental issue: "The central question for governments in Asia is—or should be—how to harness the transformative potential of this growing popular consciousness and burgeoning civil society towards greatly improving environmental performance. In essence, this means creatively bringing business and NGOs squarely into the task of environmental performance."

To be fair, the West is still experimenting with new forms of environmental governance—moving away from exclusive reliance on state-centered, command-and-control regulation—and has yet to conclusively identify a more inclusive strategy guaranteed to produce superior environmental results. Nevertheless, the West appears more willing to engage in inclusive governance enterprises in the hope that new means of mobilizing society for environmental protection will be found.

INCENTIVES FOR DISCUSSIONS

East Asian states have much to gain from taking a more proactive approach to addressing global environmental issues. A continued defensive approach will not make the issues go away. They will simply be addressed in a manner oblivious to the genuine concerns of East Asian societies. By joining the discussions, East Asian states have a chance to affect the outcome, safeguard their interests, and potentially receive benefits in return. Hideaki Shiroyama (1997: 6) has stated, "The best way to cope with the issue of trade and the environment is not to approach it directly." The day when silence was appropriate has passed.

First, discussions need to go forward to break down the barriers of suspicion and distrust that are all too common today. The perception that environmental conditions for trade are merely stalking-horses for protectionism may be justified in some cases and not in others. Discussions can begin to highlight criteria useful for distinguishing genuine environmental concern from protectionism. Applying these criteria to new PPM trade law would be a major advancement.

Second, by engaging in discussions, East Asian states would be deflecting the spotlight directed toward them—unfairly in many cases—as environmental outlaws. As Adil Najam (2000) has stated, the scapegoating of Asia is a logical result of Asia's intransigence in discussing environmental issues in a global context. Entering such discussions will reveal the distance Western societies themselves must go to be truly responsible environmental stewards.

Third, multiparty discussions will highlight the sometimes parochial approach to environmental protection practiced in the West. As noted previously, significant differences are found between environmental concerns in Western nations and those in most East Asian nations, sometimes characterized as postmaterialist concerns in the West and environmental degradation in the East. Degradation or basic livelihood issues revolve around the environment and its contribution to basic poverty in Asia. Soil erosion, gross drinking water contamination, and wholesale land conversion are distinct from issues that sometimes preoccupy the West—such as recycling, packaging wastes, and livability (quality of life) issues. Absent participation, Asian representatives will be ceding the agenda to the West. At best, this agenda will have little relevance to primary environmental concerns in Asia; at worst, it could lead to actions detrimental to Asian societies (for example, global regulation of genetically modified organisms).

Finally, by engaging in discussions, Asian societies will enhance their chances of gaining access to resources essential for them to be full participants in meaningful environmental change. Asian societies will clearly need financial resources to enhance institutional capacity, gain access to information resources, and assist in the transfer of technologies. The Clean Development Mechanism, associated with the Kyoto Protocol of the United Nations Framework Convention on Climate Change, is just one example of an institution being established to provide significant resources to developing countries. Discussions revolving around other institutions can take place if multilateral and multiparty forums are created. Moreover, willingness to directly address social issues could be a quid pro quo for getting the West to address issues of interest to Asian states (e.g., access to Western markets for textiles and agricultural products).

One can point to examples of turnarounds that indicate East Asian states are not inextricably opposed to incorporating new environmental practices into policy. The Malaysian minister of international trade and industry initially labeled the Forest Stewardship Council (FSC) a "U.S.-backed plot to impose foreign values on Malaysia" (*Tomorrow Essentials* 2000). The FSC is actually an international NGO dedicated to fostering sustainable forestry practices globally. Later, however, Malaysia reversed itself and agreed to require Malaysian loggers to abide by FSC standards (*Economist* 2001: 43). As in this example, Asian opposition to the trade-environment linkage may be less one of principle than one of priority. The unwillingness of Western states to seriously address Asian trade priorities makes Asian leaders less willing to take up the new conditions fostered by the West. Discussions in a nonadversarial environment can help distinguish real objections from those that are negotiable.

INITIATIVES OF THE
ASIA PACIFIC ECONOMIC COOPERATION FORUM

Perhaps the best venue for inclusive discussions of the environment-trade nexus would be under the auspices of APEC. As noted previously, APEC has a focused trade liberalization agenda, it includes both developed and developing member economies, and it has a separate ecotech track that concerns itself with energy and environmental issues, among others. Considerable reconceptualization of what APEC is and what it might become, however, would be required for it to play a pivotal role. The problem with APEC, as currently constituted, involves its membership and operating procedures. APEC is almost exclusively the province of states. It has opened up somewhat to business interests, but civil society representatives have not been welcomed. Indeed an APEC report recommended that the organization involve members of civil society in its deliberations (APIAN 2000).

A large number of APEC working-group meetings are cutting across the entire ecotech spectrum of activities. Reports are commissioned and completed. Very little of substance results, however, because APEC operates under rules closely associated with the ASEAN-way—for example, strictures exist against member interference in the affairs of other members, and decision making is based on "consensus." Unless uniformity among members can be found—something difficult to accomplish, given the diversity among members—action on the basis of APEC study findings languishes. Discussion of policy issues takes place behind closed doors, usually at the annual meeting of APEC heads of state.

Revitalization of APEC might begin with the creation of an APEC Civil Society Advisory Council that could provide guidance to state representatives on desirable forms of environmental governance. Zarsky and Tay (2000) have provided useful alternative models for such governance that could form the basis for ongoing discussions. A permanent APEC Business Advisory Council was created in 1996 to provide advice and counsel, and an equivalent civil society–run council could be equally useful.

APEC could also serve as a useful forum for representatives from all sectors to candidly address the environmental dimensions of globalization. The basic purpose would not be to create a formal, alternative dispute resolution mechanism (see Cameron and White 1997) but rather a setting where alternative perceptions are set forth and made the basis for discussion. By gauging the "distance" between contending views, it may be possible to determine which issues can be resolved among affected parties and which genuinely need dispute settlement by a third party such as the WTO. This could be the embodiment of the Standing Conference on Trade and Environment proposed by the International Institute for Sustainable Development (IISD 1999). It would seek to formulate practical recommendations on trade and the environment that could be introduced to the WTO or other policy forums.

Three members of APEC—Canada, the United States, and Mexico—have experience with integrating environmental issues with trade liberalization under the auspices of the North American Free Trade Agreement (NAFTA). At the behest of environmental NGOs, a side accord—the North American Agreement on Environmental Cooperation—was created, and the North American Commission for Environmental Cooperation was established to track its implementation. NAFTA support is still problematic in some quarters, but it is safe to say it would not have gone forward in the first place or been sustained without the commitment to environmental protection. APEC needs to search for this same form of consensus.

APEC members may wish to identify policy issues amenable to public policy networks. These are informal groupings of individuals from all sectors of society and the global community who join together in an attempt to find consensus on difficult policy issues (Reinicke 1999; Rischard 2000). The reputed value of these networks resides in the belief that solutions to many conflicts can be found if knowledgeable individuals from a variety of backgrounds can be assembled to function in a nonofficial, nonadversarial capacity. Examples of existing networks include the World Commission on Dams and the Global Water Partnership. It is too early to speak conclusively about the effectiveness of this policy innovation, but it constitutes an interesting, novel, and nonadversarial approach to advancing global consensus.

CONCLUSION

Fundamentally, a common understanding to approaching environmental issues must be forged among the Asia-Pacific community if the consensus goal of trade liberalization is to proceed. This chapter has highlighted critical differences in perception between East Asia and the West in terms of what constitutes legitimate environmental governance and goals. These differences must be bridged, or commerce and trade will suffer. This does not mean universal environmental standards need be imposed regardless of economic levels and circumstances. It does mean, however, that environmental concerns should become integrated components of future growth rather than afterthoughts. Trade is one important venue for this integration, but it is only a part of the broader international environmental agenda that requires cooperation across Asia-Pacific societies. As noted previously, environmental conditions in East Asia have global impacts and, as such, will be a long-standing and important component of future foreign policy.

Continued globalization of the world economy will be contingent upon the incorporation of fundamental environmental and human rights conditions into its ongoing evolution. This incorporation will not be easy or automatic. Critics of globalization are seeking its derailment, not its success. Some advocates of globalization will be playing into the hands of critics by denying that environmental and human rights issues have any relevance to the globalization process.

The mounting evidence of environmental deterioration is triggering new approaches to environmental protection, some of which will inevitably impact global commerce. The legitimacy of addressing environmental concerns in the context of trade is being sought by some and denied by others. East Asian states as a rule are laggards in recognizing this legitimacy. In general, they continue to view environmental components of trade agreements as blatant protectionism that impinges on their sovereign right to establish their own environmental standards. The case has been made in this chapter, however, that it is in the interests of East Asian states to alter their opposition, first to ensure that the globalization process—from which they have benefited—will continue and second to see that their specific environmental interests are addressed.

This change in policy will have to be accompanied by a willingness to deal directly with representatives from civil society. International environmental NGOs are leading the effort to find a comfortable fit between further globalization and environmental protection. Groups such as the International Centre for Trade and Sustainable Development, the World Conservation Union, the World Business Council for Sustainable Development, the International Institute for Sustainable Development, and Friends of the Earth have made positive contributions. The latter two, for example, have published several documents that outline ways of reconciling trade with environmental protection. These documents could provide the basis for discussions within APEC and elsewhere. All states need to recognize the value civil society brings to environmental governance and seek to both foster and channel that value in responsible ways (Esty 1997; Zarsky and Tay 2000).

The inability to reconcile trade and environment on a global scale makes efforts at a regional scale the next-best alternative. APEC, whose primary goal is trade liberalization, could be an important forum for the Asia-Pacific community to engage in a meaningful discussion of these issues. The focus should be on discussions, not negotiations. The policy distance between opposing positions is so wide that negotiations now would lead to further polarization. Discussions involving all sectors of society, not just states, are more likely to find mutually agreeable common ground that can eventually be incorporated into negotiations.

Failure to reconcile trade and the environment on a broad regional scale will bring discussions and negotiations to either a smaller subregional scale or down to the bilateral level (witness current U.S.-Singapore negotiations and proposed U.S.-Australia negotiations). This will inevitably leave millions outside the trade liberalization mainstream, denying the economic benefits that could accrue from further globalization.

The primary policy recommendation from this examination is to fundamentally change APEC's mode of operation and its agenda. APEC has great potential as a bridge between developed and developing countries but is not currently operating to fulfill that potential. A useful transformation of the organization can take place without according it the supranational powers all seek to avoid. Arguably, without bold initiatives and follow-up implementation, APEC would lose credibility as an organization (APIAN 2000). The time is right, therefore, for renewed regional efforts to come to terms with trade and environmental imperatives.

REFERENCES

Angel, David P., and Michael T. Rock, eds. 2000. *Asia's Clean Revolution: Industry, Growth and the Environment.* Sheffield, UK: Greenleaf.

Angel, David P., Michael T. Rock, and Tubagus Feridhanusetyawan. 2000. "Toward Clean Shared Growth in Asia." In David P. Angel and Michael T. Rock, eds., *Asia's Clean Revolution: Industry, Growth and the Environment.* Sheffield, UK: Greenleaf.

Annan, Kofi. 2000. "Global Values: The United Nations and the Rule of Law in the 21st Century" <http://www.un.org/partners/business/sgstate.htm>.

APEC International Assessment Network (APIAN). 2000. "Learning From Experience: The First APIAN Policy Report." Singapore: APEC Study Center.

Asian Development Bank. 2000a. *Asian Development Outlook 2000.* New York: Oxford University Press.

————. 2000b. *Asian Environmental Outlook 2001: Win-Win Policies for a Better Environment.* New York: Oxford University Press.

————. 2000c. *Sustainable Development in Asia.* New York: Oxford University Press.

Audley, John J. 2000. "Integrating Environmental Priorities Into Trade." *Economic Perspectives* [electronic journal of the U.S. State Department] (February).

Bendell, Jem. 2000. "Civil Regulation: A New Form of Democratic Governance for the Global Economy?" In Jem Bendell, ed., *Terms for Endearment: Business, NGOs and Sustainable Development.* Sheffield, UK: Greenleaf.

Brechin, Steven, and Willett Kempton. 1994. "Global Environmentalism: A Challenge to the Postmaterialist Thesis?" *Social Science Quarterly* 75, 2: 245–269.

Bruehl, Tanja, and Volker Rittberger. 2001. "From International to Global Governance: Actors, Collective Decision-Making and the United Nations in the World of the 21st Century." Paper presented at the 42nd International Studies Association Annual Convention, Chicago, 22 February.

Cameron, James, and Tanya White. 1997. "Dispute Mediation in APEC: Bridging the Legal and Cultural Gaps." Proceedings from the Joint Meeting between the Global Environment and Trade Study and Global Industrial and Social Progress Research Institute, New York, 27 June.

Central Intelligence Agency (CIA). 1999. *Handbook of International Economic Statistics.* Washington, DC: Central Intelligence Agency.

Chang-Xing, Di. 1999. "ISO 14001: The Severe Challenge for China." In Walter Wehrmeyer and Yacob Mulugetta, eds., *Growing Pains.* Sheffield, UK: Greenleaf.

Douglass, Michael, and Giok Ling Ooi. 2000. "Industrializing Cities and the Environment in Pacific Asia: Toward a Policy Framework and Agenda for Action." In David P. Angel and Michael T. Rock, eds., *Asia's Clean Revolution: Industry, Growth and the Environment.* Sheffield, UK: Greenleaf.

Dua, Andre, and Daniel C. Esty. 1997. *Sustaining the Asia Pacific Miracle.* Washington, DC: Institute for International Economics.

Dunlap, Riley E., George H. Gallup Jr., and Alec M. Gallup. 1993. "Of Global Concern: Results of the Health of the Planet Survey." *Environment* 35 (November): 7–15, 33–39.

Economic and Social Commission for Asia and the Pacific. 2000. *Review of the State of the Environment in Asia and the Pacific* [E/ESCAP/SO/MCED(00)/1] <http://www.unescap.org/enrd/environ/soe.htm>.

Economist. 2001. "Good Fellers." *Economist* (January): 43.

Esty, Daniel C. 1997. "Why the World Trade Organization Needs Environmental NGOs." Paper published by the International Centre for Trade and Sustainable Development, Geneva, Switzerland.

Gan, Lin. 2000. "Energy Development and Environmental NGOs in an Emerging Global Civil Society." In Pamela S. Chasek, ed., *The Global Environment in the Twenty-First Century: Prospects for International Cooperation.* Tokyo: United Nations University Press.

Hirsch, Phillip, and Carol Warren, eds. 1998. *The Politics of Environment in Southeast Asia.* London: Routledge.

International Institute for Sustainable Development (IISD). 1999. *A Standing Conference on Trade and Environment: Proposal by the IISD and the IUCN–World Conservation Union.* Winnipeg: International Institute for Sustainable Development.

Japan Environmental Council. 2000. *The State of the Environment in Asia 1999/2000.* Tokyo: Springer-Verlag.

Jha, Raghbendra, and John Whalley. 1999. "The Environmental Regime in Developing Countries." Paper presented at the National Bureau of Economic Research Conference, Milan, Italy, June.

Jha, Veena, Anil Markandya, and Rene Vossenaar. 1999. *Reconciling Trade and the Environment: Lessons From Case Studies in Developing Countries.* Northampton, MA: Edward Elgar.

Joyner, Christopher C., and Zachary Tyler. 2000. "Marine Conservation Versus International Free Trade: Reconciling Dolphins With Tuna and Sea Turtles With Shrimp." *Ocean Development and International Law* 31: 127–150.

Keohane, Robert O., and Joseph S. Nye Jr. 2000. "Globalization: What's New? What's Not? (and So What)." *Foreign Policy* 118 (spring): 104–119.

Lee, Yok-shiu, and Alvin Y. So, eds. 1999. *Asia's Environmental Movements: A Comparative Perspective.* Armorik, NY: M. E. Sharpe.

Mahathir, bin Mohamed. 1999. "The Green Flag of Eco-Imperialism." *New Perspectives Quarterly* 16, 2: 8–9.

Morrison, Charles E., Akira Kojima, and Hanns W. Maull. 1997. *Community-Building in the Pacific Asia.* New York: Trilateral Commission.

Najam, Adil. 2000. "Trade and Environment After Seattle: A Negotiating Agenda for the South." *Journal of Environment and Development* 9, 4: 405–425.

Newell, Peter. 2000. "Globalisation and the New Politics of Sustainable Development." In Jem Bendell, ed., *Terms for Endearment: Business, NGOs and Sustainable Development.* Sheffield, UK: Greenleaf.

O'Brien, Robert, Anne Marie Goetz, Jan Aart Scholte, and Marc Williams. 2000. *Contesting Global Governance.* New York: Cambridge University Press.

Peritore, Patrick N. 1999. *Third World Environmentalism: Case Studies From the Global South.* Gainesville: University Press of Florida.

Reinicke, Wolfgang H. 1999. "The Other World Wide Web: Global Public Policy Networks." *Foreign Policy* 117: 44–57.

Rischard, Jean-François. 2000. "The New Frontiers in Governance." Presentation at the Chatham House Conference on Corporate Citizenship: Defining the New Responsibilities, London, 23 October.

Seda, Maria, and Simon S.C. Tay. 2000. "The Environment and Regional Cooperation in Asia." Paper prepared for the Third Dialogue on Building Asia's Tomorrow, Japan Center for International Exchange, Tokyo, June.

Shiroyama, Hideaki. 1997. "Environmental Policy in APEC." Proceedings from the Joint Meeting between the Global Environment and Trade Study and Global Industrial and Social Progress Research Institute, New York, 27 June.

Tay, Simon S.C. 1998. "What Should Be Done About the Haze." *Indonesian Quarterly* 26, 2: 99–117.

————. 2000. "The South East Asian Fires and Haze: Challenges to Regional Cooperation in ASEAN and the Asia-Pacific." Paper presented to the Asia Pacific Agenda Project, Okinawa Forum, 25–26 March.

Tomorrow Essentials. 2000. Newsletter from Tomorrow Publishing, Stockholm, 14 March.

Tussie, Diana, and Patricia Vasquez . 2000. "The International Negotiation of PPMs: Possible, Appropriate, Convenient?" In Diana Tussie, ed., *The Environment and International Trade Negotiations: Developing Country Stakes.* New York: St. Martin's.

United Nations Environmental Programme (UNEP). 1999. *Global Environmental Outlook 2000.* Nairobi: UNEP.

Wallach, Lori, and Michelle Sforza. 1999. *Whose Trade Organization: Corporate Globalization and the Erosion of Democracy.* Washington, DC: Public Citizen.

World Bank. 1999. *East Asia: The Road to Recovery.* New York: Oxford University Press.

World Resources Institute. 2000. *World Resources 2000–2001: People and Ecosystems: The Fraying Web of Life.* New York: Oxford University Press.

Yencken, David, John Fien, and Helen Sykes, eds. 2000. *Environment, Education and Society in the Asia-Pacific.* New York: Routledge.

Zarsky, Lyuba, and Simon S.C. Tay. 2000. "Civil Society and the Future of Environmental Governance in Asia." In David P. Angel and Michael T. Rock, eds., *Asia's Clean Revolution: Industry, Growth and the Environment.* Sheffield, UK: Greenleaf.

5

The Asian Development Bank and Environmental Diplomacy: Limits to the Technocratic Consensus

MORTEN BØÅS

Since the early 1970s East Asia has lost half its forest cover and with it countless unique animal and plant species. A third of its agricultural land has been degraded. Fish stocks have fallen by 50 percent. No other region of the world has as many heavily polluted cities, and its lakes and rivers are among the world's most degraded. Although rapid economic development has created dynamism and wealth, East Asia has at the same time become dirtier, less ecologically diverse, and more environmentally vulnerable. All of this is the consequence of a manmade process (ADB 1997).

For too long East Asian policymakers ignored the environmental impact of rapid growth. Concerns about pollution and environmental degradation were not a priority. And once East Asian governments did adopt environmental regulations, they were ineffectively designed and inadequately implemented. The problem was that although many countries in the region introduced sophisticated environmental standards and rigid regulatory regimes, too often they neither monitored nor enforced those standards and regimes. Both the institutional capacity and the political will to enforce real implementation of the policies were lacking.

This chapter will take a closer look at an international financial institution in Asia, the Asian Development Bank (ADB), which through its environmental program has been involved in environmental diplomacy with East Asian countries since the early 1980s. The chapter will evaluate the experience of the ADB in these efforts and analyze its strategy when dealing with countries for which environmental protection was not a main priority. This experience will have several important implications for future environmental cooperation in the region because East Asian countries still do not completely accept the ADB's environmental program as legitimate. This chapter will therefore seek to make specific policy recommendations for the governments (donors and borrowing member countries) and other stakeholders involved in the policy debates on environmental issues in the ADB. In doing so, this chapter will pay particular attention to the ADB's attempt to depoliticize the environment agenda by defining the issue area of the environment in a technical and functional nonpolitical manner.

All international organizations are established to solve problems. Originally, the ADB was established to promote development in Asia. Development was seen as a linear process toward increased prosperity and closer resemblance to Western societies, facilitated through improvements in communication and infrastructure, agriculture, and industrialization. Environmental issues were not a part of the problem definition. In the early 1980s, however, this situation started to change, and the ADB was suddenly faced with a demand from nonregional donor governments and nongovernmental actors from the same countries to include environmental issues in its definition of development.

Ernst Haas (1990) suggested that change in the form of incorporation of new issue areas (or problem redefinition) can be brought about by either "adaptation" or "learning." Adaptation in this sense refers to a process in which attempts are made to resolve a problem by adding new tasks to old ones without seeking to justify and define them as means toward the organization's overall goal. This implies that neither underlying values nor the organization's purpose is seriously questioned. What is altered are the means and not the ends. Change is therefore incremental, without an attempt to place purposes in a logical order. This is what Haas calls "change by adaptation." Such a process can take place within two different institutional settings.

> One, labeled "incremental growth," features the successive augmentation of an organization's program as actors add new tasks to older ones without any change in the organization's decision-making dynamics or mode of choosing. The other, labeled "turbulent nongrowth," involves major changes in organizational decision-making: ends no longer cohere; internal consensus on both ends and means disintegrate.
> (Haas 1990: 4)

On the other hand, Haas (1990) argues that if new purposes are incorporated as part of a reflective process in which new means under new ends are subsumed in a systematic way, legitimated by different theories about development, the process of change should be referred to as learning. Consequently, learning is associated with a distinctly different model of organizational change than the one represented by adaptation. Learning takes place under a model of organizational change called "managed interdependence." The reexamination of purpose is informed by decision-making dynamics founded on the mediation of (new) knowledge. Such an approach implies that change in this respect is widely defined as the ability to deal with new demands (including those from environmental issues). It is important to keep in mind, however, that the ADB is an intergovernmental organization and is therefore dominated by political groups (e.g., country constituencies) whose behavior is subject to bounded rationality because the groups must balance objectives, means, and interests that do not necessarily cohere. This means the survival of an intergovernmental organization, such as the ADB, may have more to do with the ability to keep its most important member governments pleased than with efficiency in a narrow sense. According to Haas, "Because the states that are the masters and clients of international organizations are a heterogeneous lot, they present a similar heterogeneous 'task environment' for organizational action. The 'task' they jointly wish on the organization represents the sum of the possibly very different tasks each government faces at home" (1990: 55).

This means that compared with other social units, an intergovernmental organization confronts specific challenges when faced with a demand to incorporate new issue areas such as the environment. Its mission is never simple and straightforward because both member states and other actors in its external environment disagree on the interpretation of the mission, as well as on the tasks that need to be conducted if the mission is to be completed. The consequence is that conflict is an integral part of intergovernmental organizations. As a result, these organizations will favor one particular way of arranging and routinizing their activities. In social units that function under such circumstances, organizational routines and standard operating principles will be preferred over demands for change. According to their charters, most intergovernmental organizations are established to address technical questions in a functional manner. In other words, their programs, projects, and policies are supposedly politically neutral. Nevertheless, as noted earlier, the issue of change in such organizations cannot be addressed in a technical and functional manner. They are for all purposes political institutions, and the issue of change within them is likewise ultimately a political question.

THE ASIAN DEVELOPMENT BANK

The ADB is a regional development bank with a multipolar structure in which power is shared among the present fifty-six recipient and donor country members. The most important donor countries in the ADB are Japan and the United States, whereas the most influential recipient countries are China and India. This blend of regional members among both donors and recipient countries makes the ADB unique among the regional development banks, and it creates at least a potential for less clear-cut cleavages between regionals (recipients) and nonregionals (donors). The regional member countries hold the majority of votes: at present, they control 65 percent of the votes and the nonregionals control 35 percent.

When the ADB began operations on 19 December 1966, the Asia-Pacific region was one of the poorest regions in the world. Most regional member states struggled to develop their economic bases and improve the well-being of their people. There was a massive need for capital to develop agriculture and industry and to build basic infrastructure. The tasks facing the newly established Bank were huge.

Nearly forty years later the region has become the fastest growing in the world. Steady improvements have been made in the quality of life, and in this process the ADB has become a well-respected multilateral development bank. Although the ADB aided this process, it gained credibility mainly because of the economic growth in the region, not because it was the main engine of that growth. When Japan hosted the 30th annual meeting of the ADB in Fukuoka, however, the ADB acted like a proud parent of a child about to became an adult.[1] The meeting was meant to be the final manifestation of the maturity of both the Bank and the region it was established to serve. The meeting wanted to cultivate the image of a financially solid institution with the knowledge and institutional capacity to enter the unknown field of postindustrial development that is inhabited by difficult nexuses such as the one among the environment, indigenous people, involuntary resettlement, governance, and nongovernmental organizations (NGOs).

The annual meeting of an institution like the ADB is both a political event and a manifestation of what is going on in the institution and its regional borrowing member countries. Discussion at the ADB annual meetings are usually concerned with Bank financing and replenishment of the Asian Development Fund (ADF). Because the ADF VII negotiations were completed in Tokyo in January 1997, however, they were discussed only in passing in Fukuoka. Nevertheless, the meeting still had a strong political agenda. Criticism of the Bank was raised. NGO representatives accused the Bank of lack of accountability, transparency, and participation by stakeholders and expressed deep frustration over their perception of a wide gap between the Bank's sustainable development language and the reality of affected communities. The Bank underscored the importance of its new medium-term strategic framework—adopted in 1996—that defined the ADB agenda as promoting economic growth but also reducing poverty, supporting human development (including population planning), improving the status of women, and protecting the environment. According to the ADB, these objectives resulted from the Bank's understanding that economic growth is necessary to reduce poverty but alone is insufficient to raise the living standards of the poor, women, and other disadvantaged groups. Bank policies should therefore be directed at target populations, and economic growth had to be sustained through protection of the environment (ADB 2001: 283).

In practice, this means the ADB is officially devoted to move from a traditional role of financing growth-oriented sectors to financing promotion of sustainable development. Each country's loan portfolio is therefore to consist of a 50-50 mix of economic growth projects and social-sector projects. The problem for the Bank is that this issue is highly controversial. The idea of a new development agenda for the Bank in the twenty-first century is not popular among developing member countries (DMCs). China, India, and Indonesia have expressed deep displeasure with the new policy on mixed-loan portfolios.

The Chinese governor stated in his speech to the Fukuoka meeting that even though China agrees that economic development and social progress are complementary, without the foundation of a well-developed economy it would be difficult for developing countries to achieve social progress (Bøås 1997: 12). According to the Chinese view, issues like environmental protection, health care, and educational development are important, but it is virtually impossible for a country like China to advance beyond the reality of its economic development. The ADB's main duty should therefore be to support economic growth in its DMCs, whereas individual member countries should be responsible for the development of the social sector. This means the process of problem redefinition in the ADB remains ongoing and controversial.

To deepen understanding of this process, I shall return to the initial introduction of environmental issues to the ADB. The idea is that through such a description of the ADB's experience with environmental issues a clearer understanding will be gained of both the initial successes and limitations of a constructed technical consensus in an intergovernmental organization such as the ADB.

THE ASIAN DEVELOPMENT BANK AND THE ENVIRONMENT

TECHNOCRATIC CONSENSUS (1979–1988)

According to the ADB, it was in the late 1970s that the Bank, along with most other multilateral and bilateral agencies, began to accept that economic development often had adverse impacts on the natural environment and that the Bank had a responsibility to mitigate these impacts through environmental planning and management (ADB 1986). The *Banking on the Biosphere* report, however, had a completely different view. The report found that the ADB, during that same period, had no specific procedures or checklists to ensure that environmental impacts were considered in the loan process and did not employ even one environmental specialist (Stein and Johnson 1979). An environmental paper issued by the ADB in 1978 had paid minor attention to the issue (see ADB 1978), but by and large environmental issues were not considered important enough to included in policy statements, policy papers, and annual reports.

The *Banking on the Biosphere* report and the devastating picture it presented of environmental issues in the ADB led to a discussion by the board and among top management. It was decided to employ Jeremy Warford, a developmental economist who had worked for the World Bank. In the ADB he was assigned to the Infrastructure Department, but his work was related to environmental issues. Warford started work in the ADB in February 1979, and a year later he presented a working paper to the board entitled *Environmental Considerations in Bank Operations* (ADB 1980a). The paper outlined a general strategy by which Bank operations could systematically take account of environmental issues. The need for such a strategy was legitimized by the principles stemming from the 1972 UN Conference on the Human Environment (the Stockholm Conference) and the guidelines used by the World Bank and the U.S. Agency for International Development. Warford's general argument was that the Bank had a potential role of some magnitude in the environmental arena but that a number of important implications had to be considered if the ADB were to become involved. Anticipating resistance from the Bank's DMCs, Warford made it clear that

> The Bank is limited by the priorities that DMCs themselves place upon
> environmental protection and improvement measures and by the
> difficulty of demonstrating conclusively that such measures are indeed
> justified. Since the environmental consequences of projects and
> policies are typically not susceptible to accurate prediction, a good
> deal of reliance needs to be placed upon the subjective, but neverthe-
> less well-informed judgment of experts; however, such judgment will
> frequently be a matter of debate. The inherent complexity of environ-
> mental issues and of the relationship between environmental policies
> and social objectives of DMC governments is paralleled by the proce-
> dural difficulties that an international development institution like
> the Bank has in addressing these issues. Additional staffing and
> organizational changes within the Bank would clearly be needed, but
> these should be introduced gradually as experience is acquired. (ADB
> 1980a: 2–3)

The report therefore stated firmly that Bank lending should continue in traditional areas but that projects should be modified by the inclusion of environmental components or regulatory safeguards to ensure that environmental damage would be avoided as much as possible. Thus the approach was of an engineering problem-solving variety, and it was written in a technical language staff, management, and the board understood. Nevertheless, several executive directors (EDs) representing regional recipient countries expressed skepticism toward Bank involvement in environmental issues. They stressed the need for a balanced approach to prevent environmental experts from achieving the power to veto proposals from other departments: "Project processing should not stop just because of the fear of environmental damage. Lending should continue in the traditional areas, while at the same time the Bank should include environmental aspects" (ADB 1980b: 13). Some regional EDs even expressed fear of environmental issues becoming a new religion that could create diversion in terms of greater costs and difficulties on the path to development and progress. According to Philippine ED Roberto Melchor, "The critical issue for DMCs, particularly after the energy crisis, was survival, and poor people in these countries did not object to pollution if it meant more jobs" (ADB 1980b: 11). The other regional EDs supported Melchor's comment in principle, and several argued for a balanced approach. As they saw it, in some countries the power of environmental experts had developed to the extent where they could veto proposals from other departments, which was contrary to the development process.[2]

Nonregional EDs welcomed the report, and most supported the proposal to appoint an environmental specialist, as the World Bank had done. Some, however, also saw huge challenges for the Bank within this field. In particular, they warned that the Bank, as in many other cases, could not go faster than its client countries would permit it to do. The challenge was therefore how to encourage borrowing countries to pay more attention to the environmental consequences of projects. Thus they argued that within this issue area the Bank had an educational as well as a financial role to play. This is an interesting argument, because it highlights the main dilemma for a multilateral development bank in addressing crosscutting issues. For the ADB to play a significant role within a crosscutting issue area such as the environment, it would—at least to some extent—have to interfere in domestic policy choices of its DMCs, which is against the nature of these institutions' charters.[3]

This was the first time this dilemma had been mentioned in relation to environmental issues in the ADB, but it has been a recurring element of the Bank's policy discussions. Equally important was the way the nonregional EDs approached the issue in board discussions, which had ramifications for the debate in following years. Instead of approaching the matter in a political manner, they approached the question of Bank involvement in domestic policy choices as one of distribution and diffusion of information. Thus they focused the discussion on the part of the paper that dealt with tradeoffs between short-term economic growth and environmental objectives. They argued that in many cases solid information about these tradeoffs was crucial for decisionmakers and could be important for the country concerned in making its own judgment. The nonregional EDs thus concluded that the report provided a strong blueprint for the Bank's future work on the environment as an integrated part of Bank operations.

The Japanese ED was one of the last to speak at the meeting. His intervention was brief, but it carried clout. On one hand he welcomed the report and supported its conclusions and recommendations, but on the other hand he stressed the need for caution and a balanced approach to environmental issues. He noted that in pursuing environmental objectives, the Bank would work within the framework of the priorities of DMCs, and incorporation of environmental considerations would be incorporated in projects only after careful analysis of the costs and tradeoffs involved. In the end the whole board endorsed the report because the issue area was defined in a very modest and technical manner. This discussion, however, initially created a clear-cut donor-recipient country divide, with one important exception—Japan. The more advanced developing country economies were not interested in a dimension they perceived as a possible barrier to their industrial development, whereas the poorest regional members saw environmental protection as a luxury they could not afford. It therefore seems likely that the decision to approach this issue area in a slow and balanced manner contributed to putting the environmental question firmly on the agenda while simultaneously calming the expressed fear of regional recipient countries.

The stage was set for the development of the ADB's environmental policies, which during the first period took the Bank into the model of organizational change Haas (1990) calls "managed interdependence." By depoliticizing the environmental agenda it became possible to reexamine the ADB's purpose within the established understanding (i.e., "knowledge") of development in the Bank. Under this model, in just a few years the Bank managed to put in place most of the elements necessary to include environmental considerations in its project cycle. These events led to the employment of the Bank's first environmental specialists, the establishment of the Environmental Unit, and its subsequent upgrade to an Environmental Division. The kind of depoliticizing of the environmental agenda that took place in the Bank was not a strategy by default but part of a deliberate plan developed by the "environmentalists" in the Bank. We should interpret the next milestone in the history of environmental policies in the Bank along these lines.

The next important step toward a more full-fledged environmental policy came in 1986 when the board endorsed a working paper titled *Review of the Bank's Environmental Policies and Procedures* (ADB 1985). This report, written by the two environmental specialists, identified the scope of the ADB's future environmental activities and provided a framework for action. It was not a review forced on the Bank. The paper argued that the DMCs badly needed environmental assistance from the Bank and that the ABD should therefore seek to encourage greater environmental awareness among the DMCs and try to ensure that national environmental programs were adequately funded and interdepartmental cooperation on environmental matters improved. The document clearly spoke about the role of the Bank vis-à-vis its DMCs in a supporting role. Since an important objective, however, was also to influence domestic policy making toward increased environmental awareness, the authors of the report clearly envisioned the Bank playing a role in domestic politics. Contrary to the ADB charter, the paper saw a role for the Bank in its member countries' internal affairs.

Another noteworthy dimension of the report was the discrepancy between the agenda it defined and the modest operational and institutional implications it anticipated. The message seemed to be: just allow us to enlarge our role; you will not notice it, and it will cost you nothing. The environmentalists who wrote the report were well aware of the fear expressed by regional recipient countries that too much emphasis on environmental issues would divert attention and resources away from the kind of projects the Bank had traditionally financed. What they wanted to achieve was not necessarily more resources but an endorsement by the board that the ADB's environmental agenda could be broadened. To achieve this it was vitally important to convince the regional recipient countries that a tradeoff between traditional ADB projects and environmental awareness was less costly than they envisioned. It would be business as usual in the ADB, but it would be more environmentally friendly. This was one way of keeping politics at bay in the discussions between the ADB and its regional member countries; another was to define the entire environmental agenda of the Bank in a highly technical manner. The level of Bank involvement in national development priorities described by the 1985 report is a highly politicized issue. The report, however, was written in highly technical language. According to Julian Payne:

This issue could be approached in a technical manner, and as a technocratic institution the Bank found this quite easy to work on. It will be much harder for the Bank to approach the other crosscutting theme, which demands another approach. However, this also implies that environment in the ADB is not really addressed as a crosscutting theme, but as a technical question.[4]

Prior to the introduction of the environment and other crosscutting issues during the 1980s and 1990s, the ADB was a technical institution, a development bank run by people educated in business, economics, and engineering. Their perception of their role in the developmental process in Asia was as engineers. Development (or the lack thereof) was seen as a technical issue, not a political one. In other words, if environmental issues were defined in a technical rather than a political manner, the possibility of getting the issue accepted both among staff in the project departments and in the governments of the DMCs increased. A reexamination of purpose was therefore possible because the new knowledge such a reexamination was founded on was presented to the Bank in the same technocratic language as the old, familiar knowledge. Subsequently, by defining this new issue area in a highly technical manner and not in a political way, the authors increased their chances of getting it accepted both among staff in the project departments and in the governments of the Bank's regional recipient member countries. The strategy should therefore be seen as a deliberate attempt to depoliticize the environmental agenda in an effort to keep politics at bay. By applying this strategy, the authors of the report managed to keep discussions of the environment within the framework of standard operating procedures at the Bank.

Thus when the environment as an issue area surfaced in the ADB, it was clearly driven by nonregional donor countries and was met with skepticism and resistance by the DMCs. Nonetheless, because of the ability of the key actors involved to define this issue area in a technical manner, it became possible to keep "the political" out of policy debates. Politics could be kept at bay, and the underlying political conflicts could, at least in part, be controlled. This strategy worked remarkably well during the first period described here, but it became harder to repeat in the periods that followed. When the environmental agenda could no longer be tackled by narrow end-of-pipe approaches but needed integrated and holistic approaches that could link environmental issues to other crosscutting issue areas, the Bank found itself in difficulty. It was no longer just a matter of finding the right technical solution to a functional problem. In the post–Rio Earth Summit zeitgeist, it was more a matter of finding political solutions to an increasingly politicized issue area.

RAPID UPGRADING OF THE ENVIRONMENT? (1988–1994)

In the early part of this period, the strategy of depoliticization and technicality worked fairly well. New avenues were opened up for environmental policies and procedures, and when the Office of the Environment (OENV) was established in 1991, it played a more direct and independent role in the project preview and appraisal process than its predecessors had. Policy dialogue on environmental issues was still not a part of the agenda, however. It was not the "Asian way" of doing things. Japan's position on this issue was clear: "Aid is a co-operative joint work between two countries. Starting from this philosophy, we as a donor should be careful not to force certain economic policies on the recipients" (Ministry of Foreign Affairs, Japan 1989: 29).[5]

During this period, however, the limits of the ADB's technocratic approach started to emerge. The OENV managed to a certain degree to institutionalize its participation in the ADB's program cycle, but it was clearly not properly formalized. Participation was still ad hoc because in important parts of the process the OENV only took part, whereas the participation of other regular participants was deemed required and necessary (see ADB 1991). This suggests that the OENV as an organizational part of the Bank and the environment as an issue area for the ADB were still not on equal standing with other departments and issue areas.

One case that put its mark on the Bank in this period was the Masinloc Power Plant Project in the Philippines. According to the ADB (1991: 13), "Energy is a fundamental requirement for sustainable development, but DMC governments face an array of serious environmental issues associated with energy development and utilization." According to the Bank, it therefore focused its activities within this subsector on improved demand forecasting, optimal least-cost investment planning, and supply efficiency. It has supported technological improvements and the development of indigenous and renewable energy sources. All these efforts were supposedly carried out in the name of sustainable development, which fit the ADB's official image of itself and its activities within the energy sector in Asia. The problem was that with increased environmental awareness among the populations of East Asian countries came increased criticism of the ADB's approach.

The case of the Masinloc Power Plant Project is an example of an opposition movement that buckled under the weight of government pressure (FoE Japan 1997), but it is also a project that changed strategic thinking at ADB headquarters. The main problem was the location of the power plant. The 600-megawatt coal-fired thermal power planted was located on a formerly pristine site. According to Friends of the Earth, the community that lived there had developed a livelihood based on sustainable management of the area's mango trees and the bay's fish resources. To them it constituted "a model of successful community development" (FoE Japan 1997: 67). This tropical "paradise" was now threatened by an ADB-sponsored project. The main criticism from NGOs and the local population was that alternative sites and other types of energy generation had not been adequately considered during project design, and as such, in their view the ADB did not promote but rather destroyed sustainable development. What made this project so important for forthcoming policy debates and institutional developments in the ADB was the negative publicity it caused. Opposition and protests not only from local residents but also from national and international NGOs delayed the Masinloc project for almost four years. The peak hour for the NGO campaign came when a Philippine NGO managed to secure a promise from the Japan Export-Import Bank (JEXIM) that it would not cofinance the power plant with the ADB unless the project had "complete social acceptability." Despite continued resistance, the ADB and Philippine authorities started the bidding round for the generator in October 1993. To defeat the opposition the Philippine government resorted to carrot-and-stick approaches: making relocation promises to appease grassroots members while staging police tactics to intimidate leaders.[6] Ultimately, the opposition succumbed and agreed to move.

Some residents toured Japan and called on JEXIM to stay with its promise, but their attempt proved useless. On 22 December 1994 JEXIM announced its decision to go through with cofinancing. In mid-1995 the final opposition to the project disappeared when the last of the local owners agreed to relinquish their property. Seen in isolation, the outcome ended in defeat for the national and international NGOs, but the project and the campaign against it also constituted a disgrace for the ADB. In particular, the Bank was embarrassed that its cofinancing partner in Japan, JEXIM, made a public statement against the Bank and the project. In the end, the ADB managed to secure the outcome it desired, but it was an expensive victory. As the process around Masinloc evolved, it therefore became clear to several strategists in the Bank's top management that it could not afford too many projects like Masinloc. Mechanisms had to be established to show that the Bank was serious in its dedication to social responsibility and sustainable development.

The Masinloc project therefore had a decisive impact on the Bank's thinking, but behind both the Masinloc campaign and internal changes in the Bank lay the zeitgeist of 1992. This was the year of the UN Conference on Environment and Development (UNCED), held in Rio de Janeiro. Few international institutions escaped the influence of Rio. Sectors of the ADB would have preferred to conduct business as usual, but top management understood that it had to come up with answers in response to the UNCED call for multilateral development banks to help developing countries meet their post-UNCED commitments. The ADB therefore started to prepare a strategy and a course of follow-up actions in line with Agenda 21, the framework agreement on climate change and the biodiversity convention (ADB 1993). The questions of how to finance and implement these actions, however, were not addressed initially but would, according to the Bank, "be addressed in the future" (ADB 1993: 52). Nevertheless, the aim was that "the initiatives taken in 1992 will lay the ground for the achievement of one of the Bank's major development objectives: sound management of the environment and natural resources" (ADB 1993: 52). Thus in the coming years the ABD promised to improve the balance of its lending portfolio between traditional activities and projects/programs aimed at reducing poverty, developing human resources, and protecting the environment. The overall medium-term goal was therefore to achieve a roughly 50-50 lending mix of traditional ADB activities and these newer efforts. In the Bank's 1993 budget the first tentative steps toward executing these ideas were taken.

China, India, and Malaysia—all leading regional member countries—did not agree to these developments. They clearly expressed their distaste but initially did not take the developments very seriously. They regarded them more as lip service from the Bank to Western donors than as any real reorientation of the ADB's approach to development in Asia.

The process continued, however, and in April 1992 the Social Dimensions Unit (SDU) was established to integrate more systematically crosscutting issues of social significance into ADB operations or, seen from another angle, to identify the kind of social pitfalls the Bank fell into in the Masinloc project. Social dimensions included poverty reduction, women in development, human resources development, and the avoidance or mitigation of adverse effects from development interventions (e.g., ADB projects) on vulnerable groups that lacked the ability to absorb such shocks. Thus the Bank was now officially devoted to a participatory approach to development, gender, and social analysis and to close cooperation with NGOs to operationalize these issues. The main task of the SDU was to help Bank staff and DMCs incorporate the social dimension in their operations and projects, but the SDU had no formal power in the project or program cycle: "If important social dimensions and associated processes are found not to be adequately addressed in an activity, SDU will advise on pragmatic ways of incorporating these aspects during subsequent phases" (ADB 1993: 52). As in the 1980s, when environmental issues were introduced, the Bank's approach was once more one of small steps. This approach had worked for the Bank in the 1980s. The question was whether it would work under a zeitgeist informed by the Rio conference.

The events that took place during the 1993 annual meeting in Manila are illustrative in this respect. The meeting was marked by two main (and interlinked) issues: (1) the ADB came under increased pressure to improve its project performance, and (2) the United States opposed a capital increase, leading to increased tension between that country and Japan in the ADB.

The problem for the ADB was that whereas even internal studies showed that the Bank's project failure rate was increasing, the Bank's outgoing president, Kimimasa Tarumizu, called for donors to roughly double the ABD's authorized share capital to $46 billion by 1998. Leading the countercharge was the Clinton administration's delegate, Jeffrey Shafer, who argued that the ADB could not increase its lending every year—the plans called for a 21 percent increase only in 1993—without an objective appraisal of what everyone was getting for their money. Shafer argued that the payoff in development terms seemed to have dropped for the ADB and called on the Bank to focus more on improving the quality of loans rather than expanding the quantity. The U.S. argument against capital increase and for reform of the Bank did not sit well with Japan, which strongly came to the Bank's support. According to the Japanese governor and minister of finance, Yoshiro Hayashi, both the Ministry of Finance (MOF) and the government had "high regard for the vigorous efforts that the Bank has made to restructure its organization" (*Far Eastern Economic Review*, 20 March 1993: 53).

In the end, however, even the Bank itself had to admit that the quality of its loans was declining. The figures released at the annual meeting showed that the number of "unsuccessful" projects had risen from zero in 1983–1986 to eleven in 1990, two in 1991, and five in 1992. The long-run success rate of all evaluated projects had also deteriorated from 67 percent in 1988 to 60 percent in 1992.[7]

The Bank argued that the reason for the decline was not poor management by the ADB but the fact that the ADB now had to implement increasingly complex projects in countries where institutional constraints and lack of resilience to deal with external factors had adversely affected project performance. ADB officials even complained that projects evaluated were picked randomly and included many "soft" and socially oriented projects rather than the solid, traditional infrastructure projects customers preferred and where success were more easily achieved. Thus according to the ADB, the problems with the quality of its loan portfolio were not general but highly specific ones.

The problem for the Bank was that the only countries that wanted to listen to such arguments were the DMCs. If they could have it their way, they would be happy to return to the "good old days" of traditional ADB projects and forget all the hassle with the environment, gender, population, and the other crosscutting issues. In their interpretation, those issues were forced on the Bank by the nonregional donor countries. Malaysia was therefore applauded by most regional member countries (apart from Australia, Japan, and New Zealand) when its delegation announced at the annual meeting that Malaysia would dismiss the ADB from of a highway project and finance the road itself. The Malaysian government had asked the ADB for a loan to pay for the Sarawak portion of a highway across Borneo. The problem for the ADB was that the road construction threatened the habitat of the Sumatran rhinoceros, an endangered species of which only a few were thought to be alive in Borneo. Under pressure from environmentalists aware of the Bank's new environmental policies, the Bank raised the issue of the rhino with Kuala Lumpur. Much to the delight of several other DMCs, the Malaysian government's answer was "get out; we will finance the project ourselves and avoid your new guidelines."

Japan was clearly ambivalent with respect to the criticism by the United States because it implied criticism of Tokyo as well. As one Japanese delegate from MOF stated, "To be told that your house is dirty is a great shame" (*Far Eastern Economic Review*, 22 May 1993: 53), but Japan could not join the most vocal DMCs either. Japan needed to work closely with the United States and other nonregional donor countries if the ADB was to work. Some changes had also taken place with respect to Japan's attitude toward policy dialogue. Whereas in 1989 Japan thought that as a donor it should be careful not to force certain economic policies on recipients (Ministry of Foreign Affairs, Japan 1989: 29), in a document on Japanese ODA in 1993, Japan suddenly found it extremely important to have a policy dialogue with developing countries to conserve the environment and deepen mutual understanding of the importance of considering the environment. The document went as far as stating that Japan believed in using every available opportunity to conduct a detailed dialogue with developing countries (Ministry of Foreign Affairs, Japan 1993).

That said, this did not mean it was easy for MOF and Japan to meet the U.S request for an external review of the Bank's loan portfolio. Not only MOF itself but a considerable number of other actors saw the Bank as a "Japanese bank." Thus to meet the request for an external review would clearly entail a disgrace not only for the ADB but for MOF and Japan as well. Both senior ADB and MOF officials therefore preferred that such a review, if it had to take place, be conducted by the ADB itself. Confronted with what was more or less an ultimatum—either an internal review or no review—the United States gave in, and the outgoing president was allowed to commission one of his vice presidents, Günter Schultz of Germany, to chair an internal task force. The rest of the mess the controversies at the twenty-sixth annual meeting had created was left to the incoming president, Mituso Sato, to sort out.

The lesson we can draw from the experiences of this period is that when the crosscutting issues first arose at ADB headquarters in Manila, the Bank tried to repeat the trick that had worked so well in the 1980s. It tried to cloud difficult political questions in technical language, but the zeitgeist of the 1990s proved to be different from that which had prevailed during the

1980s. It was no longer just a matter of finding the right technical solution to a functional problem. That message had lost credibility. What was needed now were political solutions to increasingly politicized issue areas. The honeymoon days of keeping politics at bay were finally over in the ADB. The Bank's agenda became more complex and politicized. The ADB was not well equipped to deal with this new agenda, however, as debates at the Bank's 26th annual meeting in May 1993 clearly illustrate. When the environment could no longer be tackled with narrow end-of-pipe approaches, the ADB found itself in trouble. Thus in the 1990s the Bank was in a state of flux between two theoretical positions: managed interdependence and turbulent nongrowth.

THE END OF TECHNOCRATIC CONSENSUS (1994 AND BEYOND)

In 1994 the ADB found itself in a difficult situation. It was squeezed between donors who called for what seemed like a never-ending line of reforms and new policies and DMCs (in particular China and India) that vocally opposed the new direction the donors wanted the Bank to take. The *Report of the Task Force on Improving Project Quality* had just been published (see ADB 1994). The report succeeded in pacifying the United States and thereby brought about a general capital increase, but it did not stop the debate about what the ADB's mission in Asia should be. Rather, it increased the tension because the new policies took the Bank in a direction important DMCs like China and India felt was contrary to their interests. Nonetheless, it is important to keep in mind the duality of the situation: the Asian countries disliked the cultural imperialism they perceived in the arguments of the nonregionals and the feeling of being bullied by Washington, but they welcomed the capital boost—the ADB's first in ten years.

One important advantage for the ADB was that the new president understood the situation. President Sato was warmly received in Washington and Tokyo because both governments were pleased to have a president with an up-to-date vision of multilateral development assistance. Sato's reformist approach made it much harder for the Bank's critics to argue that it lacked a real development agenda. As a consequence, a new direction was spelled out for the ADB in the *Medium-Term Strategic Framework 1995–1998* (ADB 1995a). In accordance with Sato's vision, the Bank, instead of merely financing projects, would offer its DMCs an integrated package of development services linking project financing with policy review, capacity building, and regional cooperation. This realignment of the Bank's position was considered appropriate because of the changing role of government and the private sector in the DMCs (ADB 1995b). The Bank would continue to finance development projects, particularly in physical and social infrastructure sectors, but in addition a growing emphasis would be placed on strengthening policy and capacity frameworks in key sectors. This meant the Bank had to sharpen its country focus and achieve better coordination between its various departments and offices.

Economic growth was still the primary objective, but it was now recognized that sustainable growth required a mix of public-sector investment in physical infrastructure and human resources, private-sector initiatives, appropriate macroeconomic-sector policies, and protection of the environment. The ADB's goal was therefore to develop a broader-based project portfolio that more equally reflected both traditional growth projects and social projects. The Bank was therefore to make every effort to reach the 50-50 project portfolio mix. One way this was to be achieved was through the incorporation of new policies. During 1995 and 1996 the ADB introduced three new policies on governance, inspection function, and involuntary resettlement. These policies were highly controversial (Bøås 1998; Jokinen 2002).

These three new policy initiatives further antagonized the DMCs already disturbed about recent developments in the Bank. In particular, the policy on involuntary resettlement provoked China, which saw the policy as targeted against its own development vision. In China's view it was an attempt not necessarily to contain Chinese development efforts but to order China to develop in a certain way, which was not the way Europe and North America had developed. Thus at the 1996 annual meeting, Li Ruogu, Chinese ED in the ADB, said: "If there is no sacrifice, then there is no achievement. In the U.S. and Europe, your ancestors sacrificed a lot to develop your economies. In the development process, some people must sacrifice their own interests."[8]

Washington and Tokyo were pleased with the new direction, but for different reasons. Washington could tell lobbying NGOs that the ADB was moving in the right direction, whereas Tokyo could point to the fact that (1) under Sato the Bank was moving in one direction in a coherent manner, and (2) the new policies were after all the outcome of a compromise between East and West because, in the end, all three policies were approved by consensus. The Bank had thought the NGOs would be satisfied with the new policies, but they were not. According to Sahabat Malaysia, "The Policy, being a policy on Involuntary Resettlement, is unacceptable to the NGO Working Group on the ADB, who firmly hold to the position that any project that causes involuntary resettlement should not be considered by the Bank. The insistence on involuntary resettlement is a blatant contravention of human rights" (Malaysia 1996: 1).

The problem for the Bank was that different worldviews were colliding. The NGOs' position was built on what they thought they saw out in the field. For them, past experiences proved that most, if not all, projects involving involuntary resettlement not only failed to achieve their envisioned social and economic goals but also caused social and environmental destruction and further impoverished people. Even more serious for the Bank, the NGOs argued that the entire policy on involuntary resettlement was just another example proving that the so-called reorientation of the Bank under Sato's chairmanship was only rhetoric. The Bank was faking it. They argued that the Bank's policy was built on purely economic foundations. The well-being of and fairness to those displaced were secondary. Thus as the NGOs saw it, the policy was very much oriented toward economic growth. More-over, they accused the Bank of not adhering to the OECD's Guidelines for Aid Agencies on Involuntary Displacement and Resettlement in Development Projects, which call for serious consideration of alternatives to carry-ing out a project (the nonaction alternative) and the exploration of all viable alternative project designs. The NGO argument was that the Bank had not adopted these guidelines because the policy only assumed a miti-gation approach to impoverishment resulting from development projects. It did not recommend consideration of the nonaction alternative. Thus they argued that the presence of an involuntary resettlement policy in the ADB could easily be misused as a justification to carry out projects that displaced people, as long as the displacement was minimized and conse-quent problems were mitigated. These were serious accusations for the Bank because its main donors were the OECD countries who had estab-lished the guidelines.[9]

To understand this debate we have to consider that two different worldviews were colliding. The ADB made its arguments from a macroeco-nomic national point of view. The argument was that if a development project benefits the national economy and a large section of the population, re-settlement and displacement could be justified. The counterargument from the NGOs came from below: "Many projects that contribute to national economic growth have disastrous impacts on self-sufficient local economies, natural resources and social sustainability" (Malaysia 1996: 2).

The annual meeting held at Bank headquarters in Manila in early May 1996 was marked by efforts by the Bank to secure firm commitments from donor countries to replenish the ADF (ADF VII). The question of more resources for the Bank, however, was inextricably linked to transformation of the Bank. The problem for the ADB was that important figures like U.S. treasury secretary Robert Rubin made it clear that any commitment to ADF VII from the United States was dependent on institutional reform. His mes-sage to Sato was that the only way the Clinton administration could get replenishment funding to the ADF through the Republican majority in Con-gress was to sell them on the argument that the administration had been instrumental in creating the reforms implemented and those in the pipeline.[10] Nevertheless, Sato also received praise from the U.S. governor, Jeffrey Shafer, who said the Bank's image had shifted radically from a "static" institution to a bastion of development reform. Shafer acknowledged that he had ruffled some feathers when he first called for reform two years previously but went on to state: "This is a very different bank from the one then, thanks to President Sato."[11]

Japan was pleased with these statements, and they could have constituted a viable argument for the DMCs as well if they had been followed up by a firm commitment to substantially replenish the ADF. This was not the case. Rather, the United States and other major donor countries made it clear to the Bank that it would have to make do with substantially less money than it had hoped for (*Asian Wall Street Journal*, 29 April 1996). Instead, the traditional donor countries told the East and Southeast Asian newly industrialized countries to make substantial contributions to the fund. Germany's governor to the ADB, who was chairman of the board of governors, told these countries that "joining in was part of their global responsibility as part of international burden-sharing, but [was] also a question of the dragons repaying their own debt to the Asian community."[12] According to the German governor, the economic strength of the new donors was largely the result of development aid they themselves had received in the past. The problem with this strategy was not necessarily the argument about burden sharing but the fact that the request for burden sharing was combined with an insistence on even more reform and transformation of the ADB.

As the East Asian countries saw it, the traditional donor countries wanted to pay less while keeping control of the Bank's development agenda. For instance, China lashed out at the new policy of linking loans to government openness and called on the Bank to preserve its "Asian character." According to the head of the Chinese delegation to the annual meeting, Yin Jieyan, the Bank's governance policy and all the other new policies the Bank had recently established were making borrowing too complicated: "To impose conformity irrespective of the country differences and the willingness of developing member countries is not likely to work and may even produce an adverse impact on some developing members."[13] Yin went on to argue that social development was imperative for both China and the East Asia region, but the fundamental way to tackle such problems was through sustained economic growth. Helping the East Asian states to achieve economic growth should be the ADB's main objective. Social development and environmental protection should be left to the states. In the Chinese point of view the ADB should never hesitate to draw upon and promote the proven experience of East Asia's economic success. There was an "Asian way" to economic growth. Neoliberal orthodoxy was not what was needed in Asia. Elaborating on his government's position, the Chinese ED, Li Ruogu, argued that the governance policy in its present form was only meant to criticize developing countries, adding that the term *governance* was much too political. China preferred the term *development management.* The Chinese delegation underscored that it understood that several elements in the governance policy were important but that policies had to be tailored to fit country and project. Otherwise, China could not reach its development goals. Leadership of a nation's development process was the prerogative of the state, not of an international institution pushed in all directions by donors and NGOs.

China was not the only DMC to express these views. Even Philippine president Fidel Ramos, the meeting's official host, expressed similar sentiments in his opening statement to the meeting. He started by praising the Bank for some of the changes made and stated that they were in accordance with Philippine priorities: "Over the last years, the ADB has significantly shifted its orientation—by giving greater focus on such concerns as the more equitable distribution of benefits of growth, human resource development, as well as social and environmental protection. This is as it should be. It reflects the growing sophistication of our understanding of the development process, which must like the tide uplift all boats—big or small" (ADB 1996: 3). He went on, however, to warn multilateral institutions about being inflexible and insensitive to the particularities of different countries and regions:

> I speak from our Philippine experience when I say that multilateral institutions ought to proceed with great sensitivity to the peculiarity of each country's travails and the particularity of the constraints that inhibit the capacity of each government to implement the reform process. A more sure-footed, calibrated approach is, in most cases, more preferable to aggressiveness that invites a backlash. (ADB 1996: 5)

Thus if the 1996 annual meeting revealed one thing, it was that the controversies that had emerged so strongly during the 1994 annual meeting had not been resolved. Rather the meeting revealed that the ideological chasm between some donors and some borrowers had widened. The ADB and Tokyo did their best to stay out of the battle, but both were drawn into it. Some East Asian delegates accused Sato of not doing more *nemowashi*— cultivating relations with the new dragon economies of East Asia that he had asked to step up contributions to the ADF. Likewise, Tokyo was drawn into the matter when MOF was more or less forced to make a statement in support of Sato and the Bank's governance policy. The head of the Japanese delegation went on public record to state that the ADB must do more than provide capital. "Good governance and sound development management in developing countries must accompany development assistance from the Bank to ensure its impact," he said.[14]

The donor-recipient conflict was not the only conflict that marked the meeting and made the situation difficult for Sato and the ADB. The NGOs were also present. Friends of the Earth Japan demanded that the Bank should stop financing projects that required involuntary resettlement of local people. In particular, the group was critical of what it called the ADB's hands-off approach to dealing with local people. It claimed governments that had received funding from the ADB refused to compensate people who had to be relocated, and the ADB, when informed about this by the NGOs, had refused to look into the matter. According to the NGOs, the Bank had told them these matters should be left to the national governments to sort out.[15]

Tokyo was also drawn into the heated dispute between the ADB and NGOs. The NGOs argued that it was still business as usual in the ADB. According to them, the Bank was as strongly geared toward economic growth as it had always been. The new policies were more a matter of lip service than substance. Tokyo was not very interested in or well prepared for this debate. Everyone knew who would get the sympathy of the public if the choice were between a young, articulate Asian who represented a regional NGO and a conservatively dressed MOF official whose lips were basically sealed. Japan was drawn into the debate because MOF had handled the issue of Japanese NGO credentials to the 1996 meeting in a very arrogant manner, denying five of fourteen Japanese NGOs credentials. Among those rejected were the NGOs from Fukuoka that were to coordinate NGO activities at the 1997 annual meeting in Fukuoka. When this issue was brought to general attention during the 1996 meeting, it strengthened Sato's appeal for partnership between the Bank and the NGOs. Because of the general perception of a close relationship between MOF and the Bank, several observers questioned not only MOF's attitude toward NGOs but also the sincerity of the ADB's appeal for partnership with the NGOs.

The situation did not improve when a meeting between the NGO delegates to the 29th annual meeting and President Sato ended with bruised feelings on both sides. As an observer to the meeting, I felt worldviews collided. The NGOs interpreted the meeting as nothing more than ceremonial. It was much too brief (only 20 minutes long) and formal for any meaningful exchange of views. From this perspective, "The NGO meeting with President Sato failed to establish a sense of goodwill because it was abruptly ended, which caught the NGOs off guard and left them with the feeling of being short-changed and their expectations of a frank and fruitful exchange largely unfulfilled."[16] The NGOs found Sato's responses very general. As they saw it he had little to offer them. He made no clear commitments, and there was simply no time for meaningful dialogue. Thus in their point of view Sato's statement about making the NGOs an important partner in development was little more than empty rhetoric.

Sato and the Bank's top management, particularly the Asian managers, had a completely different impression of what had happened. From their point of view the meeting was first and foremost meant as a symbolic gesture, a way of showing they were willing to reach out and establish a working partnership while recognizing that this would take time and would entail many informal meetings and discussions. The Bank's top management therefore felt the NGOs were rude and obnoxious when they tried to enter into real policy discussion at this stage. The meeting should have been characterized by a general and polite exchange of credits and commitments to future cooperation, not by direct criticism. This collision may seem strange since most of the NGOs present were Asian, but we must keep in mind the generation gap and the fact that most leaders of Asian advocacy NGOs are socialized into a Western mind-set.

The NGOs felt they were making no progress in their attempt to engage in dialogue with the ADB and decided to change tactics. The next day at their press briefing they let it be known that although the Bank's rhetoric had improved, significant problems remained in project implementation. In their view these shortcomings were so serious that replenishment of the ADF would make sense only if it were linked to project quality: "The continuing problems with project quality mean that the NGOs will only support the replenishment of ADF if it is devoted primarily to primary health and education, welfare of children and environmental protection. The provision of additional Bank resources by donors must be conditional upon the Bank targeting its scare finances and adhering to its policies" (NGO Working Group 1996). From this point of view, the transformation of the Bank under Sato that had gained praise from the traditional donor countries was primarily an effort to fill the ADF's empty coffer. This statement did not improve the relationship between the Bank and the NGOs. The meeting therefore ended with two important standoffs: the first between the traditional donor countries and the DMCs, with the Bank in the middle; and the second between the Bank and the NGOs, with Japan to some degree drawn into it.

Under Sato the Bank took several important (and controversial) steps toward becoming the broad-based development institution he had promised the donor countries. Environment as an issue-area was broadened (and thereby repoliticized), and policies on other crosscutting issues were either established (e.g., involuntary resettlement) or in the pipeline (e.g., indigenous people). These developments prevented the institution from returning to the conditions present under the technical and depoliticized approach to the environment of the 1980s. Rather the controversial debate over the future direction of the institution continued. China did not accept the 50-50 project mix. As the Chinese interpreted the board decision on the mixed-project portfolio, it was related to the overall Bank portfolio and not to the individual portfolios of each and every DMC. Several Bank staff members shared this interpretation. When I interviewed staff on the China Desk at the Bank in May 1999, I discovered that they interpreted the decision in the same manner as the Chinese. Both the 1997 and 1998 annual meetings confirmed the picture of an institution in which new policies were developed and adopted but also resisted.

It is therefore no longer possible to define environmental issues solely in technical and functional language. This leads to such strong political tension that it suggests that the ADB is still caught in flux between the models of organizational change called managed interdependence and turbulent nongrowth. What we saw in this last period was that the reexamination of purpose informed by decision-making dynamics mediated by new knowledge continued. Simultaneously, the internal consensus on several of these important changes disappeared, not only between donor and borrowing member countries but also at times internally within the Bank. With an increasingly complex agenda, the Bank's policy-making procedures started to take the appearance of exogenous streams flowing through the system. These were linked to choice opportunities by their arrival and departure times and the structural constraints on access to problems, solutions, and decisionmakers. This made political maneuvering between extraregional and intraregional demands and claims increasingly difficult for the Bank. The situation clearly contributed to keeping the ADB in the stage of flux between managed interdependence and turbulent nongrowth.

CONCLUSION

The question is, then, what are the implications from this discussion for international environmental cooperation in Pacific Asia, and what kinds of policy recommendations can be made for the governments (donors and borrowing member countries) and other stakeholders involved in the policy debates on environmental issues in the ADB? For the ADB, the situation is as follows. The DMCs want to see continued emphasis from the Bank on growth-oriented projects, such as dam construction and road building. Because of the increased influence of crosscutting issues and the close scrutiny of such projects by NGOs, however, they have become very demanding for the Bank to conduct. This implies that the ADB finds itself in a situation where what it was once best at doing and what the DMCs mostly ask it to do have suddenly become the hardest projects for the Bank to undertake. To be able to continue to conduct such projects, the Bank had to put in place new policies that could be linked to the environment and act as a shield against complaints and accusations from NGOs. With these new policies the Bank had an answer when NGOs forced various donor countries to make inquiries into Bank policies and practices. The problem for the Bank was that to DMCs like China and India, these developments were seen as proof of an unwanted transformation in the ADB. This means the controversies created by the reexamination of the Bank's purpose will continue because it is impossible for the ADB to please all interests simultaneously.

Without continued transformation the cash flow will be reduced, but the more the ADB transforms itself toward a broad-based development institution, the more political challenges it will confront. Thus the ADB continues to be caught between managed interdependence and turbulent nongrowth because that is the only place it can be if it is to deal with the dilemmas it is faced with. One important implication for international environmental cooperation in East Asia is therefore that if the Bank moves too far toward a holistic developmental agenda, made up of highly politicized crosscutting issues, it will seriously annoy important DMCs like China and India. If it completely retreats to become a narrow project lending institution, it will risk a reduction in future cash flows because of increased criticism from NGOs, which will be followed by criticism and threats of reduced funding from traditional donor countries. This means future environmental cooperation in East Asia centered on the ADB must strive to uphold a delicate balance between the position of the DMCs and that of nonregional donor countries.

Concerning more specific policy recommendations, this chapter underlines the limitations of a technocratic approach to environmental issues. The discussion also revealed, however, the initial success of that approach in East Asia. There is little doubt that the incorporation of this issue area on the agendas of the ADB and its DMCs was facilitated by the technocratic approach taken by the environmentalists in the Bank. This suggests that for actors who seek to introduce environmental issues into diplomacy in East Asia, a deliberate technocratic approach is the most fruitful starting point. By depoliticizing the agenda, one can achieve a reexamination of purpose within the established framework of knowledge. As we have seen, such an approach made it easier to conduct the initial introduction of the ADB to environmental issues.

As the discussion has also revealed, however, this can be only the first stage of a much broader process during which deliberate preparedness to deal with the political dimension of the questions that will emerge must be expanded with vigor. The main fault with the process in the ADB was precisely that the political dimension was suppressed for so long. This meant the problems and challenges for Sato when he took over the presidency and tried to deal with this dimension of environmental cooperation in East Asia had grown much larger than they would have if the political dimension had been dealt with right away. As such, both the main implication for environmental cooperation in Pacific Asia and the question of what kind of policy recommendations we can draw from the ADB's experience can be subsumed by the need for a balanced approach to environmental issues, both in the ADB and in the region at large. There is little doubt that most East Asian countries should do more to protect the environment, but there is also little doubt that several of the arguments and concerns about the transformation of the ADB raised by the DMCs are valid. To avoid a regional backlash on environmental questions, a balanced approach should be pursued by the Bank and nonregional donor countries, and for the latter, calls for further reform should be followed by firm financial commitments to the ADB.

NOTES

1. This part draws on the author's personal experience as an invited guest to this meeting and on Bøås 1997.
2. Among examples used were the costs involved in the antipollution equipment at the Philippines' largest industrial project—an iron ore simmering plant in Mindanao—where the environmental production costs represented 13 percent of total project costs; and the nuclear power plant project in Bataan where it was argued the environmental measures introduced in terms of the supplier country conflicted with the more urgent need for energy production. See ADB 1980b for further details.
3. "The Bank, its President, Vice presidents, officers and staff shall not interfere in the political affairs of any members: nor shall they be influenced in their decisions by the political character of the member concerned. Only economic considerations shall be relevant to their decisions" (ADB 1966: Art. 36).
4. Interview with Julian Payne, executive director of the Canadian-Nordic-Dutch country constituency in the ADB, Manila, 11 November 1996.
5. Until the 1990s, Japan's history as a donor country is that of a donor that tried hard to avoid interference in the domestic affairs of recipient countries. The fact that the multilateral development banks, even though they are without doubt political institutions, officially advocate the doctrine of political neutrality may explain why Japan took such a keen interest in them. The ADB norm of noninterference and nonpoliticization fit well with Japanese development principles (or lack of such). For a detailed analysis of the historical relationship between Japan and the ADB, see Yasutomo 1983. For a general analysis of Japanese aid in this period see Yasutomo 1986, Orr 1990, and Koppel and Orr 1993. For a description of Japan's ODA and its organization, see Friends of the Earth–Japan 1997.
6. It was also rumored that local leaders were bought off. Originally, both the local assembly and the mayor resisted the project. In December 1992, however,

the mayor changed his position, and in April 1993 the city assembly approved plans to start construction. This change in position of both the mayor and the local assembly led to rumors about threats and bribery.

7. See *Far Eastern Economic Review,* 20 May 1993, for further details.
8. Quoted in *Emerging Markets—Asian Development Bank Daily Edition,* 2 May 1996, 1.
9. This is not to say that all OECD countries adhere to these guidelines. They do not, but that is not the main point here. The problem for the ADB was that the issue came up, and the Bank's OECD donors were forced to have an opinion. They had little choice than to say they would have preferred that the Bank had followed the OECD guidelines.
10. See *Emerging Markets—Asian Development Bank Daily Edition,* 30 April 1996.
11. Quoted in ibid., 1 May 1996, 15.
12. Quoted in ibid., 1.
13. Statement by Yin Jieyan, quoted in ibid., 2 May 1996, 1.
14. Statement by Yasuo Matsushita (head of the Japanese delegation), quoted in ibid.
15. The examples the NGOs put forward were two projects in Indonesia and one in Bangladesh. One of the Indonesian projects involved the relocation of people because a high-voltage power transmission line was built over their area, and the other involved moving people away from the site of a hydropower project. The project in Bangladesh involved the displacement of people because of the building of the Jamuna Bridge.
16. Statement by Ed Tadem, coordinator of the Hong Kong–based Asian Regional Exchange for New Alternatives, quoted in Bankwatch 1 (1996), a publication of the NGO delegation to the 29th annual meeting of the ADB.

REFERENCES

Asian Development Bank (ADB). 1966. *Agreement Establishing the Asian Development Bank.* Manila: Asian Development Bank.
———. 1978. *Environment Protection and Development Financing by the Asian Development Bank.* Manila: Asian Development Bank.
———. 1980a. *Environmental Considerations in Bank Operations.* Manila: Asian Development Bank.
———. 1980b. *Summary of Discussions at Board Meeting of 24 January 1980.* Manila: Asian Development Bank.
———. 1985. *Review of the Bank's Environmental Policies and Procedures.* Manila: Asian Development Bank.
———. 1990. *Integration of Envionmental Considerations in the Programme Cycle.* Manila: Asian Development Bank.
———. 1991. *The Environmental Programme of the Asian Development Bank.* Manila: Asian Development Bank.
———. 1993. *Annual Report 1992.* Manila: Asian Development Bank.
———. 1994. *Report of the Task Force on Improving Project Quality.* Manila: Asian Development Bank.
———. 1995a. *Medium-Term Strategic Framework 1995–1998.* Manila: Asian Development Bank.

————. 1995b. *Annual Report 1994*. Manila: Asian Development Bank.

————. 1996. *Fidel Ramos—Opening Address to the 1996 Annual Meeting of the Asian Development Bank*. Manila: Asian Development Bank.

————. 1997. *Emerging Asia: Changes and Challenges*. Manila: Asian Development Bank.

————. 2001. *Annual Report 2000*. Manila: Asian Development Bank.

————, ed. 1986. *Environmental Planning and Management: Regional Symposium on Environmental and Natural Resources Planning*. Manila: Asian Development Bank.

Bøås, Morten. 1997. "Happy Birthday? Some Reflections on the 30th Annual Meeting, 11–13 May 1997, and the Political Development Agenda of the Asian Development Bank." *NIASnytt* 2 (June): 11–13.

————. 1998. "Governance as Multilateral Development Bank Policy: The Cases of the African Development Bank and the Asian Development Bank." *European Journal of Development Research* 10, 2: 117–134.

Friends of the Earth–Japan (FoE Japan). 1997. *NGO Guide to Japan's ODA*. Tokyo: Friends of the Earth–Japan.

Haas, Ernst B. 1990. *When Knowledge Is Power: Three Models of Change in International Organizations*. Berkeley: University of California Press.

Jokinen, Janne. 2002. "Balancing Between East and West: The Asian Development Bank Policy on Good Governance." In Morten Bøås and Desmond McNeill, eds., *Framing the World: The Role of Ideas in Multilateral Institutions*. London: Routledge.

Koppel, Bruce M., and Robert M. Orr Jr., eds. 1993. *Japan's Foreign Aid: Power and Policy in a New Era*. Boulder: Westview.

Malaysia, Sahabat Alam. 1996. *Campaign Paper on ADB's Involuntary Resettlement Policy*. Manila: 1996 NGO Lobby Campaign by the NGO Working Group on the Asian Development Bank.

Ministry of Foreign Affairs, Japan. 1989. *Japan's ODA 1988*. Tokyo: Association for Promotion of International Cooperation.

————. 1993. *Basic Facts on Japan's ODA*. Tokyo: Ministry of Foreign Affairs.

NGO Working Group. 1996. Press Release of 1 May 1996. Manila: NGO Working Group.

Orr, Robert M., Jr. 1990. *The Emergence of Japan's Foreign Aid Power*. New York: Columbia University Press.

Stein, Robert, and Brian Johnson. 1979. *Banking on the Biosphere? Environmental Practice and Procedures of Nine Multilateral Development Agencies*. Lexington: International Institute for Environment and Development.

Yasutomo, Dennis T. 1983. *Japan and the Asian Development Bank*. New York: Praeger Special Studies.

————. 1986. *The Manner of Giving: Strategic Aid and Japanese Foreign Policy*. Lexington: Lexington Books.

6

Environmental Agreements in Southeast Asia: Balancing Economic Interests and Regional Politics

GIOK LING OOI, SIMON S.C. TAY, AND YUE CHOONG KOG

G lobalization has brought extended and intensified trade and investment linkages between countries around the world. It has also highlighted the environmental issues arising not only domestically within
each country but also among countries. The plethora of multilateral environmental agreements endorsed over the past few decades is evidence that
not only business but also environmental issues and concerns have been
able to negotiate and cross borders. Regional associations, such as the Association of Southeast Asian Nations (ASEAN), have been actively engaged in
multilateral environmental negotiations that have resulted in a number of
multilateral environmental agreements (Ooi 1999). The multilateralism seen
in the environmental sector is matched by that in the business investment
and trade sectors. National governments have been equally concerned about
transboundary pollution issues and the impact of global environmental agreements on business investment and trade in their economies. In Southeast
Asia there is a sense not only of shared geography and resources but also of
the need to balance national good with regional interests. This has driven
the different governments to agree on the need to cooperate in the management of several environmental issues.

Southeast Asia might be part of a globalizing world, but the ownership
and management of natural resources remain matters of national concern
and resolution. Growing regional and international trade, as well as local
responses to globalization, have allowed the region's major cities and affluent

countries to develop ecological footprints many times the size of the territories they occupy. Singapore is one example. It requires natural resources and processed materials from an area many times the size of its territory to produce the food, water, energy, and other needs that sustain its population and economy.

This chapter focuses on Singapore as a case study of multilateral agreements and bilateral relations on environmental issues in Southeast Asia. Issues Singapore faces are not unique but are also addressed by other countries that have to tackle cross-boundary pollution or negotiate with other countries for supplies of resources, such as water. Indeed these issues concern neighboring countries everywhere, such as China and Japan in the case of transboundary air pollution or China and Thailand sharing the Mekong River. The continuing importance of natural resources to the economies and trade of regions such as Southeast Asia is reflected in ongoing environmental negotiations.

SINGAPORE IN A GLOBALIZING WORLD

Global cities or city-states aspiring to be ever more integrated with the global economy, such as Singapore, can be expected to be driven by major economic as well as security considerations and concerns in shaping their foreign policies. In much the same fashion, domestic policies have been driven by concerns about the economy and economic growth, as well as internal security. Larger developmental issues, such as growing a new economy based on information technology and the life sciences, have generally subsumed sectors such as the environment. Hence the concerns about environmental issues reflected in Singapore's foreign policy have been reactive and mostly in response to international or multilateral agreements and conferences, as well as to bilateral relations that have an impact on natural resources such as water.

Singapore's policy making has been described as being based on the conviction that "goodwill alone is no substitute for astute self-interest" (Leifer 1989: 965). In its foreign policy, Singapore has cultivated cooperative relations, particularly with its closest neighbors, both bilaterally and within the regional framework and structure provided by ASEAN. Indeed a former minister of state for foreign affairs, Lee Khoon Choy, observed that "Singapore has little capacity of its own to shape the main course of world events. Essentially, for its survival and economic well-being, its foreign policy has to respond to the realities of the regional and international environment" (Lee 1976: 104). In spite of its global-city outlook, Singapore remains wedged between Malaysian and Indonesian sea and airspace. Like all states it is tied to the environment (Leifer 1989: 979). This means that although its independence is a fact of international life, the imperative of survival has not yet been superseded; and those in charge believe that in politics as in life, natural selection is the determining factor, with only the well adapted surviving (Leifer 1989: 979).

Similarly, in an increasingly interconnected world, countries in the Southeast Asian region have never been more aware of how problems in neighboring countries can spill over borders. Prior to the recent economic troubles, transboundary pollution caused by forest fires in Indonesia had already been a major source of irritation in the region, particularly for Malaysia and Singapore. The haze enveloping cities in Malaysia and Singapore also led to a downturn in the region's tourism industry. The haze problem joins an array of environmental issues traditionally shared by countries in the region, including marine pollution arising from the growth of sea traffic along shared sea-lanes, such as the Straits of Malacca.

In arguing for scholars of international relations to consider environmental ethics, John Barkdull has suggested that "international relations is usually understood as the realm of power politics, a world in which military might and the quest to survive dominate. In this world, moral concern for other human beings, much less nature, is limited or entirely lacking" (Barkdull 2000: 361). The question Barkdull posed was whether it would be possible to introduce environmental ethics' far-reaching moral claims into the competitive, militarized, and economically unequal world political system. One of Singapore's longest-serving ambassadors to both the United Nations and the United States, Tommy Koh, posed a similar question in 1987. He asked if any country could afford a moral foreign policy and then rejected the realist position because of its standard of conducting foreign policy based solely on national interest (Koh 1998: 8). He did not embrace the moralist position, however, because he recognized the need at times for a government to subordinate law and morality to its national interest. Like the Singapore government, Ambassador Koh's standpoint could be described as pragmatic.

Having said this, the discussion here of the foreign policy implications for Singapore arising from environmental concerns, as well as those related to natural resources (i.e., water), highlights the importance of environmental ethics for small states like Singapore. Environmental ethics, as Barkdull has argued, "calls on us to extend moral considerations to other living things and to natural 'wholes' such as bioregions and ecosystems" (Barkdull 2000: 361). In considering environmental agreements on both the regional and international fronts and their implications for small states like Singapore, it becomes clear how limited these agreements have been in securing cooperation among countries sharing an ecoregion.

We focus here on three areas of environmental concern—water, international environmental agreements (particularly the Montreal Protocol on

Substances that Deplete the Ozone Layer), and the haze problem arising from Indonesian forest fires—and their implications for Singapore's foreign relations. Although the natural limitations Singapore faces are significant, it has nevertheless had a strong foreign policy conducted from a strong domestic base (Leifer 1989) that is reflective of the view expressed by Barry Buzan (1983) about strong and weak states. This view considers small and militarily less important states like Singapore to be strong states because their internal and domestic consensus and political leadership are comparable to larger and militarily superior states, such as China.

Singapore's stand on multilateral environmental agreements, and the "vehicles" it has chosen to negotiate the settlement of transboundary pollution and water security, make it an interesting example that illustrates several issues related to international environmental cooperation. First, Singapore's accession to multilateral environmental agreements highlights its commitment to its domestic environmental agenda, as well as the high priority the city-state accords to trade. Such commitment, however, has not helped it secure agreement on environmental cooperation in the region, as illustrated amply by the haze caused by forest fires in Indonesia. The difficulty with securing cooperation on environmental issues in the region can be explained in part by economic competition. This is further illustrated in the bilateral negotiation between Singapore and Malaysia over water, which is crucial to Singapore's economy. The uneven process that characterizes this negotiation underscores the limits on international environmental cooperation and the tendency for economic competition to assume greater precedence.

TRADE, BUSINESS COMPETITIVENESS, AND MULTILATERAL ENVIRONMENTAL AGREEMENTS

Singapore, like many ASEAN member states, is signatory to major multilateral environmental agreements such as the Montreal Protocol on Substances that Deplete the Ozone Layer. Such international agreements introduce a political and economic dimension into the process of addressing a major environmental issue. Among countries that have acceded to these international agreements, concern has been raised about the possible erosion of business competitiveness. Studies carried out, however, illustrate that it is uncertain whether these agreements have any impact on business, particularly in the ASEAN countries (Pearson 1996).

International trade has been described as the lifeblood of the Singapore economy (Chng, Low, and Toh 1988). Unlike the larger neighboring countries of Indonesia, Malaysia, Thailand, and the Philippines, the buffer provided by domestic demand is extremely limited because of the small market. Singapore's economy depends greatly on world trade and multinational corporations located in the island-state. Not surprisingly, trade liberalization fora, as well as international agreements concerning the environment, are of paramount importance to Singapore. There is basis to assume that acceding to multilateral environmental agreements poses a major challenge to an economy as open and dependent on trade as Singapore's. Yet Singapore was one of the first countries in Southeast Asia to establish a Ministry of the Environment in the 1970s. An Anti-Pollution Unit was set up in the prime minister's office at about the same time. In spite of multinational corporations' dependence on foreign investment, Singapore introduced air and water quality standards the government has strictly enforced among its business firms since the 1970s. Observers have noted that the strict enforcement of environmental regulations has not appeared to deter foreign investors.

It is telling that although Singapore acceded to the Convention on International Trade in Endangered Species of Wild Fauna and Flora (CITES) in 1986, nature conservation remains a subject of heated debate between government planners and civil society groups like the Nature Society (Singapore). The Singapore Concept Plan, which serves as a framework for land-use development, has been qualified in its public statements concerning the time frame for conservation of the country's remaining nature reserves. The implementation of CITES led to the Endangered Species (Import and Export) Act, passed in 1989. The legislation resulted in part from pressure from the United States and the threat to the trade in tropical fish.

A liberal world economic order is so important to Singapore that it often has little choice but to join discussions concerning agreements not only on trade but also on the environment. Such active engagement in global discussions of trade and the environment has been characteristic—in spite of the difficulties—of small states such as Singapore that are active in arenas like the General Agreement on Tariffs and Trade and has depended largely on negotiations on trade liberalization between developed countries. Singapore's active engagement with the UN Convention on the Law of the Sea and the UN Conference on Environment and Development was doubtless motivated by the economic interests that have driven its foreign policies. Participation in the negotiations leading up to the Law of the Sea was important because of the interest in securing sea-lanes so vital to Singapore (which has built its economy virtually on the shipping and trading services offered by and through its port). According to Ambassador Koh, Singapore's interest and role in major global conferences on the environment have allowed it to combine virtue with self-interest: "Singapore's chairmanship of the Preparatory Committee and Main Committee of the Earth Summit has earned the country goodwill and credit. Singapore could continue to play a pro-active and leadership role in environmental diplomacy. In the decade of the 1970s, Singapore achieved prominence through its leadership role in the UN Conference on the Law of the Sea" (Koh 1998: 164).

Given the importance of engagement with multilateral environmental agreements for trade, it is not surprising that Singapore was one of the earliest countries to sign the Vienna Convention on the Protection of the Ozone Layer and the Montreal Protocol on Substances that Deplete the Ozone Layer. The Montreal Protocol is among the three major multilateral environmental agreements using trade measures to meet environmental objectives. Article 2 of the protocol contains the core provisions or signatories' obligations and is subtitled "Control Measures." According to the control measures set down, state parties to the protocol and its London amendments of June 1990 were responsible for phasing out their consumption of chlorofluorocarbons (CFCs) and other ozone-destroying chemicals by 2000. Signatories like Singapore were also to have set intermediate target levels of consumption for reduction by 1995. By 1997 those target levels were set at 85 percent.

The Singapore government has been highly effective in translating the control measures in the protocol into domestic policy. Effective implementation of those measures has enabled Singapore to stay ahead of the target levels set for developing countries in reducing consumption of controlled CFCs. In 1992 its consumption of CFCs was only 44 percent of the 1986 amount (the base year set in the protocol as a reference standard). The policy introduced to comply with the measures of the Montreal Protocol employed a quota allocation system allowing only specified amounts of the controlled CFCs and halons for use by both industrial end users and distributors of the controlled substances. The policy was implemented through "The Control of Imports and Exports (Montreal Protocol) (Chlorofluorocarbons) Order 1989," which prohibits the importation of CFCs from any country or territory that at the time of the importation is not a party to the protocol. The order was followed by an Amendment Order, passed in 1991, intended to extend the regulatory controls to halons. Both orders were eventually consolidated in the Control of Imports and Exports (Montreal Protocol) Order.

The control on CFCs led initially to an escalation of prices that in turn prompted firms to look for substitutes, alternatives, and conservation measures, as well as increased efforts at recycling. As a result the prices of controlled CFCs eventually fell by 50 percent. The control measures would have wiped out firms trading in the CFCs being phased out, but for the economy as a whole the impact appears to have been minimal—at least among firms that continued operating in Singapore after quotas were implemented on controlled CFCs. Firms that were affected, including many that were overseas subsidiaries of multinational corporations trading in CFCs, either discontinued operations or relocated to other parts of Southeast Asia.

Hotels and plants requiring cold-room facilities, like wafer fabrication plants, were less affected because of the time schedule the government had allowed for the phaseout of CFCs. Many hotels were able to phase new chillers into their financial plans over a period of years. The same was true of the plants, including pharmaceutical firms. The smaller firms observed that the implementation of regulations arising from the protocol required prohibitively expensive changes in production processes. Although government agencies had made efforts to help these firms, the efforts were expensive and took a long time to arrange. Furthermore, firms in the electronics industry point out that no level playing field exists in ASEAN as a whole, since the measures in force in Singapore are not replicated elsewhere in the region or beyond, such as in China or India. Compliance with the environmental standards set by the Singapore government as required by multilateral environmental agreements can make it difficult for Singapore firms to compete in the region's markets.

INDONESIAN FOREST FIRES AND HAZE IN SINGAPORE AND MALAYSIA

The ASEAN countries have negotiated a series of agreements on environmental conservation, although they appear to have had little impact on regional cooperation on environmental issues. A case in point would be the effort to prevent a repeat of the haze problem that has plagued the region since the major Indonesian forest fires of 1997 and 1998 (see Chapter 13).

Forest fires had burned huge areas of the old-growth tropical forests of Indonesia long before the major 1997–1998 fires that wiped out nearly 10 million hectares (Dauvergne 2000: 389). According to a 1998 report, "ASEAN Regional Cooperation on the Haze," compiled by the Centre for Strategic and International Studies (CSIS), fires and transboundary pollution in the form of haze are not new issues for ASEAN. Indeed the report noted that in 1990 ASEAN ministers agreed on efforts to harmonize their countries' pollution prevention efforts. With forest fires from Indonesia affecting the region in the 1980s, 1991, and again in 1994, the issue of fires and haze has been a recurring one. The last episode led to a regional agreement—the ASEAN Cooperation Plan on Transboundary Pollution. Yet the problem has re-emerged on a massive scale, indicating lack of implementation of the plan.

The forest fires, which were started "as an inexpensive way of clearing forest cover for palm oil plantations, also pointed to the problem of resource management in the region. It was just one example of ASEAN governments' pro-development policy to the neglect of preserving natural resources and being conscious of environmental impact" (Snitwongse and Bunbongkarn 2000: 141). The massive fires spread a choking haze across Southeast Asia, affecting not only air quality in neighboring countries of

Singapore and Malaysia but also the tourism industry in the region as a whole. According to the CSIS report, the haze that covered most of Sumatra, Kalimantan, Malaysia, and Singapore during August–October 1997 mostly originated in bush, ground, and small-holder crops, as well as large-scale plantation and forest fires in Sumatra and Kalimantan. The pall created by ashes spread over the region in 1997 and lasted for a few weeks at a time. In cities such as Kuala Lumpur in Malaysia, already struggling to keep their air clean, the haze heightened air pollution and forced schools to close. In the vicinity of the worst of the fires in Kalimantan, airports had to close, and residents were forced to flee nearby towns if they could afford to do so.

At the height of the problem, 20 million people in Singapore, Malaysia, and Indonesia were forced to breathe potentially harmful air for prolonged periods (Dudley 1997). The United Nations Environment Program declared the forest fires a global disaster. The haze and forest fires presented the greatest challenge to regional cooperation on the environment. Relief was provided only by brief periods of torrential rain. Estimates of the damage and cost of the haze—in lost production, health effects, and tourism—of US$4.4 billion were suggested by the Singapore Environment Council in June 1998. Even the usually politically apathetic business sector in Singapore was prompted to take action, with a hotelier spearheading a conference and a group of businessman forming to deal with the problem of the forest fires. At the regional level, intensive negotiations have taken place within the forum provided by the ASEAN Environment Ministers' Meeting, together with a meeting of senior environmental officers that led to a Regional Haze Action Plan. A review in early 1998 led to the agreement to create two subregional firefighting arrangements for Kalimantan and for the Sumatra/Riau provinces in Indonesia. Discussions concerning joint funding have not yielded any firm commitments.

The ASEAN agreements on the environment and the Regional Haze Action Plan notwithstanding, when pressed in Parliament for more concrete results to avert the haze, the Singapore government implied that much of potential success in this area would depend on the Indonesian government because the Singapore government had taken negotiations as far as it could. Indeed, indicating that it is resigned to the Indonesian government's ineffectual effort to help with the haze problem, the Singapore Environment Ministry issues periodic warnings to Singaporeans about the haze problem, particularly at the onset of dry weather. It seems unlikely that the regional haze problem will abate in the near future, given the Indonesian government's declared aim of overtaking Malaysia as the world's largest producer of palm oil. In 1994 plantation crops such as oil palm covered an estimated 3.8 million hectares in Indonesia. By 1998, at the height of the worst problem with regional haze, the area converted to plantations had doubled (Dauvergne 2000: 393). Given the value of the much depreciated Indonesian currency, the rupiah, and the resultant low export prices, as well as taxes, lower interest rates, and plenty of available land—together with the growing global demand for crude palm oil—the plantation sector is expected to grow much faster than before. This is especially the case if Malaysia and Indonesia cooperate to control world crude palm oil prices (Dauvergne 2000: 393). On the regional front, therefore, Singapore has had limited success negotiating cooperation to help solve the problem of haze, which has had a major impact on residents in the city-state and its tourism industry.

Clearly, the ASEAN Cooperation Plan has largely failed because of the characteristic way cooperation has been negotiated among ASEAN countries (Tay 2000). Many environmental agreements have been left to individual member states to implement, with the scheduling and nature of implementation left entirely to those states. According to Simon Tay,

> The outbreak of fires in 1997 demonstrated the lack of follow-up to the Cooperation Plan in almost all areas. Singapore's assistance to Indonesia—providing satellite imaging of fires and "hot spots"—was the lone exception. Instead of working within an agreed system of cooperation, countries were left to bilateral arrangements and emergency discussions, especially between Indonesia and Malaysia, and between Indonesia and Singapore. (Tay 2000: 174)

In many ways, such an approach to cooperation continues to emphasize national choices and capabilities rather than a unified regional procedure for dealing with the fires.

Until the onset of the economic crisis in 1997 and the fall of the Suharto regime in 1998, Indonesia had played a dominant and often leading role in ASEAN. In a way, recent political changes in Indonesia have brought developments in negotiations among affected nation-states to secure agreement on solving the haze problem. ASEAN has allowed both nongovernmental and international organizations to propose measures for solving the problem. Fires in the years after 1998, however, reflect the limits on regional environmental cooperation.

The limits to cooperation are further demonstrated on the bilateral front in negotiations between Singapore and Malaysia over water supplies. Economic competition and a shared history involving Singapore's separation from Malaysia have not facilitated negotiations for the water Singapore needs from Malaysia to meet commercial and domestic household uses. Problems in bilateral relations have led to threats by Malaysia, veiled and otherwise, to end water pacts between the two countries and cut off Johor's water supply to Singapore.

FOREIGN RELATIONS, BILATERAL NEGOTIATIONS, AND SHARED RESOURCES

Bilateral as well as multilateral relations are in full play over questions of trade and the sharing of water and other resources. In the past, such issues have created tension among countries like Malaysia, Singapore, and Indonesia. The need for trade and sharing of resources among the nation-states of the Asian region will grow over time. With diminishing supplies of such resources and contestation over them for even domestic needs, tensions are likely to grow within and among countries. Furthermore, great differences exist in the incomes of countries in the region. Industries that create more pollution could move from the richer to the poorer countries because of differences in environmental standards. Fortunately, the problem has not been serious, judging from of studies conducted, although some incidents suggest that unless the region as a whole adopts and effectively enforces common environmental standards, the likelihood of the problem emerging as a potential source of conflict and tension will remain.

Water is a case in point. Water has always been in very short supply in Singapore. It is a crucial aspect of the country's national security and is included as part of its civil defense strategy. The fact that the lack of water was a key factor that hastened the fall of Singapore to the Japanese during World War II serves as a painful reminder of how crucial water is to the country's security. When the British blew up the causeway connecting Singapore to the mainland in anticipation of an invasion from the north, they also cut off water mains from Johor (see Simson 1970). Water supply is also a crucial aspect of Singapore's economic security. Although the Malaysian government guaranteed Singapore's water supply in a Separation Agreement deposited at the United Nations, Singapore's leadership has stated that the Singapore Armed Forces would move into Johor if necessary to restore the water supply to Singapore if the guarantee is ever breached (Lee 2000).

The supply of water is also an issue in bilateral relations between Singapore and Malaysia for another reason. The Malaysian state of Johor depends largely on a supply of treated water from Singapore. This is the result of the earlier Water Agreement between Singapore and Malaysia by which Johor sells raw water to Singapore at three Malaysian cents per 1,000 gallons and buys back treated water for fifty Malaysian cents per 1,000 gallons. Clearly, this arrangement has become increasingly unacceptable to the Malaysian government, judging from the recent Malaysian Cabinet decision to approve $318 million Malaysian ringgit for the construction of a water treatment plant in Johor. When this plant is completed, Johor will have its own water supply (*Straits Times*, 19 August 2000).

According to the Department of Statistics, Singapore, in the period since 1963, when Singapore was part of the Malaysian union, the population of Singapore has increased from 1.8 million to 4 million people. In the same period per capita consumption of water has also more than doubled, from 154 liters to 327 liters per person per day. Consequently, water consumption for Singapore as a whole has increased 4.7 times, from 273,912 m^3 per day to 1,276,000 m^3 per day. Clearly, the increase in water consumption in the past thirty-nine years has outpaced population growth, and factors such as the larger economy and higher standards of living have influenced the increase in Singapore's water consumption.

Given the acute water situation in Singapore and its dependence on neighboring and foreign territories for much of its water supply, great care has been taken with management of the island-state's own water sources and supply. Around half of its total land area is harnessed for water resources (Lim and Lim 1999). Total storage capacity for reservoirs in Singapore and Johor is estimated to be 142 × H10^6 m^3 and 787.5 × H10^6 m^3, respectively (Yap 1995). If the water stored in the reservoirs in Johor is no longer available for use by Singaporeans, Singapore will have about four months to sort out problems with the Malaysian government.

In bilateral negotiations the Malaysian government has been reluctant to commit itself to supply water to its neighbor for the next 150 years, a feature of the new water pact Singapore is seeking with Malaysia. The Malaysians have also accused Singapore of profiteering in the resale of water (Singh and Zulfakarin 1999). Similarly, some unhappiness has been expressed in Indonesia over selling water to Singapore on the grounds of ecological damage and Singapore's "exploitation" of Indonesia (*Straits Times,* 29 June 1991, 1 December 1993).

Singapore is in practice managing water resources in Malaysia, and it proposes to do the same in Indonesia. Accepted state practice, however, does not allow Singapore to intervene directly in the management of catchments in Malaysia and Indonesia. The quality of the water is controlled by the environmental policies and enforcement practices of the territory in which the water catchments are located. Hence pollution control in these catchments becomes a regional concern, and skillful diplomatic handling of the pollution problem is required to resolve the issue. At times, however, it may be necessary to close down a treatment plant, as was done with Skudai Water Treatment Works in Johor in 1991 while technical problems were being resolved.

Although Malaysia's supply of water to Singapore is a testimony to international cooperation and friendship, it must be pointed out that water supply agreements were concluded before Singapore gained full independence—that is, while Singapore and Malaysia were still under British rule.

The continuing negotiations between the two countries over water supply illustrate that bilateral relations and foreign policy are important aspects of environmental cooperation within the ASEAN region.

CONCLUSION

International relations and diplomacy remain important dimensions in resolving environmental issues in ASEAN and beyond. This brief case study of a small state—Singapore—illustrates the types of environment-related negotiations that have been conducted at both regional and global levels. International environmental cooperation remains a key strategy in Singapore's position on trade and other economic interests. On the international front, the importance of trade to Singapore's economy has driven it to take part in international negotiations on environmental issues. If negotiations on the regional front have proven less remarkable in terms of Singapore's ability to influence regional environmental cooperation, the city-state has nevertheless had to implement measures required by multilateral environmental agreements to which it has been a signatory. Former prime minister and now senior minister Lee Kuan Yew once explained Singapore's interest in complying with international agreements when he stated that Singapore's foreign policy had to encourage the world's major powers to help the island-state. To that end Singapore found it necessary to offer the world a continuing interest in the type of society Singapore projects (Lee 1966: 9). Being a player in negotiations to meet environmental needs at the global level has proven important in projecting Singapore's image as an environmentally conscious society and polity. Singapore's dependence on markets in the United States and Europe mandates its cooperation with multilateral environmental agreements. To be sure, in negotiations at the international front, continuing concern has been expressed about the impact of such agreements on Singapore's business competitiveness. Yet not subscribing to international environmental cooperation would fly in the face of the Singapore government's expressed with to be increasingly integrated with global markets and the global economy.

Singapore has had limited success securing cooperation on the environment within the region, as is illustrated by the effort to resolve the problem of haze from Indonesian forest fires. In its bilateral relations with Malaysia, water resources have featured often and sometimes prominently in foreign policy discussions. Negotiations to maintain the supply of water from Malaysia have highlighted other related environmental issues, including the need to safeguard water quality. This requires cross-border cooperation as much as good bilateral relations. Important though the issue is, it is one of many examples that illustrate why Singapore's foreign policy has been aptly described by Michael Leifer (2000) as "coping with vulnerability."

Regional cooperation on the environment is clearly needed. Not only the entire region but also Singapore, as a small and environmentally vulnerable city-state, benefit from such cooperation. The effort to secure greater regional cooperation on the environment has typically meant a flurry of meetings among political leaders and bureaucrats, followed by declarations of good intent. Unfortunately, this has not always been followed by real commitments to international or regional cooperation on major environmental issues facing individual nation-states.

REFERENCES

Barkdull, John. 2000. "Why Environmental Ethics Matters to International Relations." *Current History* (November): 361–366.

Buzan, Barry. 1983. *People, States, and Fear: The National Security Problem in International Relations.* Brighton: Wheatsheaf.

Centre for Strategic and International Studies (CSIS). 1998. *ASEAN Regional Cooperation on Haze: Memorandum for the ASEAN Economic Forum.* Unpublished paper, Jakarta, Indonesia.

Chng, Meng Kng, Linda Low, and Mun Heng Toh. 1988. "Trade Policy Options for Singapore." In Mohammed Ariff and Loong Hoe Tan, eds., *The Uruguay Round: ASEAN Trade Policy Options.* Singapore: Institute of Southeast Asian Studies.

Dauvergne, Peter. 2000. "Globalisation and Environmental Change: Asia's 1997 Financial Crisis." *Current History* (November): 389–395.

Dudley, Nigel. 1997. *The Year the World Caught Fire.* Gland, Switzerland: World Wide Fund for Nature.

Koh, Tommy. 1998. *The Quest for World Order: Perspectives of a Pragmatic Idealist.* Singapore: Institute of Policy Studies and Federal Publications.

Lee, Koon Choy. 1976. "Foreign Policy." In C. V. Devan Nair, ed., *Socialism That Works: The Singapore Way.* Singapore: Federal Publications.

Lee, Kuan Yew. 1966. "We Want to Be Ourselves." Singapore: Ministry of Culture.

———. 2000. *From Third World to First—The Singapore Story: 1965–2000.* Singapore: Times Media.

Leifer, Michael. 1989. "The Conduct of Foreign Policy." In Kernial Sandhu Sandhu and Paul Wheatley, eds., *Management of Success: The Moulding of Modern Singapore.* Singapore: Institute of Southeast Asian Studies.

———. 2000. *Singapore's Foreign Policy: Coping With Vulnerability.* London: Routledge.

Lim, William C.H., and Lim Ngin See. 1998. "Urban Stormwater Collection for Potable Use." Paper presented at the 11th IWSA-ASPAC Regional Conference, Sydney, Australia, 1–5 November.

Ooi, Giok Ling. 1999. "Trade and the Environment in Southeast Asia." In Tai-Chee Wong and Mohan Singh, eds., *Development and Challenge: Southeast Asia in the New Millennium.* Singapore: Times Academic.

Pearson, Charles. 1996. "Theory, Empirical Studies and Their Limitations." In Simon S.C. Tay and Daniel C. Esty, eds., *Asian Dragons and Green Trade.* Singapore: Times Academic.

Simson, Ian. 1970. *Singapore: Too Little, Too Late: The Failure of Malaya's Defence in 1942*. Singapore: Asia Pacific.

Singapore, Department of Statistics. Various years. *Yearbook of Statistics*. Singapore: Department of Statistics.

Singh, Harpajan, and Zulfakarin Mergawati. 1999. "Look Elsewhere for Extra Water, Singapore Told." *Star* (5 June).

Snitwongse, Kusuma, and Suchit Bunbongkarn. 2000. "New Security Issues and Their Impact on ASEAN." In Simon S.C. Tay, J. Estanislao, and Hadi Soesastro, eds., *A New ASEAN in a New Millennium*. Jakarta: Centre for International and Strategic Studies.

Tay, Simon S.C. 2000. "Institutions and Processes: Dilemmas and Possibilities." In Simon S.C. Tay, J. Estanislao, and Hadi Soesastro (eds.), *A New ASEAN in a New Millennium*. Jakarta: Centre for International and Strategic Studies.

Yap, Adriel Lian Ho. 1995. "Water for Singapore: Management of a Resource in a Subregional Economic Zone." Unpublished academic exercise, Department of Geography, National University of Singapore.

7

Emerging Norms of International Justice: Global Warming and China's Changing Environment

DONALD A. BROWN

Nations are usually assumed to be responsible for environmental problems within their borders. For a number of environmental issues, however, there is growing recognition of some nations' responsibility for environmental problems experienced by others. This responsibility is encompassed by many principles of international distributive justice (Harris 1996: 274–275, 2000b: 2–5). Theories of distributive justice are concerned with ways of fairly distributing benefits and burdens of human activities throughout society (Harris 2000b: 33–37). Principles of distributive justice assert that benefits and burdens should be distributed according to equality or merit or some combination thereof, and often attempt to resolve the tension between treating people equally and making distributions on the basis of merit or deservedness (Benn 1967).

This chapter examines some principles of international distributive justice as they relate to two environmental problems experienced by China—global warming and deforestation. These principles are potentially the basis for attributing some responsibility to other nations for China's environmental problems, as well as China's potential responsibility for damage to other nations' environments.

The world has only recently realized the relevance of distributive justice to international environmental issues. The 1992 United Nations Conference on Environment and Development in Rio de Janeiro is widely seen as one catalyst for this awakening because it involved serious consideration of the twin problems of global environmental deterioration and grinding poverty. The Rio conference, generally referred to as the Earth Summit, is also seen as the place where principles of international distributive justice were first seriously and widely considered as relevant to these emerging global issues. At the heart of the agreements reached in Rio were two ideas. The first was that the problems of poverty and environment were interrelated. Therefore the international community needed to work on environmental, economic, and social issues simultaneously if it hoped to make progress on any of these issues. The second idea was that a new partnership between rich and poor nations was needed to move the world toward environmentally sustainable development.

To move the world in this direction, five documents were signed in Rio. They included Agenda 21, the UN plan of action on the environment and development (United Nations 1992a); the UN Framework Convention on Climate Change (FCCC) (United Nations 1992b); the Convention on Biological Diversity (1992); the Rio Declaration on Environment and Development (United Nations 1992c); and the statement on forest principles (United Nations 1992d). All of these documents in one way or another recognized new equitable responsibilities between rich and poor nations (see Harris 2001: 44–69). For instance, Agenda 21 stated, "The development and environmental objectives of Agenda 21 will require a substantial flow of new and additional financial resources to developing countries" (United Nations 1992a: sec. 33). Under the FCCC, nations agreed to

> Protect the climate system for the benefit of present and future
> generations of humankind, on the basis of equity and in accordance
> with their common but differentiated responsibilities and respective
> capabilities. Accordingly, the developed country Parties should take
> the lead in combating climate change and the adverse effects thereof.
> (United Nations 1992b: art. 3)

The Convention on Biological Diversity acknowledged that "special provision is required to meet the needs of developing countries, including the provision of new and additional financial resources and appropriate access to relevant technologies" (Convention on Biological Diversity 1992: preamble). The Rio Declaration on Environment and Development provided that

> States shall cooperate in a spirit of global partnership to conserve,
> protect and restore the integrity of the Earth's ecosystem. In view of the
> different contributions to global environmental degradation, States
> have common but differentiated responsibilities. The developed
> countries acknowledge the responsibility that they bear in the interna-
> tional pursuit of sustainable development in view of the pressures

their societies place on the global environment and the technologies and technical resources they command. (United Nations 1992c: prin. 7)

The statement on forest principles declared that "specific financial resources should be provided to developing countries with significant forest areas which establish programs for conservation of forests, including protected natural resource areas" (United Nations 1992d: sec. 7[b]). In addition to these provisions, many other sections of the Rio documents—including those on international finance of sustainable development, trade and the environment, and technology transfer—drew distinctions between the obligations of developed and developing nations, thereby establishing new standards of international distributive justice in relation to environmental responsibility.

Several commentators on the 1992 Earth Summit saw profound historical significance in these and similar provisions in the Rio documents because they established different environmental protection obligations for rich and poor nations. For instance, Holmes Rolston declared that the Rio documents created two new principles of international order (Rolston 1994: 270): the right to an equitable international economic order and the right to protection of the environment. Because these rights raise questions about the obligations of one nation to another, the Rio documents can be understood to indicate heightened recognition of the need to apply principles of international distributive justice to environmental controversies.

The Rio Earth Summit created hope that the world would finally confront questions of justice between nations. Yet by 1997, at the five-year review of Rio, bitter fights had broken out between rich and poor nations over implementation of Earth Summit agreements. The poorer nations charged that the rich nations had failed to live up to promises made in Rio, and the richer nations claimed many poorer nations had repudiated some of their environmental commitments (Brown 1998: 31–47). In some cases it had become clear that many of the developed nations' most important promises had been broken. For instance, in Chapter 33 of Agenda 21 the richer nations agreed to increase foreign aid to poorer nations when they promised:

> Developed nations reaffirm their commitments to reach [the] accepted United Nations target of 0.7 percent of Official Development Assistance and, to the extent that they have not yet achieved that target, agree to augment their aid programs in order to reach that target as soon as possible and to assure prompt and effective implementation of Agenda 21. (United Nations 1992a: sec. 33)

At the five-year review of Rio, not only had the rich nations failed to make progress on this financial target, but foreign assistance to poorer nations had actually declined from 1992 levels. For this reason among many others, the developing nations at the review often bitterly accused the richer nations of bad faith in living up to Rio promises (Brown 1998: 31–47). Other disagreements occurred over implementation of more general provisions, such as the previously mentioned provision in the Climate Change Convention calling on developed nations to reduce their greenhouse gas emissions to equitable and just levels.

For these reasons, principles of distributive justice, which could help provide substantive content to such abstract concepts as equity, have become not only important theoretical questions but also burning practical matters because distributive justice could be the basis for resolving disputes that constitute the greatest barriers to international cooperation on emerging international environmental problems. Unless the poorer nations believe they are being treated fairly by richer nations, they are not likely to agree to cooperation on global environmental problems (Harris 2000b: 5). China, one of the most important developing nations, is a case in point.

CHINA'S ENVIRONMENTAL PROBLEMS

Notwithstanding remarkable recent economic growth, China is threatened by a host of staggering environmental problems, most of which have grown in severity in proportion to China's almost 10 percent yearly economic growth since the early 1990s. The sobering statistics include the following. Over half of China's population (nearly 700 million people) lacks access to clean water and consumes drinking water contaminated with animal and human waste that exceeds the maximum permissible level (Word Resources Institute 2000). Organic pollution is very prevalent in China's main rivers, and nonpoint source pollution is becoming increasingly serious (China 1999). In 1999, 40.1 billion tons of industrial and urban sewage was discharged into China's rivers, 600 million tons more than the previous year (China 1999). According to the World Bank, at least 5 of the 9 most polluted cities in the world are in China, and 500 major cities in China do not meet the World Health Organization's air quality standards (cited in Mufson 1997: 22).

Most factories built before the 1980s have no pollution control equipment and are fueled by coal, which the government calls "the chief source of pollution in China" (Karasov 2000: 455). No other large developing nation relies as heavily as China on coal for cooking, heating, and electricity. The country currently relies on coal for three-quarters of its energy. Largely because it burns coal for electrical power, China emits one-twentieth of the world's mercury pollution (Karasov 2000: 455). Per capita usable land resources are very low, only 0.078 hectares, and they will continually decrease in quantity and quality because of population and industrialization pressures unless solutions can be found. A shortage of land resources has become the major limitation to sustainable economic development (China 1997). As China's population has grown, its farmland has been shrinking. As a result, many farmers have replaced dwindling cropland with marginal lands too fragile to support crops. The result has been increased desertification (Karasov 2000: 457). As we will see, China's forest resources have been greatly damaged by past practices and are increasingly threatened by climate change.

Although China's environmental problems are daunting, it has recently demonstrated a serious commitment to environmental protection. In recent decades China has added environmental protection to its constitution, built an extensive body of environmental laws, participated in the drafting of many international protection agreements, supported the development of science and technology to address environmental issues, and created government infrastructures to educate its people and enforce regulations (Karasov 2000: 454).

The environmental problems in China raise questions of responsibility and international justice. Problems examined in this chapter, as mentioned previously, include global warming and protection of forests. These two environmental concerns are considered here because the first represents a problem that is obviously global in scope, whereas the second is (usually) considered a domestic issue. Because forests are usually thought to be resources within the control and responsibility of individual nations, questions of international distributive justice are not obviously relevant to forest protection. In fact, since Rio the poorer nations have insisted that nation-states have the right to fully control the natural resources within their borders. This idea is summarized in Principle 2 of the Rio Declaration, which asserts that

> States have, in accordance with the Charter of the United Nations and the principles of international law, the sovereign right to exploit their own resources pursuant to their own environmental and development policies, and the responsibility to ensure that activities within their own jurisdiction or control do not cause damage to the environment of other States or of areas beyond the limits of national jurisdiction. (United Nations 1992c: prin. 2)

Therefore nations are usually assumed to be responsible for managing natural resources within their jurisdictions. By examining both a global-scale problem and a natural resource problem believed to be a matter of national concern and responsibility, I will consider whether principles of international distributive justice may be relevant to national-scale environmental problems.

CHINA'S RESPONSIBILITY FOR GLOBAL WARMING

The Intergovernmental Panel on Climate Change (IPCC) has predicted that human-induced climate change may cause global temperatures to rise between 2.5 and 10 degrees Fahrenheit by the end of the twenty-first century (IPCC 2001a: 13). This temperature change will cause rising sea levels; create changes in local weather, including increases in drought and floods; endanger human health; threaten already vulnerable ecosystems; further stress marginal agricultural production; and adversely affect some water supplies. Climate models show that the world's poorest people—including hundreds of millions in China—are the most vulnerable to climate change because their ecological systems are most at risk, and they are vulnerable to storms, flooding, and rising sea levels. The health of the poor worldwide is especially at risk from global warming because of increases in the intensity and duration of heat waves, increases in potential transmission of vector-borne infectious diseases (e.g., malaria, dengue, yellow fever, and viral encephalitis), some increases in nonvector-borne infectious diseases (e.g., salmonella, cholera, and giardiasis), limitations on freshwater supplies, and aggravation of air pollution. The food supplies of the poor are also at risk from global warming. And the poorest people have the fewest financial and institutional resources to adapt to climate change (IPCC 2001b: 5–17).

China is vulnerable to these impacts and has already suffered from unusual climate events. For instance, in 1998 and 1999 China experienced droughts in the north and floods in the south; abnormally dry weather in winter and spring in most areas; unusually warm summer temperatures; and seventeen tropical storms in the northwest Pacific and the South China Sea, five of which landed in China (China 1999). China clearly has much to lose from global warming and has much more at stake than many developed nations that are less vulnerable. Eric Eckholm has illustrated this by describing the immense hardship and suffering created by lack of rainfall and desertification in parts of China.

> The rising sands are part of a new desert forming here on the eastern edge of the Qinghai-Tibet Plateau, a legendary stretch once known for grasses reaching as high as a horse's belly and home for centuries to ethnic Tibetan herders. The spread of wastelands on these 9,000-foot-high steppes, and across the pastures and farmed hillsides of a broad swath of northern China, is threatening to rend patterns of life that depend intimately on the land and to strand millions of herders and farmers who have no other place to go in a country with virtually no decent, unused land. (Eckholm 2000: 1)

Eckholm points out that no one knows for sure whether these climate changes are temporary or part of a human-induced global warming many scientists in China and abroad believe has already begun. Some Chinese also believe recent crop failures caused by droughts are attributable to human-caused changes in climate.

China is not only a potential victim of global warming but also a major contributor to the global climate problem. In fact, as the country with the world's largest population and one of its most rapidly growing economies, China is constituting a larger portion of the global warming problem. China currently emits almost 13 percent of the world's greenhouse gases. Between now and 2020, China may account for 50 percent of growth in major greenhouse gases (Karasov 2000: 455). China's greenhouse gas emissions have been steadily mounting as its economy has grown at extraordinary rates in the past few decades. China is already the second-largest emitter of greenhouse gases after the United States, although its per capita emissions are relatively low. By comparison, in 1999 U.S. per capita energy consumption was 5.5 times the world average and slightly over 14 times China's per capita energy use (U.S. Energy Information Administration 2001: 3).

China has been somewhat successful in decoupling carbon emissions from economic growth (Zhang 2000: 590). Its economy grew by over 10 percent from 1980 to 1997, but carbon dioxide emissions increased only 5.2 percent (Zhang 2000: 591). This success was the result of policies adopted for economic rather than environmental reasons (Zhang 2000: 593). These policies sought to conserve energy, and since the early 1980s China has enacted thirty energy conservation laws (U.S. Energy Information Administration 2001: 4). China may have had considerable recent success in reducing greenhouse gas emissions (Eckholm 2001), although there is disagreement over the magnitude of the reductions. It was originally reported that between the mid-1990s and April 2001 China's greenhouse gas emissions were reduced by 17 percent at the same time gross domestic product (GDP) grew 36 percent (Eckholm 2001). These figures have been challenged on the grounds that some of China's greenhouse gas statistics are unreliable (Pomfret 2001). Yet some researchers have concluded that China has nevertheless substantially reduced emissions of greenhouse gases, probably between 6 and 14 percent—even if one agrees with concerns about the statistics on which the 17 percent reduction conclusion was based (Natural Resources Defense Counsel 2001: 1). This achievement has resulted from China's shift to market prices for fuels, including ending coal subsidies, and its programs to encourage energy conservation and fight urban air pollution, mainly by curbing coal burning (Zhang 2000: 591; Eckholm 2001).

CHINA'S FAIR SHARE OF GREENHOUSE GAS EMISSIONS

As noted earlier, distributive justice is concerned with the ways benefits and burdens of a problem should be shared. Given China's historical and current share of global greenhouse emissions relative to other nations and its vulnerability to damage from global warming, a number of questions can be asked. What is China's fair share of an atmospheric greenhouse gas stabilization target? Who should pay for unavoidable damages from global warming experienced by China?

The goal of the Framework Convention on Climate Change is to stabilize greenhouse gases in the atmosphere at levels that do not dangerously interfere with the climate system (United Nations 1992b: art. 2). Future international negotiations will have to decide precisely what this level should be. Once that level is determined, total global emissions will need to be allocated among nations. As we saw earlier, signatories to the FCCC—including China and the United States—agreed that they would reduce emissions based on equity (United Nations 1992b: art. 3).

One can ask what principles of international equity and distributive justice specifically apply to notional greenhouse gas allocations. In the global warming negotiations held in Geneva in 1991, the Indian government introduced the idea that equity requires that national emission caps be based on a global per capita calculation. The Indian representative said, "The problem of global warming is caused by excessive levels of per capita emissions of these [greenhouse] gases. . . . An equitable solution can only be found on the basis of significant reductions in levels of per capita emissions in industrial countries, so that, over a period of years, these converge with rising per capita emissions in developing countries" (ECO 1997: 121). Following the 1997 Kyoto conference of parties to the FCCC, many developing nations—including China—continued to argue that equity demands that national allocations be based on equal per capita shares of the global target (Harris 2000a: 34). These per capita–based allocations could be calculated by first deciding on a safe concentration of greenhouse gases in the atmosphere and then dividing the total number of tons of emissions thereby determined by the world's population.

For instance, the IPCC suggested 450 parts per million (ppm) as a safe concentration level, although even at this level a temperature increase of 0.7 degrees centigrade and sea-level rise of 10–65 cm will occur. In this case the worldwide per capita entitlement in 1990 would have been 1.1 tons of carbon equivalent (tC) per capita. The European Union spoke of a 550-ppm limit, which would require per capita emissions of 1.5 tC (Centre for Science and the Environment 2000: 3). In the United States, per capita emissions in 1996 were 5.37 tC, and in the same year Chinese per capita emissions were 0.7 tC (U.S. Energy Information Administration 1999). Therefore if China were to accept a per capita allocation to stabilize greenhouse gases at either 450 or 550 ppm, the Chinese would have to prevent per capita emissions from increasing much above present levels (U.S. Energy

Information Agency 2001). If China exhibited the same per capita energy consumption as the United States in 1997, China would have consumed approximately 448 quadrillion British thermal units, approximately 17 percent more than the amount the entire world used (U.S. Energy Information Agency 2001: 4). By comparison, if the United States were to accept a per capita allocation to stabilize greenhouse gases at these levels, the country would have to reduce its emissions by 70 to 80 percent below 1990 levels. For this reason the United States has strongly resisted greenhouse targets derived through per capita calculations (Brown 2002). Given that even under a very aggressive U.S. global warming program it will take decades to replace power plants that burn fossil fuel and that most of the transportation sector runs on gasoline, it would be impossible for the United States to implement a per capita–based national greenhouse gas allocation in the very short term.

Because of the long phase-in time that would be required to move toward per capita allocations in the developed nations, those developing nations pushing for per capita allocation—including China—have proposed an approach usually referred to as "contraction and convergence" (Centre for Science and the Environment 1999). Contraction and convergence refers to an allocation that would allow large emitter nations enough time, perhaps thirty or forty years, to reduce their emissions by replacing greenhouse-emitting capital and infrastructure and to converge on a uniform per capita allocation (Meyer 2000). Support for contraction and convergence has been building around the world, with the European Parliament, among other government bodies and organizations, recently calling for its adoption (Meyer 2000).

A per capita allocation would be consistent with principles of distributive justice because (1) it treats all individuals as equals, (2) it would implement the ethical maxim that all people should have an equal right to use the global commons, and (3) it would implement the widely accept "polluter-pays" principle affirmed at the 1992 Earth Summit. The principle states that "national authorities should endeavor to promote the internalization of environmental costs and the use of economic instruments, taking into account the approach that the polluter should, in principle, bear the cost of pollution, with due regard to the public interest and without distorting international trade and investment" (United Nations 1992c: prin. 16). A per capita allocation would implement the polluter-pays principle because by accepting a per capita share of safe atmospheric carbon levels, no nation would be polluting at a level greater than its fair share. Because the very essence of distributive justice is that burdens and benefits of actions should be shared equally or in accordance with merit, a per capita allocation would be just and would comply with the polluter-pays principle.

Of course, not all nations have accepted a per capita allocation for determining equitable national responsibility. As a result of the intense political opposition to acceptance of the per capita approach to carbon targets, some alternative approaches to equitably based allocations have surfaced—including one based on emissions/GDP ratios and one proposed by the Pew Center for Global Climate Change (Brown 2002; Clausen and McNeilly 1998). Both approaches have been proposed by representatives of developed nations and would require those nations to make much smaller reductions than per capita allocations would require to reach atmospheric carbon stabilization levels. They are arguably inconsistent with principles of distributive justice (Brown 2002). For this reason the approaches are not supported by developing nations. As a result, future negotiations between developed and developing nations over equitable national allocations of maximum carbon emissions are likely to remain contentious.

UNAVOIDABLE DAMAGE TO CHINA: WHO SHOULD PAY?

The IPCC has concluded that strong evidence indicates that global warming caused by human activities is already experienced around the world (IPCC 2001a: 4–5). Along this line, the Chinese have asserted that they believe recent devastating floods and reduced agricultural harvests as a result of drought have been caused at least in part by human-induced climate change (Ruqui 2001: 9). Before the Industrial Revolution, carbon dioxide levels had been relatively stable at 260 ppm for thousands of years (Center for the Study of Carbon Dioxide and Global Change 2001). Since then, the level of carbon dioxide has risen to over 370 ppm. The developed world is largely responsible for this buildup. The Preamble to the 1992 United Nations Framework Convention on Climate Change noted that "the largest share of historical and current global emissions of greenhouse gases originated in developed countries, that per capita emissions in developing countries are still relatively low and that the share of global emissions in developing countries will grow to meet their social and development needs" (United Nations 1992b: preamble). Because it is too late to stabilize carbon dioxide at levels lower than 450 or 550 ppm, China and other nations are likely to experience additional unavoidable damage from global warming.

Distributive justice requires a fair sharing of human problems. To determine who is responsible for global warming damage on the basis of distributive justice, most observers believe it would be necessary to calculate the relative contribution of each nation to the buildup of greenhouse gases in the atmosphere. This would identify which nations are responsible for the existing problem and allow attribution of responsibility based on historical causation. As we have seen, the international community, under the polluter-pays principle, has already acknowledged the normative legitimacy of this approach.

Several practical difficulties must be overcome to calculate national responsibility for unavoidable global warming damage. The first will be the challenge of identifying what damage would have occurred even without human climate intervention. To do this it will be necessary to separate natural damage from human-caused damage because it is reasonable to assume that some weather-related damage would have been experienced in the absence of human-induced climate changes. For instance, even if floods did not increase as a result of human interference with the climate system, some flood damage would no doubt still be experienced. For this reason it will be very difficult to point to any damage and prove that it was caused by human activity.

Another problem, involving assigning responsibility for specific global warming damage experienced by China, would be to determine whether any of China's own actions have led to the damage, even assuming the climate-caused damage was human induced. For instance, China has recently experienced great flooding many believe has been caused by global warming. Yet some of the damage from the flooding would not have occurred if China had not allowed its forests to be logged. Therefore at least some of the extensive damage caused by global warming–induced flooding may also be a consequence of China's forest policy. For this reason it may be very difficult to attribute China's flooding damage to external causes.

As China's emissions remain below a fair share of the level needed to stabilize greenhouse gases at a safe level in the atmosphere, according to accepted principles of distributive justice the developed world and those elements of the developing world that are exceeding their fair share of acceptable global emissions are potentially responsible for global warming damage in China. Yet China's current carbon emission trajectory could make the country responsible for climate damage in other nations in the years ahead, according to the same principles. Thus China could become responsible for global warming damage in other nations if it does not reduce its projected emissions to an equitable share of total safe global emissions.

CHINA'S RESPONSIBILITY FOR PROTECTING ITS FORESTS

By the mid-twentieth century China had lost much of its forested land to logging, development, clearing to support farming, and other forest exploitation activities. After thousands of years of forest exploitation, by 1950 China's forests had declined to 5.2 percent of its total area. As the result of changes in forest policy implemented in the last few decades, forests are now estimated to cover 13.4 percent of China's land (Zhang et al. 2000: 2135). This is still much lower than the international average of 31 percent and is significantly less than is needed to meet domestic demand for wood products

(World Bank 2000). For this reason China is a net importer of wood products and is likely to remain so in the years ahead (World Bank 2000). China began to reverse its forest policy in the 1960s (World Bank 2000; Zhang et al. 2000: 2135). At first the new policies were not effective, but after the 1980s forest cover increased as a result of extensive planting programs (Zhang et al. 2000: 2135). Data suggest that forest cover in China increased 15 percent between 1980 and 1993 (World Bank 2000).

By the 1990s the Chinese government acknowledged that its forest protection practices had led to disastrous consequences, including degradation of landscapes, loss of biodiversity, unacceptable levels of soil erosion, and catastrophic flooding (Zhang et al. 2000: 2135). One flooding event on the Yangtze River in 1998 left 13,656 people dead and immersed 64 million acres of land (Pomfret 1998). China banned logging in some provinces, including the 4.63 million hectares of the Chuanxi forest in Sichuan Province, for the disaster (Adhikari 1998). The government later banned all nationwide logging in natural forests, allowing only planted trees to be used for wood products (*People's Daily* 2000). The logging ban immediately resulted in layoffs of many logging workers, but the government said they would be hired to manage natural forests and tree plantations (Adhikari 1998). Since then, hundreds of thousands of logging workers across China are now planting rather than cutting trees (Xiaoming 1999).

In 1998 China announced a very ambitious new forest policy called the Natural Forest Conservation Program (NFCP) (Zhang et al 2000: 2135). Its purposes were to restore natural forests in ecologically sensitive areas, to plant forests for soil and water protection, to increase timber production in forest plantations, to protect existing natural forests from excessive cutting, and to maintain a multiple-use policy in natural forests. To implement the NFCP, China invested $500 million in 1998, $750 million in 1999, and $875 million in 2000 (Zhang et al. 2000: 2136). Some of the financing came from foreign support, including major loans from the World Bank (Word Bank 2000). China's forests are still greatly threatened by urbanization and industrialization despite the aggressive provisions of the NFCP. Initial statistics from the first two years of implementation of the NFCP indicated that timber production control, land conservation, and resettlement of forest dwellers have been successful (Zhang et al 2000: 2136).

Implementation of forest policy will challenge China. The NFCP has tremendous short- and medium-term social and economic costs. For instance, it has already reduced timber supply and will likely continue to affect employment, incomes, and government revenues (World Bank 2000). Therefore the program's long-term success has yet to be determined.

China's forest problems create extraordinary challenges of distributive justice for national policy because environmental policy, including that related to forests, cannot focus on resource protection alone. Most environmental problems in China, including deforestation, raise serious questions about how humans will be affected by various policy options. China's 1.2 billion people force environmental decisionmakers to focus on the consequences of policy options for people in ways developed nations have been able to avoid. For instance, in the United States most forests are relatively uninhabited, so most forest policy has been able to avoid facing issues about how people living in forests should be resettled following new restrictions on forest use. China does not have that luxury. In China over a million foresters have been laid off under the NFCP (Zhang et al. 2000: 2136). Millions of farmers will also be affected by the NFCP because restoring China's forests at the level necessary to meet NFCP goals will mean farmland will have to be reforested. China has responded to the immense social problems created by the NFCP by giving farmers who lose their land free food for thirty years after conservation starts and by reeducating, training, and paying for resettlement of foresters who lose their jobs (Zhang et al. 2000: 2136).

Unlike the global warming problem per se, it is much more difficult to point to foreign responsibility for China's diminished forests because they have mostly been under the control of the Chinese people. Moreover, as we have seen, the developing world has consistently argued that each nation has the right to exploit its own natural resources. For this reason it is much more difficult to rely on principles of international distributive justice to determine responsibility for China's forest problems. Despite this difficulty, however, arguments can be made that other nations have some responsibility for China's forests.

INTERNATIONAL RESPONSIBILITY FOR DAMAGE TO CHINA'S FORESTS

Because the damage to China's forests has largely been caused by the country's initial unenlightened forest policy rather than by actions of other nations, principles of distributive justice do not provide a basis for international responsibility for China's forest restoration. If (and only if) it could be demonstrated that China's forest problems have been caused at least in part by human-induced climate change, however, arguments could be made that distributive justice requires that nations that have caused global warming should share with China the costs of forest damage. As recognized earlier, however, the difficulty with this line of reasoning is the complexity of segregating human-caused damage from damage that would have occurred without human-induced climate change.

What is more, if restoration of China's forests benefits people in other nations, distributive justice might involve allocating the burden of forest restoration to them. Forests provide many ecological benefits to the world, not least of which is that they store carbon after removing it from the atmosphere during photosynthesis. Thus the entire world benefits from intact forests in China, and an argument can be made that part of the China's reforestation costs should be paid by nations that will benefit and that rely on China's forest restoration efforts to help limit global warming. This is one line of reasoning behind the Clean Development Mechanism, one of the trading mechanisms under the Kyoto Protocol that provides for developed nations to pay for carbon sink projects in the developing world. Allowing developed nations to finance forest restoration projects in China (or other developing nations) so they receive credit against domestic carbon reduction targets constitutes a recognition that the developed nations have an interest in the quality of developing nations' forest resources. The logic of the Clean Development Mechanism is consistent with some principles of distributive justice that require that government policy reward "deservedness" or "merit." That is, to the extent that China's forests need to be restored to achieve extraterritorial objectives of providing carbon sinks for all nations, some principles of distributive justice support allocating the burden of forest restoration programs to those nations that want to benefit from them.

CONCLUSION

Emerging norms of international distributive justice have profound importance for international environmental cooperation. Developing nations expect to be treated equitably if they are to take the steps necessary to limit global warming. The case of China is illustrative. Other nations may be responsible in part for global warming damage experienced by China, especially as long as its greenhouse gas emissions remain below its equitable share of safe global greenhouse gas emissions. If China exceeds its equitable share of safe emissions, however, it may become proportionally liable for global warming damage in the rest of the world.

As we have seen, responsibility for protecting national environmental resources such as forests is usually seen to be the obligation of the nation in which the resources are located. Because global environmental problems are affecting the quality of what were once viewed as purely national environmental resources, however, principles of international distributive justice support finding foreign responsibility for damages to those national resources in some circumstances. Determining the degree of foreign nations' responsibility for damage to domestic environmental resources raises difficult questions of causation. These questions will be particularly troublesome for those nations that have failed to fulfill domestic responsibility to protect the resources in question. To protect domestic resources from emerging global environmental problems such as global warming, insofar as they are able to do so, China and other developing nations should limit their contribution to global warming and adapt to its consequences. Doing so should make it easier for them to argue that they are entitled to financial support from developed nations. Such aid would in turn help developed and developing nations cooperate in addressing a global problem that will increasingly affect Pacific Asia.

REFERENCES

Adhikari, Pushpa. 1998. *Environment China: New Green Policy Put to the Test.* World News Service (6 December) <http://www.oneworld.org/ips2/Dec98/ 04_27_008.html>.

Benn, Stanely. 1967. "Justice." In Paul Edwards, ed., *Encyclopedia of Philosophy.* New York: Macmillan and Free Press.

Brown, Donald. 1998. "The Need to Face Conflicts Between Rich and Poor Nations to Solve Global Environmental Problems." In Laura Westra and Patricia Werhane, eds., *The Business of Consumption, Environmental Ethics and the Global Economy.* Lanham: Rowman and Littlefield.

———. 2002. *American Heat: An Ethical Analysis of the United States Response to Global Warming.* Lanham: Rowman and Littlefield.

Center for the Study of Carbon Dioxide and Global Change. 2001. *The Last 10,000 Years* <http://www.co2science.org/subject/otherco2con_tenthousand.htm>.

Centre for Science and the Environment. 1999. *Shades of Equity* 7, 19 (28 February) <http://www.cseindia.org/html/dte/dte990228/dte_cross.htm>.

———. 2000. "Equal Rights to the Atmosphere." Equity Watch (22 November) <http://www.cseindia.org/html/cmp/climate/ew/art20001122_4.htm>.

China, People's Republic. 1997. *State of the Environment: China 1997* <http:// svr1-pek.unep.net/soechina/>.

———. 1999. *State of the Environment: China 1999* <http://www.sepa.gov.cn/ soechina99/index.htm>.

Clausen, Eileen, and Lisa McNeilly. 1998. "Equity and Global Climate Change: The Complex Elements of Global Fairness." Arlington: Pew Center for Climate Change <http://pewclimate.org>.

Convention on Biological Diversity. 1992. 31 *International Legal Materials*: 822.

Eckholm, Eric. 2000. "Chinese Farmers See New Desert Erode Their Way of Life." *New York Times* (30 July) <http://www.nytimes.com/library/world/asia/ 073000china-farmers.html>.

———. 2001. "China Said to Sharply Reduce Carbon Dioxide Emissions." *New York Times* (14 June) <http://www.climateark.org/articles/2001/2nd/ chsaidt1.htm>.

Environment Congress (ECO). 1997. "India Throws Down the Gauntlet." From *ECO* NGO newsletter 2 (20 June 1991). In Makund Govind Rajan, ed., *Global Environmental Politics: India and the North-South Politics of Global Environmental Issues.* Delhi: Oxford University Press.

Harris, Paul G. 1996. "Considerations of Equity and International Environmental Institutions." *Environmental Politics* 5, 2 (summer 1996): 274–301.

Donald A. Brown

———. 2000a. "Climate Change: Is the United States Sharing the Burden?" In Paul G. Harris, ed., *Climate Change and American Foreign Policy*. New York: Saint Martin's.

———. 2000b. "Defining International Distributive Justice: Environmental Considerations." *International Relations* 15, 2 (August): 1–39.

———. 2001. *International Equity and Global Environmental Politics*. Aldershot: Ashgate.

Intergovernmental Panel on Climate Change (IPCC). 2001a. "Working Group I (Science), Summary for Policymakers, Third Assessment Report" <http://www.ipcc.ch/pub/spm22–01.pdf>.

———. 2001b. "Working Group II (Impacts), Summary for Policymakers, Third Assessment Report, February 2001" <http://www.usgcrp.gov/ipcc/wg2spm.pdf>.

Karasov, Corliss. 2000. "On a Different Scale: Putting China's Environmental Crisis in Perspective." *Environmental Health Perspectives* 108, 10: 452–459.

Meyer, Aubrey. 2000. *Contraction and Convergence: The Global Solution to Climate Change*. Devon: Green.

Mufson, Steven. 1997. "Rising Coal Consumption Makes China a World Leader in Pollution." *Washington Post* (30 November): 22.

Natural Resources Defense Council. 2001. "Second Analysis Confirms Greenhouse Gas Reductions in China" <http://www.nrdc.org/globalWarming/achinagg.asp>.

People's Daily. 2000. "Government Stumps Deforesters" (13 November) <http://www.peopledaily.co.jp/english/200011/13/eng20001113_55009.html>.

Pomfret, John. 1998. "Yangtze Flood Jolts China's Land Policies Development." *Washington Post* (22 November) <http://www.tibet.ca/wtnarchive/1998/11/22_4.html>.

———. 2001. "Research Casts Doubt on China's Pollution Claims." *Washington Post* (15 August) <http://www.climateark.org/articles/2001/3rd/recastsd.htm>.

Rolston, Holmes. 1994. "Environmental Protection and Equitable International Order: Ethics After the Earth Summit." In Donald Brown, ed., *Proceedings on the Conference on the Ethical Dimensions of the United Nations Program on Environment and Development, Agenda 21* Camp Hill, PA: Earth Ethics Research Group [on file with author].

Ruqui, Ye. 2001. "Studies on Climate Change Problems and Response Measures in China." Chinese Environmental Protection Agency <http://www.uccee.org/CopenhagenConf/yeruqiu.htm>.

United Nations. 1992a. Agenda 21: The United Nations Program on Environment and Development. UN Doc. A/CONF.151/26, Rio de Janeiro.

———. 1992b. United Nation Framework Convention on Climate Change. UN Doc. A/CONF.151/26, New York.

———. 1992c. Rio Declaration on Environment and Development. UN Doc. A/CONF.151/5, Rio de Janeiro.

———. 1992d. Statement of Principles for Global Consensus on the Management, Conservation and Sustainable Development of All Types of Forests. UN Doc. A/CONF.151/26, Rio de Janeiro.

U.S. Energy Information Administration. 2001. "China's Environmental Issues" <http://www.eia.doe.gov/cabs/chinaenv.html>.

World Bank. 2000. "China: From Afforestation to Poverty Alleviation and Natural Forest Management" <http://wbln0018.worldbank.org/oed/oeddoclib.nsf/>.

World Resources Institute. 2000. "The Environment and China" <http://www.wri.org/china/>.

Xiaoming, Liu. 1999. "China's Perspective on the Environment." *Proceedings of the Mayors' Asia Pacific Environmental Summit* <http://www.csis.org/e4e/MayorOPLiu.html>.

Zhang, Peichang, Guofan Shao, Guang Zhao, Dennis C. Le Master, George R. Parker, John B. Dunning Jr., and Qinglin Li. 2000. "China's Forest Policy for the 21st Century." *Science* 288 (23 June): 2135–2136.

Zhang, ZhongXiang. 2000. "Can China Afford to Commit Itself to an Emissions Cap? An Economic and Political Analysis." *Energy Economics* 22: 587–614.

II

Regime Building, Interstate Cooperation, and Environmental Diplomacy

8

Ecological Interdependence and Environmental Governance in Northeast Asia: Politics vs. Cooperation

SANGMIN NAM

N
ortheast Asia faces significant regional environmental problems, including increased transboundary air pollution, deterioration of the marine environment of regional seas, and the loss of biodiversity. These environmental issues have not only local and regional impacts but also global implications considering the significant scale of population, resource consumption, and environmental deterioration in the region. The region, however, lacks experience in collective problem solving in both environmental and political arenas. Northeast Asian countries have sought to develop and expand opportunities for regional environmental cooperation since the early 1990s. Increased global environmental diplomacy and regionalization of environmental protection, rather than the region's enlightenment about its environmental condition, induced the start of intergovernmental cooperation among Northeast Asian countries. Rapid changes in international politics after the end of the Cold War were also critical in providing the countries with a new opportunity for modest diplomatic dialogue. In particular, after a long history of intraregional colonialism and political antagonism that had ruled the region during most of the twentieth century, the receding Cold War encouraged Northeast Asian countries to test intergovernmental cooperation in nonpolitical areas, including the environmental field.

Current environmental issues and cooperation processes in Northeast Asia have shown, however, that environmental cooperation is not a nonpolitical agenda but a showcase of political reality portraying the socio-economic heterogeneity among the countries and the region's poor capacity for collective action and policy coordination. As a result, the countries have not achieved visible relaxation of the political aspect of regional environmental governance and thus have made sluggish progress in such governance. Moreover, the cooperation processes have revealed crucial obstacles the region faces in establishing effective institutional vehicles that are urgently needed to resolve the emerging negative aspects of ecological interdependence. These obstacles include the heterogeneity of economic and environmental conditions, a lack of scientific and political consensus on regional environmental problems, and a deficiency of national capacities necessary to comply with new rules of regional governance.

This chapter first describes regional environmental issues to present the need for regional environmental governance. These issues concerning common pool resources have significant global and regional implications and have become a focal point for regional environmental governance since its beginning. The chapter then briefly describes multilateral and bilateral environmental cooperation in the region and analyzes the process of regional environmental governance. This assessment of the environment and governance in Northeast Asia aims to conceptualize the big picture of environmental governance in Northeast Asia and to enhance understanding of the current state and process of governance. Finally, geopolitical conditions in environmental governance and other major impediments to effective collective activities will be analyzed to present ways to address regional environmental issues in Northeast Asia. The analysis, however, focuses on the activities and attitudes of key members of regional governance—China, Japan, and South Korea—because of their active roles, but does not concentrate on other countries in the region—Russia, North Korea, and Mongolia—because they have been less active in regional governance as a result of different geography, economic situations, or political capabilities.

GROWING ECOLOGICAL INTERDEPENDENCE IN NORTHEAST ASIA

DEMARCATING NORTHEAST ASIA

What is Northeast Asia? A review of commonly cited attributes of regional designations reveals the three most common conditions for defining regions: geographic proximity, regularity and intensity of interactions, and shared perceptions of the region (Katzenstein, 1997: 8). Nevertheless, discourses on Northeast Asia suggest that the boundaries of the region are inevitably the construct of an analyst's object of study. Economic discourses on Northeast Asia commonly include Hong Kong and Taiwan as main actors in the region, whereas others exclude those "quasi-sovereign" entities. Some include all territories of the Russian Far East (Kirchbach 1997: 47), and attempts have also been made to include Alaska in the region because of its strong economic tie with Northeast Asia (Cho 1999: 1). These examples thus indicate that Northeast Asia as a natural economic territory has flexible boundaries. Cultural studies of Northeast Asia, however, mostly exclude Russia from the region because of the feebleness of racial and cultural commonalities as well as historical contacts between societies. Therefore the boundary of the region is not clearly defined but tends to change according to the research topic (Mack and Ravenhill 1995: 6–7).

This fluid definition of the region raises questions regarding its boundaries in environmental discourses. Since regional common pool resources such as the atmosphere do not respect political boundaries, it is necessary to draw a new boundary for this chapter by examining biophysical, geographical, and political determinants (Hayes and Zarsky 1994: 283). Given the conditions of regional ecological interdependence, "Northeast Asia" for the purpose of this research encompasses Japan, Mongolia, northeastern China (Heilongjiang, Jilin, Liaoning, Hebei, Henan, Shanxi, Shandong, and Jiangsu[1]), the Russian Far East, North Korea, and South Korea.[2]

The vast array of political, demographic, and economic characteristics among the countries presents enormous obstacles to the development of a regional identity and hence to the ability to become a regional community. Current negative environmental trends in the region, however, increase ecological interdependence among countries and societies in Northeast Asia and force them to seek collective actions to cope with these trends. Here the prerequisite concept of *ecological interdependence* entails the physical and biological interconnections of the environment that cause the actions of each actor in the environment to impinge on the welfare of the others (Young 1994: 20–23). Thus the concept encapsulates not only the interconnections of environmental changes across time and space but also the intertwined relationship among ecological, economic, and political factors (Lipschutz and Conca 1993: 9).

Air Pollution: Creating an Ecological Community

Geographical proximity and climate contiguity may seem to constitute what shapes a region into a single ecological community, but that is not necessarily the case. Rather, deterioration of regional common pool resources drives the region to become a destined ecological community. The resources not exclusively utilized by a single entity or source are defined as common pool resources, which include high seas and the atmosphere.

Transboundary air pollution in particular is a critical source of deteriorating regional common pool resources in Northeast Asia. The Regional

Air Pollution Information and Simulation (RAINS)–Asia model,[3] assessing regional acidification and policy options and developed under a World Bank initiative in 1991, shows that long-range transport of pollutants and acidic deposition in Northeast Asia have greatly deteriorated atmospheric common pool resources, as well as terrestrial and marine ecosystems (Carmichael and Arndt 1997: 16; Hayes 1995: 17.) In particular, the model reveals that China contributes 17 percent of total acid deposition in Japan and 35 percent of the total in North Korea, even if China's 83 percent of the total emission is deposited in its own territory.[4] South Korea is also a major source of cross-border acid deposition in North Korea and Japan, and it received 16 percent of the total deposition from Chinese-originated pollutants in 1990 (Carmichael and Arndt 1997: 6).[5]

This complex cross-border acid deposition issue is inevitable because of geographical proximity. South Korea's most populous area, the Seoul metropolitan zone, is only 400 km from one of China's major air polluters, the Shandong region. Moreover, the distance between Japan's nearest coastal areas and Ulsan, one of the most polluted industrial area in South Korea, is only 250 km.[6] Dust containing sulfate can travel as far as 1,000 km from source areas, which places countries under the same polluted sky and into the same ecological community (Kim et al. 1997: 75). In particular, each spring the region as a whole is affected by westerly flows of yellow dust originating from the central China deserts. Moreover, the RAINS-Asia project revealed that acid deposition is not the only cause of increased risk of damage to natural ecosystems and agriculture in the region; atmospheric concentration of air pollutants, including sulfur dioxide, also causes direct damage (Hettelingh et al. 1995: 52–53).

The worsening acid precipitation not only enhances the vulnerability of ecosystems but also causes substantial economic loss. According to a 1995 report of China's State Environmental Protection Agency, direct economic damages in two of the country's most severely affected provinces, Sichuan and Guizhou, were $170 to $190 million per year (Sinton 1997: 3).[7] The rapid increase of energy consumption combined with the high rate of economic growth in Northeast Asia is likely to result in a significant increase of regional sulfur dioxide emissions, from 14.7 million tons per year in 1990 to 20.7 million tons by 2020, even if advanced control technologies are applied to China's industrial and power sectors (Streets 1997: 10).

Critical trends of pollution concentration in the atmosphere also occur in carbon dioxide emissions, which have not only regional but global implications. Three countries in Northeast Asia—China, Japan, and South Korea—are in the top ten carbon emitters in the world and accounted for 19.5 percent of world emission in 1998 (IEA 2000: 48). The growth rate of carbon emissions from South Korea—82.5 percent—during the period 1990–

1996 was the highest in the world. China also ranked at the top in terms of absolute growth, with a 29.3 percent increase in emissions (Flavin and Dunn 1997: 16). Unfortunately, this rapid increase in carbon emissions in Northeast Asia will not change significantly during the first quarter of the twenty-first century. Since climate change has disproportional effects according to latitude and socioenvironmental conditions and has a heavier impact on countries in the middle latitudes, the current trend is likely to have significant adverse impacts on Northeast Asia's regional environment. Thus the constant increase of concentrations of sulfur dioxide and carbon dioxide in the atmosphere not only deteriorates regional common pool resources but also contributes to aggravation of national ecological and economic assets and global common pool resources.

MARINE POLLUTION AND DYING SEAS

Marine pollution is another critical environmental issue in Northeast Asia, destroying regional common pool resources and defining the countries as members of an ecological community. The region has two semienclosed seas—the Yellow Sea, bordered by China and the Korean Peninsula, and the East Sea (Sea of Japan),[8] bordered by Japan, the Korean Peninsula, and the Russian Far East.

The Yellow Sea is ecologically fragile because of its relative shallowness, with an average depth of just 44 meters and a maximum depth of about 100 meters. Sluggish and confined patterns of currents contribute to accumulation of pollutants in the sea, causing rapid deterioration of the marine environment (Valencia 1996: 75). In addition, human activities along its borders discharge pollutants into the sea at a level exceeding its assimilative capacity. The Yellow Sea has been exposed to various types and sources of marine pollution, including industrial wastewater from growing industries of coastal states; domestic sewage from coastal areas; oil spills from oil and gas exploration, tankers, and ports; and organic and nuclear waste dumping (Lee 1997: 117). The Yellow River of China carries 750 tons of heavy metals into the sea each year, producing concentrations 1,000 times the permissible level of some pollutants (Valencia 1996: 175). In particular, the influx of wastewater into the Bohai Gulf—encircled by Liaoning, Hebei, and Shandong Provinces of China and a major part of the Yellow Sea— amounts to 8.7 billion tons annually, which is 32 percent of the total wastewater discharged from China while the gulf constitutes just 1.6 percent of China's coastal zone (*Donga Daily*, 1 August 2000). Moreover, in 1999 the gulf received 2 million tons of oil-containing sewage and 42 tons of oil from eight oil and gas fields (SEPA 2000). As a result, the environmental condition of over half of the 80,000-km²-wide gulf falls exceedingly short of the national environmental standard (Guan 2000: 35).

Petroleum hydrocarbons from oil exploration and accidents have also severely contaminated the Yellow Sea. In particular, Korea's coastal environment has been seriously exposed to oil contamination from oil spills, mostly from vessels. During the 1990s, 1,067 oil spills occurred along the Yellow Sea's South Korean coastline, releasing 17.5 million liters of oil into the sea (NMPA 2000). As a result, a Worldwatch Institute report designated the Yellow Sea one of the seven "dying" seas in the world and argued that a more accurate name for the sea might be "the Brownish-Red Sea" (Platt 1995).

Among the most visible evidence of deterioration of the marine environment is the notable increase in frequency and scale of red tide occurrences along the coastal areas of China and South Korea over the past few decades. In particular, in the 1990s in the seas adjacent to South Korea, red tides not only occurred along seashores more frequently but also spread extensively to the open seas (Lee 1999: 7; NFRDI 1999). During that same decade China also experienced an increase in the frequency and duration of red tides and in the magnitude of damage to the aquatic environment. One of the most severe red tides, which covered 5,000 km^2 and remained for forty days, occurred in Bohai Gulf in 1998 and resulted in a direct economic loss of over 120 million yuan (Guan 2000: 35). As major fisheries become more vulnerable to pollution, the countries of Northeast Asia—which are dominant world fishery countries—encounter significant conflicts with each other in the competition for marine fisheries resources.[9]

The East Sea (Sea of Japan) is in much better condition than the Yellow Sea because of its relatively large assimilative capacity created by its depth and water circulation. The East Sea, however, has drawn the world's attention as a result of radioactive contamination from nuclear waste disposal by the former Soviet Navy. It was reported that the navy dumped eighteen decommissioned nuclear reactors and 13,150 containers of radioactive waste into the East Sea between 1978 and 1993 (Yoon and Lee 1998: 75). The analysis of radionuclides concentration in the East Sea resulting from Russian radioactive waste dumping in 1993 found no definite evidence of additional accumulations of radionuclides such as plutonium and cesium as a result of the dumping and concluded that global radioactivity fallout from nuclear weapons tests was primarily responsible for the level of radionuclide deposition in the sea (Ikeuchi et al. 1999; Hong et al. 1999). The longer-term effects of radioactivity dumping into the sea are unknown, however, particularly after the containers corrode. Since research projects on the effects of the dumping have only focused on the level of radionuclides concentration in the water with a limited number of expeditions, proper analysis of ecological consequences has not yet been carried out, and the consequences remain unclear.

GOVERNING ECOLOGICAL INTERDEPENDENCE
IN NORTHEAST ASIA

THEORETICAL FRAMEWORK

The concept of governance in international relations has been developed to elaborate the emergent structures of world politics such as simultaneous occurrences of integration and fragmentation of political systems, rising interdependencies among the members of international society, and emerging webs of large, differentiated and autonomous actors (Rosenau 1992: 2; Smouts 1998: 85; Young 1997: 273). James Rosenau's term *governance without government* also exemplifies the changing concept of the word (Rosenau 1992: 7). The term implies that governance is not necessarily backed by any legal or sovereign power, which is the basis for government activities.

Although the use and concept of governance vary widely according to different research topics and scholars, literature on global governance allows us to draw a consensual definition of the concept. Governance is not only a set of arrangements (e.g., rules, norms, principles) guiding expectations and activities of actors but also includes activities and continual interactions during the process from establishment of rules to their implementation. The arrangements include both formal and informal systems. The definition is also flexible in scope; it applies whether the subject is general or specific. These conceptual flexibilities of governance also help expand the membership of actors in the establishment and operation of governance from state to nonstate actors. Since the scope of governance embraces diverse activities, governance does not necessarily require a physical entity or organization to be defined (Finkelstein 1995: 369; Rosenau 1992: 5; Smouts 1998: 86). *Governance* is therefore a flexible term covering any network of activities from its structural framework to its implementation.

Some have argued that the concepts of governance and regimes are ambiguous. Like governance, regimes are conceived "as sets of implicit or explicit principles, norms, rules, and decision-making procedures around which actors' expectations converge" (Krasner, 1983:2) and that sustain and regulate activities across national boundaries.[10] Nevertheless, proponents of governance theory argue that a prime difference exists between regimes and governance. They state that regimes are "more specialized arrangements that pertain to well-defined activities, resources, or geographical areas" or that converge "in a given area of international relations" (Young 1989: 13). They argue that governance "in a global order is not confined to a single sphere of endeavor" and is more encompassing than regimes (Rosenau 1992: 8–9).

The notion of governance has also become an important theoretical base for analyzing the relationship between growing ecological interdependence and institutionalization of national activities on global and regional environmental imperatives (Young 1994: 15). The concept is also useful to illustrate the dynamic process of environmental cooperation in Northeast Asia. The processes of evolution in the region, from institutional vacuum to burgeoning environmental institutionalization, cannot be categorized as primarily regime-building processes because of dispersed and diverse activities. In particular, the governance concept is more effective than regime theory in analyzing the processes because regime theory that focuses on state-centric and issue-specific mechanisms cannot fit all aspects of environmental cooperation in Northeast Asia into its simple analytical frame.

Puzzles remain, however, in analyzing environmental governance in Northeast Asia. What are the main factors in governance formation and persistence? The institutionalization trend of international environmental governance has corresponded with two advances in natural and social sciences concerning causality of environmental problems and transnational consensus on policy options (Tolba and El-Kholy 1992: 605–644). Knowledge constitutes the basic foundation of environmental governance by presenting an elaborate picture of a new issue to be governed. As the content of knowledge shapes states' perception of environmental issues and affects their preference regarding internationally coordinated actions, it is also crucial to examine the heterogeneity of knowledge among states. It is not knowledge, however, but the interplay of national interests that shapes the main course of governance. As the purpose of creating a governance mechanism is to alter the socioeconomic practices in participating countries, the evolution of the governance process inevitably facilitates political negotiation and bargaining practices among different national interests (Sprinz and Vaahtoranta 1994: 79; Zartman 1997: 58–60). As a result, the process of international governance illustrates that knowledge and national interest are dominant factors in the institutionalization of governance.

Another puzzle is, What role do nonstate actors play in formal mechanisms of governance? The role of nonstate actors, international organizations, and nongovernmental organizations (NGOs) in environmental governance has substantially expanded during the past few decades. They are particularly effective in creating new agendas, diffusing new knowledge, and mobilizing political forces for new governance (Princen, Finger, and Manno 1995: 47–51; Young 1993: 146). Having considered that the serious environmental situation in Northeast Asia cannot be ameliorated by state actors alone but requires active involvement of all stakeholders, it is critical to test nonstate actor roles in regional governance.

ENVIRONMENTAL GOVERNANCE IN NORTHEAST ASIA

The environmental deterioration of regional marine and atmospheric common pool resources calls on countries in the region to pursue urgent collective actions that are not only desirable but essential if solutions to these problems are to be found and implemented. The heterogeneity of political, socioeconomic, and other characteristics of current domestic environmental issues among the countries, however, has prevented effective collaboration on common pool resource management and cooperation on a range of environmental issues. In addition, bilateralism has dominated both political and economic relations in Northeast Asia, which has also contributed to the deferment of regional governance on environmental issues.

Changes in international relations after the Cold War and rapid integration of regional trade and economies since the early 1990s, however, have allowed the region to explore a common understanding of regional environmental issues. In particular, the United Nations Conference on Environment and Development (UNCED) in 1992 greatly contributed to the inclusion of regional environmental issues as an important intergovernmental agenda item. Furthermore, the growing importance of environmental diplomacy encouraged countries of the region to engage in processes of establishing regional environmental governance so they could be recognized as good neighbors working on environmental issues in good faith.

Current regional governance on the environment in Northeast Asia can be categorized in three areas: multilateral meetings as forums of policy dialogue, regional regimes on common resources, and NGO networking with or without governmental channels.

INSTITUTIONALIZING INTERNATIONAL COOPERATION

Regional environmental governance focuses on multilateral meetings as forums for policy dialogue on comprehensive agendas rather than as meetings for specific regime building. This direction resulted from the fact that Northeast Asian countries have been bounded by the priority to establish a common ground for understanding regional environment and cooperation. Thus multilateral meetings have been devoted to sharing information and exploring possible specific agendas, essentially acting as stepping-stones to build a comprehensive regional environmental regime in the future, in addition to the regime-building–oriented channels on marine and atmospheric environment already in existence.

The first intergovernmental dialogue on regional environment among Northeast Asian countries is the Northeast Asian Subregional Program of Environmental Cooperation (NEASPEC), in which all six countries in the region participate. This program was established in 1993 at the initiation of the South Korean government and the Economic and Social Commission for Asia and the Pacific (ESCAP), and it acquired an institutional foundation in 1996 (MoFAT 1996: 9–12). NEASPEC is a diplomatic channel and regime-oriented meeting that aims to shape a comprehensive mechanism for environmental cooperation. That characteristic is also reflected by its origin and the name of the annual meeting—Meeting of Senior Officials on Environmental Cooperation in Northeast Asia—which acts as the governing body of NEASPEC while ESCAP functions as the interim secretariat. The third meeting of NEASPEC in 1996 adopted three priority areas: energy and air pollution, ecosystem management, and capacity building (MoFAT 1998a: 231–233). In addition, with financial support from the Asian Development Bank (ADB), since 1996 the program has carried out pilot projects on training for sulfur dioxide mitigation in coal-fired power plants, demonstration of clean coal-fired power plant technology, and techniques for environmental data collection and analysis (ESCAP 2000a: 1). At the sixth conference in 2000 this program reached agreement on establishing a core fund that will be based on the voluntary contributions of participating countries and agreed to develop a comprehensive program for regional environmental cooperation by 2002. The meeting also decided to establish the Northeast Asian Center for Environmental Data and Training and the Northeast Asian Training Center for Pollution Reduction in Coal-Fired Power Plants (ESCAP 2000b: 19; MoFAT, 2000a: 9).

Whereas NEASPEC is a meeting of senior officials from ministries of foreign affairs, the North-East Asian Conference on Environmental Cooperation (NEACEC) is an annual meeting of working-level officials of environmental ministries among Northeast Asian countries except North Korea. The program was established in 1992 through annual seminars on environmental science held from 1988 to 1991 by the Japanese and South Korean governments. The program does not aim to perform an instrumental role in promoting intergovernmental projects or developing a regional environmental framework but has mainly pursued intergovernmental exchange of information and policy on national as well as regional environment affairs and common understanding of environmental governance (Taguchi 2000: 1–2). The ninth meeting of NEACEC, held in Mongolia in 2000, came to a consensus to promote the program as a policy forum in which not only government officials but also various environmental sectors—including NGOs—participate to facilitate free discussion of environmental issues (MoE 2001: 590–591).

The Environment Congress for Asia and the Pacific (ECO-Asia) is a regional meeting in which Northeast Asian countries participate but that also encompasses South Asian and Pacific countries. The Environmental Agency of Japan initiated the program in 1991 and has hosted annual meetings since that time. The immediate purpose of the first meeting was to prepare the Asia and Pacific's statement for UNCED involving further cooperation in the region (ECO-Asia 1991: 2). ECO-Asia's most important goal is to draft a long-term perspective on the environment and development in the Asia-Pacific region by examining environmental issues and their links to economic and social conditions and identifying policy options. This eight-year project, which started in 1993, is expected to provide decisionmakers in the region with a scientific basis for proper policy formulation for sustainable development and to contribute to building human and institutional capacity (ECO-Asia 1999: 1–3; Taguchi and Iwaya 2000: 21). Since the Japanese government has organized most activities and secretariat functions of ECO-Asia and the geographic scope of the program has expanded to forty countries, the program is limited as the driving force in framing Northeast Asia's environmental governance.

A new multilateral environmental meeting is the Tripartite Environment Ministers Meeting of China, Japan, and South Korea (TEMM), which had its first annual meeting in 1999. This high-level meeting is expected to play a guiding role in streamlining complicated and inefficient regional environmental channels, since the three countries are dominant actors in those channels. TEMM is the only regular ministers' meeting among the three countries. Thus TEMM has tried not to contest national interests but has sought to carry out projects that help each country's environmental interests. The first and second meetings decided to focus on cooperative activities such as developing common programs on environmental education and information sharing, organizing roundtables on the environmental industry, assisting China's activities for preventing desertification, developing mitigation measures for water pollution, and carrying out joint programs on atmospheric and marine pollution (MoE 2001: 588–590; TEMM 2000a: 1).

In addition to various levels of multilateral environmental governance, bilateral mechanisms through intergovernmental environmental agreements and cooperative activities have also emerged in the region. Government-to-government bilateral agreements for environmental cooperation were formed among countries of the region, particularly since UNCED in 1992. South Korea signed bilateral agreements with both Japan and Russia in 1993 and with China in 1994 (MoFAT 1998a: 242–248). Japan signed an environmental agreement with Russia in 1991 and one with China in 1994 (EAJ 1997: 443). China signed agreements with North Korea in 1992 and with Russia in 1994 (Choi 1995: 95; SEPA 1994).

Some Northeast Asian governments have preferred bilateral relations because it is difficult to find a comfortable niche in multilateral relations on the regional environment. This preference reflects the geopolitical situation and economic heterogeneity of the region. The countries are reluctant to choose or accept the political leadership of a neighboring country in multilateral discussions. Moreover, the countries' economic and environmental heterogeneity has puzzled governments in their quest to find common interests in collective regional activities.[11] Thus the governments have utilized bilateral relations to find common interests and cooperative activities. In particular, the Japanese government has led bilateral environmental initiatives in the region. Japan focused considerable resources on linking official development assistance (ODA) to environmental protection during the 1990s (Schreurs 1998: 209–210). The environmental sector's share of total Japanese ODA has increased substantially since the early 1990s and exceeded 25 percent of the total in 1996 (MoFA 1999a: 43). In 1991 the Japanese Ministry of International Trade and Industry also established a new form of ODA, the Green Aid Plan, which spurred environmental technology transfer to Asia. The Green Aid Plan stretched into various environmental issues and programs during the mid-1990s and has played an important role in promoting bilateral environmental relations with China and Russia (Brettell and Kawashima 1998: 98–102). For instance, in 1998 Japan pledged 10 billion yen to support a program on technical capacity building in China, conducted by the Japan-China Friendship Environmental Protection Center, a project that began in 1992 and was established as a center in 1996 (MoFA 1999b).

The South Korean government has also vigorously pursued strengthening bilateral relations with other countries. Since signing agreements with Japan in 1993 and with China in 1994, South Korea has cohosted annual meetings on environmental cooperation with each government. Through those meetings the South Korean and Chinese governments have reached consensus on conducting joint monitoring and assessment projects on marine pollution in the Yellow Sea and joint research and information exchange on acid rain (MoFAT 1997: 18–20). Bilateral activities between South Korea and Japan include annual meetings for cooperation on the protection of migratory birds and joint projects regarding endocrine-disrupting chemicals and improvement of water quality (TEMM 2000b: 11–12).

GOVERNING THE COMMON RESOURCES

Regional regimes on governing common resources, including the marine environment and the atmosphere, have evolved since the early 1990s but are still in the early stages of formation. The current mechanisms focus particularly on the two most important regional environmental issues: deterioration of marine environments in the Yellow Sea and the East Sea (Sea of Japan) and transboundary air pollution.

In 1989 the United Nations Environment Program (UNEP) proposed an action plan for protecting and managing the marine and coastal environment of the region as one of fourteen regional seas programs (Kim 1998: 2). Following a series of meetings of experts and policymakers beginning in 1991, the Northwest Pacific Action Plan (NOWPAP) was adopted at the first intergovernmental meeting held in 1994 with China, Japan, Russia, and South Korea participating. The geographic scope of NOWPAP encompasses the Yellow Sea and the East Sea (Sea of Japan).[12] This program focuses on the assessment of causes of environmental problems, the management of environmental data and information, and the establishment of preventive policy on marine pollution (MoFAT 1994: 11). To carry out these objectives, at the intergovernmental meeting in 1998 the member countries decided to establish regional activity centers within each country's existing research organization: the Marine Pollution Prevention Center in South Korea, the Marine Information and Data Center in China, the Marine Environment Monitoring Center in Russia, and the Special Monitoring and Coastal Environmental Assessment Regional Activity Center in Japan (MoFAT 2000b: 13–14). Launching the standing secretariat and trust fund has been slow. Member countries—especially Japan and South Korea—have competed to host the secretariat, the Regional Coordinating Unit, which is a fundamental prerequisite to enter the implementation phase of NOWPAP (Natori 2000: 13). Japan and South Korea finally decided to compromise and proposed a new "joint secretariat," which was approved by the UNEP Governing Council in 2001 (UNEP 2001: 11). The member countries, however, have been unable to agree on the permanent rate for each country's financial contribution, and as a result the establishment of the financial structure for the program has been delayed (MoFAT 2001).

Since marine environmental deterioration is one of the most critical regional issues, NOWPAP is regarded not only as the foundation of collective activities for marine environmental conservation but also as a stepping-stone for developing broad regional environmental governance. As participating governments and academics have pointed out, however, NOWPAP's slow progress highlights the seriousness of geopolitical impediments to regional environmental governance (Valencia 1998: 14–17).

Concern over regional acid rain has also led to multilateral mechanisms for enhancing concerted activities among Northeast Asian countries on monitoring, research, and policy implementation. Instead of shaping a regional regime, however, the countries are still building common understanding through cooperative assessments of the state of the regional atmosphere. RAINS-Asia, the World Bank–sponsored regional program on acid rain, takes precedence in current regional programs on acid rain even though it does not focus solely on Northeast Asia. Since 1991, government research organizations and academic groups in Southeast and Northeast Asian countries have carried out this program, which follows the experience and model of RAINS-Europe. RAINS-Asia aims not only to develop an acid deposition dispersion model in East Asia but also to conduct research on energy-economics analyses, ecosystem sensitivity evaluation, and proper institutional development (Hordijk, Foell, and Shah 1995: 8–9).

One intergovernmental mechanism is the Acid Deposition Monitoring Network in East Asia (EANET), which has evolved into a core multilateral mechanism on the regional acid rain issue. EANET formed as a meeting of experts at the initiation of the Environmental Agency of Japan in 1993 and encompasses Southeast and Northeast Asian countries. Since its establishment, EANET has held four expert meetings sponsored by the agency and led the way toward the adoption of a proposal for the "design of the acid deposition monitoring network in East Asia" at the expert meeting in 1997 (EANET 1997). This adoption enabled EANET to obtain the status of a formal regional institution by hosting the first intergovernmental meeting of EANET in 1998 and establishing the Interim Network Center and the Interim Scientific Advisory Group (JEQ 1998; MoFAT 1998b). The network's secretariat, to be run by UNEP, was established at the second intergovernmental meeting in 2000. It was also at that meeting that the Acid Deposition and Oxide Research Center of Japan was officially designated the Network Center to act as EANET's core body, handling all scientific and technical matters of the network (EANET 2000: 3). EANET's main activity is to monitor acid deposition in participating countries in line with standardized monitoring guidelines and technical manuals, to analyze the results and develop a report on the state of acid deposition in East Asia, and to promote technical cooperation among participating countries (Toda 2000: 2).

Whereas the geographic scope of the two programs just discussed covers all of East Asia, the Joint Research Project on Long-Range Air Pollutants (LTP) focuses on three Northeast Asian countries: China, Japan, and South Korea. This project was created through three annual tripartite meetings of officials and government institutions of the countries starting in 1995 and consists of the interim secretariat and two subworking groups on modeling and monitoring (Shim 2000: 25–26). The subworking group meeting in 1999 adopted five-year joint monitoring and modeling plans on long-range transboundary air pollutants that will monitor the pollutants by implementing emissions inventory and numerical simulations from 1999 to 2004 (TEMM 2000b: 1–2). South Korea's Ministry of Environment and its affiliate organization, the National Institute of Environmental Research (NIER), which acts as the program's secretariat, initiated the LTP to consolidate conditions for promoting a regional agreement on transboundary air pollution (MoFAT 1998a: 240). Although the program puts more emphasis on modeling than EANET does and its geographical scope is much smaller than EANET's, its relationship is competitive as a result of duplicative aspects of covering the same area and overlapping membership of the three most important state actors—China, Japan, and South Korea—in Northeast Asia's environmental governance.

Moreover, a decision at the sixth meeting of NEASPEC, held in Seoul in 2000, appended a new mechanism on governing Northeast Asia's atmosphere. At the meeting the ADB announced its decision to provide financial assistance to the Northeast Asian Center for Environmental Data and Training, a core component of NEASPEC's Environmental Monitoring, Data Collection, Comparability, and Analysis Project (ESCAP 2000c: 5–6). The center was established at NIER, which had prepared to host the project since its endorsement at the fourth meeting in 1998. The project and center are designed to collect and analyze emissions data, identify the needs of technical and institutional capacity building, and conduct activities to enhance data comparability among the countries (ESCAP 2000a: 2–3). The NEASPEC meeting also raised concerns that the project endorsement and establishment of the center might duplicate existing mechanisms (ESCAP 2000c: 11). Having considered this issue, NIER proposed that the center should cover data not only on air pollution but also on water pollution, which NEASPEC accepted (NIER 2000: 5)—even though adding a responsibility does not resolve the issue of duplication.

BUILDING NGO NETWORKS AND EPISTEMIC COMMUNITIES

NGOs have emerged as important actors in international environmental governance and have been increasingly incorporated into the previously "state-only" governance activities since the 1980s (Raustiala 1997: 721–723). In particular, they play an active role by providing information, linking local environmental issues and the global environmental agenda, and harnessing transnational linkages (Levy et al. 1993: 399; Princen 1994: 38–41). This enables observers to proclaim that "NGOs actually become nascent forms of transnational governance" (Rosenau 1995: 23), and further "it is possible that they are emerging as alternative forms of political authority" (Conca 1995: 6).

The processes of Northeast Asia's environmental governance have revealed, however, that the role of NGOs in regional governance is still in its infancy. The limited role of NGOs reflects a combination of domestic influences common to each country, only one or two decades of NGOs' existence as a result of political conditions that restricted environmental activism in most countries of the region, the overwhelming local and domestic environmental issues preoccupying NGOs, little experience in international activities, language barriers, and limited financial and human resources for NGOs (Yu 1999: 7). Japanese NGOs have been free from some of these impediments, but that has not guaranteed active participation in shaping regional governance since activism also requires vigorous partnership. In addition, the short history of international activity–oriented environmental groups that emerged in the early 1990s, and the dispersed and grassroots-level characteristics of Japanese NGOs, also explain their limited role in regional governance (Lee 1998: 152–165).

South Korean environmental NGOs began to appear during the liberalization from dictatorial governments in the mid-1980s, and their organizational basis and scope of activities have expanded greatly since the early 1990s (Lee et al. 1999: 232–235). In particular, some groups—including the Korean Federation of Environmental Movements and Green Korea United—became the biggest environmental NGOs in Asia and at the same time gained substantial political influence in domestic environmental issues. Their activities in regional environmental issues, however, are only at the beginning stage despite having accumulated experience in international activism since UNCED.

The history and activity of Chinese NGOs are very limited. Chinese NGOs that are not government-organized groups but are analogous to Western-style NGOs have emerged since the mid-1990s. In particular, Friends of Nature and Global Village Environmental Culture Institute of Beijing, which mainly carry out programs on environmental education and nature conservation, are prominent organizations and quickly made outreach efforts to international society (Chu 1999; Knup 1997: 12–13). Their outreach, however, has been driven from the position of recipients of international assistance, not necessarily as actors in regional environmental governance (Liao 2000; 4).

The disadvantaged history of NGOs in Northeast Asian countries imposes constraints on carrying out substantial joint programs to institutionalize regional governance while they are still forming loose networks among themselves. The Northeast Asian governments also recognize the necessity of NGO participation in state-initiated mechanisms. The ninth meeting of NEACEC in 2000 agreed to promote NGOs' participation, which is important for NEACEC's future as a central, open-ended environmental policy forum in Northeast Asia (MoE 2001: 591). The vision statement of the sixth meeting of NEASPEC in 2000 also noted the importance of NGOs' involvement in that mechanism (ESCAP 2000c: 20).

Currently, the only standing environmental NGO network in Northeast Asia is the Atmosphere Action Network East Asia (AANEA), which consists of NGOs in China, Japan, Korea, Mongolia, Hong Kong, Taiwan, and Russia and was established in 1995 with financial assistance from the Japanese Fund for Global Environment (AANEA 1997: 105). The main objectives of AANEA are enhancing common understanding of the state of air pollution and climate change in the region, linking Northeast Asian NGOs and other regional NGO networks on transboundary air pollution and climate changes, and promoting cross-sectional cooperation for improving the atmospheric environment (Park 2000: 43; Yoo 1999: 8). Since its inception, the network has held annual meetings that present each country's atmospheric situation and NGOs' activities on the issue. The network has not conducted joint projects, but it did carry out a survey on the atmospheric environment and related policy in each country (AANEA 1997: 119–166). Through a series of international meetings, the network has played a significant role in developing NGOs' common positions on regional and global atmospheric issues and at the same time mobilizing participating NGOs' domestic efforts in each country.

The role of epistemic communities, which are "transnational networks of knowledge-based communities" (Hass 1995: 41), has evolved during various regional and global regime formations by providing authoritative consensual knowledge to regime actors and diffusing new ideas into society (Breitmeier 1997: 91; Hass and Hass 1995: 260). Since information has increasingly become a central feature of most international environmental governance (Krueger 2000: 6), epistemic communities can play a decisive role in regime formation or implementation depending on the political and technical characteristics of the subject of the regime (Vogler 1995: 204–206). The role of epistemic communities in environmental governance in Northeast Asia has not been very visible, but the participation of experts in intergovernmental meetings has influenced the expansion of consensual knowledge among bureaucrats of Northeast Asian countries (Kim 1999: 78). There are currently not only various academic meetings but also a growing number of joint research projects and regular meetings among experts in the mechanisms of bilateral and multilateral agreements among China, Japan, and South Korea in particular.

The Northeast Asia and North Pacific Environmental Forum is an important driving force for building epistemic communities in Northeast Asia. The forum was conceived at the Seoul International Environmental Symposium in 1992 as a Northeast Asia environmental network encompassing China, Japan, Mongolia, South Korea, and Russia. At the next meeting in Russia, held in 1993, the forum decided to include U.S. organizations as members with the commitment of the Tokyo office of the Asia Foundation—a U.S. organization—to support sustainability of the network (Han 1999: 70; Konigsberg 1994: 3–4). Since then the forum has held annual meetings in each member country. The forum became a standing network of participating experts at its the sixth meeting in 1998, which set up an executive committee consisting of a representative from each country and a permanent secretariat at the Institute for Global Environmental Strategies—a Japanese governmental body in Kanagawa (Inman 1998: 2).

The main purposes of the forum are linking environmental leaders in the region, strengthening NGOs' capacity, and promoting constructive engagement among NGOs, national and local governments, and business (Asia Foundation 1997: 1). The forum's meetings have particularly addressed migratory birds, multinational environmental cooperation, and biodiversity issues in Northeast Asia. Its Khabarovsk meeting in 1997 emphasized its function of developing strategies for ecosystem management in the transboundary areas of China and Russia and of North and South Korea (Asia Foundation 1997: 3). The series of meetings illustrates that the forum has provided academics with vital opportunities to establish links, but either its aims need to be transformed or the scope of its agenda has to be streamlined because the forum has neither successfully facilitated participation of NGOs nor carried out joint programs for domestic NGO capacity building (Asia Foundation 1996: 1–14).

The East Asian Biosphere Reserve Network (EABRN), a United Nations Educational, Scientific, and Cultural Organization (UNESCO)–initiated network, is also an important platform for building an epistemic community for ecosystem conservation in Northeast Asia. The inception of this network resulted from two meetings of the East Asian Biosphere Reserves cooperative scientific study in 1994 and the adoption of "Statutes of the EABRN" at its third meeting in 1995 (UNESCO 1994: 1; K. Kim 1999: 244). UNESCO, with a proposal from South Korea and support from other Northeast Asian countries to strengthen cooperation in implementing the action plan for a biosphere reserve, launched a cooperative scientific study program and prepared a draft plan for the establishment of EABRN (Ishwaran 1995: ii–1). In addition, UNESCO's Jakarta offices and its national committees in Northeast Asian countries have played pivotal roles in facilitating the network's annual meetings and activities. This role is attributed to UNESCO's initiation of the concept of a biosphere reserve in 1974 and its organization of regional and international networks of the reserve beginning in 1976 (UNESCO 1995: iii–1).

Since its inauguration, EABRN has carried out various activities focusing on ecotourism in biosphere reserve areas and transnational cooperation for conservation of transborder biosphere reserves and has functioned as an effective channel for exchanging information, comparing each country's experience and developing common guidelines on reserve management (K. Kim 1999: 242–244).

The regular meetings and activities show that EABRN has become a core base in building an ecological epistemic community by regularly exchanging information, conducting joint research, and enhancing shared principles and beliefs. The network's unique status has facilitated North Korea's practical participation, which indicates its meaningful position in regional environmental governance. Comparative research on EABRN activities also reveals, however, that the network has a long way to go to fulfill its role in offering comprehensive views and substantial direction for conservation of the biosphere reserve. In particular, there is great need to promote more effective joint studies and sufficient information exchange and to upgrade EABRN's loose consultative status within UNESCO programs. Moreover, the network needs to launch human resource development programs if it aims to contribute significantly to improving reserve management (K. Kim 1999: 254–265).

ASSESSING REGIONAL ENVIRONMENTAL GOVERNANCE

Although emerging multi- and bilateral environmental cooperation mechanisms in Northeast Asia have achieved some progress in enhancing understanding of regional environmental problems, they reveal great limitations in promoting effective national and regional responses to those problems. In particular, the current mechanisms lack a sense of ownership from participating countries and exclude wide participation of experts and institutions. The limitations are rooted in part in the history of deep and abiding political tensions between countries, in different levels of socioeconomic development that account for differing dominant environmental issues in each country, and in the poor capacity of environmental institutional systems in most countries. As a result, the various multi- and bilateral systems have not achieved visible outcomes in developing and implementing collective actions to mitigate regional environmental problems. Slow and sometimes embittered negotiation of the mechanisms clearly unveils such causes of minimal progress in shaping and implementing regional environmental governance.

GAPS IN POLITICAL INTERESTS

Northeast Asian countries have displayed a wide gulf of political interests among themselves. In particular, Japan and South Korea, two major initiators of the regional environmental program, have exposed political differences during the negotiation and initiation of regional mechanisms.

Japan has been reluctant to be involved in multilateral mechanisms in Northeast Asia but has pursued a vigorous role in building broad regional cooperation, which includes not only Northeast Asia but also Southeast Asia and the Pacific. This preference is based in part on Northeast Asia's geopolitical situation in which subregional multilateral cooperation (i.e., Northeast Asia as the subregion) poses limits on Japan in exercising its political leadership while at the same time Japan is expected to be a main financial contributor to regional environmental programs and a source of technology transfer. Thus bilateral or Japanese-initiated multilateral cooperation extending beyond the subregion provides comfortable leadership and a more visible role in intergovernmental environmental cooperation (MoFAT 1998a: 253; Valencia 1996: 16).

South Korea, however, a middle-power country located between adjacent political and economic giants, has pursued exclusive multilateral environmental cooperation for the subregion since its initiation of NEASPEC. The political motivation of this preference is also reflected by geopolitical circumstance, which is that environmental cooperation allows the government to act as a visible leader, as an initiator or mediator in a way it may lack in other domains of international relations in Northeast Asia.[13]

China actively participates in multilateral and bilateral discussions of the regional environment but has not shown an intention to exercise a leadership role. Moreover, China is extremely sensitive about the use of terms such as *transboundary, standardization,* and *strategy* in the texts of regional mechanisms because those terms have the potential to formalize China's negative role in the regional environment and the coordination of national environmental policies (ESCAP 2000b: 6; MoFAT 1996: 27). China, however, feels the necessity to commit to regional governance to a certain extent. China's dual position is based in part on the fact that regional governance gives China the chance to receive financial and technical assistance that is imperative to combat domestic environmental deterioration (Sinton 1996: 3; Wu 2000: 2).

The founding process of EANET clearly illustrates the geopolitics of institutionalizing regional activities. Even though EANET was formed as a multilateral body, the Japanese government has dominated the development process by hosting all experts' meetings and financing EANET activities (Toda 2000: 183–184). Moreover, the government drafted the design of the network at informal expert meetings organized and dominated by the Environmental Agency of Japan and its own experts, with the design then presented to the first intergovernmental meeting of EANET (EAJ 1997; Triendl 1998: 1). This process led other governments to officially express suspicion about Japan's political motivation and to emphasize "the need to enhance full transparency in organization and operation of the network."[14]

The problem of one party–dominant development of multilateral mechanisms also influenced the Chinese government's decision to participate in the network not as a member but as an observer party (MoFAT 1998c). The Chinese government finally announced its participation as a gift at the 1998 summit meeting when President Jiang Zemin visited Japan (Yonemoto 2000: 16). South Korea also tried to retard the official launch of EANET because the government had an imperative need to clarify the relationship between EANET and Korean government–initiated regional programs so as not to lose its institutional credibility (MoFAT 2000c: 1–2).

The geopolitics of regional governance results not only in slow progress in institutionalizing regional actions but also in duplication of activities by establishing different channels for similar tasks because of limited financial and human capacity. States and international organizations are unanimous in recognizing that duplication wastes time and resources and is unlikely to guarantee sound competition. Thus they unhesitatingly accept the need for streamlining current multilateral channels (ESCAP 2000c: 11; Han 1999: 88), but they are indecisive about entering into dialogue on changes required for effective governance.

LACK OF CONSENSUAL KNOWLEDGE AND COMMON INTERESTS

Lack of common interests among Northeast Asian countries has also played a critical role in posing obstacles to regional environmental cooperation. Moreover, this issue occurs among not only diplomats but also scientific communities in the countries. Researchers represent different perceptions and knowledge of regional environmental status, with their results often justifying their own country's political position on regional environmental issues and confirming the existing lack of consensual knowledge. As mentioned previously, these gaps in understanding of environmental issues in the region result from the heterogeneity of economic, political, and environmental conditions among the Northeast Asian countries. Heterogeneity, however, is a double-edged sword. It can both promote and discourage intergovernmental cooperation through complementary effects (Martin 1995: 72). Unfortunately, heterogeneity among Northeast Asian countries has played more negative than positive roles in environmental governance, in particular by encouraging a lack of common interests.

The past experience of regional conventions on transboundary air pollution in Europe and North America shows that scientific consensus on ecological, social, and economic impacts of air pollution on source and adjacent countries is critical to overcome political impediments to the establishment of regional programs (Levy 1993: 76). Northeast Asia seriously lacks consensus among countries on regional issues, including acid rain and marine environment, which again illustrates the causes of scant development of regional programs. This problem has manifested not only in the political domain or in institutional mechanisms for regional cooperation but also in scientific understanding of the magnitude of current regional environmental problems.

As an example, the research results on source-receptor relationships of acid deposition in Northeast Asia show substantial differences between Japanese and Chinese academics. Their calculations of Chinese-originated long-range air pollutants to Japan's overall acid deposition present markedly different results. Experts at the Chinese Academy of Science (Huang et al. 1995: 1925) estimate that China accounts for only 3.5 percent of Japan's total sulfur deposition. In contrast, Japanese experts (Ichikawa and Fujita 1995: 1931) conclude that China is responsible for half of the anthropogenic wet sulfur deposition. Various research projects confirm that wet sulfate deposition accounts for 60–70 percent of total deposition in Japan (Carmichael and Arndt 1997: 7). Thus the results of Chinese and Japanese research show the extensive knowledge gap and the difficulty in building consensual knowledge on transboundary air pollution issues in Northeast Asia. Furthermore, conclusions from other Chinese and Japanese research also strongly represent this difference (Brettell and Kawashima 1998: 109). In addition, China refused to acknowledge the outcome of RAINS-Asia work, justifying its stance by pointing out methodological problems (Shim 2000: 22). The RAINS-Asia model was expected to build consensual knowledge on the state of regional acid rain and concluded that China is responsible for 17 percent of the acid deposition in Japan.

The lack of consensual knowledge is again tied to the limited experience of academic exchange that results from economic, social, and political heterogeneities among the countries. Despite these heterogeneities, it is possible to have a positive perspective on building consensual knowledge. Joint research programs that have been mushrooming with the evolution of environmental governance will work to stitch the knowledge gap. A great need also exists for building not only consensus on scientific issues but also broad regional perspectives on the direction of regional environmental governance among ecological epistemic communities and NGOs. Building consensual perspectives will be critical in reducing the states' wide disparity on the direction and required level of institutionalization.

SHARING FINANCIAL BURDENS

A lack of consensus on sharing financial burdens has also retarded the development and implementation of regional environmental cooperation. Discussions of ways to finance national and regional environmental investment have explored the possibility of establishing a trust fund or a regional environment and development bank (Hirono 1998: 10–11; Zarsky 1995: 126). During the negotiation processes of regional environmental programs, the countries argued about national financial contributions to those programs. Regional environmental programs have received financial support from UN organizations and international financial organizations including the United Nations Development Program, ESCAP, the ADB, and the World Bank to implement cooperative projects (ESCAP 1998a; Hordijk, Foell, and Shah 1995: 8). This financial support, however, constitutes only a portion of the amount the region needs to implement and strengthen regional environmental governance.

The most significant issue in financing regional environmental activities is the gap in understanding the national financial responsibility for regional programs. The negotiation processes for national distributions of the

NOWPAP trust fund clearly revealed each country's diplomatic maneuver on sharing financial burdens, significantly impeding the program's progress. The Japanese government argued that the "principle of equal responsibility and equal contribution" among participating countries should be applied for sharing the financial burden. In contrast, the Chinese government stressed the "principle of voluntary contribution and of common but differentiated responsibility," which would be applied according to the different economic development stages of the member countries. South Korea compromised by suggesting consideration of "common participation and shared responsibility" and "capacity to pay" combined. Russia preferred voluntary payment and an option to pay in kind (UNEP 1996: 4, 1998: 4). The countries have repeated their positions at most regional meetings. Although they came to a tentative decision on each state's contribution by combining a 5 percent basic contribution for all countries and an additional 3 to 20 percent contribution depending on each country's economic condition,[15] the total contribution makes up only 63 percent of the targeted amount for the fund (MoFAT 2000b: 12; UNEP 1996: 5). Russia, however, was unable to make any financial contribution during the 1990s. Japan made no payments in 1998 because of its budgetary situation (UNEP 2000: 4).

NEASPEC also represents the countries' reluctance to share financial burdens. NEASPEC's activities have faced financial constraints because they have mainly functioned on a project basis, with limited funding from the ADB. As a result, NEASPEC has experienced delays or renunciation of the implementation of some endorsed projects and cannot progress beyond its current activities (ESCAP 1998b: 8, 2000d: 5). Thus the establishment of a trust fund or tentative "Northeast Asia Environmental Cooperation Fund" has been an important item at the annual meetings of NEASPEC since 1996. At the 2000 meeting, however, the governments were only able to agree on the establishment of a core fund with voluntary contributions from the governments, international organizations, and donor countries. This agreement was reached despite the governments' recognition of the low possibility of outside financial assistance for regional cooperation (ESCAP 2000b: 4). The countries know that without demonstrating a strong commitment to their own region it is impractical to expect outsiders to make financial contributions to Northeast Asia's governance while the region contains the world's top donor country—Japan—and a new donor member, South Korea (ESCAP 1999: 10; Yang 1998).

LIMITED ROLE OF INTERNATIONAL ORGANIZATIONS AND NGOS

The processes of international environmental governance have proved that the quality of executive leadership is a critical determinant in shaping collective actions (Underdal 1998: 103). In addition, an implicit or explicit consensual leadership exercised by a certain country in the region is also recognized as key to successful regional cooperation (Hass 1998:4). The gap in political interests and lack of regional cooperative experience among Northeast Asian countries impedes leadership. This situation has caused Northeast Asian countries to rely on international organizations to create regional environmental governance.

The role of international organizations in the formative and operative stages of environmental governance includes setting agendas for new governance, distributing technical information, drafting normative statements and rules, facilitating negotiations, promoting national capacity, and monitoring implementation (Breitmeier 1997: 93–95; Peterson 1998: 416). International organizations in Northeast Asia have played these roles since the early 1990s. ESCAP and UNEP in particular have been important initiators or mediators in setting agendas, guiding negotiations, and drafting frameworks for shaping current regional governance.

The role of international organizations, however, has not been visible as basic building blocks for regional governance beyond the early stage of setting agendas and facilitating initial governmental meetings. Their limited political and instrumental leadership capacity has not allowed these organizations to press the countries to be active in regional governance, even if it is required.[16] In particular, international organizations have not helped to promote efficient utilization of limited financial resources or to prevent the region from duplicating projects. Instead they have kept a low-key profile, their activities not going beyond distributing basic information and assisting intergovernmental meetings.

The discussions on strengthening NEASPEC can serve as an example to explain the limited capacity and internal dilemma of international organizations. ESCAP implicitly forced participating countries to set up their own secretariat and trust fund, since all countries unanimously acknowledged the lack of continuity and efficient coordination in the current NEASPEC mechanism. ESCAP faced severe financial and human resource problems in continuing as an interim secretariat as a result of organizational reductions mandated by the UN reform (ESCAP 2000d: 6). Thus ESCAP proposed new institutional and financial mechanisms at its Moscow meeting in 1998. The proposal contained new options for establishing a standing organization or changing the membership of NEASPEC by including local governments and NGOs. ESCAP, however, only succeeded in blocking productive discussions, and the countries opted to stay with the current mechanism. This failure resulted in part from the organization's subjective interpretation of current conditions and new options without adequately measuring the participating countries' positions (MoFAT 1998d: 144–147), which illustrates its low capacity in instrumental leadership.

Bear in mind, however, that the limited role of international organizations results from more than internal factors. Many external factors also restrict their roles. In particular, the interplay of tense geopolitics in environmental governance and the nominal alliances with NGOs and epistemic communities have not helped their performance.

Although NGOs and experts have created and operated their own forms of regional governance, their involvement in formal mechanisms has been extremely limited. Those who might be regarded as members of existing or potential epistemic communities have been involved in formal mechanisms, but their participation has been mostly as resource persons or advisers upon request of their governments, not as representatives of epistemic communities. The situation for NGOs is little different. Most formal mechanisms have no channels for NGO participation and have not conducted activities that require input from NGOs. Although meetings of both NEASPEC and NEACEC in 2000 decided to promote NGOs' participation in their mechanisms, the meetings in 2001 did not meet the provisions. NEASPEC made no effort to bring NGOs to its meeting. NEACEC invited NGOs and arranged discussions on the role of NGOs in regional environmental cooperation as a main agenda topic of the meeting. Only the South Korean government invited active NGOs, however, so the meeting did not facilitate meaningful input from active NGO communities in Northeast Asia generally (Kim 2001). This situation also derives from the fact that formal mechanisms are not equipped with sufficient space for NGOs because most are still at the formative stage, which focuses on intergovernmental discussions and negotiations. In addition, the current state of NGO networking in Northeast Asia is not strong enough to demand a niche in the mechanisms.

CONCLUSION

As we have seen, Northeast Asia has experienced the emergence and evolution of various forms of multi- and bilateral environmental governance since the early 1990s. The governance mechanisms have made different degrees of progress in institutionalization. Some mechanisms that contain specific scope of actions—EANET and NOWPAP—have moved further than broad policy forums such as NEASPEC and NEACEC by moving toward establishment of organizational and financial foundations. Nevertheless, most mechanisms have suffered from similar symptoms: significant gaps in national interest, lack of financial sources and consensual knowledge, and nominal roles of nonstate actors. It is also important to bear in mind that the ultimate purpose of institutionalization of ecological interdependence is not the establishment of institutional mechanisms overseeing intergovernmental or regional environmental issues but the strengthening of a foundation that carries out effective implementation of environmental activities.

Effective implementation implies bringing about not only behavioral changes of actors through governance but also substantial amelioration of environmental quality. In that context, regional governance has a long way to go.

Successful stories of environmental governance in other regions have illustrated that the promotion of effective regional environmental governance can be achieved without eradicating these overwhelming symptoms and existing heterogeneities but by altering each participant's incentives. Basic provisions for the alteration of incentives in regional environmental governance in Northeast Asia could include the incremental performance of activities targeted to assist each country's domestic environmental needs that contain regional aspects. The creation of multidimensional consensual leadership is also important in altering national interests because it mitigates the current political conflict by helping to eliminate dominant leadership and by distributing leadership to each participant according to an environmental area and the participant's capacity and enthusiasm. Furthermore, active participation of NGOs and epistemic communities in regional governance is crucial not only to urge states to implement and comply with activities defined by certain governance but also to promote desirable norms and principles of regional governance in Northeast Asia.

NOTES

1. This definition is based on consideration of the geographic proximity to neighboring countries and the interaction between local pollution and the regional environment, in particular the source-receptor relationship of transboundary air pollutants. Hayes and Zarsky (1994: 283), however, define the Inner Mongolian Autonomous Region and Heilongjiang, Jilin, and Liaoning as China's northeast provinces.

2. Certain countries are excluded from the objective of this analysis according to the scope of environmental issues, but the six countries' central governments were subjected to this research because they represent the political authority of the members of the region.

3. The institutional genesis of this project is rooted in a meeting of international specialists on acid rain in Bangkok, 1989, recognizing potential regional environmental problems resulting from the massive growth of fossil fuel use in Asia. Through various discussions the project was developed using a model and experiences from acid rain assessment in Europe (Hordijk, Foell, and Shah 1995: 7).

4. The calculated source-receptor relationship shows great differences according to models and researchers, even though the predictions of total deposition are consistent between them. Huang and colleagues (1995: 1925) estimated that China accounts for only 3.5 percent of Japan's total sulfur deposition. In contrast, the estimation of Ichikawa and Fujita (1995: 1931) concluded that China is responsible for half of the wet deposit.

5. According to research of the National Environmental Institute of South Korea, China was responsible for about 12–17 percent of deposited sulfate in South Korean territory during the four years after 1995. The level was 39 percent when there was a northwesterly wind (*Chosun Daily*, 28 April 1999).

6. This proximity causes certain areas in each country to suffer from neighbor-produced sulfate more than from their own emissions. Such is Kyushu-Okinawa, the southern part of Japan, which receives slightly more acid deposition from Korea than it emits (Carmichael and Arndt 1997: 5).

7. China began a comprehensive survey of acid deposition in 1982 and currently operates monitoring facilities in eighty-four major cities (SEPA 1998).

8. The name of this sea is an important political issue in the region because of the absence of international agreements. Japan calls the sea "Sea of Japan." South Korea calls it "East Sea." For North Korea it is "East Sea of Korea." As a result, scholarly literature and international organizations' documents on regional environmental issues use both names. The National Geographic Society had named the sea the Sea of Japan but decided to use both names starting in 2001 for its updated map because the organization "recognized . . . the term Sea of Japan was legitimately disputed" (National Geographic Society 2001).

9. The operation of illegal fisheries by Chinese vessels in South Korean territory rapidly increased during the 1990s, with estimates of over 3,000 cases from 1988 to 1999 (*Chosun Daily*, 26 April 1999). Tensions between South Korean vessels and the Japanese government also became common. Forty-eight South Korean vessels were captured by the Japanese government between 1994 and 1996 (*Chosun Daily*, 8 July 1997). Moreover, in 1998 a few Chinese and North Korean fishery workers were shot by the Russian Navy during armed conflicts caused by their illegal operation in Russian territory (*Chosun Daily*, 1 June 1998).

10. This definition has been widely quoted in scholarly discussions of regimes, but some question whether it is precise enough to preclude disputes about a proper description of any given regime (Hasenclever, Mayer, and Rittberger 1997: 12). For example, Keohane (1989: 4) avoids using the complex apparatus of principles, norms, rules, and procedures and puts all terms into the single concept of "rules."

11. This problem has appeared in most regional discussions, including NOWPAP and EANET (Kim 1998: 4; Triendl 1998: 1; Yoon and Lee 1998: 85).

12. Actually, the official geographic scope of the program defines seas from about 121 to 143 degrees east longitude and from approximately 52 to 33 degrees north latitude. During the initial phase of NOWPAP, the program encountered strong disputes over naming the geographic scope of NOWPAP between Japan and South Korea, and it took five years to resolve the issue. The key point involved naming one of the two regional seas either the Sea of Japan or the East Sea because no international agreement on a geographic name exists for this sea, which is acceptable to all countries in the region. After much dispute between the two countries, the member countries decided to specify the geographic scope of NOWPAP in terms of longitude and latitude instead of names (UNEP 1996: 3; Kim 1998: 3).

13. The political motivation is explicitly explained by the Ministry of Foreign Affairs and Trade, South Korea, in an official publication, *Environmental Diplomacy* (MoFAT 1998a). The South Korean government also hosted the first Tripartite Environmental Ministers Meeting of China, Japan, and Korea in January 1999 (TEMM 2000a).

14. Statement from a South Korean delegate about the Japanese proposal during the first meeting (Triendl 1998).

15. The contribution rate is 25 percent for Japan, 3 percent for China, 20 percent for South Korea, and 10 percent for Russia. North Korea is a member country and participated in the preparatory process for NOWPAP, but it has not participated in any intergovernmental meeting since its inception and thus has no condition of financial contribution.

16. Instrumental leadership is "based on authority as well as engineering skill and capacity" (Andresen and Wettestad 1995: 130). During the negotiations for establishing the Mediterranean Action Plan, UNEP successfully exercised this leadership by not only allocating financial sources and disseminating information but also designing politically feasible solutions (Skjærseth 1990: 328).

REFERENCES

Acid Deposition Monitoring Network in East Asia (EANET). 1997. "Summary of the Fourth Expert Meeting on Acid Deposition Monitoring Network in East Asia" <http://www.eic.or.jp/eanet/e/emad/summ04.html> (accessed 15 November 1999).

———. 2000. "Report of the Meeting of the Sixth Working Group Meeting on the EANET." EANET/WG 6/9, Niigata, Japan.

Andresen, Steinar, and Jorgen Wettestad. 1995. "International Problem-solving Effectiveness: The Oslo Project Story So Far." *International Environmental Affairs* 7, 2: 127–149.

Asia Foundation. 1996. "Participants in Past NEANPEF Conferences." Internal memorandum, Tokyo.

———. 1997. "Amur River Workshop: Transboundary Environmental Challenges and Opportunities." Internal memorandum, Tokyo.

Atmosphere Action Network East Asia (AANEA). 1997. *Proceedings and Report of Workshop on Atmospheric Pollution in East Asia, 25–27 January.* Hong Kong: Conservancy Association.

Breitmeier, Helmut. 1997. "International Organizations and the Creation of Environmental Regimes." In Oran Young, ed., *Global Governance: Drawing Insights From the Environmental Experience.* Cambridge: MIT Press.

Brettel, Anna, and Yasuko Kawashima. 1998. "Sino-Japanese Relations on Acid Rain." In Miranda A. Schreurs and Dennis Pirages, eds., *Ecological Security in Northeast Asia.* Seoul: Yonsei University Press.

Carmichael, Gregory R., and Richard Arndt. 1997. "Baseline Assessment of Acid Deposition in Northeast Asia" <http://www.nautilus.org/papers/energy> (accessed 10 January 2000).

Cho, Leejay. 1999. "Regional Economic Cooperation and Integration in Northeast Asia for the Twenty-first Century." Paper presented at the Conference on

Economic Cooperation in Northeast Asia: Challenges and Opportunities, Ulaanbaatar, Mongolia, 9 June.

Choi, Byungdoo. 1995. "Environmental Cooperation Between Korea and Neighboring Countries." *Environment and Life* 7: 84–97 (in Korean).

Chu, Jangmin. 1999. "Protection Movement of the Friends of Nature." *Environmental Movement* (June): 69 (in Korean).

Conca, Ken. 1995. "Global Environmental Governance: Causes, Components and Consequences." Occasional paper 6, Harrison Program on the Future Global Agenda <http://www.bsos.umd.edu/harrison/papers/paper06.htm> (accessed 6 October 1999).

EAJ (Environment Agency of Japan). 1997. *White Paper 1997*. Tokyo: EAJ.

ECO-Asia. 1991. "Environmental Congress for Asia and the Pacific: Declaration and Report" <http://www.ecoasia.org/congress/1991jul.htm> (accessed 17 November 1999).

———. 1999. "Chair's Summary of the Eighth Environmental Congress for Asia and the Pacific" <http://www.ecoasia.org/congress/1999sep.html> (accessed 17 November 1999).

Economic and Social Commission for Asia and the Pacific (ESCAP). 1998a. "Northeast Asia Sub-regional Program for Environmental Cooperation" <http://www.unescap.org/enrd/environ/neaspec> (accessed 17 November 1999).

———. 1998b. "Report of the Meeting of Senior Officials on Environmental Cooperation in Northeast Asia." ENR/SO/ECNA(4)/Rep.

———. 1999. "Implementation of the Framework of the NEASPEC: Institutional and Financial Mechanisms." ENR/SO/ECNA(5)/3, Bangkok.

———. 2000a. "Programme Planning and Implementation: Endorsement of New Projects and Assessment of Implementation of Ongoing Projects." ENR/SO/ECNA(6)/2, Bangkok.

———. 2000b. "Report of the Preparatory Meeting for the Sixth Meeting of Senior Officials on Environmental Cooperation in Northeast Asia." ENR/SO/ECNA(6)/Rep, Bangkok.

———. 2000c. "Report of the Preparatory Meeting for the Fifth Meeting of Senior Officials on Environmental Cooperation in Northeast Asia." ENR/SO/ECNA(6)/Rep, Bangkok.

———. 2000d. "The Vision for Environmental Cooperation in Northeast Asia: Focusing on the Role of NEASPEC in a New Era." Paper presented at the Sixth Meeting of Senior Officials on Environmental Cooperation in Northeast Asia, Seoul, 3–10 March.

Finkelstein, Lawrence S. 1995. "What Is Global Governance?" *Global Governance* 1: 367–372.

Flavin, Christopher, and Seth Dunn. 1997. *Rising Sun, Gathering Winds: Policies to Stabilize the Climate and Strengthen Economies*. Washington, D.C.: Worldwatch Institute.

Guan, Daoming. 2000. "Marine Environmental Quality and Marine Environmental Protection in China." In *Proceedings of International Workshop on Environmental Peace in East Asia*, 5–7 July. Seoul: Korean National Commission for UNESCO.

Han, Taekhwan. 1999. "Current Status of and Long-Term Vision for Environmental Cooperation Mechanisms in Northeast Asia." Paper presented at the Expert Group Meeting on Environmental Cooperation Mechanisms in Northeast Asia, in Particular NEASPEC and NOWPAP, Seoul, 10–11 November.

———. 2000. "Current Status of and Long-term Vision for Environmental Cooperation Mechanisms in Northeast Asia." In *Proceedings of the Expert Group Meeting on Environmental Cooperation Mechanisms in Northeast Asia, in Particular NEASPEC and NOWPAP,* 10–11 November. Seoul: Ministry of Foreign Affairs and Trade.

Hasenclever, Andreas, Peter Mayer, and Volker Rittberger. 1997. *Theories of International Regimes.* Cambridge: Cambridge University Press.

Hass, Peter M. 1995. "Obtaining International Environmental Protection Through Epistemic Consensus." In Ian Rowlands and Malory Greene, eds., *Global Environmental Change and International Relations.* Hampshire: Macmillan.

———. 1998. "Prospects for Effective Marine Governance in the Northwest Pacific Region." Paper presented at the ESENA Workshop, 11–12 July. Tokyo: Nautilus Institute.

Hass, Peter M., and Ernst B. Hass. 1995. "Learning to Learn: Improving International Governance." *Global Governance* 1: 255–285.

Hayes, Peter. 1995. "Acid Rain in a Regional Context." In *Proceedings of the Seminar on the Role of Science and Technology in Promoting Environmentally Sustainable Development,* 13–15 June. Seoul: Science and Technology Policy Institute.

Hayes, Peter, and Lyuba Zarsky. 1994. "Environmental Issues and Regimes in Northeast Asia." *International Environmental Affairs* 6, 4: 283–319.

Hettelingh, Jean-Paul, Michael Chadwick, Harald Sverdrup, and Dianwu Zhao. 1995. "Impact Module." In Wes Foell et al., eds., *Rains-Asia: An Assessment Model for Air Pollution in Asia* <http://www.iiasa.ac.at> (accessed 11 December 1999).

Hirono, Ryokichi. 1998. "The Role of Japan, the Republic of Korea, China, and Russia in the Promotion of Environmental Cooperation in the Northeast Asian Region." Source unknown.

Hong, Gilhoon, et al. 1999. "Artificial Radionuclides in the East Sea (Sea of Japan) Proper and Peter the Great Bay." *Marine Pollution Bulletin* 38, 10: 933–943.

Hordijk, Leen, Wes Foell, and Jitendra Shah. 1995. "Introduction." In Wes Foell et al., eds., *Rains-Asia: An Assessment Model for Air Pollution in Asia* <http://www.iiasa.ac.at> (accessed 11 December 1999).

Huang, Meiyuan, et al. 1995. "Modeling Studies on Sulfur Deposition and Transport in East Asia." *Water, Air, and Soil Pollution* 85: 1921–1926.

Ichikawa, Yoichi, and Shinichi Fujita. 1995. "An Analysis of Wet Deposition of Sulfate Using a Trajectory Model for East Asia." *Water, Air, and Soil Pollution* 85: 1927–1932.

Ikeuchi, Yoshihiro, et al. 1999. "Anthropogenic Radionuclides in Seawater of the Far Eastern Seas." *Science of the Total Environment* 237–238: 203–212.

Inman, Jerry. 1998. "The Sixth NEANPEF Workshop." Unpublished internal report, Asia Foundation, Tokyo.

International Energy Agency (IEA). 2000. *Key World Energy Statistics*. Paris: IEA.

Ishwaran, Natarajan. 1995. "The Status of the East Asian Biosphere Reserve Network." In *Proceedings of the Third Meeting of the Cooperative Scientific Study of East Asian Biosphere Reserves*, 29 May. Seoul: UNESCO Office-Jakarta.

Japan Environmental Quarterly (JEQ). 1998. "Acid Deposition Monitoring Network in East Asia." *Japan Environmental Quarterly* 3, 4: 3.

Katzenstein, Peter J. 1997. "Introduction: Asian Regionalism in Comparative Perspective." In Peter J. Katzenstein and Shiraish Takashi, eds., *Network Power: Japan and Asia*. Ithaca: Cornell University Press.

Keohane, Robert. 1989. *International Institutions and State Power: Essays in International Relations Theory*. Boulder: Westview.

Kim, Chooni. 2001. International coordinator of Korean Federation for Environmental Movement. Interview with author. 24 October.

Kim, Dongyoung. 1999. Case Study on the Role of Epistemic Communities in International Environmental Issues: Case of Korean Expert Groups in Northeast Asia's Air Pollution Issues. Master's thesis, Seoul National University (in Korean).

Kim, Hyunjin. 1998. "Marine Environmental Cooperation in Northeast Asia." Paper presented to the ESENA Workshop, 11–12 July. Tokyo: Nautilus Institute.

Kim, Jeongwoo, et al. 1997. *China's Air Pollution Problems and Civil Cooperation*. Seoul: Center for Environment and Development (in Korean).

Kim, Kwigon. 1999. "The Evaluation of the East Asian Biosphere Reserve Network." In *Report on the 6th Meeting of the East Asian Biosphere Reserve Network: Ecotourism and Conservation Policy in Biosphere Reserve and Other Similar Conservation Areas*, 16–20 September. Sichuan: UNESCO.

Kirchbach, Friedrich von. 1997. "The Normalization of Economic Relations in Continental Northeast Asia: Recent Development and Implications." In Henri-Claude de Bettingnies, ed., *The Changing Business Environment in the Asia-Pacific Region*. London: International Thomson Business Press.

Knup, Elizabeth. 1997. "Environmental NGOs in China: An Overview." *China Environment Series 1*. Washington, D.C.: Woodrow Wilson International Center for Scholars.

Konigsberg, Jan. 1994. "Upcoming Meeting of Northeast Asia and North Pacific Environmental Forum." Personal letter to Northeast Asia Forum members.

Krasner, Stephen D. 1983. *International Regimes*. Ithaca: Cornell University Press.

Krueger, Jonathan. 2000. "The Role of Information in Environmental Governance: The Case of the Rotterdam PIC Convention." Paper presented at the 2000 Annual Meeting of the American Political Science Association, Washington, DC, 31 August–3 September.

Lee, Sanggon. 1997. "Transboundary Pollution of the Yellow Sea." In Edward English and David Runnalls, eds., *Environment and Development in the Pacific: Problems and Policy Options*. Melbourne: Addison-Wesley.

Lee, Soohoon, et al. 1999. "The Impact of Democratization on Environmental Movements." In Yokshiu F. Lee and Alvin Y. So, eds., *Asia's Environmental Movement: Comparative Perspective*. London: M. E. Sharpe.

Lee, Wonduk. 1998. "Japan's Environmental Issues and the Role of Environmental NGOs." In Myunwoo Lee, ed., *The Studies of Japanese NGO Activity.* Seoul: Sejong Institute (in Korean).

Levy, Marc A. 1993. "European Acid Rain: The Power of Tote-board Diplomacy." In Peter M. Hass, Robert O. Keohane, and Marc A. Levy, eds., *Institution for the Earth: Sources of Effective International Environmental Protection.* Cambridge: MIT Press.

Levy, Marc A., et al. 1993. "Improving the Effectiveness of International Environmental Institutions." In Peter M. Hass, Robert O. Keohane, and Marc A. Levy, eds., *Institutions for the Earth: Sources of Effective International Environmental Protection.* Cambridge: MIT Press.

Liao, Xiaoyi. 2000. "Individual Changing the World: An Interview With Sophie Prize 2000 Winner Liao Xiaoyi" <http://www.gvbchina.org/sophieprize/gvbrepor.html> (accessed 6 February 2001).

Lipschutz, Ronnie D., and Ken Conca. 1993. "The Implications of Global Ecological Interdependence." In Ronnie D. Lipschutz and Ken Conca, eds., *The State and Social Power in Global Environmental Politics.* New York: Columbia University Press.

Mack, Andrew, and John Ravenhill. 1995. *Pacific Cooperation: Building Economic and Security Regimes in the Asia-Pacific Region.* Boulder: Westview.

Martin, Lisa. 1995. "Heterogeneity, Linkage and Commons Problems." In Robert O. Keohane and Elinor Ostrom, eds., *Local Commons and Global Interdependence: Heterogeneity and Cooperation in Two Domains.* London: Sage.

Ministry of Environment, South Korea (MoE). 2001. *Environment White Paper 2000.* Seoul: MoE (in Korean).

Ministry of Foreign Affairs, Japan (MoFA). 1999a. *Japan's Official Development Assistance: Annual Report 1999.* Tokyo: MoFA.

————. 1999b. "Overview of Environment Center Projects (six countries)" <http://www.mofa.go.jp/policy/oda/summary/1999/ov3_1_02.html#c_1_4> (accessed 10 January 2001).

Ministry of Foreign Affairs and Trade, South Korea (MoFAT). 1994. *The Report on Results of the First Intergovernmental Meeting of NOWPAP.* Seoul: Ministry of Foreign Affairs and Trade of the Republic of Korea.

————. 1996. *The Report of the Third Meeting of Senior Officials on Environmental Cooperation in Northeast Asia.* Seoul: Ministry of Foreign Affairs and Trade of the Republic of Korea.

————. 1997. *The Report of the 4th Meeting of the PRC-ROK Joint Committee on Environmental Protection.* Seoul: Ministry of Foreign Affairs and Trade of the Republic of Korea.

————. 1998a. *Environmental Diplomacy* (in Korean). Seoul: Ministry of Foreign Affairs and Trade of the Republic of Korea.

————. 1998b. *Global Environment Report, No. 27* (in Korean). Seoul: Ministry of Foreign Affairs and Trade of the Republic of Korea.

————. 1998c. *Global Environment Report, No. 25* (in Korean). Seoul: Ministry of Foreign Affairs and Trade of the Republic of Korea.

————. 1998d. *The Report of the Fourth Meeting of Senior Officials on Environmental Cooperation in Northeast Asia.* Seoul: Ministry of Foreign Affairs and Trade of the Republic of Korea.

————. 2000a. *The Report of the Sixth Meeting of Senior Officials on Environmental Cooperation in Northeast Asia*. Seoul: Ministry of Foreign Affairs and Trade of the Republic of Korea.

————. 2000b. *The Result Report of the 5th Intergovernmental Meeting of NOWPAP.* Seoul: Ministry of Foreign Affairs and Trade of the Republic of Korea.

————. 2000c. *Negotiation Instruction on the EANET,* 13 March (in Korean). Seoul: Ministry of Foreign Affairs and Trade of the Republic of Korea.

————. 2000d. *Global Environment Report, No. 39* (in Korean). Seoul: Ministry of Foreign Affairs and Trade of the Republic of Korea.

————. 2001. *The Result Report of the Sixth Intergovernmental Meeting of NOWPAP.* Seoul: Ministry of Foreign Affairs and Trade of the Republic of Korea.

National Fisheries Research and Development Institute, South Korea (NFRDI). 1999. "States of Red Tides Occurrence" <www.nfrda.re.kr/dcenter/kored/kored3.html> (accessed 10 July 1999).

National Geographic Society. 2001. "Atlas Update: Sea of Japan" <www.nationalgeographic.com/maps/atlas_updates/html> (accessed 1 February 2001).

National Institute of Environmental Research, South Korea (NIER). 2000. "Report on the Project Northeast Asian Center for Environmental Date and Training." Seoul: NIER.

National Maritime Police Agency, South Korea (NMPA). 2000. "Prevention of Marine Pollution" <http://www.nmpa.go.kr/an_sys7.htm> (accessed 27 January 2001).

Natori, Yoshihiro. 2000. "Progress in the Implementation of NOWPAP." In *Proceedings of the Kyobo International Symposium on Review of Environmental Cooperation in Northeast Asia and Prospects for the New Millennium,* 5–6 October. Seoul: Kyobo Foundation.

Park, Hyesook. 2000. "A Success Story of the AANEA: The Only One Environmental NGOs' Network for East Asian Cooperation." In *Proceedings of the Kyobo International Symposium on Review of Environmental Cooperation in Northeast Asia and Prospects for the New Millennium,* 5–6 October. Seoul: Kyobo Foundation.

Peterson, M. J. 1998. "Organizing for Effective Environmental Cooperation." *Global Governance* 4: 415–438.

Platt, Anne E. 1995. "Dying Seas." *Worldwatch Magazine* (January-February) 8, 1: 10–19.

Princen, Thomas. 1994. "NGOs: Creating a Niche in Environmental Diplomacy." In Thomas Princen and Matthias Finger, eds., *Environmental NGOs in World Politics: Linking the Local and the Global.* London: Routledge.

Princen, Thomas, Matthias Finger, and Jack Manno. 1995. "Nongovernmental Organizations in World Environmental Politics." *International Environmental Affairs* 7, 1: 42–58.

Raustiala, Kal. 1997. "State, NGOs, and International Environmental Institutions." *International Studies Quarterly* 41: 719–740.

Rosenau, James N. 1992. "Governance, Order and Change in World Politics." In James N. Rosenau and Earst-Otto Czempiel, eds., *Governance Without Government: Order and Change in World Politics.* New York: Cambridge University Press.

————. 1995. "Governance in the Twenty-first Century." *Global Governance* 1: 13–43.

Schreurs, Miranda A. 1998. "The Future of Environmental Cooperation in Northeast Asia." In Miranda A. Schreurs and Dennis Pirage, eds., *Ecological Security in Northeast Asia.* Seoul: Yonsei University Press.

Shim, Sangkyu. 2000. "Transboundary Air Pollution in the Northeastern Asian Region." In *Proceedings of International Workshop on Environmental Peace in East Asia,* 5–7 July. Seoul: Korean National Commission for UNESCO.

Sinton, Jonathan. 1996. "China's View of Acid Rain in Northeast Asia and Regional Cooperation Strategies for Mitigation" <http://www.glocom.ac.jp/eco/esena/resource/sinton/AcidRain.html> (accessed 5 June 1999).

Skjærseth, Jonbirger. 1990. "The Effectiveness of the Mediterranean Action Plan." *International Environmental Affairs* 2, 3: 313–335.

Smouts, Marie-Claude. 1998. "The Proper Use of Governance in International Relations." *International Social Science Journal* 155: 81–89.

Sprinz, Detlef, and Tapani Vaahtoranta. 1994. "The Interest-based Explanation of International Environmental Policy." *International Organization* 48, 1: 77–105.

State Environmental Protection Agency, China (SEPA). 1994. *Agreement on Environmental Protection Between the Government of the People's Republic of China and the Government of the Russian Federation.* Beijing: SEPA.

————. 1998. "State of the Environment, China '97" <http://svr1-pek.unep.net/soechina> (accessed 16 November 1999).

————. 2000. "State of the Environment, China '99" <http://www.sepaeic.gov.cn/SOE/99gb> (accessed 27 January 2001).

Streets, David. 1997. "Energy and Acid Rain Projections for Northeast Asia" <http://www.nautilus.org/papers/energy/streetESENAY1.html> (accessed 19 June 1999).

Taguchi, Hiroyuki. 2000. "An Outline of the Northeast Asian Conference on Environmental Cooperation (NEACEC)." Paper presented at the Preparatory Meeting for the 6th Senior Officials Meeting of NEASPEC, 8 March. Seoul: ESCAP.

Taguchi, Hiroyuki, and Tomoko Iwaya. 2000. "ECO-Asia and Its Related Activities." In *Proceedings of the Kyobo International Symposium on Review of Environmental Cooperation in Northeast Asia and Prospects for the New Millennium,* 5–6 October. Seoul: Kyobo Foundation for Education and Culture.

Toda, Eisaku. 2000. "Acid Deposition Monitoring Network in East Asia (EANET)." Paper presented at the 6th Senior Official Meeting of NEASPEC, 8–10 March. Seoul: ESCAP.

Tolba, Mostafa K., and Osama A. El-Kholy. 1992. *The World Environment 1972–1992: Two Decades of Challenges.* London: Chapman and Hall.

Triendl, Robert. 1998. "Asian States Take 'First Step' on Acid Rain." *Nature* (2 April).

Tripartite Environment Ministers Meeting (TEMM). 2000a. *The Tripartite Environmental Ministers Meeting Among Japan, Korea and China: 1999–2000.* Tokyo: Environment Agency of Japan.

————. 2000b. *Progress Report on the Tripartite Environmental Ministers Meeting Among China, Japan and Korea.* Tokyo: Environment Agency of Japan.

Underdal, Arlid. 1998. "Leadership in International Environmental Negotiation: Designing Feasible Solutions." In Arlid Underdal, ed., *The Politics of International Environmental Management*. Dordrecht: Kluwer Academic.

United Nations Education, Scientific, and Cultural Organization (UNESCO). 1994. *The First Meeting of the Cooperative Scientific Study of East Asian Biosphere Reserve, 13–23 March, Beijing*. UNESCO Office-Jakarta.

———. 1995. *The Third Meeting of the Cooperative Scientific Study of East Asian Biosphere Reserve, 29 May–June 2, Seoul*. UNESCO Office-Jakarta.

United Nations Environment Program (UNEP). 1996. Preparatory Meeting of Experts and National Focal Points for the Second Meeting on the NOWPAP. UNEP(WATER)/NOWPAP WG.7/5.

———. 1998. Preparatory Meeting of Experts and National Focal Points for the Third Intergovernmental Meeting on the Northwest Pacific Action Plan. UNEP(WATER)/NOWPAP WG.9/7.

———. 2001. The Fifth Intergovernmental Meeting on the NOWPAP. UNEP/ NOWPAP IG.5/6.

Valencia, Mark. 1996. *A Maritime Regime for Northeast Asia*. Hong Kong: Oxford University Press.

———. 1998. "Ocean Management Regimes in the Sea of Japan: Present and Future." Paper presented at the ESENA Workshop, 11–12 July. Tokyo: Nautilus Institute.

Vogler, John. 1995. *The Global Commons: A Regime Analysis*. Chichester: John Wiley and Sons.

Wu, Hailong. 2000. Statement by Mr. Wu Hailong, Head of the Chinese Delegation at the Sixth Meeting of Senior Officials of the NEASPEC. Seoul, 9 March.

Yang, Chaofei. 1998. Opening Statement at the Third Intergovernmental Meeting on NOWPAP. UNEP (Water)/NOWPAP IG.3/7, Annex II.

Yonemoto, Shohei. 2000. "Japan's Diplomacy Strategy for Dealing With Acid Rain." *Japan Echo* (August): 15–17.

Yoon, Esook, and Hongpyo Lee. 1998. "Environmental Cooperation in Northeast Asia: Issues and Prospects." In Miranda A. Schreurs and Dennis Pirages, eds., *Ecological Security in Northeast Asia*. Seoul: Yonsei University Press.

Young, Oran. 1989. *International Cooperation: Building Regimes for Natural Resources and the Environment*. Ithaca: Cornell University Press.

———. 1993. "International Organization and International Institutions: Lessons Learned From Environmental Regimes." In Sheldon Kamieniecki, ed., *Environmental Politics in the International Arena: Movements, Parties, Organizations, and Policy*. New York: State University of New York Press.

———. 1994. *International Governance: Prospecting the Environment in a Stateless Society*. Ithaca: Cornell University Press.

———. 1997. "Global Governance: Toward a Theory of Decentralized World Order." In Oran Young, ed., *Global Governance: Drawing Insights From the Environmental Experience*. Cambridge: MIT Press.

Yu, Jachyun. 1999. "Cooperation Issues for Resolving Environmental Problems in Northeast Asia." *Bulletin of Korea Environmental Preservation Association* 21, 322: 7–11 (in Korean).

Zarsky, Lyuba. 1995. "The Prospects for Environmental Cooperation in Northeast Asia." *Asian Perspective* 19, 2: 103–130.

Zartman, I. William. 1997. "Negotiation, Governance and Regime Building." In Mats Rolen, Helen Sjöberg, and Uno Svedin, eds., *International Governance on Environmental Issues*. Dordrecht: Kluwer Academic.

9

Building Environmental Regimes in Northeast Asia: Progress, Limitations, and Policy Options

SHIN-WHA LEE

lthough theoretical disputes arise among the academic and policy communities over "securitizing" environmental matters and uncertainty continues about identifying environmentally induced conflict (see Chapter 2), there is increasing global consensus and recognition that environmental cooperation among nations is needed to address transboundary and regional environmental problems. An example of environmental threats facing the globe can be found in the increase of greenhouse gases produced by human activities, which are disrupting atmospheric balance and causing global climate change. In addition, an increasing list of regional and international environmental problems includes disintegration of stratospheric ozone, loss of biological diversity, tropical deforestation, depleted fisheries, and transboundary air, soil, and water pollution. Also, it is a matter of time before the problem of acid rain and marine pollution in Northeast Asia—with no feasible way of reversing the effects of environmental degradation—will have a devastating impact on the Northeast Asian ecosystem.

Such environmental problems, which are either inherently international or localized in particular countries but influencing many others, have the potential to complicate interstate relations unless they are properly addressed. No single country can successfully address these problems. Not only sustainable development practices for environmental protection within a state but also interstate cooperation and policy coordination are required at the regional level. In fact, growing concerns over cross-border environmental problems have led many states to engage in regional and international environmental negotiations and to establish regional environmental networks and multilateral organizations to collectively address environmental issues. In this context it can be said that transnational environmental issues, although a source of interstate conflict, present a prime opportunity for regional cooperation.

With this in mind, this chapter discusses how transboundary ecological issues render strong incentives for collective environmental cooperation within a region and how such cooperation in turn paves the way for establishing regional confidence building to promote peace in the region. The countries chosen for discussion are China, Korea, and Japan in the Northeast Asian region.[1]

TRANSNATIONAL ENVIRONMENTAL ISSUES IN NORTHEAST ASIA

Northeast Asian countries, located within a short distance of each other, occupy parts of a single ecological region and influence each other environmentally, thus making them both producers and recipients of cross-border air and water pollution. Over the past two to three decades the region's economic development process has increasingly confronted various environmental problems. Japan is now an economic superpower, South Korea has achieved phenomenal economic growth, and China has achieved one of the world's fastest rates of development in less than two decades. This remarkable economic performance has been occurring against continued environmental degradation caused by overconsumption of resources and energy and a huge increase in industrial pollution and wastes. For instance, China is expected to almost quadruple its electricity-generating capacity by 2010 compared with 1995, and growing Chinese demands for energy bring serious environmental concern at both domestic and regional levels. Two-thirds of China's energy currently comes from coal, which has a large amount of sulfur dioxide (SO_2).

Air Pollution

China's atmosphere is seriously polluted. During the 1990s of the world's ten most polluted cities named by environmental nongovernmental organizations (NGOs), from five to nine of China's cities have been included. Around 110,000 Chinese people suffer serious health problems related to indoor air pollution, mainly caused by burning coal for cooking and heating. High SO_2 and nitrogen oxide emissions from coal-fired power plants in China are also a primary source of transfrontier air pollution (i.e., acid rain), causing problems at the regional level in Northeast Asia.

Emissions from Manchurian China are a cause of major regional concern, as Korea and Japan have suffered the most from acid rain originating in China and carried by natural air circulation. Several islands in the western part of Korea, including Baekryung Island, are directly exposed to the polluted air that blows across the Yellow Sea from China. Since the 1980s, however, China has been preoccupied with the national objective of rapid economic development, indicating little sign of reducing its emissions. China has even increased its reliance on coal to cope with the shortage of other energy sources, particularly oil. As China's coal consumption is expected to double the 1990 level by 2010, the scale and impact of cross-border acid rain deposition will likely increase (Economy 1997). It is encouraging to note that in recent years China has begun to pay increasing attention to environmental degradation, publishing Agenda 21—the *White Paper on China's Population, Environment, and Development in the 21st Century*—which coordinates the development of the country's economy, society, resources, and environment. Such efforts by China should be expanded not only for regional environmental sustainability but also for China's own economic development. China's plan to develop for its own sake at the cost of Korea's and Japan's environments is likely to invite economic and diplomatic sanctions and cause interstate disputes. Paradoxically, such sanctions, if they take place, will hamper China's further development.

RECENT YELLOW DUST

The phenomena of yellow dust, known as *Hwangsa* (the major long-distance polluting agent), which are blown from Mongolia and China to the Korean Peninsula through the prevailing westerlies every spring, have worsened. There is a high possibility that the sulfurous acid gas and carbon monoxide pollution, which had been greatly reduced in Seoul, may have been remitted on the surface of yellow dust.[2] In particular, the recent discovery of large amounts of SO_2 and nitrogen dioxide (NO_2) in research findings increases the chances of acid rain.

For thousands of years the natural yellow dust that came in the spring was not a concern until China began to industrialize. Before the 1990s yellow dust occurred only twice between March and May. Starting in the 1990s, however, yellow dust sometimes occurred more than five times in a year. During the springs of 1998 and 2000 *Hwangsa* occurred in all of Korea and many parts of China, causing many people to suffer from respiratory difficulties and eye trouble. Yellow dust is also drastically raising the body temperature of citizens, and the tiny particles can affect the organs of young children.

The amount of dust in the atmosphere is increasing greatly. In 2000 alone there were six instances of yellow dust.[3] With drought spells around the Yellow River and the depletion of the Huang He River as a result of industrialization, the soils were very dry and subject to be blown by strong winds caused by high temperatures and dryness in northwestern China. During 2000 the level of dioxin in Busan City's atmosphere was three times the amount before the yellow dust passed by. It is difficult to forecast the path of yellow dust, and even when its appearance is detected by satellite, its destination cannot always be assumed. Unless the effects of natural disasters and environmental destruction are addressed, *Hwangsa* is expected to continue to become more severe.

In addition, air pollution blown across the East Sea (Sea of Japan) from Korea may lead to interstate tensions with Japan (Winnefeld and Morris 1994). For instance, large amounts of yellow dust polluting agents are moving according to Korea's atmospheric flow, which carries them to Japan.

MARINE POLLUTION

Marine pollution is another transboundary environmental problem facing the region. The Yellow Sea is a semienclosed water area surrounded by China and the Korean Peninsula, whose coastal areas contain industrial facilities. The East Sea (Sea of Japan)—which is shared by the Russian Federation, China, Japan, North Korea, and South Korea—also has industries along its coastal rim. As ocean vessel traffic in both seas grew as the result of a remarkable increase in the volume of trade among nations since the end of the Cold War, routine discharge of oil from ships as well as factory wastes have been disrupting the aquatic system of Northeast Asia. Yet the level of government activity and public attention, as well as the number of interstate agreements on transfrontier marine pollution issues, is much less than that regarding air pollution issues.

The Yellow Sea has suffered the most from marine pollution. As both Korea and China developed industrial facilities along their coastal rims on the Yellow Sea, the coastal waters on both sides became contaminated by industrial wastewater and domestic sewage, as well as by the high volume of oil spills. For example, the number of oil spills along the western coastline of South Korea tripled between 1987 and 1991, and since 2000 an estimated 10,000 tons of oil have been spilled every year along the Chinese coastline of the Yellow Sea (Yoon and Lee 1998: chapter 4). The Yellow Sea is already one of the world's seven "dying seas" (i.e., the Black Sea, Yellow Sea, North Sea, Barents Sea, Red Sea, Arabian Sea, and Caspian Sea) and is the second-most polluted after the Black Sea. The East Sea, despite being relatively less polluted by oil spills than the Yellow Sea, has also suffered from industrial waste dumping.[4] Some coastlines on the East Sea have also been polluted by marine oil spills and radioactive wastes (Yoon and Lee 1998). Furthermore, in the marine areas of Northeast Asia—that is, the Northwest Pacific area—the coastal eutrophication resulting from excessive nutrient input is increasingly a major concern.[5] Also, red tide incidents are reported regularly in the region's coastal areas.[6]

In addition to marine pollution, depletion of fishery resources is a problem in Northeast Asia. According to the World Research Institute, the Northwest Pacific fisheries were fully fished by 1998, and many other species such as sea grass, coral, mollusks, shrimp, and lobsters are endangered (WRI 1999). Also, the boundary delimitation of the overlapping Exclusive Economic Zones (EEZs) among China, Japan, and South Korea is a controversial maritime issue. The 1982 UN Convention on the Law of the Sea, to which these Northeast Asian countries are signatories, legitimatized the 200-nautical-mile EEZ. The distance from one coast to another in the region's seas, however, never exceeds 400 miles, so regulation of the shared waters and fishing arrangements has been problematic (Lee 2001).

Table 9.1 documents environmental problems facing the Northeast Asian region. In recent years these problems have offered opportunities for domestic and regional discussion of environmental protection and sustainable development.

Table 9.1—Common Environmental Problems in Northeast Asia

TRANSFRONTIER AIR POLLUTION	Acid precipitation and deposition *Hwangsa* (yellow dust)
MARINE POLLUTION	Oil spills Dumping of radioactive and other industrial wastes Coastal runoff and eutrophication
RESOURCE SCARCITIES	Overpopulation and growing demands Heavy dependence on energy and food imports Strong need for alternative energy sources (e.g., nuclear energy) Access to clean water Depletion of fishery resources
ECOLOGICAL MANAGEMENT	Protection of migratory fish and birds Sustainable forest development Regional trade-related environmental issues Boundary delimitation of the overlapping EEZ among the countries in the region

PROGRESS ON ENVIRONMENTAL COOPERATION IN NORTHEAST ASIA

Regional cooperation on the environment has grown significantly in all regions during the past few decades. Most regions have active programs that aim to establish a regional environmental database to strengthen policy-making capacities and to develop regional institutional and legislative frameworks, regional environmental networks, and high-level policy forums. Since the late 1980s strong calls have been made for regional regimes for cooperative environmental management in Northeast Asia. South Korea, Japan, and China have been engaged in bilateral and multilateral dialogues to establish or promote regional ecological cooperation to address their common environmental problems

BILATERAL ENVIRONMENTAL COOPERATION

Bilateral environmental cooperation involving China, South Korea (Korea hereafter), and Japan developed only in the 1990s. The "Agreement Between the Government of the Republic of Korea and the Government of Japan on Cooperation in the Field of Environmental Protection" was signed by Korea and Japan in June 1993. Since the first meeting in January 1994, the Korea-Japan Environmental Cooperation Joint Committee has conducted environmental management. Cooperative research is also under way between Korea's National Institute of Environmental Research and Japan's National Institute for Environmental Studies. Although the need for cooperative environmental management was driven by ecological imperatives, national competition in part led Japan and Korea to launch environmental initiatives in the Northeast Asian region.

Since the late 1980s Japan has greatly increased its budget for environmental projects in China and elsewhere in the Asian region. By 1990 the percentage of Japan's environmental aid to its official development aid had tripled from the amount in 1986. Japan's environmental assistance increased further at the UN Conference on the Environment and Development in 1992 and constituted 16 percent of the country's total official development aid in 1994. Also, the Institute for Global Environmental Strategies, aiming to promote sustainable development in the Asia-Pacific region, was established in Japan in early 1998 and is expected to provide financial assistance to those who study environmental issues in the region. Japan further promotes policy dialogues through such conferences as the Environment Congress for Asia and the Pacific (ECO-ASIA), which is becoming an annual gathering of environmental ministers in the Asia-Pacific region.

Japan has two primary reasons for promoting environmental protection initiatives in the region. First, strong environmental imperatives exist for promoting regional cooperation. For instance, since Japan lies downwind of the Asian continent, growing awareness of what transfrontier acid rains mean for Japan's environment drove the country to aid China in achieving efficient energy use. Throughout the 1990s China was a major recipient of Japan's environmental aid. Also, the Environmental Agency of Japan created an acid rain monitoring network in the region. Second, as the region's richest nation but with constitutional restrictions on the use of the military, Japan wants to play a leading role in establishing a cooperative regional regime for the environment.

Korea has also been playing a visible role in regional ecological cooperation—for example, by taking initiatives for establishing a regional environmental regime, which since 1992 has developed into the Northeast Asian Conference of Environmental Cooperation (NEACEC). On International Environmental Day in June 1997, the Korean government adopted the "Seoul Declaration on Environmental Ethics" to promote national and regional coordinating mechanisms for sustainable development and the implementation of Agenda 21. Furthermore, Korea will soon establish regional environmental cooperation at the level of Northeast Asia and the Asia-Pacific Economic Cooperation Forum (APEC). Such Korean initiatives are not only considered ecological imperatives but also play a role in Korea's aspiration to enhance its role in the region.

In October 1993 Korea and China signed the "Agreement on Environmental Cooperation Between the Government of the Republic of Korea and the Government of the People's Republic of China," thus establishing the Korea-China Joint Environmental Cooperation Committee. At the first meeting in June 1994 the two countries agreed to carry out eighteen joint projects, including one to prevent cross-border air pollution. The two countries agreed to undertake joint research on Yellow Sea pollution at the second meeting in May 1995 and since that time have made much effort to prevent sea pollution caused by oil spills (DFT 1998). Korea and China held the second Korea-China Regional Workshop (January 18–19, 2000) and the third meeting of the Steering Committee for the Yellow Sea Large Marine Ecosystem (YSLME) project (January 20, 2000) in Beijing.[7] In November 2000 Korea and China started a five-year project called "Monitoring of the Ecosystem in the Yellow Sea," which is open to North Korea's participation. Meanwhile, Japan and China agreed on an environmental cooperation treaty in 1994, calling for joint research on acid rain and the exchange of observation data between the two nations.

MULTILATERAL ENVIRONMENTAL COOPERATION

Intergovernmental dialogues have also occurred at the multilateral level. In 2000 regional environmental cooperation in Northeast Asia made great progress. NEACEC is the annual conference at which environmental authorities from Korea, China, Japan, Mongolia, and Russia participate to exchange information on policies and issues regarding the region's environmental situation. Nine rounds of NEACEC meetings were held between 1992 and 2000. One of NEACEC's important accomplishments is that it has facilitated several sectors—such as governments, international organizations, NGOs, and groups from the private sector—coming together and addressing environmental issues in the region.

The Northeast Asian Subregional Program of Environmental Cooperation (NEASPEC), launched in 1993 under the supervision of the Economic and Social Commission for Asia and the Pacific (ESCAP),[8] is a cooperative body among South Korea, North Korea, China, Japan, Russia, and Mongolia. At the Sixth Senior Officials Meeting of NEASPEC, held in March 2000, a vision statement on the future activities of NEASPEC was adopted, and a Core Fund was created for Northeast Asian environmental cooperation. The members were making efforts to adopt the Northeast Asian Environmental Cooperation Program by 2002. The Meeting of Senior Officials on Environmental Cooperation in Northeast Asia was initiated by ESCAP. This meeting, first held in Seoul in February 1993, was the first attempt at the official level to promote subregional environmental cooperation in the Northeast Asian region. The second Environment Ministerial Meeting of South Korea, China, and Japan, held in 2000, laid the foundation for an annual meeting of the environment ministers in Northeast Asia. Considering these three countries' importance in Northeast Asian environmental cooperation, the three-party ministerial meeting may be able to guide such cooperation in Northeast Asia.

The Northwest Pacific Action Program (NOWPAP) was set up by South Korea, China, Japan, and Russia to establish a database to prevent and clean up ocean pollution. At its sixth government-level meeting in December 2000, the participating countries discussed establishing a joint Korea-Japan secretariat for NOWPAP. This could become a new cooperation forum the Northeast Asian environment once Korea and Japan overcome the problem of coordination in operating a joint secretariat. Also, the Global Environment Facility (GEF) has decided to support a few environmental cooperation activities in Northeast Asia. The Environmental Preservation Project of the Tumen River Region, whose participating members include South Korea, China, Russia, and Mongolia, is a two-year project that started in July 2000.

Government efforts to foster regional environmental cooperation have extended beyond the Northeast Asian region. Several examples of multilateral intergovernmental environmental cooperation are seen at the level of East Asia and of Asia and the Pacific as a whole. For instance, the Acid Deposition Monitoring Network in East Asia (EANET) was created in 1998 to promote cooperation among member countries on researching and monitoring acid deposition in East Asia. At the second government-level meeting of EANET in October 2000, ten Association of Southeast Asian Nations (ASEAN) member countries—as well as Korea, China, and Japan—

participated and decided to launch EANET as an official intergovernmental institution with an independent secretariat. Meanwhile, the Japan-initiated ECO-ASIA has met nine times since 1991 and played a leading role in facilitating environmental policy dialogue in Asia and the Pacific region. Also, APEC and the Asia-Europe Meeting have been instrumental in providing important forums to address common environmental issues in the Asia and Pacific region.

YELLOW DUST AND KOREA-CHINA-JAPAN COOPERATION

Cooperation between Korea and China is at an infant stage concerning yellow dust/sand. In the past, when China raised the issue of yellow dust, it believed Korea's claim that the dust carried polluting agents had no foundation. China maintained this attitude until January 1999, when the annual Tripartite Environment Ministers Meeting (TEMM) of Korea, China, and Japan was established. Various joint projects—such as International Joint Research for Long-range Transboundary Air Pollutants in Northeast Asia, the Ecological Conservation Project in Northwest China, and the Acid Deposition Monitoring Network in East Asia—have been suggested by TEMM and implemented jointly by all three nations. In the fourth TEMM in April 2002, substantial measures to control yellow dust were discussed in detail as a continuation of joint efforts among the three countries.

International concern over yellow dust has recently increased, especially since yellow dust was discovered in pollution measurements of the U.S. West Coast in April 1998. As a result, under the auspices of International Global Atmospheric Chemistry (IGAC) in Kosan, a collective aerosol measurement project was scheduled to be launched in March 2001.[9] This project, in which thirty research teams from twelve countries—including the United States, Australia, and Japan—are participating, uses satellites, aircraft, and ships to record aerosol levels in the Northeast Asian region. In particular, the distribution of yellow dust molecules and chemical structures, together with the characteristics of its long-distance movement, will be closely examined.

In addition to government efforts to achieve environmental cooperation, private organizations are actively cooperating. In 1995 NGOs from seven countries—China, Korea, Japan, Mongolia, Hong Kong, Taiwan, and Russia—established the Atmospheric Action Network East Asia. This is the only environmental NGO network for East Asian cooperation that aims to promote improvement of regional and global atmospheric conditions by strengthening NGO capacity building and collective and equitable efforts. Members meet every year to exchange data on atmosphere pollution and formulate ways to reduce long-distance moving polluting agents (Park 2000).

LIMITATIONS OF NORTHEAST ASIAN
ENVIRONMENTAL COOPERATION

Despite various attempts to address environmental problems, regional environmental cooperation in Northeast Asia, and in East Asia more generally, is still in its infancy compared with that in Europe where multilateral environmental institution building began in the early 1970s. In Europe the process of regional environmental institution building was long and painful, since it required environmental capacity building and changes of some member states' values. Although institution-building efforts began in the late 1950s when the European Economic Community (which later became the European Community [EC] and is now the European Union [EU]) was established, the primary objectives were to promote industrialization and economic growth. Only after the first UN Conference on the Human Environment, held in Stockholm in 1972, did EC activities expand to the social and environmental arenas. And it was not until the late 1980s that the EC formed the Single European Act, which formulates common environmental standards and environmental laws that supersede those of member states (Schreurs 1997).

To compare, efforts to enhance economic cooperation in East Asia began with the establishment of ASEAN in 1967. Although ASEAN has been instrumental in enhancing economic dialogue and easing security tensions among the member states, little effort was made to protect the environment until the 1980s. In 1989 APEC was formed to facilitate free trade among Asia-Pacific states.[10] APEC provided a common ground for interstate negotiations among diverse member states. Still APEC, like ASEAN, was established mainly to promote economic cooperation. In the 1990s many East Asian states began to recognize the seriousness of environmental deterioration resulting from rapid economic growth in the region and have sought to develop regional activities for environmental protection. ASEAN and APEC have also expanded their activities to noneconomic issues.

As the European experience proved, however, the transformation of Asian states' position on environmental issues requires normative changes by and the political will of the countries involved. This is particularly true for Northeast Asian countries. Although common environmental problems facing the region provide some opportunities to promote regional cooperation in Northeast Asia, the region is far from implementing concrete cooperative projects and actions with long-term vision or a legally binding agreement (Han 2000). In fact, skepticism exists over establishing a sustained cooperative institution for regional environmental protection because of preexisting confrontations and distrust in the region throughout the colonial period, World War II, the Korean War, and the Cold War. Even with the end of the Cold War, several potential risk spots stand out in traditional (military) security terms: the long-standing confrontation between the two Koreas and possible renewal of a Korean civil war, conflict over Chinese territorial claims to Taiwan, growing concerns about Japan's major rearmament, and a possible struggle for regional hegemony between China and Japan.

A further weakness of the development of regional cooperation is insufficient proof of transfrontier environmental damage. Despite regional awareness of cross-border pollution problems, no country in Northeast Asia has officially claimed grave environmental damage. The serious impact of acid rain from China's coal burning on ecological conditions in Korea and Japan has yet to be reported. Despite the serious impact of yellow dust on the Korean Peninsula, it is risky to place responsibility on China without much thought. The first step should be to collect data on the amount of pollution produced by each county and to conduct long-term observation and analysis. In Korea no long-term research has been carried out on how far polluting agents are carried, how they are carried, and when pollution occurs. In addition, there is no consistent solution regarding the effect yellow dust has on Korea.[11] Concerning marine pollution, only occasional reports implying ecological deterioration in some coastal areas are available. Furthermore, the level of public awareness and political motivation to address the region's environmental issues remains low while the traditional political agenda is given priority.

The great differences in economic levels among countries in Northeast Asia have impeded facilitation of regional environmental cooperation efforts. Despite recognizing environmental imperatives to promote effective interstate cooperation, no single country is willing to risk its national welfare and interests or to allow encroachment on its sovereignty in the area of environmental policy. For example, notwithstanding diplomatic pressures from South Korea and Japan, the Chinese government has shown little sign of reconciling its growth-oriented economic plan with the concept of environmentally sustainable development. Facing a shortage of other energy sources, China continues to rely on coal, even though its coal consumption increases the scale and impact of cross-border acid rain deposition. There are also problems of duplication and unnecessary competition among environmental institutions within and across Northeast Asia. Consensus is lacking "to build up a Northeast Asia–specific forum which covers overall regional environmental issues, and eventually leads to legally binding agreements" (Han 2000: 138).

Finally, at least five factors are required for the establishment of an institutional mechanism for regional environmental cooperation—national leadership, involvement of international institutions, involvement of transnational scientific networks, active presence of NGOs, and significant public concern (Haas 1998). Unfortunately, none of these factors has been strong enough in Northeast Asia to facilitate a regional environmental regime.

In summary, current developments in environmental cooperation in Northeast Asia resemble those in Europe in the early 1970s. It is thus too early to assess the impact of such efforts to address environmental questions in the region.

POLICY SUGGESTIONS

Turning to policy suggestions, the first priority should be to ensure population and food security. Increasing the number of people and their resource-intensive industrial activities places growing demands on natural resources—including water, land, and forests—and leads to an increased demand for food. It is thus imperative that Northeast Asian countries improve agricultural productivity and build better mechanisms for food distribution, especially to marginal groups and sectors. Empowering communities to seek and find their own solutions and resources is a key element to promoting sustainable agricultural systems. A regionwide community outreach program should be created or expanded to facilitate the identification and establishment of a regional environmental network of committed individuals and groups.

Second, managing overpopulation problems in environmentally fragile areas is critical. Yet it is argued that northerners telling southerners to expedite fertility decline to the replacement level and to slow their economic development for the sake of the global ecosystem is hypocritical and nonpersuasive, since developed nations previously exploited much of the natural system while they industrialized. Northern support for southern sustainable development is imperative to prevent human and ecological catastrophes around the globe. With regard to ensuring a sustainable population level, responsibility lies with both developed and developing countries. European countries that have achieved or are approaching zero population growth should provide the Third World with financial and technical assistance for successful family planning programs,[12] as well as for immediate needs. In the densely populated Third World, vigorous government-supported population policies (e.g., South Korea in the 1960s and 1970s and China in the 1980s and 1990s) and individual recognition of the need for contraception should be accompanied by social and economic progress. Third World countries that have effectively reduced birth rates can also help other poor countries develop family planning strategies.

Third, when it comes to entwining economic growth and environmental protection, each Asian country has its own priority issues because of the gross disparities in their industrial or environmental circumstances and degree of development. Efforts to reduce gross economic disparities are prerequisite for enhancing interstate cooperation in the region. Technology and financial transfers to less-developed states from industrialized countries in the region are suggested. It is encouraging to note that in 1991 the Japanese Ministry of International Trade and Industry established the Green Aid Plan as part of official development assistance. Under this plan Japan helped China, Indonesia, and Thailand build environmental centers. Also, Japan has actively promoted the transfer of its first-rate environmental technology and energy efficiency know-how to China and Southeast Asia by training technicians from these areas or dispatching environmental advisers to Asian nations (Schreurs 1998).

Fourth, if one country suffers environmental degradation, all other nations in the region could be affected. Therefore cooperative efforts between any two countries alone are insufficient for the region's environmental protection. Although sustained attention should be given to bilateral environmental collaboration, further efforts to build multilateral institutions and networks are required. Several intergovernmental institutions have been established at the subregional level to promote interstate environmental cooperation. Such subregional cooperation can be further consolidated if all governments in the region agree to work together to facilitate regional ecological interdependence on a collective basis. For this, the region's ongoing bilateral and multilateral cooperation should be reinforced by the establishment of a comprehensive Northeast Asian Environmental Regime that includes a dispute settlement mechanism (for disputed regional environmental issues) and crisis prevention and management (for natural and human-induced ecological disasters) (Lee 2000).

Fifth, the United States used to play a major role in regional security matters in Northeast Asia (see Chapter 3). But changes are occurring as the United States is turning inward and minimizing its commitment to foster regional stability with the demise of Soviet threats in the region and with the U.S. focus on wars against terrorism. Still, growing concerns about environmental deterioration in Northeast Asia have forced the United States to consider "whether it is in the best interest of the developed countries to support the modernization of raw material producing or primitive economies, or to risk the acute conflicts that would surely follow failure to modernize" (Winnefeld and Morris 1994: 99–100). In such a context, U.S. efforts to shape changes in Pacific policies should include financial and technical assistance to improve the efficiency of resource and energy use in the region, particularly in China.

Sixth, although Asian countries do not necessarily replicate the European experience, some lessons from the EU can be applied to Asia. The history of EU environmental policy provides an example of how member states have managed to integrate environmental protection requirements into all other relevant EU policies and harmonize national environmental policies at the European level. With no institution equivalent to the EU (e.g., little codification of regional environmental institutions and law and few multilateral environmental agreements or networks), Northeast Asia has a long way to go before regional environmental protection initiatives will reach the level of what EU environmental policy making has achieved. Still, regional environmental cooperation in Northeast Asia should move forward by integrating environmental protection requirements into its economic and trading institutions such as ASEAN, APEC, and, more recently, ASEAN plus Three. Also, all the diverse states of the region should make every effort to formulate flexible multilateral agreements under which they come to consensus on environmental priorities and policy responses and work together to establish the framework for sustainability.

Seventh, the efforts of international organizations and foreign donor countries in supporting sustainable development in Third World countries can contribute to lessening or preventing ecological disruption and related humanitarian crises. To begin with, multinational cooperation through international organizations such as the United Nations and the World Bank can play a vital part in checking harmful development policies through economic sanctions and diplomatic pressure. It is encouraging that the World Trade Organization, the UN Conference on Trade and Development, and the UN Environment Program have begun to consider ways to make trade and environment mutually supportive, including how to tie the objectives and principles of the multilateral trading system to the provisions of multilateral environmental agreements.

Eighth, most academic writing and policy dialogue has centered on approaches to environmental issues, such as effective methods to achieve and implement environmental agreements and install cooperative systems at the central government level. Such approaches suffer from the "hypocrisies and delays" of intergovernmental cooperation because of issues of national sovereignty and state interests (Vogler 2001). Efforts to resolve environmental problems should therefore be made by promoting cooperative relations through subgovernmental or informal channels within countries, in addition to continuing cooperative efforts at the central government level. This lower-level governmental relationship can broaden the scope of activities between the countries involved without the political and diplomatic constraints of national-level exchanges (Lee 2001; Moon 1998).

Ninth, the international media that has "shrunk" the planet should play a more substantial role in monitoring development policies conducted by sovereign states. In doing so the media should inspire global villagers to enforce rules and put international pressure on states to correct harmful policies. The role of NGOs in Northeast Asia has been particularly important in the process of building regional environmental cooperation. With their expert knowledge and innovative ideas about environmental issues in the region, their strong commitment to the common good that transcends national interests, and their representation of the populace at a grassroots level, NGOs have emerged not only as key actors in addressing regional environmental problems but also as operational partners for national governments and regional organizations. Yet many NGOs have difficulty maintaining their independent organizational vision as they have increased their dependence on funding from their home government or subcontracted with the government or international organizations. Thus governments should more actively assist the development of cooperative networks among NGOs. NGOs in the field can help reduce environmental refugee problems by fulfilling an "early warning" role in revealing the status of "invisible" indigenous groups at environmental risk. In addition, the media and NGOs can encourage the international community to promote sustainable development.

Contrasting the scale of the world's developmental needs with the evidence of the earth's environmental limits presents governments with a paradox. Public opinion should play a leading role in pushing governments and international organizations to consider how to solve the political, practical, and theoretical difficulties of reconciling economic development with ecological sustainability.

CONCLUSION

The position of many Northeast Asian states on the environment remains passive and ex post facto. Unless a dramatic environmental catastrophe within one country spills over to affect the entire region, different interpretations and emphasis of environmental standards and values will remain a continued barrier to a regional regime-building process. The high environmental interdependence of countries in Northeast Asia, however, makes it imperative to create a framework to promote greater cooperation within the region. Given that the region lacks institutions for regionwide dialogue and cooperation, the formation of an effective regional environmental regime will be a long-term process. Yet the process itself is pivotal, as it can increase dialogue and exchange from which a regional environmental regime can evolve (Conca 1998; Lee 2001). It is hoped that an understanding of the destabilizing environmental implications for security will lead academics, policymakers, and the public to recognize the importance of common action through interstate cooperation and to take action. More optimistically, environmental security can be defined by considering its positive effect—environmental confidence building, which can provide political opportunities to further security and peace.

NOTES

1. Because both environmental issues and security concerns are broad subjects for inquiry and because Northeast Asia—including China, Russia, Japan, both Koreas, Mongolia, Hong Kong, and Taiwan—is a large region, I have defined the boundary of my research and have omitted important concerns, topics, and countries. This can be expanded in later research to encompass larger or different portions of my subject.

2. The actual composition of yellow dust is almost the same as that of ordinary earth. Silicon, aluminum, and iron are the main elements. Heavy metals including lead, cadmium, and zinc, however, which are toxic to the human body, are also included.

3. This does not mean the tendency to increase is mandatory. In 1994 the flow was so uneven that it was impossible to record it in the Korean Peninsula.

4. Japan was reported as the world's largest marine dumper; as of 1996 the country had dumped 4.5 million tons into the Pacific Ocean and the East Sea (Valencia 1996: 189).

5. "Nutrient loads from agriculture and sewage and atmosphere and rivers, formation of anoxic water masses due to the decomposition of organic matter are the causes of eutrophication in the region. This problem is closely related with red ties (harmful algal blooms) and changes in phytoplankton communities" (Han 2000: 126).

6. "Red tides have pronounced negative effects including damage to aquaculture and fisheries [and] deterioration of water quality with regard to recreation and human health" (Han 2000: 127).

7. The YSLME is a joint project among Korea, China, and the United Nations Development Program for preserving the ecosystem of the Yellow Sea. GEF provided Korea and China with funding of US$349,650 in 1997 for preparation of the YSLME project, which is now in its third stage <http://www.mofat.go.kr>.

8. ESCAP is the intergovernmental forum for the entire Asia-Pacific region to promote economic and technological development in the region.

9. The IGAC project aims to work to understand how the chemistry of the global atmosphere is regulated and the role of biological processes in producing and consuming trace gases <http://web.mit.edu/igac>.

10. APEC members include the six ASEAN states (Brunei, Indonesia, Malaysia, the Philippines, Singapore, and Thailand) plus twelve states (South Korea, Japan, Taiwan, the People's Republic of China, Hong Kong, Australia, New Zealand, Papua New Guinea, the United States, Mexico, Canada, and Chile).

11. To compare, despite the fact that yellow dust rarely occurs in Japan, since the early 1980s Japan has conducted in-depth research and collected data on the issue.

12. Antiabortion forces in donor countries often oppose this policy, however.

REFERENCES

Agenda 21. *White Paper on China's Population, Environment, and Development in the 21st Century* <http://www.acca21.org.cn/ca21pa.html>.

Conca, Ken. 1998. "Environmental Confidence Building and Regional Security in Northeast Asia." In Miranda A. Schreurs and Dennis Pirages, eds., *Ecological Security in Northeast Asia*. Seoul: Yonsei University Press.

Department of Foreign Affairs and Trade (DFT). 1998. *Environment Diplomacy* (*Hwan Kyung Woi Kyo Pyon Ram* in Korean). Seoul: Bureau of International Economy.

Economy, Elizabeth. 1997. "China and East Asia." In Robert S. Chen, W. Christopher Lenhardt, and Kara F. Alkire, eds., *Consequences of Environmental Change—Political, Economic, Social*. Proceedings of the Environmental Flash Points Workshop, 12–14 November, Reston, Virginia.

Haas, Peter M. 1998. "Prospects for Effective Marine Governance in the Northwest Pacific Region." Paper presented at the ESENA Workshop Energy-Related Marine Issues in the Sea of Japan, July, Tokyo, Japan.

Han, Tak-Whan. 2000. "Assessment of Environmental Cooperation in North-East Asia." In *Proceedings of Kyobo International Symposium on Review Environmental Cooperation in Northeast Asia and Prospects for the New Millennium*. Seoul: Kyobo Foundation for Education and Culture.

Lee, Shin-wha. 2000. "Safeguarding the Environment: An Agenda for Regional Cooperation in South Korea, Northeast Asia, and Beyond." In Carolina G. Hernandez and Gill Wilkins, eds., *Population, Food, Energy, and the Environment: Challenges to Asia-Europe Cooperation*. Tokyo: Council for Asia-Europe Cooperation.

————. 2001. "Environmental Regime-Building in Northeast Asia: A Catalyst for Sustainable Regional Cooperation." *Journal of East Asian Studies* 1, 2 (August): 182–217.

Moon, Chung-in. 1998. "South Korea." In Paul B. Stares, ed., *The New Security Agenda: A Global Survey*. Tokyo: Japan Center for International Exchange.

Park, Hye-Sook. 2000. "A Success Story of the AANEA (Atmosphere Action Network East Asia): The Only One Environmental NGOs' Network for East Asian Cooperation." In *Proceedings of Kyobo International Symposium on Review Environmental Cooperation in Northeast Asia and Prospects for the New Millennium*. Seoul: Kyobo Foundation for Education and Culture.

Schreurs, Miranda A. 1997. "Environmental Cooperation in the Northeast Asian Region." Paper presented at the conference "Dynamic Transition and Cooperation in Northeast Asia," November, Seoul.

————. 1998. "The Future of Environmental Cooperation in Northeast Asia." In Miranda A. Schreurs and Dennis Pirages, eds., *Ecological Security in Northeast Asia*. Seoul: Yonsei University Press.

Valencia, Mark J. 1996. *A Maritime Regime for Northeast Asia*. New York: Oxford University Press.

Vogler, John. 2001. "Environment." In Brian White, Richard Little, and Michael Smith, eds., *Issues in World Politics*. New York: Palgrave.

Winnefeld, James A., and Mary E. Morris. 1994. "The Environmental Dimension of Security in East Asia." In James A. Winnefeld and Mary E. Morris, eds., *Where Environmental Concerns and Security Strategies Meet: Green Conflict in Asia and the Middle East*. Santa Monica: RAND.

World Resource Institute (WRI). 1999. *World Resources, 1989–1999.* New York: Oxford University Press.

Yoon, Esook, and Hong Pyo Lee. 1998. "Environmental Cooperation in Northeast Asia: Issues and Prospects." In Miranda A. Schreurs and Dennis Pirages, eds., *Ecological Security in Northeast Asia.* Seoul: Yonsei University Press.

10

Problems of Environmental Cooperation in Northeast Asia: The Case of Acid Rain

WAKANA TAKAHASHI

Since the 1972 United Nations Conference on the Human Environment, the world has witnessed enhanced environmental cooperation at the regional level. Many regional and subregional environmental programs and plans have been adopted and implemented all over the world. Some have developed into legally binding agreements or treaties for controlling transboundary pollution. The Long-Range Transboundary Air Pollution (LRTAP) Convention, endorsed by the United Nations Economic Committee for Europe (UNECE), has been cited as one of the most successful examples of such regional initiatives. Following the launch of the European Monitoring and Evaluation Program (EMEP) in 1977, countries in Europe and North America adopted the LRTAP framework convention in 1979. It has provided a solid basis for its member states to negotiate and conclude several protocols regulating specific pollutant emissions.

Agenda 21, adopted during the 1992 United Nations Conference on Environment and Development (UNCED), states that the convention and its protocols "have established a regional regime in Europe and North America, based on a review process and cooperative programs for systematic observation of air pollution, assessment and information exchange. . . . These programs need to be continued and enhanced, and their experience needs to be shared with other regions of the world" (United Nations 1993: chapter 9). The statement spurred collaboration in other regions of the

221

world, particularly Asia. In South Asia the Malé Declaration on Control and Prevention of Air Pollution and Its Likely Transboundary Effects was adopted in 1998 by eight countries in the region and has been implemented with the support of the United Nations Environment Program (UNEP), the South Asia Cooperative Environment Program (SACEP), and the Stockholm Environment Institute (SEI). In Southeast Asia smoke and haze from forest fires in Indonesia in 1991, 1994, and 1997 have devastated the biophysical and socioeconomic environments of neighboring countries and spurred Association of Southeast Asian Nations (ASEAN) environment ministers to adopt the Cooperation Plan on Transboundary Pollution in 1995 and the Regional Haze Action Plan in 1997. ASEAN countries are currently engaged in negotiations on an ASEAN agreement on transboundary haze.

In Northeast Asia, where the adverse effects of acid deposition were about to become a serious problem, the Acid Deposition Monitoring Network in East Asia (EANET) was created by the Environment Agency of Japan (now the Ministry of Environment). In parallel, the National Institute of Environmental Research (NIER) of South Korea has held regular meetings on long-range transboundary air pollutants in Northeast Asia, in which representatives and experts from South Korea, China, and Japan have participated. A five-year research plan on joint monitoring and modeling was agreed upon in 1999. In addition, several other regional collaborative activities on air pollution/acid rain have commenced.

The creation of such regional initiatives in Northeast Asia, however, in no way guarantees that a regime addressing long-range air pollution (acid rain) based on accumulated scientific knowledge—as with the European model—will be created in the region. In fact, the progress of each initiative has been slow. Some initiatives have stagnated because of weak institutional and financial structures. Little formal affiliation or coordination exists among the several initiatives, resulting in redundancies. This deficiency applies not only to the case of acid rain but also to other environmental issues. In fact, a number of regional environmental initiatives, started in the post-UNCED period, have little political clout. The mechanisms for cooperation have been characterized as unsatisfactory, with insufficient links between each pair of initiatives.

This chapter first attempts to expose such deficiencies of the cooperation mechanisms as a whole by surveying existing and ongoing major multilateral environmental programs and plans and examining the actors involved. Second, the chapter reviews major cooperative activities on acid rain and analyzes how the weaknesses and inadequacies of the environmental cooperation mechanisms as a whole have influenced and hindered the progress of cooperation on acid rain. The chapter then considers whether and how regional cooperation on the acid rain issue may be promoted.

MULTILATERAL ENVIRONMENTAL COOPERATION IN NORTHEAST ASIA

In this chapter Northeast Asia refers to China, Japan, the Republic of Korea (South Korea), the Democratic People's Republic of Korea (North Korea), Mongolia, the Russian Far East, and Chinese Taipei (Taiwan).[1] The climates in the subregion extend from Arctic to semitropical zones. High population densities, high rates of consumption of natural resources, and the pressures of rapid industrialization with inadequate environmental management have made Northeast Asia one of the most polluted subregions in the world. Northeast Asia has suffered environmental deterioration in terms of air pollution (including acid rain), coastal and inland water pollution, soil pollution, loss of biodiversity, and desertification. Some of this damage has extended beyond national boundaries.

Northeast Asia lacked a centralizing political, economic, or social force until the late 1980s because of the Cold War and a diversity of political and economic systems. Except for certain bilateral initiatives, little cooperation occurred on environmental issues. The Ministerial Conference on Environment and Development (MCED), held by the United Nations Economic and Social Committee on Asia and the Pacific (UNESCAP) in 1985, was a milestone in Asian environmental cooperation. Since 1985 the MCED, held every five years, has provided a forum for environment ministers in the Asia-Pacific region to review the state of the environment and promote collective actions for the environment among the countries. The Regional Action Programme on the environment and development was thus developed in 1995.

Considering the broad geographical scope and diverse economic and political systems of the Asia-Pacific region, UNESCAP has long emphasized collaboration at the subregional rather than the regional level. UNEP also emphasized the promotion of subregional environmental cooperation. In response, several environmental programs and plans were developed in some subregions—namely, the ASEAN Sub-Regional Environmental Programme (1977), the creation of SACEP (1981), and the South Pacific Regional Environment Programme (1982). No environmental programs or plans were created in Northeast Asia. The end of the Cold War, however, led to joint efforts to promote multilateral environmental cooperation in the region. Agenda 21, agreed upon during the Rio Summit in 1992, helped promote collaboration efforts at the subregional level. A number of cooperative programs, plans, and forums were advocated and extended through multiple channels in the 1990s (see Table 10.1).

Table 10.1—Major Events in Multilateral Environmental Cooperation in Northeast
Asia

Year	Major Events/Action Plans/Programs
1985	1st UNESCAP Ministerial Conference on Environment and Development (MCED)
1988	Japan-Korea Environmental Symposium
1990	Regional Strategy for Earth Summit (adopted at 2nd UNESCAP-MCED)
1991	Establishment of Environment Congress for Asia and the Pacific ECO-ASIA)
1992	Inauguration of North-East Asian Conference on Environmental Cooperation (NEACEC) Inauguration of North-East Asian Subregional Program on Environmental Cooperation (NEASPEC)
1994	Adoption of an Asia-Pacific Economic Cooperation (APEC) Environmental Vision Statement
1995	Regional Action Programme 1996–2000 (adopted at 3rd UNESCAP-MCED) Establishment of Asia-Pacific Network for Global Change Research (APN) Adoption of Memorandum on Understanding on Environmental Principles Governing the Tumen River Area Development Program (TRADP)
1998	Inauguration of Tripartite Environment Ministers Meeting (TEMM) among South Korea, China, and Japan
2000	Regional Action Programme 2001–2005 (adopted at 4th UNESCAP-MCED)

NORTH-EAST ASIAN CONFERENCE ON ENVIRONMENTAL COOPERATION

The origins of multilateral environmental cooperation in the Northeast Asian subregion can be traced back to 1988, when the Japan-Korea Environmental Symposium was held. The symposium was cohosted by the respective environment ministry/environment agency of Japan and South Korea, with the cooperation of UNEP, participation of China, and the attendance of the Soviet Union and Mongolia as observers. The symposium thus developed into a forum for exchanging information and exploring possibilities for regional cooperation among the five countries. With the Rio Summit in 1992 as a trigger, the symposium was renamed the North-East Asian Conference on Environmental Cooperation (NEACEC).

NEACEC gave the environment ministries and agencies from five countries in Northeast Asia—Japan, South Korea, China, Mongolia, and Russia—and international organizations such as UNEP and UNESCAP the chance to meet every year to exchange information, share experiences, and discuss future actions. Researchers, local government officials, and representatives of nongovernmental organizations (NGOs) have been also invited to conferences. Various issues have been placed on the agenda, from global and local environmental issues to specific policy instruments. The conference itself does not create projects or program-oriented activities. Member countries have hosted the conference on a rotating basis.[2]

NORTH-EAST ASIAN SUBREGIONAL PROGRAM ON ENVIRONMENTAL COOPERATION

Whereas NEACEC is an informal forum for policy dialogue among environmental government organizations, local governments, and specialists, the North-East Asian Subregional Program on Environmental Cooperation (NEASPEC) represents cooperation on environmental issues through foreign ministries (Overseas Environmental Cooperation Center 1994). The program was established at the first Meeting of Senior Officials of Environmental Cooperation in North-East Asia held in Seoul in 1993. The meeting was attended by six countries—China, Japan, South Korea, North Korea, Mongolia, and Russia—and was hosted by UNESCAP. The motivating force behind NEASPEC was the government of South Korea. Since then, the senior official meeting has been held every one or two years to decide on program activities.

The senior officials identified three priority subject areas—energy and air pollution, ecosystem management, and capacity building. Since 1997 several fundamental projects on energy and air pollution have been identified and implemented with financial assistance from the Asian Development Bank (ADB).

The secretariat for the program has been provisionally situated at UNESCAP until 2002 (UNESCAP 1999: 2). Although NEASPEC did not have its own financial mechanisms until recently, relying exclusively on ad hoc project-based funding, in March 2000 the participating governments agreed to establish a core fund to which participating countries are expected to make voluntary contributions. At the meeting South Korea expressed a voluntary contribution of US$100,000 to the fund (UNESCAP 2000: 1).

TRIPARTITE ENVIRONMENT MINISTERS MEETING

Concerted efforts at the ministerial level have also begun.[3] Following a proposal from South Korea during the sixth United Nations Commission on Sustainable Development in May 1998, the Tripartite Environment Ministers Meeting (TEMM) among China, Japan, and South Korea has been held annually since 1999. At the first meeting, held in Seoul in January 1999, the three countries recognized the need to cooperate and to improve the level and quality of environmental cooperation in the subregion. The countries agreed on four priority areas requiring increased cooperation: (1) raising awareness of the countries' "environmental community" and stimulating information exchange; (2) strengthening cooperation on global environmental issues, such as biodiversity and global warming; (3) preventing air pollution and protecting the marine environment; and (4) enhancing cooperation on environmental technology, the environmental industry, and environmental research. The need for more cooperation among not only their respective governments' environmental agencies but also among NGOs, research organizations, local governments, and private sectors was also emphasized.

The second ministerial meeting was held in Beijing in February 2000, at which the ministers agreed to develop and work on specific projects—focusing particularly on raising the consciousness of the environmental community, preventing freshwater pollution and land-based marine pollution, and cooperating in the field of environmental industry. The three countries have begun designing project proposals and have taken steps toward implementation.

TUMEN RIVER AREA DEVELOPMENT PROGRAM

The Tumen River Area Development Program (TRADP) is facilitated by the United Nations Development Program (UNDP) with the aim of promoting regional economic cooperation among China, South Korea, North Korea, Mongolia, and Russia.[4] This river area has achieved economic development at the expense of the environment and been threatened by environmental degradation—inland and coastal water pollution, biodiversity loss, deforestation, and air pollution.

In response to these environmental problems, a Memorandum of Understanding on Environmental Principles governing the TRADP was adopted in 1995. The countries created a strategic action program on the environment with the goal of developing an effective long-term regional strategy for dealing with international water pollution and biodiversity loss. The Global Environment Facility (GEF) sponsored the development of the action plan with US$5 million over a two-year period, and the project was launched in May 2000. In parallel, the Tumen Program Environmental Action Plan was also developed, focusing on transborder pollution and other forms of regional environmental damage, such as trade in endangered species. The action plan identified four program areas with detailed project proposals. TRADP member states are currently seeking investment and donor assistance for implementing the projects.

ASIA-PACIFIC ECONOMIC COOPERATION

Covering a much broader geographic area of the Asia-Pacific region, the Asia-Pacific Economic Cooperation (APEC) forum, inaugurated in 1989 and including eighteen member economies, also began to work toward integrating environmental and economic concerns. The member economies from Northeast Asia include China, Japan, South Korea, Russia, and Taiwan.

The First Environmental Ministerial Meeting, held in 1994, developed an "APEC Environmental Vision Statement." Since this statement and other declarations, APEC has developed a three-pronged environmental work program: (1) integration of environmental and economic considerations in APEC working groups; (2) attention to sustainable cities, clean technologies, and the marine environment; and (3) long-term focus on food, energy, the environment, economic growth, and population.

ASIA-PACIFIC NETWORK FOR GLOBAL CHANGE RESEARCH

The Asia-Pacific Network for Global Change Research (APN), established in 1995, is an intergovernmental network for the promotion of global environmental change research and links between science and policy making in the Asia-Pacific region. APN has funded a number of multicountry research projects related to long-term changes in the earth's climate, oceans, and terrestrial systems, as well as related physical, chemical, biological, and socioeconomic processes. The network also sponsors international workshops, symposiums, and conferences to strengthen interactions among scientists and policymakers, providing scientific input to policy decision making, and disseminating scientific knowledge to the public. Rules and procedures for the operation of all APN activities, research priorities, and programs and projects to be undertaken or financially supported by the APN are decided by annual intergovernmental meetings. The network secretariat is located in Kobe, Japan. Five of the twenty-one member states are from Northeast Asia: China, Japan, South Korea, Mongolia, and Russia.

ENVIRONMENT CONGRESS FOR ASIA AND THE PACIFIC

Inspired by the 1992 UNCED, the Environment Agency of Japan (now the Ministry of Environment) initiated the Environment Congress for Asia and the Pacific (ECO-ASIA), with the objective of fostering policy dialogue and cooperation among environmental ministers of participating countries. This meeting is held annually in Japan, with the financial support of the government of Japan. Although ECO-ASIA was originally intended as an informal forum for information exchange among ministers, it has developed the ECO-ASIA Long-term Perspective Project, which seeks to identify environmental policies that can contribute to the long-term sustainable development of the Asia-Pacific region. The project identifies major environmental issues confronting the region, examines their connection to socioeconomic issues, and forecasts social economic and environmental issues that may arise from various development scenarios for the region.

ACTORS IN ENVIRONMENTAL COOPERATION

In addition to these initiatives, collaboration focusing on single subjects also began in the 1990s.[5] Thus several questions are raised: Why were so many programs, plans, and forums established in parallel within a decade? How do they differ from each other? How are they linked? Analysis of the actors involved will help answer these questions.

REGIONAL ORGANIZATIONS

Among the major actors in the multilateral environmental cooperation arena are regional organizations. They play significant roles in addressing, identifying, coordinating, and implementing joint environmental activities for regional environmental cooperation. This is demonstrated by a number of European Community (EC) or European Union (EU) efforts to unify environmental standards in connection with economic activity, such as trade and manufacturing. In the case of long-range transboundary air pollution control, the convention itself was facilitated and coordinated by the UNECE. Data quality and compliance control within the air pollution regime have been significantly improved through the EC's efforts. The EC, however, has issued a number of pieces of common environmental legislation, such as directives limiting the emission of certain air pollutants from large combustion plants. It is assumed that those directives, reinforced by strict enforcement mechanisms, have caused EU member states to comply with the commitments of the LRTAP Convention and its protocols. Also, EC/EU financial and technology transfer mechanisms have official and unofficial links with the LRTAP Convention that apparently made it easier for member states to comply with the convention and its protocols (Nordberg 2000).

In Asia, since ASEAN has no strong central bureaucracy as does the EC/EU, it has provided minimal, largely administrative support to member states through the ASEAN secretariat (Tay 2000). ASEAN has drafted many regional environmental action plans, three environmental programs (1978–1992), two strategic action plans (1994–), and transboundary pollution action plans (1995–) (ASEAN Secretariat 1995).

Northeast Asia is characterized by the fact that no comprehensive regional organizations equivalent to the EC/EU and ASEAN exist, resulting in the emergence of several independent initiatives on environmental cooperation. The functions and activities of each subregional program, plan, and forum may overlap. In fact, redundancies seem inevitable in Northeast Asia.

The absence of a regional organization also affects the institutional and financial arrangements of each initiative, since they must start negotiations from scratch. The locations of the secretariat vary from one initiative to another: UNEP, UNESCAP, China, and Japan. No initiative has decided the location of the secretariat; instead, participating countries have taken the responsibility on a rotating basis. Accordingly, the status of participating states differs from one initiative to another, depending on diplomatic relations among countries within the region and the international membership of the host organizations.[6]

INTERNATIONAL ORGANIZATIONS

UN organizations have conducted various activities underlining their catalytic and coordinating roles in promoting regional and subregional cooperation in the environmental field. The most notable contribution of UNEP in promoting subregional cooperation lies in its role in coordinating and initiating the Regional Seas Program, which includes the Northwest Pacific Action Plan, East Asian Seas Action Plan, and South Asian Seas Action Plan.[7] Attaching a high priority to subregional approaches, UNEP has also provided substantial support to the drafting of action plans in most subregions, together with technical and financial assistance for a number of projects developed under subregional environmental programs (Natori 2000).

UNDP, which helps developing countries adopt integrated approaches to natural resource management to improve the lives of people living in poverty, has also provided financial and technical assistance to subregional environmental initiatives in the developing world. GEF has provided technical assistance grants to proposed biodiversity and climate change projects in Asia, including a project to prepare a Strategic Action Program for the Tumen River Area Development Program.

International banks such as the ADB and the World Bank have provided large amounts of financial assistance for environmental activities in the region. In particular, the ADB's regional technical assistance grants have played a significant role in facilitating multilateral environmental programs.

UNESCAP, which holds ministerial meetings on the environment and development every five years, develops regional action programs for sustainable development with five-year time frames as a follow-up to UNCED. To ensure implementation of the programs, ESCAP conducts consultations on a subregional basis. In keeping with this purpose, subregional efforts—including several plans endorsed by ASEAN, NEASPEC, and SACEP—were examined at the fourth ESCAP ministerial meeting, held in 2000 in Japan (Ichimura 2000). ESCAP has also devoted itself to maintaining and facilitating subregional meetings, particularly in the case of Northeast Asia. Upon request from countries of the subregion, UNESCAP has acted as the interim secretariat of NEASPEC since 1997 and has coordinated its activities. Furthermore, ESCAP held a senior officials meeting in Central Asia, where no regional organizations for environmental cooperation exist, and initiated the process of formulating subregional environmental programs in the late 1990s (Karim 1999).

Except for bilateral financial and technical assistance to China and other developing countries, Northeast Asia receives less funding from international organizations than other subregions—such as South Asia and Southeast Asia—for implementing multilateral environmental programs and plans, since the region contains two developed countries, Japan and South Korea. Instead, international organizations have given more attention and resources to supplementing the poor political relations in the region (Shrestha 2000). This is true for the Northwest Pacific Action Plan (NOWPAP) and NEASPEC. The former is administered by UNEP, whereas the latter has been managed by UNESCAP. There is, however, a limit to the role of international organizations. For example, UNESCAP wants to give up the position of secretariat of NEASPEC after 2002. Countries in Northeast Asia, however, want UNESCAP to continue to take the responsibility.

NATIONAL GOVERNMENTS

National governments are the most important actors among those involved in environmental cooperation. Regional cooperation should be based on spontaneous initiatives between countries. Transboundary pollution and even global environmental problems are rooted in human activities taking place at the local and national levels and are therefore best dealt with at the level closest to the source (Kato 2001). Without the commitment of national governments, regional cooperation cannot be successful.

It seems that countries in Northeast Asia, however, have not reached the point where concrete commitments can be negotiated. Because of the great diversity in their level of economic development and political systems, countries in the region have expressed different views and approaches to environmental cooperation—especially China, Japan, and South Korea.

China, suffering from devastating environmental deterioration including heavy industrial pollution, desertification, and inland water and coastal pollution, believes subregional cooperation should be focused on these issues. China also believes developed countries in the subregion should offer substantial financial support for the establishment and operation of environmental programs, as well as technical assistance for projects in their priority areas. China has been sensitive to the use of the term *transboundary*, as it does not wish to be seen by other countries as causing pollution that threatens environmental conditions in territories outside its borders (Brettell and Kawashima 1998).

Japan believes it has long worked to satisfy China's demands through bilateral official development aid. Some point out that Japan also appears wary of multilateral initiatives out of concern that such initiatives could become another channel for development assistance (Valencia 1998). Japan prefers to focus on monitoring the state of the environment and transboundary pollution.[8] Multilateral initiatives undertaken or endorsed by Japan target the wide region of East Asia or the entire Asia-Pacific region rather than focusing on Northeast Asia. Japan has also suggested that countries attending an initiative should share the burden to the extent possible under their present circumstances.

South Korea is keener to promote multilateral environmental cooperation focusing on Northeast Asia. It apparently believes multilateral initiatives should include both technical projects as preferred by China and monitoring-type environmental management projects as preferred by Japan (Valencia 1998). South Korea has tried to reconcile the approaches of both China and Japan by proposing that NEASPEC give priority to energy and air pollution projects. South Korea seemingly prefers the presence of international organizations in such multilateral initiatives. It has suggested that coordinating mechanisms for environmental cooperation channel financial and technical assistance from international organizations, including UNDP, UNESCAP, and the ADB.

International relations within Northeast Asia have been dominated by strong bilateral relations with the United States rather than multilateral cooperation among countries of the subregion. This is particularly true for Japan. Recent evidence indicates, however, that China has begun to show interest in multilateral relations. It can safely be said that now is the time to enhance multilateral cooperation in various fields in Northeast Asia. This is not an easy task, considering the absence of regional organizations, different and sometimes competing perspectives of national governments, and lack of expertise in multilateral diplomacy.

NGOs, CITIZENS, AND ACADEMICS

International NGOs and NGO networks are among the new emerging actors in environmental governance in Asia. Although most target single countries on single issues, several NGOs and networks have taken regional approaches to environmental protection. Some NGOs are linked to regional institutions endorsed by international and regional organizations and national governments.[9]

Nevertheless, NGO participation in multilateral environmental cooperation has thus far been limited in every subregion in Asia. A number of critics have suggested that regional initiatives to address environmental issues are often top-down, with little involvement of civil society, local governments, and NGOs—especially at the decision-making level (Nicro and Apikul 1999). Appropriate mechanisms for bringing the public and NGOs into play do not currently exist.

Academics—universities, research institutes, and individual technical and scientific specialists—are another newly emerging actor in regional environmental cooperation in Asia. Academics play significant roles in identifying environmental threats, drafting action plans and agreements, and monitoring implementation of the agreements in cooperation with officials from international organizations and national governments. In fact, the decision-making processes of several action plans and agreements of ASEAN and SACEP involved a number of lawyers and scientific specialists from several academic institutes, such as the Asia-Pacific Center for Environmental Law (Singapore), the Institute of Southeast Asian Studies (Singapore), the Asian Institute for Technology (located in Thailand), the Thailand Environment Institute, and the Tata Energy Research Institute (India).

Although collaboration has occurred mostly on a single-project basis, some research institutes have started to deal with more comprehensive tasks, such as creating regional plans and institutions and following up on their implementation. This is particularly true for the SEI. Taking advantage of its well-developed expertise on the regional approach to long-range transboundary air pollution control in Europe, the institute assisted UNEP and SACEP in drawing up the Malé Declaration on Control and Prevention of Air Pollution and Its Likely Transboundary Effects for South Asia. The institute has also assisted SACEP and its member states with developing common monitoring guidelines, provided technical and financial assistance, and reviewed implementation processes.

International joint research among academics has also been expanding since the 1990s. The creation of mechanisms to support such research efforts, such as APN, has accelerated the trend. This is not to say that such efforts are sufficiently advanced to create transnational "epistemic communities," or communities of experts sharing common values and approaches to policy problems.[10] Peter Haas (1989: 384) attributes the success of regional efforts to control marine pollution in the Mediterranean Sea to "the involvement of ecologists and marine scientists who set the international agenda and directed their own states' support to international efforts and toward the introduction of strong pollution control measures at home." It seems the time has not yet come for such a community to emerge in Asia.

On the contrary, most links between international and national governmental organizations and academics or between academics and other academics are on an ad hoc basis. These insufficient links sometimes cause friction between scientists, between scientists and policymakers, and among policymakers from different countries. In several cases some have criticized the fact that scientists from a single country consulted with decisionmakers on regional initiatives and took over the decision-making process.

CHARACTERISTICS OF COOPERATION MECHANISMS

The characteristic features of existing programs and mechanisms for environmental cooperation in Northeast Asia can be summarized as follows.

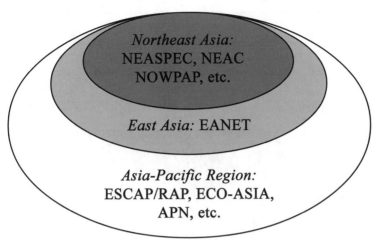

10.1 Multilayered Structure of Environmental Cooperation

1. Parallel institutions (see Table 10.2)—Several programs, plans, and forums for environmental cooperation were established through different channels, including environmental ministries, official diplomatic channels, and officers of environmental ministries and agencies, with little
coordination among the various channels. Consequently, some institutions contain material that is redundant.

Table 10.2—Major Cooperation Initiatives by Channel

Issue/Channel	Comprehensive	Sectoral
Ministerial	TEMM	
Diplomatic	NEASPEC	NOWPAP
		EANET
Environmental ministries	NEAC	EC
Citizens/NGOs	NAPEP*	

*North Asia–Pacific Environment Partnership

2. Multilayered structure (see Figure 10.1)—The geographic coverage of
environmental cooperation institutions ranges from global and wider-
than-regional to subregional. Some multilateral institutions target Northeast Asia, and some target the entire East Asian region or, even more
broadly, Asia and the Pacific. South Korea tends to focus on Northeast
Asia, whereas Japan focuses on the broader region (East Asia) or the
entire Asia-Pacific region.

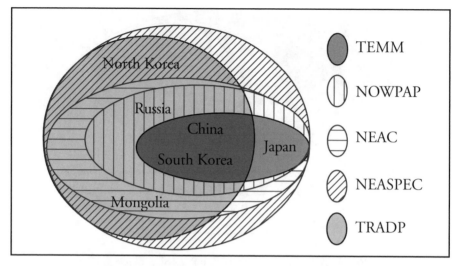

10.2 Membership of Major Environmental Initiatives

3. Different membership (see Figure 10.2)—The status of participating states differs from one institution to another, depending on diplomatic relations between countries and on the international membership of the host organization.
4. Weak institutional/financial structure—Most initiatives have poor organizational structures and weak financial foundations because each must start negotiations from scratch in the absence of regional organizations that can administer regional environmental plans and programs. Therefore cooperation has made slow progress.

The weaknesses and inadequacies of environmental cooperation mechanism in Northeast Asia can be observed in the case of single issues, such as acid rain and marine pollution control.[11] The latter part of this chapter takes up the case of acid rain to analyze the problem of cooperation in detail. First it explains how and by whom the issue of acid rain has been addressed, identified, and framed at the regional level. It then discusses how further progress on cooperative efforts on acid rain has been impeded by deficiencies of environmental cooperation mechanisms as a whole.

REGIONAL INITIATIVES ON ACID RAIN

The favorable economic trends observed in Northeast Asia in the 1980s and 1990s were accompanied by growing threats to the environment. Energy consumption in this region, which is highly dependent on coal, is expected to increase drastically, leading to a significant increase of emissions of acidifying pollutants such as sulfur dioxide (SO_2) and nitrogen oxides. In particular, emissions by China are causing great concern. Assuming that the countries of Northeast Asia will not take countermeasures other than those existing today, sulfur dioxide emissions were expected to increase from 14.7 million metric tons (mt) in 1990 to 40.5 mt in 2000 (Streets 1996). Nitrogen oxide emissions are projected to increase from 11.1 mt in 1990 to 38.9 mt in 2020 (Streets 1996). It is assumed that some air pollutants, carried by prevailing winds, will be transported across national boundaries. Within the next twenty to thirty years the human health and ecosystems in Northeast Asia will be seriously endangered by acidification.

In the early 1990s policymakers in some states in Northeast Asia became aware that the region was facing threats from air pollution and acid rain and hence needed to take preventive measures. Agenda 21, as adopted during the 1992 UNCED, spurred the awareness, stating that European experience in controlling long-range transboundary air pollution "based on a review process and cooperative programs for systematic observation of air pollution, assessment and information exchange . . . needs to be shared with other regions of the world" (Agenda 21, Chapter 9, 26).

The need for regional cooperation to investigate and monitor acid deposition has been repeatedly stressed at regional and subregional intergovernmental and interagency conferences, such as ECO-ASIA and NEACEC.

ACID DEPOSITION MONITORING NETWORK IN EAST ASIA

The first collective regional initiative on acid rain was the establishment of the Acid Deposition Monitoring Network in East Asia. The Environment Agency of Japan (now the Ministry of Environment) hosted four Expert Meetings between 1993 and 1997, inviting experts from all interested countries in East Asia,[12] together with representatives from the U.S. National Acid Precipitation Assessment Program and other concerned international organizations.[13] At the first meeting it was stated that "considering the expanding economies in the region, it was feared that adverse effects of acid precipitation would become a critical problem in certain areas in the future although evidence of the effects of acid precipitation on ecosystems has yet to be determined" (Interim Secretariat of EANET 1998: 41). The meeting agreed that a need existed to develop guidelines suitable for collaborative monitoring to address the region's lack of reliable monitoring data, resulting in part from the use of different monitoring methods by different countries and in part from the lack of skills and funding in certain countries. In 1997 the expert group finalized three technical manuals and one set of guidelines for monitoring acid deposition, as well as the "Design of an Acid Deposition Monitoring Network in East Asia," which addressed major activities and institutional and financial arrangements of EANET.

The Japanese prime minister conveyed Japan's intention to promote the establishment of an acid deposition monitoring network in East Asia, as part of the Japanese Initiatives for Sustainable Development Toward the 21st Century, at the 1997 UN General Assembly Special Session on Environment and Development. Simultaneously, the Japanese government initiated training programs inside and outside Japan and provided monitoring-related equipment to developing countries in the region as a part of Japanese overseas development assistance. Moreover, the Japanese government suggested holding an intergovernmental meeting of EANET in March 1998, together with a Working Group Meeting in preparation for the intergovernmental meeting. At the first intergovernmental meeting the participants agreed that EANET would begin preparatory-phase activities in April 1998 that would continue for two years.

The core activity of the network is to link ten participating countries and their monitoring sites and to collect, compile, and evaluate monitoring data on acid deposition (wet deposition, dry deposition, soil and vegetation, and inland aquatic environment) using shared guidelines and technical manuals. During the preparatory phase, participating countries prepared their national monitoring plans and designated and opened several monitoring sites in remote rural and urban areas. Monitoring data collected at respective monitoring sites were gathered at the Acid Deposition and Oxidant Research Center (ADORC), an interim network center, by national monitoring centers in each country. Quality assurance, quality control, and training programs were also developed and implemented.

The institutional structure during the preparatory phase consisted of four major organs: an interim scientific advisory group, consisting of representatives from each participating country, designated to implement tasks concerning scientific aspects of the monitoring activities; a working group, consisting of participating countries' representatives, assigned the task of reviewing preparatory-phase activities and preparations for future full-operation activities; the secretariat, provisionally located within the Environment Agency of Japan; and the interim network center, based at ADORC, which was established and located in Niigata, Japan (Interim Secretariat of EANET 1998).

The government of Japan contributed all operational costs—except certain local costs—for the preparatory-phase activities on a voluntary basis. Following the two-year interim activities the government of Japan hosted the second intergovernmental meeting, together with the working group meeting, in October 2000. The meeting concluded that "the preparatory-phase activities of EANET" have been successful in demonstrating EANET's feasibility and stated that activities "on a regular basis" would be inaugurated in January 2001 (Interim Secretariat [of EANET] and Interim Network Center [of EANET] 2000).

It was also decided that all organs of the institutional structure would continue to serve on an interim basis except for the location of the network secretariat. UNEP expressed its readiness to serve as the secretariat if so requested and was designated the secretariat for EANET after 2002 (Decision 3/IG.2) (Interim Secretariat [of EANET] and Interim Network Center [of EANET] 2000).

Currently, regulatory activities are in progress. A number of technical, institutional, and financial issues remain to be settled and elaborated. Financial matters are among the most pressing problems. EANET has depended exclusively on voluntary contributions by Japan. Although the second intergovernmental meeting encouraged participating countries to make voluntary financial and in-kind contributions to EANET activities, a firmer financial mechanism should be elaborated. Participating countries' sense of ownership should also be enhanced.

RAINS (REGIONAL AIR POLLUTION INFORMATION AND SIMULATION)-ASIA PROJECT

In the European experience with combating long-range transboundary air pollution, a long-range transport model called RAINS, developed by the International Institute for Applied System Analysis (IIASA), has played a significant and critical role in the LRTAP Convention.[14] The model exposes source-receptor relationships of acidification pollutants, assesses sulfur deposition and ecosystem protection levels resulting from different energy pathways and emission control strategies, and provides various control options and costs. It was officially admitted as a policy tool for the LRTAP Convention and was used to determine each country's commitment to limit and reduce emissions of pollutants, along with information about concrete policy options. In the 1990s this integrated model was altered for use in Asia. The new integrated model is called RAINS-ASIA.

IIASA and the Wageningen Agricultural University in the Netherlands took the initiative on integrating the model. The governments of the Netherlands, Norway, and Sweden provided funding through the World Bank and the ADB. A number of scientific institutions, together with individual scientists in Asia and Europe, collaborated on the model.[15] The model is expected to offer an analytical tool for decisionmakers in the region, allowing them to analyze future trends in emissions, estimate the regional impacts of resulting acid deposition levels, and evaluate the costs and effectiveness of alternative mitigation options.

MODEL INTER-COMPARISON STUDY OF LONG-RANGE TRANSPORT AND SULFUR DEPOSITION IN EAST ASIA PROJECT

RAINS-ASIA, as explained earlier, was considered a valuable first attempt toward integrated assessment of future SO_2 emissions in Asia. The model, however, contains great uncertainty on some important components, such as the sensitivity of ecosystems and critical load calculations (Hayes and Zarsky 1995). Uncertainty also exists with respect to long-range pollutant transport models.

Recognizing that long-range transport models would play a critical and significant role in policy analysis, a number of research institutes in both Asia and Europe have attempted to improve the models. There are, however, great differences between these models, as well as gaps in information about the processes involved, giving rise to differences in predicted outcomes. For example, one Chinese research institute estimated that China accounts for only 3.5 percent of Japan's total sulfur deposition and that the remainder comes from Japanese anthropogenic or volcanic sources. In contrast, Yoichi Ichikawa and Sshin-ichi Fujita estimated that China is a major source of wet sulfate deposition in Japan, calculating that it accounts for nearly half of that deposition (Ichikawa and Fujita 1995).

Convinced that a great need exists to determine the cause of the wide range of estimates, in 1998 an international joint project, Model Inter-Comparisons of Long-Range Transport and Sulfur Deposition in East Asia (MICS-ASIA), was initiated through nonofficial channels (Ichikawa and Hayami 1999). The collaborating research institutes include IIASA in Austria, the Central Research Institute of the Electric Power Industry of Japan, the University of Iowa, and several research institutes and experts from South Korea, Taiwan, Japan, Sweden, and China. The project has been cofunded by IIASA and the Central Research Institute of the Electric Power Industry of Japan, and they have sought new contributors. They are currently consulting on the matter ADORC, the EANET network center.

JOINT RESEARCH PROJECT ON LONG-RANGE AIR POLLUTANTS IN SOUTH KOREA, CHINA, AND JAPAN

This joint research project was initiated by the Ministry of Environment in South Korea. NIER has hosted Expert Meetings on long-range transboundary air pollutants annually since 1995, inviting experts and policymakers from South Korea, China, and Japan. In 1999 the expert groups decided to conduct joint research on long-range transboundary air pollutants in Northeast Asia and worked out five-year joint monitoring and modeling research plans. Major components of the plan include development of emissions inventories, numerical simulations, ground monitoring, and aircraft observations.

1999 ESCAP EXPERT GROUP MEETING ON EMISSION MONITORING AND ESTIMATION AND 1999 NEASPEC SENIOR OFFICIAL MEETING

Along with monitoring and modeling activities, the need for emissions monitoring and estimates has been addressed as another important step toward constructing a scientific infrastructure to understand acidification in the region. UNESCAP, in collaboration with the Environment Agency of Japan and together with the EANET interim network center, hosted an Expert Group Meeting on Emission Monitoring and Estimation, inviting government officers and experts from China, Japan, South Korea, Mongolia, Indonesia, Malaysia, the Philippines, Thailand, and Vietnam and international organizations such as the ADB, UNEP, and UNECE. Recognizing that a wide range exists of methods and quality of emissions monitoring and estimation of respective countries, the meeting recommended that guidebooks on the issue should be developed. In response, UNESCAP examined the potential for implementing the project within the framework of NEASPEC, funded by the ADB.

The recommendation was submitted to the senior-official meeting of NEASPEC in 1999, which agreed to launch the regional project on air pollution with the financial assistance of the ADB. The recommendation, however, was not included in the project. Among the major components of the project was the creation of a regional data clearinghouse for environmental pollution data monitoring and analysis, located at NIER in South Korea. Its duties include the collection, comparison, and analysis of environmental pollution data and the facilitation of environmental information exchanges among member states through the Internet.

UNDP/UNDESA (UN Department of Economic and Social Affairs) Project on Transboundary Pollution Modeling in Northeast Asia

The UNDP and UNDESA, in cooperation with government officers and scientists, have initiated a regional project to address air pollution associated with massive use of coal in Northeast Asia (RAS/92/461 Energy, Coal Combustion and Atmospheric Pollution). As part of the project the UN Workshop on Transboundary Pollution was held in China in 1997, at which government officers and scientists from four participating countries—China, North Korea, Mongolia, and South Korea—agreed to launch a project on transboundary pollution modeling in Northeast Asia. The major objective of the project is to develop models for the regional impacts of transboundary air pollution as a quantitative basis for regional planning.

Among the major achievements of the project to date are the development of a manual for preparation of emissions inventories for use in transboundary air pollution modeling and the establishment of an electronic, Internet-based clearinghouse. The former was drafted by the SEI, commissioned by UNDESA and UNDP, and modified by experts from member countries. The latter was implemented by the State Environmental Protection Administration of China and the Shenzhen Environmental Training Center, with the goal of sharing information on transboundary air pollution issues among groups carrying out air pollution modeling in Northeast Asia.[16]

ATMOSPHERE ACTION NETWORK EAST ASIA

The Atmosphere Action Network East Asia (AANEA) is an international NGO network established in 1994 to encourage regional cooperation between NGOs and to address the concerns of governments and citizens on atmospheric problems, including transboundary air pollution and climate change. The network consists of seventeen NGOs from seven East Asian countries (China, Hong Kong, Japan, Korea, Mongolia, Russia, and Taiwan). AANEA held a workshop in 1998 during which a project for joint monitoring of air pollution in East Asia was proposed.

INSTITUTIONAL BARRIERS
TO FURTHER COOPERATION ON ACID RAIN

As described earlier, the 1990s witnessed the launch of a number of regional initiatives on acidification. That is not to say, however, that every state and relevant actor has actively participated in the process or that collaborative initiatives have gone smoothly and without controversy.

PARALLEL INSTITUTIONS

Among the critical problems of regional cooperation on acid rain are redundant activities among several parallel initiatives. This is particularly the case for monitoring activities. EANET, launched by the government of Japan, is devoted to monitoring acid deposition in ten East Asian countries, whereas AANEA has also established a network for monitoring acid deposition in East Asia. Similarly, NIER in Korea has established a regional data clearinghouse for environmental pollution data monitoring and analysis, but with broader thematic coverage. The Joint Research Project endorsed by South Korea also includes monitoring as one of its major activities. Nevertheless, little coordination has occurred among the government of Japan, AANEA, and NIER regarding these similar initiatives.

MULTILAYER STRUCTURE AND DIFFERENT MEMBERSHIP

The geographical coverage of the different initiatives ranges from three-country groups composed of Japan, China, and South Korea to all Northeast Asian countries to the broader East Asian region. This multilayer structure makes the situation complicated and can sometimes be a restraint on regional cooperation (see Figure 10.3). For example, as mentioned earlier, NEASPEC declined the proposal to develop guidebooks on emission monitoring and estimation made by the 1999 ESCAP expert group meeting. NEASPEC covers six countries of Northeast Asia, whereas ESCAP tar-

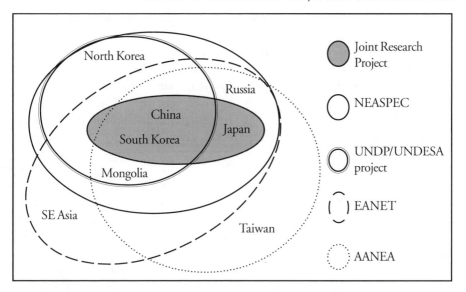

10.3 Multilayered Structure and Membership of Major Initiatives on Acidification

geted nine countries in East Asia. It is assumed that the different geographical coverage of the two groups resulted in the rejection of the proposal.

WEAK INSTITUTIONAL/FINANCIAL STRUCTURE

Most initiatives suffer from weak institutional and financial foundations. In particular, securing financial sources is a critical need. One exception is EANET, whose operating costs have been voluntarily financed by the government of Japan. Nevertheless, Japanese representatives want each participating country to carry some of the financial burden so that every country enhances its sense of ownership. Most other countries, however, believe Japan should shoulder the entire burden.

The development of several initiatives on acid rain per se is expedient, since it indicates a high level of concern by regional countries and their willingness to investigate the problem of acid rain. The lack of formal affiliations among the different initiatives, however, means cooperative mechanisms on acid rain as a whole are overly complicated and inefficient. Although coordination among initiatives is needed, some initiatives compete with one another. It might safely be said that countries have a halfhearted attitude toward regional initiatives they do not endorse.

Anna Brettell and Yasuko Kawashima (1998: 111) argue that the Chinese "have concerns about national sovereignty that manifest at times, as an unwillingness to participate, or to share or grant access to data and information." This reluctance has frustrated many scientists who wish to improve their long-range transport models. The lack of openness is not a problem exclusively of China but is common for most initiatives guided by national governments in the region. The lack of openness and transparency in regional initiatives seems to mirror the domestic policy-making process of each country, which exemplify a lack of transparency in decision-making processes, limited disclosure, and insufficient accountability. Furthermore, insufficient links between national governments and scientists and between groups of scientists causes friction among them, further complicating the situation.

CONCLUSION

The evidence, as analyzed here, shows that institutional and political barriers exist to further cooperation on acid rain in Northeast and East Asia. The question is whether and how the region can escape the existing stagnation. Considering that no regional organization exists, international organizations and NGOs hold the key to improving the situation, as they can act as intermediaries for the countries of Northeast Asia. To this end the initiatives endorsed by international organizations, such as the UNDP/UNDESA project, should play a significant role. Although Japan is not a member of the project since it is not a member of UNDP, it has started attending project activities as an observer. The NEASPEC project (regional data clearinghouse located in the National Institute for Environmental Research in South Korea) is also endorsed by an international organization (UNESCAP). EANET will be a new addition to the list, since UNEP took on the responsibility of the network secretariat in 2001. It is hoped that all relevant actors will endeavor to create links between initiatives and to clarify their respective roles, with the three initiatives (UNDP/UNDESA project, NEASPEC project, and EANET) as the central focus.

MICS-ASIA, initiated by nonofficial scientists who share common beliefs, is significant because it shows that an "epistemic community" is developing. International organizations should ensure that the research outcomes of high-quality international projects are reflected in regional policy-making processes.

Taiwan has no access to many regional initiatives since its position in international politics is uncertain and it is not a member of the United Nations. Although Northeast Asia needs to create a framework in which all parties in the region can participate, this cannot be easily achieved because of the political sensitivities and security situation that prevail. Only NGOs can remedy this deficiency for the time being. In this regard an international NGO network, such as AANEA, might act as an intermediary. Scientists from Taiwan have access to nonofficial channels such as MICS-ASIA. The flexibility and openness of MICS-ASIA should be maintained.

At the same time, countries in the region and the relevant actors need to improve their diplomatic relations and skills to handle the complex and difficult problems of different political systems and perspectives. This is particularly true for Japan and South Korea. For example, the two countries had major arguments over the name of a sea area—the Sea of Japan/East Sea—which has nothing to do with environmental collaboration in essence and caused a meeting to stagnate.[17] Although the two countries have much in common in that both are willing to promote and lead the various environmental initiatives, they are working without linking up with each other. The result has been parallel institutions and stagnation. Both countries need to develop and share strategies for regional cooperation that incorporate their own as well as the other country's interests and the common interests of the region.

The next question is how to develop effective regional plans to control acidification in Northeast Asia based on accumulated scientific facts and knowledge. In the case of Europe, the first step taken was to gather scientific facts on acid deposition, pollutant emissions, and reaction, transport, and diffusion mechanisms. During this period participating countries agreed to the LRTAP Convention. The second step was to develop efficient strategies for acid rain control based on the accumulated scientific knowledge and information. During the process several protocols regulating specific air pollutants were adopted under the framework convention. The third step was to implement a pollution abatement and prevention process, mostly at the domestic and local levels. The East Asian region is currently at the first step, with a status equivalent to that of Europe in the mid-1970s. It seems unlikely that legally binding treaties or protocols, similar to the LRTAP Convention, will appear in East Asia, given the fundamental differences that exist between the two regions. It is more difficult for East Asia to reach a consensus because it lacks Europe's relative economic, political, and social homogeneity (Takahashi 2000).

One of the biggest differences between Europe and East Asia is that the third step has already started to take shape in East Asia. That is, countries in the region are paying more attention to, and strengthening national laws and regulations on, controlling air pollution and acid rain. A large amount of environmental investment has been made in China through both official development assistance and foreign private investment.

Considering these facts, it might safely be said that a significant degree of collaboration has already taken place on the issue of acid rain in Northeast Asia. Much of this collaboration has unfortunately been undertaken in a fragmented manner. Therefore the region needs to form links between individual initiatives and financial mechanisms, between bilateral and multilateral aid programs, between donor agencies, and between regional cooperation institutions and financial aid mechanisms.[18] To make this real, the first step would be to maintain openness and full disclosure. Recently, some initiatives have started to open their information through Web pages. This trend should be further enhanced.

NOTES

1. See Takahashi 2001 for detailed information on topics addressed in this section.
2. Japan, South Korea, and China have hosted NEACEC in turn, and in 2000 Mongolia hosted the ninth meeting for the first time.
3. See its Web page for detailed information on TEMM.
4. See its Web page for detailed information on TRADP.
5. These include NOWPAP, adopted in 1984, and EANET, which is discussed in more detail later in this chapter.
6. For example, North Korea does not attend most subregional programs except those hosted by UN organizations. North Korea cannot receive assistance from the ADB, to which it does not belong. Taiwan has no access to many initiatives because its position in international politics is uncertain, although it is a member of APEC and ADB.
7. The Regional Seas Programs endorsed by UNEP took off from the regional-level approach recommended at the 1972 Stockholm Conference and led to remarkable developments as subsequent action plans were formulated—the Mediterranean Action Plan of 1975 and the Barcelona Convention of 1976. The approach has spread to other regions of the world, and fourteen Regional Seas Programs are now in operation, with more than 140 seacoast countries participating in various plans (UNEP 1997).
8. Japan places a high priority on multilateral programs in areas such as marine pollution, acid rain, and air and water pollution. Japan has recently expressed deep concern over climate change.
9. One encouraging example is a program of the International Union for the Conservation of Nature (IUCN) on regional aquatic ecosystems of Asia. IUCN has maintained strong ties with the Mekong River Commission and has conducted environmental assessments of developments in the lower river basin to create new protected wetlands areas, support national agencies, increase institutional capacity, assist governments with implementation of the Ramsar Convention, disseminate information, and promote communication among various actors (IUCN 2000). Another example is migratory waterbird protection. The late 1990s witnessed the emergence of several waterbird networks, administratively managed by Wetlands International–Asia Pacific. The networks link researchers, conservationists, government officers, and any other parties concerned about waterbird protection in an open manner and provide a basis for joint research and conservation activities.
10. According to Haas (1990: 55), an epistemic community is "a professional group that believes in the same cause-and-effect relationships, tests to assess them, and shares common values. As well as sharing an acceptance of a common body of facts, its members share a common interpretive framework, or

'consensual knowledge,' from which they convert facts or observations to policy-relevant conclusions."

11. See Valencia 1998 and Haas 1998 for the case of marine pollution control.
12. They include China, Indonesia, Japan, South Korea, Malaysia, Mongolia, the Philippines, Singapore, Thailand, and Russia.
13. They include UNEP, EMEP, the World Bank, and others.
14. The RAINS model was developed at IIASA as a computer-based tool for the integrated assessment of alternative strategies to reduce acid deposition in Europe. The RAINS model provides data on energy scenarios, emission control technologies and abatement costs, atmospheric transport, and critical loads. RAINS allows the user to examine the costs and effectiveness of different emission control strategies under various energy-use scenarios. IIASA is a nongovernmental research organization located in Austria. The institute conducts interdisciplinary scientific studies on environmental, economic, technological, and social issues in the context of human dimensions of global change. It is sponsored by its national member organizations in North America, Europe, and Asia. See IIASA Web page for detailed information.
15. Collaborators from Asia include the Asian Institute of Technology (Bangkok), Bangladesh Council of Scientific and Industrial Research, Research Center for Eco-environmental Sciences (China), Tata Energy Research Institute (India), Institute of Technology (Indonesia), University of Tokyo (Japan), Korea Energy Economics Institute (South Korea), University of Sains Malaysia (Penang), Pakistan Atomic Energy Agency (Pakistan), Environmental and Protection Monitoring Division (Philippines), Institute of Energy (Vietnam), Center for Atmospheric Sciences (United States), Indian Institute of Technology (India), Jahangir Nagar University (Bangladesh), Hong Kong Polytechnic University, Malaysian Meteorological Service, Department of Hydrology and Meteorology (Nepal), Ajou University (South Korea), Taiwan National University, Research and Training Center (Thailand), and Institute of Chemistry (Vietnam). See IIASA 1999 for detailed information.
16. See Shenzhen Environmental Training Center Web page for detailed information.
17. The sea area is called Sea of Japan in Japan and East Sea in South Korea. In a document prepared by the EANET network center (located in Niigata, Japan) during the second EANET intergovernmental meeting in 2000, a sentence described the location of the network center using the term "Sea of Japan." The delegation of South Korea asked to replace it with "Sea of Japan/East Sea," but the Japanese delegation did not agree. The chairperson reconciled the situation, and at last it was decided simply to cut "Sea of Japan" from the document.
18. To this end the creation of the China Council, which consists of China and its donor countries and coordinates efficient assistance to China, is a step in the right direction.

REFERENCES

ASEAN Secretariat. 1995. *ASEAN Cooperation Plan on Transboundary Pollution.* Jakarta: ASEAN Secretariat.

Brettell, Anna, and Yasuko Kawashima. 1998. "Sino-Japanese Relations on Acid Rain." In Miranda A. Schreurs and Dennis Pirages, eds., *Ecological Security in Northeast Asia*. Seoul: Yonsei University Press.

Haas, Peter M. 1989. "Do Regimes Matter? Epistemic Communities and Mediterranean Pollution Control." *International Organization* 43, 3: 377–405.

———. 1990. *Saving the Mediterranean: The Politics of International Environmental Cooperation*. New York: Columbia University Press.

———. 1998. "Prospects for Effective Marine Governance in the Northwest Pacific Region." Paper presented at the Energy, Security, and Environment in Northeast Asia Workshop "Energy-Related Marine Issues in the Sea of Japan," Tokyo, Japan, 11–12 July.

Hayes, Peter, and Lyuba Zarsky. 1995. "Acid Rain in a Regional Context." Nautilus Institute <http://www.nautilus.org/papers/enviro/acidrain.html>.

Ichikawa, Yoichi, and Sshin-ichi Fujita. 1995. "An Analysis of Wet Deposition of Sulfate Using a Trajectory Model for East Asia." *Water, Air and Soil Pollution* 85: 1927–1932.

Ichikawa, Yoichi, and Hiroshi Hayami. 1999. "Report on Workshop on the Transport of Air Pollutants in Asia." *Taiki Kankyo Gakkai-shi* [journal for atmospheric environment] 34, 6: A53 (in Japanese).

Ichimura, Masakazu. 2000. Expert on environmental policies, Environment and Natural Resources Department Division, UNESCAP. Interview with the author, Thailand, 20 November.

Interim Secretariat of EANET. 1998. Acid Deposition Monitoring Network in East Asia, the First Intergovernmental Meeting, the First and the Second Meeting of the Working Group. Yokohama, Japan.

Interim Secretariat [of EANET] and Interim Network Center [of EANET]. 2000. *Summary of the Second Intergovernmental Meeting on the Acid Deposition Monitoring Network in East Asia (EANET)*. Niigata, Japan, 25–26 October.

International Institute for Applied System Analysis (IIASA). IIASA Web page <http://www.iiasa.ac.at/>.

———. 1999. "RAINS (Regional Air Pollution Information and Simulation)-Asia" <http://www.adorc.gr.jp/mirror/docs/index.html>.

International Union for the Conservation of Nature (IUCN). 2000. *IUCN in Asia: Moving Forward From Kota Kinabalu*. Pakistan: IUCN–World Conservation Union.

Karim, Rezaul. 1999. Chief, Environment and Natural Resources Development Division, UNESCAP. Interview with the author, Bangkok, Thailand, 6 October.

Kato, Kazu. 2001. "An Analytical Framework for a Comparative Study of Sub-regional Environmental Programs in Asia." In *IGES Environmental Governance Project 2001: Regional/Subregional Environmental Cooperation in Asia and the Pacific*. Shonan, Japan: IGES.

Natori, Yoshihiro. 2000. Deputy regional director, UNEP Regional Office for Asia and the Pacific. Interview with the author, Thailand, 20 November.

Nicro, Somrudee, and Christine Apikul. 1999. "Environmental Governance in Thailand." In *IGES Environmental Governance Project 1999. Environmental Governance in Four Asian Countries*. Shonan, Japan: IGES.

Nordberg, Lars. 2000. Former deputy director, Environment and Human Settlements Division, UN Economic Commission for Europe. Interview with the author, Geneva, Switzerland, 17 March.

Overseas Environmental Cooperation Center [of Japan]. 1994. *Report of the Meeting: The Second Northeast Asian Conference on Environmental Cooperation,* commissioned by Environmental Agency of Japan. Tokyo: Overseas Environmental Cooperation Center.

Shenzhen Environmental Training Center, State Environmental Protection Administration of China, Information Clearinghouse. "Trans-boundary Air Pollution Modelling in Northeast Asia Region" <http://www.chinasetc.org/>.

Shrestha, Surendra. 2000. Regional coordinator, UNEP/EAP-AP. Interview with the author, Asian Institute of Technology, Bangkok, Thailand, 11 November.

Streets, David G. 1996. "Energy and Acid Rain Projections for Northeast Asia." ESENA Project <http://www.glocom.ac.jp/eco/esena/resource/streets/index.html>.

Takahashi, Wakana. 2000. "Formation of an East Asian Regime for Acid Rain Control." *International Review for Environmental Strategies* 1: 97–117.

———. 2001. "Environmental Cooperation in Northeast Asia." In *IGES Environmental Governance Project 2001: Regional/Subregional Environmental Cooperation in Asia.* Shonan, Japan: IGES.

Tay, Simon. 2000. "The South East Asian Fires and Haze: Challenges to Regional Cooperation in ASEAN and the Asia-Pacific." Paper presented at Asia Pacific Agenda Project, Okinawa Forum, Okinawa, Japan, 25–26 March.

Tripartite Environment Ministers Meeting (TEMM). TEMM Web site <http://www.temm.org/>.

Tumen River Area Development Program (TRADP). TRADP Web site <http://www.tradp.org/>.

United Nations. 1993. *AGENDA 21: Program of Action for Sustainable Development, Rio Declaration on Environment and Development,* and *Statement of Forest Principles.* New York: United Nations Publications.

United Nations Economic and Social Committee on Asia and the Pacific (UNESCAP) (NEASPEC secretariat). 1999. "Institutional and Financial Mechanisms for North-East Asian Subregional Program on Environmental Cooperation (NEASPEC)." Distributed at the Expert Meeting on Environmental Cooperation Mechanisms in North-East Asia, Seoul, 10–11 November.

———. 2000. ENR/SO/ECNA(6)/Rep. "Report of the Sixth Meeting of Senior Officials on Environmental Cooperation in North-East Asia," Seoul, 9–10 March.

United Nations Environment Program (UNEP). 1997. *Regional Seas: Action Plan for the Protection, Management and Development of the Marine and Coastal Environment of the Northwest Pacific Region.* NOWPAP Publication 1.

Valencia, Mark. 1998. "Ocean Management Regimes in the Sea of Japan: Present and Future." Paper presented at the ESENA workshop "Energy-Related Marine Issues in the Sea of Japan," Tokyo, Japan, 11–12 July.

II

Toward a Greener Peace?
Nuclear Reprocessing, Security,
and International Cooperation in East Asia

STEPHANIE TAI, ANDREW B. LOEWENSTEIN, TODD BISSETT,
AND ERIC O'MALLEY

O ver the next few decades Asia will be a testing ground for energy
development, as major economic ambitions requiring multilateral
cooperation must overcome deeply rooted ethnic suspicion and
substantial political barriers. One thing is certain: this experiment will require energy resources at an unprecedented scale. Whether Asian goals of
expanding energy resources can be met in an environmentally sustainable
manner is a linchpin question that has been inadequately addressed, given
the stakes involved. Asian nations currently or on the verge of experiencing
rapid industrialization see nuclear power as the most workable solution,
even as Western developed nations increasingly eschew this source of energy,
mainly for political reasons. Few if any Asian nations, however, credibly
envision running an autonomous nuclear energy program. Such a program
would involve the generation of plutonium, a highly fissile end product that
can be reprocessed and reused in specialized reactors but that is also the
material used to make high-yield nuclear bombs.

An autonomous nuclear energy program would also require adequate
and accessible supplies of uranium, established processing and refining

The views and analysis presented by Stephanie Tai are her own and should not be
interpreted as reflecting those of the United States or of the U.S. Department of
Justice.

capabilities, safe and efficient generators, and permanent disposal methods for waste. Although different Asian countries possess many of these resources, no single country has them all. This imbalance of nuclear assets consequently presents an opportunity for long-standing regional conflicts to cede to domestic necessities, fostering cooperation and improving regional stability.

The Republic of Korea (ROK) and the People's Republic of China (PRC) are poised as Asia's pioneers in commercial plutonium trading. The next stage of economic development of both the ROK and the PRC is expected to be powered increasingly by nuclear energy, resulting in an enormous amount of high-level spent nuclear wastes, including weapons-usable plutonium. The PRC is expected soon to have the technology and facilities necessary to reprocess the waste generated by itself and the ROK into a reusable source of nuclear energy, greatly protracting the life span of primary nuclear fuels, as well as addressing—at least in part—the problem of spent fuel management. But these are not ordinary commodities, and moving plutonium across national borders is one of the most controversial issues facing the nuclear industry. Such trade is fraught with environmental and political costs that reach far beyond the borders of any two nations.

SPENT FUEL REPROCESSING

One universally recognized concern over nuclear power is its generation of spent fuel in the form of uranium and plutonium waste (Carter and Pigford 1999: 8; Williams and Deese 1979: 9–29). These wastes pose enormous human and environmental health risks, as exposure to radiation from high-level nuclear wastes can kill almost instantaneously. Because uranium and plutonium high-level waste remains radioactive for over 100,000 years, storage facilities for this waste must have the capacity to handle the material for that lengthy period of time (Office of Nuclear Waste Management 1980). The storage of spent nuclear fuel is complicated by difficulties predicting the stability of geological repositories and maintaining the stability of surface or underground storage facilities (Nuclear Energy Agency 1993: 99–110; Krauskopf 1990). In addition, significant political pressure against storage facilities often prevents them from being sited (Carter and Pigford 1999: 8).

These storage concerns have led some countries to consider reprocessing as a means of managing the waste produced through their commercial reactors. Through reprocessing, plutonium and uranium are separated from the highly radioactive fission products contained in spent fuel. This separated plutonium (in the form of plutonium oxide) and uranium (in the form of uranium oxide) in turn can be refabricated into mixed-oxide fuels and used as reactor fuel for breeder reactors and light water reactors. Proponents view spent fuel reprocessing as a way to reduce spent fuel stockpiles (and thereby reduce the monetary costs and environmental hazards involved with storing spent fuel) while recapturing some of the remaining energy content in the spent fuel. Furthermore, these proponents regard reprocessing as a means for nations to address their energy needs without boosting greenhouse gas emissions.

In Asia, these storage concerns are especially salient. At the November 2000 Pacific Basin Nuclear Conference, held in Seoul, officials from Japan, the ROK, and Taiwan discussed the fact that the Asian public has become more concerned about the nuclear dangers involved with storing spent fuel "as densely populated countries near political decisions about siting repositories in the limited space available" (Hibbs 2000d: 12). This led conference speaker James Lake, president of the American Nuclear Society, to suggest that this "greater concern for the environment may make it increasingly less desirable to bury spent fuel in the ground" and in turn may lead to a reassessment of spent waste management policies "favoring geological disposal of spent fuel over reprocessing" (Hibbs 2000d: 12).

DIRECT PHYSICAL COSTS ASSOCIATED WITH REPROCESSING

The option of reprocessing spent nuclear fuel, however, comes with its own safety concerns. Indeed the 11 March 1997 accident at a Japanese nuclear fuel reprocessing facility best illustrates critics' fears about the hazards of reprocessing spent nuclear fuel ("Tokaimura Reprocessing" 1997). During the accident a fire and explosion occurred at the nuclear fuel reprocessing facility in Tokai, Japan. Thirty-seven plant workers were exposed to radiation. Toxic plutonium was released into the atmosphere and detected as far as twenty-three miles away (Pollack 1997).

The cause of the accident was traced to the ignition of asphalt, which was used to give nuclear waste a slurry consistency before being poured into drums for temporary storage (Crowell and Mutsuko 1997). When the asphalt was mixed with nitric acid, contained in liquefied nuclear waste, a chemical reaction occurred. The reaction generated heat and set the asphalt—which has a low ignition point—on fire ("Chemical Reaction" 1997). As a result of operator error, the sprinkler system used to put out the fire was left on for only one minute (Pollack 1997), and the fire was inadequately extinguished. About ten hours later the asphalt slurry exploded, knocking out windows and a door and providing a route for radioactive materials to escape into the atmosphere.

Although no one died as a result of the accident, many found its low-tech nature to be cause for concern (Pollack 1997). The plant's containment system failed to function properly, allowing the radiation to leak further into an adjacent building. Workers at the plant were not evacuated until twenty-four minutes after the fire was noticed. Reporting was lax— Tokai village officials were not informed of any radiation leakage until four hours after the explosion. Similar mistakes had led to a coolant leak just two years earlier at a Japanese fast-breeder reactor facility, indicating that the instances of human error at Tokai were not isolated.

At the time, the Tokai facility was Japan's only domestic reprocessing plant, handling about 12 percent of the spent fuel from the country's nuclear power plants. Japan, however, sent and continues to send additional spent fuel abroad for reprocessing. After the accident the Tokai plant was shut down for over four years. It has reopened but is engaging only in research and development of reprocessing technologies rather than in the actual reprocessing of nuclear fuel ("Nuclear-Fuel Reprocessing" 2000). Currently, a larger reprocessing plant is under construction in Rokkasho and is expected to become operative in 2005 (Fukada 2000).

The accident at Tokai was only one of many accidents that have occurred at nuclear reprocessing plants. In 1993 an explosion and fire occurred at the Tomsk-7 nuclear reprocessing plant in Siberia, also resulting from a chemical reaction involving nitric acid (Ivanov and Perera 1993). The British Nuclear Fuels nuclear reprocessing plant at Sellafield has also had a history of accidents, all attributable at least in part to human error. The incidents include the large-scale discharge of low-level liquid waste into the Irish Sea and the release of radioactive sulfur into the atmosphere (Ahlstrom 1998; Lean 1998).

Reprocessing plants have also been accused of discharging radioactive residue into the air and sea during their "normal" course of operation (Forwood 1999; Gibson 2000). Ireland and Denmark have long criticized reprocessing plants as the largest source of artificial radioactivity in the northeast Atlantic. Indeed in June 2000 Denmark sponsored a resolution—supported by twelve of the sixteen members of the 1997 Ospar Convention on preventing and reducing marine pollution in the northeast Atlantic Ocean— that urged all parties to the convention to abandon reprocessing (MacLachlan, Marshall, and Sains 2000). The Danish proposal was weaker than the one Ireland put forth, which urged the United Kingdom to completely halt reprocessing at the controversial Sellafield site.

In addition, reprocessing plants such as Sellafield have been accused of causing significant health problems for their workers and surrounding communities. The Sellafield dormitory town of Seascale has ten times the U.K. national average of childhood leukemia, and many reports find a statistical connection between reprocessing and cancers in surrounding communities (Forwood 1999; MacMahon 1992). And a year 2000 study sponsored by the Irish government suggested that the radioactive discharge from Sellafield into the Irish Sea has caused a 60 percent greater risk of leukemia and a 40 percent greater risk of cancer for residents directly opposite Sellafield on the Irish coast ("Revealed" 2000).

Accidents can also occur while the spent nuclear fuel is being transported from nuclear power plants to reprocessing facilities, which are often in separate locations—often even in different countries. Although a major transport accident has yet to occur, neither method of transporting spent nuclear fuel—rail or ship—is fail-safe. In Bridgewater, Somerset, material from nuclear flasks has leaked onto train tracks (Gruner 2000). Trains carrying spent nuclear fuel from a Swiss power plant to a French reprocessing facility have been detected with levels of radioactivity much higher than permitted. Even though plant officials noted that the higher radiation rates (1,400 becquerels per square centimeter, compared to accepted levels of 4 becquerels) did not pose an actual threat to the health of railway workers, the radiation seepage was sufficient to cause the Swiss power plant to temporarily suspend transporting of the nuclear waste ("Swiss Deny" 1998). Spent fuel containers carried by ship are vulnerable to dangers at sea—ranging from typhoons to terrorists. To prepare for such potentialities, these containers must be built to withstand the high pressures of the ocean floor and the high temperatures of shipboard fires (sometimes up to 2000 degrees C) and must be accompanied by armed escort ships (Helm 1992). Fears of potential sabotage and shipping accidents have caused leaders of sixteen South Pacific nations to appeal to Japan to provide tougher safety and liability measures for the transport of spent nuclear fuel by sea ("Pacific Leaders" 1999).

It is unclear whether the PRC or the ROK has a long-term plan to address safety measures regarding the transport of spent fuel to reprocessing facilities. The PRC has solicited bids from foreign firms to transport spent fuel from its Daya Bay facility in Guangdong to a pilot plant in Lanzhou (Hibbs 2000c). The spent fuel assemblies must be moved by road, however, because the rail connections from Guangdong to north-central China are deemed inadequate for the secure transfer of nuclear materials.

With all its associated problems, reprocessing does not completely dispose of the waste generated by the initial fuel cycle. Even after separating the plutonium and uranium from the spent fuel, significant quantities remain in the reprocessing wastes. Some analysts have suggested that the radioactivity of the material remaining in reprocessing wastes is so high that no meaningful environmental benefits from waste reduction are gained from reprocessing (Albright and Feiveson 1987), and they point out that an Organization for Economic Cooperation and Development study has demonstrated that the once-through fuel cycle followed by direct disposal is 57 percent cheaper than the cost of reprocessing (MacLachlan 1995).

GENERAL POLITICAL COSTS

In addition to the physical dangers, many political costs are associated with reprocessing. Although each country faces its own individual costs, some of the more generalizable costs are mentioned here. First, reprocessing invokes significant nonproliferation concerns, as plutonium oxide can be directly used in nuclear explosives without having to be reduced to its nonoxide, metal form. Rogue terrorist organizations could build fission bombs using just 5 to 10 kilograms of diverted reactor-grade plutonium (Abrahamson and Swahn 2000: 41–42). Therefore countries that currently engage in reprocessing must provide stringent security measures for the transport and storage of reprocessed fuel if they wish to protect it from being diverted by terrorists.

Both safety and nonproliferation concerns may also lead to increasing strains between a reprocessing nation and its border countries. The discord between the Nordic nations and the United Kingdom over U.K. reprocessing facilities is one example of the tension created by safety concerns. Another example is the conflict between South Pacific nations and Japan over Japan's shipments of spent nuclear fuel, resulting in part from fears that the ships will be subject to terrorist attacks. In certain situations these tensions may exacerbate existing regional conflicts. Indeed recent shipments of plutonium mixed-oxide fuel to Japan have met with protests from the Pusan chapter of the Korean Federation of Environmental Movement, expressing its "opposition to Japan's transport of its plutonium through the Korea Strait, for fear of environmental hazards, and to Japan's long-term sea-born shipment program itself" (Seok-jae 2001). Given the current opposition to the Japanese shipments, direct transport of spent nuclear fuel between the PRC and the ROK likely increase.

In addition, citizens of many countries greatly distrust nuclear technologies, especially when the public perceives a history of concealment on the part of the plant or government officials (Abrahamson and Swahn 2000: 39–40). Even if such distrust is irrational and is based on an instinctive association with military uses of nuclear power, opposition may still be expressed in the form of protests and lost political credibility (Yasuhiko 2000). Consequently, political leaders in countries in which citizens have avenues for public participation might avoid establishing reprocessing facilities to avoid political backlash, even if they wish to adopt such technologies.

Finally, some critics might find the further entrenchment of the nuclear fuel economy to be, in and of itself, a long-term political cost. The high initial costs of reprocessing facilities may make it difficult for a country to withdraw from reprocessing once it has made initial investments in the facilities, especially if economic structures have developed around the facilities. For instance, if the Sellafield nuclear plant were to close, the local unemployment rate would be expected to rise to 25 percent. At this point the effect of closing Sellafield would be devastating to the local economy (McCarthy 2000).

TRADE DYNAMICS, REPROCESSING EFFORTS, AND POLICY CONCERNS BETWEEN CHINA AND THE REPUBLIC OF KOREA

Ultimately, although their ties are deeply impacted by relations with North Korea, the United States, and other world powers, PRC-ROK relations have strengthened into a powerful bond in and of themselves. A detailed analysis of the events leading to this about-face in relations is beyond the scope of this chapter, but the mere existence of this unlikely partnership raises intriguing questions and provides valuable insight into international relations—specifically in the complex Asian arena. In particular, although the bulk of trade relations between the PRC and the ROK may be relatively benign in nature, trade in nuclear materials raises additional concerns, as outlined in the preceding section. The approach taken toward nuclear power in general, and toward trade in nuclear materials specifically, is much different in the PRC and the ROK than that found in the United States and elsewhere in the West.

BACKGROUND: TRADE RELATIONS

Prior to 1990, relations between the People's Republic of China and the Republic of Korea were extremely limited. The chances of *any* significant trade or cooperation between the two nations, let alone trade or cooperation involving nuclear materials, would have been considered extremely low. From the time of the Korean War through the entire Cold War period, relations were frosty to nonexistent (Cha 1999). During this period policies of containment and nonrecognition were dominant; the PRC and the ROK refused even to open dialogues with each other. With the end of the Cold War, however, relations changed dramatically, most notably through expanding trade. This expansion was evident across the board, and in 1991 trade offices were opened in both countries to facilitate it.

Overall trade between the PRC and the ROK has grown from negligible levels in the late 1970s to a level of major importance (Lee 1996). Currently, the ROK is one of the PRC's largest trading partners, with trade between the two likely to increase (Meise 1997). Reciprocal most-favored-nation status was granted in 1991, and reciprocal protection of investments was put in place in 1992. Today the ROK is one of the PRC's most important trading partners, outstripping North Korea in trade volume many times over (Lee 1996). These powerful economic ties create a strong connection between the PRC and the ROK that has remained intact despite the disrupting influence North Korea represents.

POLICY PRIORITIES IN CHINA AND THE REPUBLIC OF KOREA

Trade in nuclear materials, where the PRC is concerned, seems less a question of security issues than of environmental and economic concerns.

Considering security first, the PRC has a long-standing practice of trading in nuclear technology and materials and seems to follow no particular ideological pattern (Cha 1999). Indeed the PRC has been a major worldwide supplier of equipment and materials necessary for nuclear bomb and missile production. It sometimes markets entire systems, supplying comprehensive production assistance and technology (Kellman and Gualtieri 1996: 667). Although the PRC is a member of the Non-Proliferation Treaty, there appears to be no legal bar to those transfers under current international law as long as the PRC successfully qualifies its nuclear transfers as peaceful, which it can and does with materials for nuclear reprocessing (Woodard 2000). Until very recently the PRC was the only nuclear weapon state that lacked an explicit policy of nuclear weapons nonproliferation, and it was not until 1998 that President Clinton certified that the PRC had finally met the requirements of nonproliferation under U.S. law (Woodard 2000).

If the PRC has a single overarching goal it is to maintain the country's economic growth, which remains the primary foundation on which the power and legitimacy of the Chinese Communist Party (CCP) are based. Should it come to a direct conflict, environmental concerns will more than likely be superseded by other development goals (Zhong 2000). Indeed in stating the government's commitment to environmental issues, the official mouthpiece of the CCP—the Xinhua News Agency—stated that "China's basic state policy is to save natural resources, protect the environment and realize sustainable development" ("Environmental Protection" 1999). This statement touches on all of the most important factors leading to the PRC's increasing use of nuclear power and thus to its trade in nuclear materials. The PRC is aware of environmental pollution and ecological destruction and has made environmental protection one of its top priorities since the early 1980s (Luo 2000). Additionally, the PRC was involved in most international environmental discussions during the 1990s and has signed most international environmental treaties (Lieberthal 1995; Liebman 1998). The PRC's most pressing environmental difficulty, however, is not concerned with nuclear power—quite the opposite, in fact, as it views increased nuclear power production as a solution to its environmental problems rather than as a danger in and of itself.

Currently, the PRC's use of coal as its primary energy source makes it the second-largest world contributor of greenhouse gas (GHG) emissions, behind only the United States (Cooper 1999). The emissions from coal-fired plants in 1998 caused over 500 major Chinese cities to fail to meet the clean air standards set by the World Health Organization (Spodak 1998). Respiratory diseases caused by air pollution have become the leading cause of death in the PRC, and crop yields have been significantly affected by such pollution (Brown and Flavin 1996; Pimentel et al. 1998). Coal currently provides nearly three-quarters of the PRC's energy needs, and extremely large deposits of the fuel remain to provide such energy in the future (Zhong 2000).

As the PRC's power requirements expand over time, so will its use of coal unless alternate power sources are developed. Oil, natural gas, hydro-electricity, and various other power sources are also used in the PRC, but none shows significant promise as a potential replacement for burning coal to produce energy. Nuclear power plants, however, produce forty to one-hundred times less GHGs than fossil fuel power plants ("Nuclear Energy" 1996). In contrast to coal, large uranium deposits exist in the PRC, transportation of uranium is much more efficient than coal transportation, and uranium generates more energy than coal. In addition, the long-standing nuclear weapons programs in the PRC make public acceptance of the nuclear industry relatively easy to establish ("Nuclear Power" 1999). All of these factors, combined with the PRC's need to increase energy efficiency and the increasing demand for energy in the aggregate, seem to assure increased use of nuclear power in China (Zhong 2000).

NUCLEAR POWER AND REPROCESSING IN CHINA AND THE REPUBLIC OF KOREA

Although nuclear power plants provide over 15 percent of the world's power, nuclear energy represents only about 1 percent of the PRC's energy needs ("Westinghouse Reaffirms" 1999). Yet the PRC is well situated to greatly expand its nuclear power production. The PRC has over 1.5 billion tons of uranium in extensive reserves. It also has significant experience with nuclear power production and use and the technical knowledge necessary to develop a strong nuclear power industry (Spodak 1998). Currently, the PRC plans to significantly expand its generation of nuclear power and to fulfill 5 percent of its energy needs with nuclear power by 2020 ("China: Country Needs $20 Billion" 1996).

Although the dangers associated with both nuclear power generation and the transport and reprocessing of nuclear materials are known in the PRC, it is highly unlikely that they will significantly impact the PRC's decision to expand its nuclear power plant and reprocessing plans. The rate of growth of the country's energy efficiency remains well below its economic growth rate (Spodak 1998), and economic growth is the linchpin of CCP authority in Beijing. As well, the dangers nuclear power represents will not be of great concern in the PRC because the dangers associated with the burning of coal are currently more pressing.

Given the volume of nuclear power generation anticipated in the PRC and the level of technology available, the major challenge the country will face will be nuclear waste management, especially long-term storage. Although the United States has rejected the reprocessing of nuclear waste because it yields weapons-grade plutonium, other powers—including France and Japan—have adopted reprocessing to deal with waste storage problems (Gross 1998). The PRC, too, appears set to engage in reprocessing, with a pilot reprocessing facility in Lanzhou in its final stages of construction in April 2002. Chinese officials anticipate that this facility will be able to handle 500 kilograms of heavy metals per day (Hibbs 2000a). The Chinese National Nuclear Corporation has also discussed prospects with the U.K.-based British Nuclear Fuels and French-based Cogema for long-term cooperation on developing an industrial reprocessing infrastructure for the PRC (Hibbs 2000b).

In fact, France, the United Kingdom, and the PRC are the only nations planning to conduct or already conducting civilian reprocessing operations in their own facilities (Kellman and Gualtieri 1996: 692). Other countries such as Japan currently transport spent fuel to France and the United Kingdom for reprocessing.

The ROK as well has long utilized nuclear power and also has the technology to reprocess nuclear waste, with the associated costs already discussed, although its plans to engage in reprocessing are less solidified than those of the PRC. As long ago as 1975, the United States and Canada threatened financial and export sanctions to persuade the ROK not to buy a French reprocessing plant that could produce weapons-grade nuclear materials (Pires 1994). The country has nevertheless expressed continued interest in reprocessing, although the ROK recently abandoned attempts to convince the United States to allow it to export spent fuel to France for reprocessing (USDOE 1998: 45). Although the ROK is not currently considered a nuclear power, it is—along with Japan and Taiwan—developing a large civil nuclear program that will provide large quantities of nuclear material that could potentially be used for weapons ("New Players" 1992; "Tick, Tick, Tick" 1994). Part of this program is expected to involve the reprocessing of nuclear materials, and trade relations between the PRC and the ROK already include fissile materials to supplement both countries' nuclear power industries.

Of course, all relations between the PRC and ROK must be considered in the unique context North Korea provides. The PRC's long-standing relationship with the North, combined with the dual influences of North-South efforts at partnership despite still existent hostility and the ever-present influence of other powers—most notably the United States—must be taken into account. North Korea's use of nuclear power has long been a security concern, particularly its access to technologies that may contribute to its drive to develop nuclear weapons. Indeed a North Korea with nuclear weapons could easily lead to the possession of such weapons by Japan, the ROK, and other states to counter the threat (Meise 1997). Nevertheless, the PRC appears to have deliberately chosen not to dissuade North Korea from its efforts to obtain nuclear weapons materials and technology (Meise 1997). This has led to concern in the West because the PRC possesses the materials and technology North Korea might want, and Western ties with the ROK and others might be insufficient to block such trade with the North.

With this overarching political complexity confusing the issue, it may be virtually impossible to determine what part the factors unique to trade in nuclear materials may play. Nevertheless, considered in the larger context of Asia and beyond, PRC-ROK trade relations may provide a useful model for theorists in understanding relations in this difficult corner of the world.

THE POLITICS OF PLUTONIUM TRADE IN EAST ASIA

Asia has no regional authority to regulate its emerging nuclear industry, although nongovernmental organizations and institutes have made various proposals (Cossa 1998: 12–13; Kaneko 2000). Also lacking is a single vision about how to deal with spent fuel, specifically plutonium, and about whether a regional authority should handle its regulation (Roberts and Davis 1996). Both the PRC and the ROK have established nuclear energy programs, and for them at least the issue of managing waste is of immediate concern. In 1997 the PRC was storing around 170 tons of spent nuclear waste (in tons of heavy metal), and the ROK had around 3,700 tons (in tons of heavy metal). And the amount in both countries is growing (Dyck and Crijns 1998: 26).

Other Asian nations currently more consumed with developing the infrastructure necessary to support a nuclear industry will inherit circumstances, relationships, and practices generated by the PRC and the ROK. In the worst-case scenario, trade in plutonium and related technologies would develop ad hoc, with inadequate oversight and little accountability for environmental accidents or materials diverted to other parties.

Although the economics of plutonium recycling has been questioned (Albright and Feiverson 1987), plans for a mammoth nuclear industry spanning Asia, combined with the promise of a permanently renewable resource and energy independence, may be too tempting a prospect for Asia's developing economies to ignore (Roberts and Davis 1996). Over the next decade as much as two-thirds of the world's new electricity-generating capability will develop in Asia. Roughly one-tenth of that electricity will come from nuclear power. Advanced countries such as Japan and the ROK will rely on nuclear energy to meet nearly half of their electricity demands. India has sixteen nuclear power plants in operation and plans for nearly a dozen more. Smaller developing nations such as Indonesia, Thailand, Pakistan, Taiwan, Vietnam, and the Philippines all have at least one research reactor in operation and plans for one or more operational reactors within the next several years (Uranium Information Centre 2000). Asia's plans for a nuclear industry are extensive, and no nation to date has openly rejected the option of recycling.

The debate over reprocessing plutonium for use in civilian reactors is long-standing, and transnational trade in civilian-use plutonium is hardly novel. Perhaps just a matter of luck, problems with reprocessing and transporting used fuels have been relatively minor. Although the current system of oversight is far from fail-safe, the United States has introduced important accounting and inspection practices through its bilateral trade agreements (Suzuki 1996). EURATOM, the agency immediately responsible for regulating Europe's nuclear trade and industry, has adopted and expanded upon many of those safeguards. For example, under Article 80 of EURATOM's charter, any by-products of Europe's civilian nuclear industry classified as "special fissile materials" are deposited with or otherwise controlled by the agency (Suzuki 1996). The cooperative approach, in theory, improves accountability.

At present it appears unlikely that a similar regime capable of regulating the Asian nuclear industry will develop, at least before bilateral trade and reprocessing has been firmly established—first between Taiwan and Japan and now between the PRC and the ROK. Nor is an adequate body likely to develop independently in the near future. Whereas European trade developed within an established framework of preexisting institutions such as EURATOM and the EEC, the geopolitical climate in today's Asia is immensely different than early Cold War Europe. Along with promoting civilian use of nuclear technology, one of EURATOM's primary objectives was nuclear nonproliferation. In contrast, the Asian commitment to this objective appears subordinate to other goals, at least in the case of the PRC. Moreover, the regional authority governing Europe's plutonium trade was a strategic response to perceived exigencies created by Soviet-U.S. relations (Suzuki 1996). Currently, no such overriding ideological impetus exists, and the primary—if not the only—incentive to cooperate is purely economic. Short-run economic objectives might very well prevail over long-term stability interests.

Commercial trade in plutonium for civilian uses will likely develop along different lines in Asia, probably bilaterally, without an overarching administrative authority. Consequently, affected third-party nations will have to use normal diplomatic channels and existing agreements to voice concerns about environmental safeguards or the diversion of weapons-usable materials. The ability of the United States to influence and control the world's nuclear industry will diminish once again—just as it did several decades before with respect to the Soviet Union. Whether existing market incentives and international pressures are sufficient to ensure that this trade is environmentally and politically responsible should be of great interest to politicians, scientists, and theorists (Roberts and Davis 1996).

Although the United States may be ineffectual in preventing trade between the PRC and the ROK, its interests in the matter are substantial. Officially, the United States does not engage in and in fact discourages the practice of reprocessing, especially in countries—such as the PRC—with poor records of adhering to nonproliferation agreements (Dooley 1996). This is especially true because uranium ore, once thought to be in short supply, is now stockpiled in quantities necessary to meet world demand for the next several decades. The destabilizing effect of too much nuclear fuel is exacerbated by a glut in existing plutonium created by dismantled U.S. and former Soviet warheads. As one spokesman for the U.S. State Department explained, "There is simply too much plutonium out there" (Dooley 1996: 20).

On the other hand, the abundance of plutonium stocks and the equally troublesome alternatives to disposing of nuclear waste have also led the United States to reconsider its blanket objections to burning plutonium in commercial reactors. Moreover, the United States would appear hypocritical if it steadfastly opposed bilateral trade between the ROK and the PRC on purely economic grounds while concurrently engaging in a similar bilateral practice with Japan. Under this agreement, the United States retains control over U.S.-origin fuels after they have been spent in Japanese reactors. In this way the United States is able to manage the end of Japan's fuel cycle to a degree beyond the authority provided by the International Atomic Energy Agency. Whether the PRC, the ROK, or other Asian nations would be as demanding in their agreements is unclear. But prior practices indicate that such trade could develop without adequate safeguards in place, at least not formally or permanently in an institution.

Although a loosely regulated trade in nuclear materials may be worrisome, the development of regional or national nuclear programs may also have a destabilizing effect in an area of the world that has enjoyed a generation of comparative stability (Roberts and Davis 1996). If Asian nations decide to pursue reprocessing, as is their sovereign right, a trade regime might provide a desirable alternative to each nation attempting to develop programs independently. The hazardous nature of nuclear energy has already led North and South Korea to establish the groundbreaking Korean Peninsula Energy Development Corporation. In sum, Asian nations do have a sophisticated understanding of trade, and numerous incentives for cooperation exist. But the theoretical complexities are underdeveloped, and whether they would hold fast in practice is at best uncertain.

THEORETICAL PERSPECTIVES
ON ASIAN NUCLEAR REPROCESSING

According to the traditional understanding of international relations, the touchstone of any state's foreign policy was to maximize its security, narrowly defined in strictly military terms (Grieco 1988; Morganthau 1978; Waltz 1979). All other considerations, including economic and environmental concerns, were considered subservient or even irrelevant when compared with a state's overriding need to safeguard its military position. Thus it was taken as axiomatic that if given the choice, a state would eschew the economic benefits of trade and give short shrift to environmental protection if it meant preserving an advantageous military position.

In recent years, however, this view of international relations has been challenged by those who see in the thickening web of international institutions a willingness of states to forego focusing purely on achieving military advantage in their foreign policies for the economic benefits of international cooperation (Keohane and Nye 1989). As this debate between realists and institutionalists has progressed, some have begun to argue that the concept of "security" itself should be expanded. No longer should a state's security be conceived solely in terms of relative military power vis-à-vis potential adversaries. Rather, according to this new perspective, analysis of a state's security should comprehend all significant phenomena that threaten to jeopardize stability. As Jessica Tuchman Matthews (1989: 162) has suggested, the definition of security should extend beyond just military or even economic matters and encompass "resource, environmental, and demographic issues."

As this new approach to security gains wider currency, environmental concerns increasingly receive the attention of international relations scholarship (Hass 1990; Hurrell and Kingsbury 1992; Myers 1989). Grouped under the rubric of "environmental security," environmental degradation and ecological concerns generally are increasingly seen, if not on par with traditional military matters, at least as of great importance to states in setting their national interests (Brunnee 1995). As former U.S. secretary of state Madeleine K. Albright remarked, "Not long ago, many believed that the pursuit of clean air, clean water, and healthy forests was a worthy goal, but not part of our national security. Today environmental issues are part of the mainstream of American foreign policy" (Graffy 1998: 406).

Nonetheless, environmental issues, although accepted as ultimately affecting the security of states and thus deemed to warrant study, are frequently viewed as part of a discrete topic and are consequently seen as analytically distinguishable from the sorts of military or even economic concerns usually understood to be the integral components of a state's national security calculus. Access to clean water, for example, is viewed in this manner—such access is crucial to a state's well-being and thus in some sense to its ultimate security, yet it is still conceptually distinguishable from national security in its narrower military sense. The same may be said for concerns over global climate change, which is clearly of great importance to a state for its effects on agriculture and sea levels yet poses different challenges and concerns and thus is understood very differently than threats to military security. In other words, even if one accepts an expanded definition of security that is construed broadly enough to encompass pressing environmental concerns such as access to water and climate change, environmental and ecological issues are still often seen as falling into their own distinct category within the ambit of an overarching security rubric.

Although this hiving off of environmental security from other aspects of security may be appropriate in some instances, it would be a serious mistake to conclude that environmental security issues are necessarily distinct from economic and military ones. To the contrary, acute environmental concerns may themselves overlap, have critical ramifications for, or even be coterminous with national security in its more conventional, narrow sense. The Asian trade in reprocessed nuclear fuels is one such case and provides a valuable case study illustrating how such competing interests as military security, economic development, and environmental concerns interact in the formation of foreign policy.

This three-dimensional character of nuclear reprocessing forces the states of East Asia to face what might be termed a *trilemma*. Any attempt to maximize one of the three variables—military security, economic wealth, and environmental stability—necessarily affects, often detrimentally, the other two. Consequently, each state is required to tacitly determine the extent to which it is willing to maximize military, economic, or environmental security at the expense of a marginal loss of security in the other two areas. According to the traditional understanding of international relations, states should, presumptively, grant primacy to security concerns over economic or environmental ones. Nonetheless, despite the fact that trade in reprocessed materials carries significant risk of spreading nuclear weapons capabilities to nonnuclear states and even terrorist groups, the PRC and the ROK have consciously chosen to assume that risk to attain what they perceive as economic advantages.

The evidence suggests that the PRC and the ROK, in balancing the relative weights of these three considerations, have decided that the economic advantages of engaging in extensive nuclear reprocessing outweigh the resultant military and environmental dangers caused by this course of conduct. What explains this phenomenon? First, one must appreciate the full extent of the political leadership's concern over the Asian impending energy crisis and its fears that failure to adequately prepare will doom plans for economic development. The nuclear option is increasingly seen as the solution. Consequently, since Asia's burgeoning energy requirements necessitate increasing reliance on nuclear power and therefore increased generation of spent fuels, the reprocessing of nuclear fuels is becoming a critical component of maintaining economic security. Nowhere is this more clearly demonstrated than in the PRC's decision to power its economic development by shifting from coal to an increasing reliance on nuclear power, with plans for nuclear energy to increase fivefold as a percentage of total energy use in the PRC. Moreover, the link between environmental and economic security is accentuated by the fact that no Asian state is capable of running a self-sufficient nuclear reprocessing program. The result is transnational trade in reprocessing materials, as users and reprocessors of nuclear energy—such as the PRC—seek economic gain and spent fuel management by reprocessing the spent fuel generated in other markets, such as South Korea.

This economic calculus by which the PRC and the ROK seek to maximize their developmental potential, however, has been inextricably intertwined with environmental issues. But here the task of arriving at the optimal balance is not easy. Evidence of the danger posed to the environment by nuclear power and reprocessing is at least plausibly offset by two factors: the fact that reprocessing may help manage some of the spent fuels produced in primary nuclear power generation, and the fact that utilization of nuclear energy avoids emitting the harmful greenhouse gases produced by burning coal—currently the predominant fuel source in the PRC. Thus from the perspective of East Asian policymakers, evidence of the ecological problems associated with nuclear energy generally and reprocessing specifically may be outweighed by countervailing arguments that a better environmental balance may be struck by reprocessing spent fuels to avoid storage concerns and by looking instead to the nuclear option to satisfy swelling energy demands, thereby decreasing reliance on coal-based power (with its attendant greenhouse emissions). Although this conclusion is subject to dispute, the logic that nuclear power is an environmentally sound alternative to coal nonetheless remains persuasive for many Asian policymakers. As a result, environmental concerns have not proved significant enough to counterbalance the purported economic benefits of reprocessing.

On the military side of the equation, states considering whether to engage in nuclear reprocessing and trade in reprocessed materials must assay the security risks of proliferation against its predicted economic and even debatable environmental benefits. Policymakers recognize that the plutonium oxide created by reprocessing can be used directly in nuclear devices without having to be further reduced to its nonoxide, metal form and thus that the decision to engage in reprocessing carries obvious and significant military implications—particularly if the reprocessed material must be transported, making it susceptible to theft and thus to inadvertent nuclear proliferation. The United States has banned reprocessing because of these proliferation concerns. The recognized proliferation risks, however, have not dampened enthusiasm in East Asia for trading reprocessed materials. This may be explained by the fact that whether proliferation is conceived as a threat to security is a matter of perception, and one not necessarily perceived uniformly. Indeed the risk of proliferation caused by trading reprocessed materials may be much more serious for those other than the immediate parties to the economic transaction. That is almost certainly the case here: because the most likely candidates for proliferation represent threats not to the PRC but rather to the United States and its allies, fears that trading reprocessed materials could lead to them gaining nuclear weapon capabilities have not proved, and are unlikely to prove, effective in dissuading countries from engaging in reprocessing.

REFERENCES

Abrahamson, Dean, and Johan Swahn. 2000. "The Political Atom." *Bulletin of the Atomic Scientists* 56, 4 (July-August): 39–44.

Ahlstrom, Dick. 1998. "BNFL Confirms Recent Incidents." *Irish Times* [Dublin] (17 January): 9.

Albright, David, and Harold Feiveson. 1987. "Why Recycle Plutonium?" *Science* 235 (27 March): 1555–1556.

Brown, Lester R., and Christopher Flavin. 1996. "China's Challenge to the United States and to the Earth." *World Watch* 8, 5 (19 September): 10–13.

Brunnee, Jutta. 1995. "Environmental Security in the Twenty-First Century: New Momentum for the Development of International Environmental Law?" *Fordham International Law Journal* 18 (May): 1742–1747.

Carter, Luther J., and Thomas H. Pigford. 1999. "The World's Growing Inventory of Civil Spent Fuel." *Arms Control Today* 29, 1 (January-February): 8–14.

"Chemical Reaction Suspected as Cause of Tokai Plant Fire." 1997. *Japan Economic Newswire* (29 March).

Cha, Victor D. 1999. "The View From Korea." In Alastair Ian Johnston and Robert S. Ross, eds., *Engaging China—The Management of an Emerging Power.* London: Routledge.

"China: Country Needs $20 Billion Investment for Energy Production Goal, Official Says." 1996. *Daily Environment Reporter* [Washington, DC] 200 DEN (16 October): A-1.

Cooper, Deborah E. 1999. "The Kyoto Protocol and China: Global Warming's Sleeping Giant." *Georgetown International Environmental Law Review* 11: 401–434.

Cossa, Ralph A. 1998. "PACATOM: Building Confidence and Enhancing Nuclear Transparency." A Report from the International Working Group on Confidence and Security Building Measures, organized by the Council for Security Cooperation in the Asia Pacific <www.csis.org/pacfor/opBuildConf.pdf>.

Crowell, Todd, and Murakami Mutsuko. 1997. "Japan: Hot Zone." *AsiaWeek* [Hong Kong] (28 March): 22–23.

Dooley, John. 1996. "Civil Use of Plutonium: A U.S. Position Paper." Washington, DC: Office of Nuclear Energy Affairs, U.S. Department of State.

Dyck, Peter, and Martin J. Crijns. 1998. "Rising Needs: Management of Spent Fuel at Nuclear Power Plants" 40, 1: 24–27 <http://www.iaea.or.at/Periodicals/Bulletin/Bull401/article6.html>.

"Environmental Protection Vital to Sustained Development." 1999. *World News Connection* (15 September).

Forwood, Martin. 1999. "Sellafield: The Ugly Duckling." *The Ecologist* 29, 7 (1 November): 417–418.

Fukada, Takahiro. 2000. "Japan's Sole Spent Nuclear Fuel Reprocessing Plant to Resume Operations." *Agence France-Presse* (27 October).

Gibson, Helen. 2000. "Confidence Meltdown." *Time International* 155, 14 (10 April): 27.

Graffy, Colleen P. 1998. "Water, Water Everywhere, Nor Any Drop to Drink: The Urgency of Transnational Solutions to International Riparian Disputes." *Georgetown International Environmental Law Review* 10: 399–440.

Grieco, Joseph M. 1988. "Anarchy and the Limits of Cooperation: A Realist Critique of the Newest Liberal Institutionalism." *International Organization* (summer): 485–507.

Gross, Neil. 1998. "Science and Technology: Nuclear Waste Between a Rock and a Hot Place." *Business Week* (April 20): 134.

Gruner, Peter. 2000. "Ban Nuclear Trains From the Capital, Urges Expert." *Evening Standard* [London] (11 September): 18.

Hass, Peter. 1990. *Saving the Mediterranean: The Politics of International Environmental Cooperation.* New York: Columbia University Press.

Helm, Leslie. 1992. "Nations on Route of Japan's Plutonium Ship Voice Fears." *Los Angeles Times* (7 October): 4.

Hibbs, Mark. 2000a. "Chinese Pu Lab to Operate in 2002, but Interim Storage Now Foreseen." *Nuclear Fuel* 25, 22: 9.

———. 2000b. "Chinese Reprocessing Program Awaiting Decision on Pu Needs." *Nuclear Fuel* 25, 7: 3.

———. 2000c. "China's Plutonium Separation Program at Least Three Years Behind." *Nuclear Fuel* 25, 9: 3.

———. 2000d. "Security, Environmental Concerns May Refocus Pacific Rim." *Nucleonics Week* 41, 44: 12.

Hurrell, A., and B. Kingsbury, eds. 1992. *The International Politics of the Environment: Actors, Interests, and Institutions.* Oxford: Oxford University Press.

Ivanov, Andrei, and Judith Perera. 1993. "Environment: Ecologists Question Tomsk-7 Investigation." *Inter Press* [Rome] (19 April).

Kaneko, Kumao. 2000. *Nuclear Energy and Asian Security in the 21st Century: A Proposal for ASIATOM.* University of California Institute on Global Conflict and Cooperation, Policy Paper 37 <http://wwwigcc.ucsd.edu/publications/policy_papers/pp37.html>.

Kellman, Barry, and David S. Gualtieri. 1996. "Barricading the Nuclear Window— A Legal Regime to Curtain Nuclear Smuggling." *University of Illinois Law Review* 1996: 667–741.

Keohane, Robert O., and Joseph S. Nye. 1989. *Power and Interdependence.* Boston: Scott, Foreman.

Krauskopf, Konrad B. 1990. "Disposal of High-Level Nuclear Waste: Is It Possible?" *Science* (14 September): 1231–1232.

Lean, Geoffrey. 1998. "Sellafield Shut Down After New Leak." *Independent* [London] (19 July): 2.

Lee, Chae-jin. 1996. *China and Korea: Dynamic Relations.* Stanford: Hoover.

Lieberthal, Kenneth. 1995. *Governing China: From Revolution to Reform.* London: W. W. Norton.

Liebman, Benjamin L. 1998. "Autonomy Through Separation? Environmental Law and the Basic Law of Hong Kong." *Harvard International Law Journal* 39: 231–298.

Luo, Jackie. 2000. *China Environmental Status* <http://www.ifce.org/pages/environment.html> accessed: 27 October 2000.

MacLachlan, Ann. 1995. "NEW Study Chief Says Once-Through Cycle 57% Lower Cost Than That of Reprocessing." *Nuclear Fuel* (2 January): 10.

MacLachlan, Ann, Pearl Marshall, and Ariane Sains. 2000. "U.K., France Say They Won't Heed Ospar Exhortation on Reprocessing." *Nuclear Fuel* (10 July): 10.

MacMahon, Brian. 1992. "Leukemia Clusters Around Nuclear Facilities in Britain." *Cancer Cases and Control* 3: 283–288.

Matthews, Jessica Tuchman. 1989. "Redefining Security." *Foreign Affairs* 68, 2 (spring): 162–177.

McCarthy, F. T. 2000. "Running Scared: Scaling Back the Sellafield Nuclear Plant Would Be a Big Blow to Cumbia." *The Economist* (8 April).

Meise, Gary J. 1997. "Securing the Strength of the Renewed NPT: China, the Lynchpin 'Middle Kingdom.' " *Vanderbilt Journal of Transnational Law* 30: 539–577.

Morganthau, Hans. 1978. *Politics Among Nations: The Struggle for Power and Peace.* New York: Knopf.

Myers, N. 1989. "Environment and Security." *Foreign Policy* 74 (spring): 23–41.

"New Players in the Nuclear Club." 1992. *Toronto Star* (19 December).

Nuclear Energy Agency, Organisation for Economic Co-operation and Development. 1993. *The Safety of the Nuclear Fuel Cycle.* Paris: OECD.

"Nuclear Energy: Nuclear-Based Electricity Could Soar if Linked to Greenhouse Gas Cuts, NEA Says." 1996. *International Environment Daily (BNA)* [Washington, DC] (6 September).

"Nuclear-Fuel Reprocessing Plant to Resume Operations." 2000. *Kyoto News* (23 October).

"Nuclear Power Sector Battles Skepticism." 1999. *China Daily* (3 May).

Office of Nuclear Waste Management, U.S. Department of Energy. 1980. *Final Environmental Impact Statement on Management of Commercially Generated Radioactive Waste.* DOE/EIS-0046 F. Washington, DC: U.S. Department of Energy.

"Pacific Leaders to Appeal to Japan Over Nuclear Shipments." 1999. *Agence France-Presse* [Paris] (5 October).

Pimentel, D., et al. 1998. "The Ecology of Increasing Disease: Population Growth and Environmental Degradation." *Bioscience* 48, 817 (October).

Pires, Jeong Hwa. 1994. "North Korean Time Bomb: Can Sanctions Defuse It? A Review of International Economic Sanctions as an Option." *Georgia Journal of International and Comparative Law* 24: 307–346.

Pollack, Andrew. 1997. "Nuclear Accident Rankles Japanese." *Portland Oregonian* (25 March).

Stephanie Tai, Andrew B. Loewenstein, Todd Bissett, and Eric O'Malley

"Revealed, the Terrible Cancer Toll on Children Living Near Sellafield." 2000. *The Express* [London] (2 April).

Roberts, Brad, and Zachary Davis. 1996. "Nuclear Cooperation in the Asia-Pacific: A Survey of Proposals." In Ralph A. Cossa, ed., *Asia Pacific Multilateral Nuclear Safety and Non-Proliferation: Exploring the Possibilities.* Honolulu: Council for Security Cooperation in the Asia Pacific.

Seok-jae, Kang. 2001. "Puan Environmentalists Stage Rally to Protest Japan's Planned Plutonium Shipments." *Korea Herald* [Seoul] (16 March).

Spodak, William M. 1998. "Power Struggle." *China Business Review* (March-April).

Suzuki, Tatsujiro. 1996. "Lessons From EURATOM for Possible Regional Nuclear Cooperation in the Asia-Pacific Region (ASIATOM)." In Ralph A. Cossa, ed., *Asia Pacific Multilateral Nuclear Safety and Non-Proliferation: Exploring the Possibilities.* Honolulu: Council for Security Cooperation in the Asia Pacific.

"Swiss Deny Nuclear Trucks Were Radioactive When Sent to France." 1998. *Agence France-Presse* [Paris] (7 May).

"Tick, Tick, Tick, Tick Them Off: Should the World Worry About the Spread of Nuclear Weapons, Ask Jimmy Burns and Bronwen Maddox." 1994. *Financial Times* (5 August).

"Tokaimura Reprocessing Nuclear Accident May Be the Worst." 1997. *Japan Energy Scan* [Tokyo] (24 March).

United States Department of Energy (USDOE), International Policy and Analysis Division, Office of Arms Control and Nonproliferation. 1998. *Major Commercial Nuclear Programs of the World* <http://www.nn.doe.gov/docs/majorcom.pdf>.

Uranium Information Centre. 2000. *Asia's Nuclear Energy Growth, Nuclear Issues Briefing Paper Two* <http://www.uic.com.au/nip02.htm>.

Waltz, Kenneth. 1979. *Theory of International Politics.* Reading, Mass.: Addison-Wesley.

"Westinghouse Reaffirms Its Nuclear Policy." 1999. *China Daily* [Beijing] (9 May).

Williams, Frederick C., and David A. Deese, eds. 1979. *Nuclear Nonproliferation: The Spent Fuel Problem.* New York: Pergamon.

Woodard, Jon L. 2000. "International Legal Frameworks Relating to China's Nuclear Exports to Iran: Safeguarding the Transfer of Dual-Use Nuclear Technology." *North Carolina Journal of International Law and Commercial Regulations* 25: 359–379.

Yasuhiko, Yoshida. 2000. "Nuclear Safety Issue Jars Japan to Reconsider Its Policy, Program." *Japan Quarterly* 56 (1 January).

Zhong, Ling. 2000. "Nuclear Energy: China's Approach Towards Addressing Global Warming." *Georgetown International Environmental Law Review* 12: 493–522.

Politics of the South China Sea: Diplomacy, Cooperation, and Environmental Regimes

TOM NÆSS

The South China Sea region is unique because of its abundance of coral reefs, mangroves, sea grass, and fruitful estuaries—creating a biodiversity that is of great importance regionally as well as constituting what one might call a heritage of humankind, which makes it important from a global perspective too. The environmental threats to these rare natural resources have been well documented (Coulter 1996; Gomez 1988; Soegiarto 1994; UNEP 1999). The degraded quality of the water in the world-famous Ha Long Bay off Hai Phong Province in Vietnam is a case in point. Pollution and man-made changes to the environment threaten coral reefs, marine life, and the livelihood of fishermen and hoteliers. An extract from an article published in the *South China Morning Post* [Hong Kong] (28 April 1999) is indicative:

> The director of Haiphong's Oceanology Institute said Halong Bay had "been invaded by sediments, heavy metals and wastewater." In 10 years, 900 million tonnes of polluted earth has been carried into the sea by rivers which traverse nearby coal-mining zones. Underwater "hills of mud" up to 30 metres high have been created. Adding to the damage

This chapter is based on research conducted in association with the project on Energy and Security in the South China Sea at the Centre for Development and the Environment, Oslo.

is the discharge every year of close to nine million cubic metres of wastewater contaminated by lead and petrol. The coral reefs are also victims of dynamite fishing by Cat Ba Island fishermen, and untreated wastewater from Haiphong, Vietnam's third-largest city with two million inhabitants, pollutes the bay. The institute also estimates that hundreds of visitor boats spill about two tonnes of oil each day.

As we can see, environmental problems in the Ha Long [Descending Dragon] Bay are complex. The bay, which because of its thousands of volcanic islands has been called one of the world's great wonders, suffers from problems that will lead to further degradation of the marine environment.

To policy analysts the South China Sea is known as an area over which China and Taiwan stand against their Southeast Asian neighbors in an unresolved sovereignty conflict over the Spratly Islands. The South China Sea, however, is not just a potential scene of military conflict; it is also a rich maritime environment. Environmental security is therefore pertinent.[1] High economic growth, often coupled with depletion of natural resources, intensifies conflicts like the one in the South China Sea.

From the issues at stake in this complex conflict I focus on the efforts by various actors to create multilateral cooperation on environmental issues in the South China Sea. Environmental issues have long been discussed at the national political level in Asia, but interstate cooperation on environmental issues around the South China Sea is fairly recent. I shall examine regime-building processes connected to the management of environmental problems and, finally, will discuss the likelihood that these efforts will succeed in making environmental issues take precedence in regional politics.

I make three preliminary conclusions regarding the question of whether environmental politics is taking precedence in regional politics.

- The South China Sea Workshops and the United Nations Environment Program (UNEP) initiative have been successful in spreading information and knowledge about environmental problems and necessary steps to be taken to prevent those problems from growing larger.
- An implicit maritime regime based on various arrangements and agreements between two or more Association of Southeast Asian Nations (ASEAN) states has emerged. A sort of "Asian multilateralism," experienced through the South China Sea Workshops, has prevented armed conflict in the region and has even succeeded in engaging China and Chinese Taipei (Taiwan) in multilateral endeavors. The process of informal interstate discussions is led by leading marine scientists concerned about the environmental status of the South China Sea.
- Obvious institutional weaknesses exist in the region. At the national level, the multiplicity of agencies dealing with the maritime environment and

the lack of interest at the highest political level make efficient and inte-grative ocean policy almost impossible. This problem is even worse at the regional level, where no agency exists that can coordinate efforts at improving the maritime environment. In the future UNEP may be the integrative force that can merge national and regional policies more effectively.

Throughout the 1980s growing concern for the environment resulted in new forms of state cooperation. Relevant examples can often be found in the context of international environmental diplomacy, where man-made harm to the environment has caused transboundary pollution (acid rain, damage to ecosystems, oil tanker spills, and similar problems), requiring that states cooperate in a wide range of areas. When students of interna-tional relations try to identify regimes, they either look for explicit rules or practices or seek evidence of some sort of pattern of communication among state actors. A regime is a kind of political system guiding states' behavior in a certain policy area, and most theories of international regimes presuppose that states have an interest in cooperating with each other (Krasner 1983).

I focus here on two existing regime-building initiatives related to the South China Sea: first, a set of informal multilateral meetings that, under the leadership of Ambassador Hasjim Djalal and Professor Ian Townsend-Gault, have taken up issues relevant to the South China Sea every year since 1990; and second, an attempt by the littoral countries of the region, in coop-eration with UNEP, to establish an environmental action plan for the South China Sea. The question I will try to answer is, to what extent are the South China Sea Workshops and the UNEP initiative promoting regional environ-mental policies?

THE STATUS OF THE SOUTH CHINA SEA ENVIRONMENT

The South China Sea is the maritime heart of a region binding southern China to Southeast Asia. The sea is of great economic, political, and envi-ronmental importance to surrounding nations: China and Taiwan, the Phil-ippines, Vietnam, Brunei Darussalam, Malaysia, Indonesia, Cambodia, Singapore, and Thailand. The sea produces fish, sea grass, and other living and nonliving resources for one of the most populous regions in the world. In the Southeast Asian region alone more than 70 percent of the population lives in coastal areas, and they depend greatly on the sea for resources and as a means of transportation. Fisheries in the Southeast Asian region repre-sented 23 percent of the total catch in Asia and about 10 percent of the total world catch in 1992 (Soegiarto 1994: 1–2). At the same time, high economic growth is overshadowing environmental problems like overfishing, destruc-tive fishing methods, habitat devastation, and marine pollution.

Some major environmental problems are described here:

- Erosion: Logging and "slash-and-burn" agriculture create millions of tons of sediments that are transported through the rivers to coastal areas and river deltas.
- Solid waste: Rivers are used as depositories for solid waste and garbage generated by large cities along the coast.
- Sewage: Like solid waste, sewage is often discharged directly into the sea, creating red tide phenomena and often bacterial contamination of entire bays.
- Industrial waste: A result of economic activity along the coast, this waste goes straight into the ocean without prior treatment.
- Fish: The pressure on coastal fish stocks is growing as a result of the introduction of modern fishing techniques like trawling. At the same time, primitive destructive fishing methods are still used in Indonesia, Vietnam, China, and the Philippines and to a limited extent in Thailand and Malaysia. The use of explosives and chemicals destroys coral reefs and habitats of species, as well as their breeding grounds.
- Coral reefs are under severe threat from the environmental problems described here. Roughly 30 percent of the world's coral reefs are found in Southeast Asia. These reefs are very diverse, and they are important because they are the nursery and breeding grounds for 12 percent of the world's total fish catch. It has been estimated that coral reefs contribute 30 percent of East Malaysia's total catch and 25 percent of that in the Philippines (Brookfield and Byron 1993; Gomez 1988; Low, Goh, and Chou 1996). Reefs fix nitrogen and sequester carbon, and they provide a visual display of color and life unmatched anywhere on earth, thereby constituting a tourist magnet that has been exploited for many years—especially in Thailand, Malaysia, Indonesia, and the Philippines. Future income from tourism and fisheries is important in the further development of coastal nations.
- Mangrove forest: Thirty percent of the world's mangrove forest, covering 50 000 km^2 of coastal areas, is found in the South China Sea region. Mangroves have important economic and environmental value. Mangrove trees are harvested for use as fuel, building materials, and other products; they also support productive fisheries (as nursery grounds) and prawn production and protect coastal areas against the impact of storms (Low, Goh, and Chou 1996). Products and ecological services provided by the mangrove systems of the South China Sea region are estimated to be worth about $US15.984 million a year (UNEP 1999).
- Sea grass is a basis for many complex marine ecosystems and provides a valuable nursery for commercially important fish and other living re-

sources (e.g., shrimp, crabs). Sea grass binds sediment to the bottom, thereby preventing erosion of the sea floor.

• Estuaries and wetlands are normally associated with river deltas and coastal areas where land and sea meet. These areas may include mangrove forests, swamps, and fens. Wetlands and estuaries are seasonal homes to migratory birds, have their own animal and plant diversity, and serve as nursing grounds for fish and crabs. They also trap nutrients and prevent erosion, as well as being used for aquaculture and agricultural purposes. The estimated value of these areas in the South China Sea region is US$190.726 million a year (UNEP 1999).

As shown in the Ha Long example earlier, environmental problems are serious and visible enough to arouse public concern. The loss of coral reefs, mangroves, estuaries, and sea grass beds can have serious long-term consequences because of the time these ecosystems need to recover from damage. All countries in the South China Sea region have degraded reefs. Ninety-five percent of the coral reefs around Hainan are damaged, as is an unknown amount along the coast of Vietnam. The original mangrove area has decreased by 70 percent since 1930. If the current trend continues, all mangroves will be lost by 2030 (UNEP 1999: 14).

REGIONAL ENVIRONMENTAL ORGANIZATIONS

The United Nations Environment Program, established in 1972, aims at promoting international cooperation on the environment and policies that adhere to the sustainable development concept. Most important in this context are its Regional Seas Programs, which cover 140 countries and constitute one of UNEP's major successes. The regional headquarters in Asia are in Bangkok, Thailand; and the first East Asian Action Plan was adopted in 1981. Indonesia, Malaysia, Singapore, and Thailand signed the plan with the intention of promoting development and protecting the environment and coastal areas. The Coordinating Body on the Seas of East Asia (COBSEA) is the secretariat for the program. With technical assistance from UNEP and the member countries, various projects have been implemented that aim to support management of the coastal and marine environment (Bleakley and Wells 1999). In the South China Sea region most activities have been directed at ASEAN countries, and three consecutive ASEAN Environment Programs have been implemented since 1977. The UNEP partnership with ASEAN has resulted in the foundation of the ASEAN Expert Group on Environment and ASEAN Senior Officials on Environment, which have been central players in the development of the first ASEAN Strategic Plan of Action on the Environment for the period 1994–1998. The environmental policies of the ASEAN countries, however, are much less integrated than those in the European Union: "Marine affairs and maritime security issues [in this region] are generally kept separate from proposals to deal with the question of regional maritime security in its broadest sense" (Thayer 1999: 13).

The Southeast Asian Program in Ocean Law, Policy, and Management (SEAPOL) is another nongovernmental network of scholars, government officials, private-sector representatives, and people with an interest in the Southeast Asian maritime region that has held regular meetings since 1981. The network consists of more than 250 government and academic specialists from the region and 50 associates from outside the region. Canada mainly provides the funding, as it does for the South China Sea Workshops. The Canadian International Development Agency (CIDA) is the main contributor.

As a capacity-building institution on Southeast Asian legal maritime affairs, SEAPOL "aims to facilitate the exchange of information and ideas related to current ocean law, policy and management in the region" (SEAPOL 2002). SEAPOL started out discussing the implementation of the United Nations Convention on the Law of the Sea (UNCLOS) in the South China Sea region, but today the agenda embraces a growing number of problems and issues in coastal management and other critical sectors of ocean governance. Most participants' backgrounds are in law, but as UNCLOS also encompasses ocean development and management, maritime experts now take part in the workshops. SEAPOL is also assisting national programs and institutes like the Maritime Institute of Malaysia, the Philippine Institute of Marine Affairs, and the Thailand Institute for Marine Affairs.

REGIME-BUILDING EFFORTS
IN THE SOUTH CHINA SEA REGION

If we compare the South China Sea with other semienclosed seas, it becomes clear that the South China Sea is different in that it lacks formalized cooperative instruments that integrate and coordinate efforts by littorals at managing and protecting the marine life, as well as regulating marine economic activities of the region.[2] The nations of the South China Sea region have not established conventions or legal frameworks for common governance of the marine environment. Fisheries, ecosystems, shipping, pollution, and similar issues are discussed at meetings of scientists and at various levels of government, but attempts to address these important questions multilaterally, including among all ten states surrounding the sea, remain at what might be called an elementary stage.

Since the early 1990s, attempts have been made to bring the states of the South China Sea region together. These attempts at regime building have included, first, a set of informal multilateral meetings that have taken up issues relevant to the South China Sea every year since 1990. This multilateral political process, called Managing Potential Conflicts in the South China Sea (hereafter South China Sea Workshops), has involved workshops in different Indonesian provinces, with funding from Canada and the participant countries.[3] Workshops were conceived and have been led by two experts on law of the sea questions: Ambassador Hasjim Djalal (Jakarta)[4] and Professor Ian Townsend-Gault (Vancouver).[5]

Second, the littoral countries of the region, in cooperation with UNEP, have attempted to establish an environmental action plan for the South China Sea. This initiative emerged as a collaborative project between littoral countries and UNEP with initial funding from the Global Environment Facility. A transboundary diagnostic analysis (TDA), a study of issues and problems and their societal root causes, was formulated by UNEP and senior marine scientists in the region in the period 1996 to 1998. The TDA was later used as a basis for the development of a draft Strategic Action Program for the South China Sea. In preparing these documents, scientists and government agencies from seven littoral states—Thailand, Malaysia, Cambodia, Indonesia, Vietnam, China, and the Philippines—have been involved in conducting country-specific studies used as a basis for the transboundary diagnostic analysis, as well as for the Strategic Action Program.

> Important transboundary environmental problems of the South China Sea region have been identified by the UNEP in cooperation with the national committees. The TDA identifies the priorities among water-related problems and concerns, their socio-economic root causes, the sectoral implications of actions needed to mitigate them and the extent to which the problems are transboundary in either origin or effect. . . . The actions proposed in the framework of the Strategic Action Program are wide ranging in both context and proposed areas for action. Successful implementation of the Program will depend upon co-ordination of actions by diverse organizations, agencies, non-governmental organizations, private sectors, and stakeholder groups at both the national and regional levels. Recognizing the mandate of the United Nations Environment Program to co-ordinate environmental action across the United Nations System, the widest possible range of appropriate partners at national and regional levels will be encouraged and assisted to participate in the execution of the Program. It is the intention of the participating countries that all actions be undertaken in a spirit of collaboration and partnership, to enhance the synergy between on-going initiatives at national and regional levels, and eliminate duplicative and conflicting actions." (UNEP 1999: 4)

Whether these two initiatives are examples of a new trend of integrative cooperation in the South China Sea region will be further discussed later.

Djalal and Townsend-Gault say the South China Sea Workshops have aimed at

> Encouraging confidence building between the states of the South China Sea region, thus easing tensions arising from sovereignty and jurisdictional disputes over the Spratly and Paracel island groups, and ocean space adjacent to the littoral states. Cooperation will be encouraged in such a way as to *implement a regime* for the South China Sea compatible with the regime for semi-enclosed seas as set forth in the United Nations Convention on the Law of the Sea 1982, which serves a model for project purposes.[6] (my italics)

The conveners of the workshops refer here to the future establishment of (according to Krasner's [1983] definition of a regime) a cluster of commitments to a given issue area (management and protection of natural resources in the South China Sea) where a negotiated combination of norms, rules, principles, and decision-making procedures creates a formal and regional multilateral agreement or gives premises for state action in the South China Sea. The lack of formal and binding cooperation in the South China Sea means there is no regulation of fisheries, no regional regulation of or cooperation on combating pollution. Overlapping claims to maritime zones make it impossible to decide which state is responsible for environmental protection and management, and there is no sense of any temporary shared responsibility, although many speak of joint development or joint management.

This sounds much like a situation Garrett Hardin (1968) referred to as the "Tragedy of the Commons."[7] As the South China Sea is not partitioned according to UNCLOS in Exclusive Economic Zones (EEZ), where the individual state has jurisdiction over the resources within the zone, large areas of sea—especially the living resources in these areas—are left to those who manage to catch them. This means one littoral state has the opportunity to exploit and deplete the living resources that belong to all littoral states in the area. According to Oran Young (1994: 20), there are roughly three ways to regulate this problem. One is to solve the sovereignty question with reference to ideas developed in UNCLOS. Normally, this would lead to a delimitation agreement among all claimants on how to define the limits of EEZs and solve the question of sovereignty over islands. This is not likely to happen in the near future. A second solution is to establish a joint development zone in the disputed area, share the cost and responsibility for development, and divide the benefits of resource exploitation. This is what China and Taiwan have suggested in principle since the early 1990s (Lee 1999a: 127–131)—without, however, presenting any concrete proposals. No joint development zone is likely to be established in the near future. China's understanding of joint development also seems to imply that the other participants must negotiate with China bilaterally, not multilaterally. The third option is to create a regime or formalized agreement in which all states in the region join forces to set up a joint management regime (to oversee fisheries regulation, environmental protection, and marine scientific research) while abstaining from drilling oil and gas. This may be the aim of the conveners of the South China Sea Workshops: a regime to carry out the obligations of UNCLOS 123 (regarding semienclosed seas). The normative and principled contents of such a regime are sketched in the UNCLOS paragraph, and the workshops are based on the suggested fields of cooperation in the convention.[8]

But we must also remember that these workshops, as well as the UNEP initiative, take place within an Asian setting. The countries of East and Southeast Asia are less experienced in multilateralism than are European and North American countries.[9] In other words, the effort to implement international regimes in the regional context of the South China Sea has important aspects that make this region stand out from others. The "Asian way" of diplomacy is important in this respect. Another central aspect is the contribution of scientists to establish cooperative regimes. What role are scientists playing in influencing governments to cooperate? Could environmental cooperation lead to cooperation in other areas?

REGIME BUILDING AND THE REGIONAL SCIENTIFIC COMMUNITY

Regional scientists have actively participated in the South China Sea Workshops, as well as contributed to the formulation of the Strategic Action Program for the South China Sea. The UNEP initiative and the workshops should probably be seen as parts of the same regime-building effort. In this section I analyze efforts to build a cooperative regime: What characterizes it, and what role have scientists from various disciplines played in the process?

Regional environmental regime formation has been analyzed by Gareth Porter and Janet Brown in terms of four consecutive but overlapping stages (1996: 69): issue definition, fact-finding, bargaining on regime creation, and regime strengthening. Between the fact-finding and bargaining stages one might add Young's (1994: 83) *prenegotiation* stage, which he defines as "the process through which an issue initially finds it way onto the international agenda, gets defined or framed as a topic for international consideration, and reaches the sufficiently prominent place on the agenda to justify expending the time and effort involved in explicit negotiations." Scientific evidence and knowledge advanced by communities of marine scientists may eventually attract the attention of decisionmakers, who will change their policies accordingly. The extent to which the scientific community in the

South China Sea region has been successful in gaining governments' attention and making them cooperate on environmental issues in the region will be discussed later.

ISSUE DEFINITION AND FACT-FINDING

Issue definition is understood here as efforts to bring the issue to the attention of the international community and identify the scope and magnitude of environmental threats, as well as the action required to address the issue. The fact-finding process consists of collecting information to assess the scope and nature of the problem and present policy options (Porter and Brown 1996: 69–70). In the South China Sea a wide range of environmental issues need to be acted upon. Through participation in the South China Sea Workshops' Technical Working Group on Marine Scientific Research (TWGMSR) and work on the UNEP Strategic Action Program for the South China Sea, the regional scientific community has documented and informed the governments of the environmental challenges they are facing. The TWGMSR has provided a forum for the regional scientific community to discuss various aspects of marine scientific research, as well as being an important arena for presenting data, project proposals, and common denominators on which to base cooperation.

In 1998 the TWGMSR drew the attention of UNEP, and discussions emerged on how to integrate the TWGMSR and other Technical Working Groups with the Strategic Action Program for the South China Sea.[10] Although a biodiversity proposal had been discussed for a number of years within the TWGMSR, the proposal was not implemented. The biodiversity proposal seemed to be the factor that might pave the way for cooperation on other issues, but lack of funding has prevented the proposal from being implemented. This was the reason UNEP was invited to the Group of Experts Meeting on Biological Biodiversity in November 1998. UNEP wanted to integrate the biodiversity proposal into its Strategic Action Program for the South China Sea, which was to be finished in this period. John Pernetta, from UNEP headquarters in Nairobi, and Liana Talaue-McManus, responsible for formulating the Strategic Action Program for the South China Sea, participated in the meeting.

I believe UNEP and the regional scientific community have succeeded in bringing environmental issues of concern to the attention of the governments in the region, have succeeded in pinpointing the important issues, and have prescribed the steps to be taken. In the TWGMSR the scientists discussed important issues such as fisheries research; biological diversity; nonconventional energy; environmental phenomena; marine circulation; training, networking, and information; and mechanisms for cooperation and joint research. From these seven areas three project proposals were selected: proposals on database and information networking, sea-level and tide monitoring, and biodiversity.[11] The first project in the workshop process that is about to be implemented, the biodiversity proposal, is funded in part by Brunei Darussalam, Singapore, and Indonesia (Townsend-Gault 1998: 186). The project proposals worked out within the TWGMSR appear to be the most successful, suggesting that the marine scientists and their understanding of the current situation in terms of marine environmental status have influenced the participating governments in approving, funding, and adopting projects.

In the Strategic Action Program for the South China Sea, priorities for action are spelled out as endorsing a legal framework for regional cooperation, preparing maps and inventories to achieve the program's aims, developing a network of databases throughout the region to facilitate program goals, developing criteria for management plans for ecosystems and fisheries, enhancing capacity building in terms of education technology exchange, and diffusing knowledge on all levels (UNEP 1999: 78). Through the work on the Transboundary Diagnostic Analysis and the formulation of the draft Strategic Action Program for the South China Sea, marine scientists in the region have been allowed to document the major environment-related transboundary problems governments of the region are facing.

The willingness to implement the biodiversity proposal within the South China Sea Workshops and the willingness of Malaysia, Vietnam, the Philippines, Thailand, Cambodia, and Indonesia to sign the draft Strategic Action Program can be taken as proof that the countries of the region are serious about combating environmental problems. It may also prove that the regional scientific community has achieved success in getting attention, framing issues, and prescribing the necessary remedies. In other words, the regional scientific community has been successful in influencing the governments of the region to include the marine environment as an important issue in the environmental regime-building process. This is not to say that the scientific community has influenced the governments to cooperate on environmental issues, but in the issue definition and fact-finding process scientists have been influential in bringing marine environment–related issues to the attention of decisionmakers. COBSEA's decision to initiate work on a South China Sea Strategic Action Program and the decision to add discussions of marine scientific research and environmental protection to the main South China Sea Workshops support the idea that scientists are gaining attention on the regional level.

Although agreement seems to exist on the initiatives (the South China Sea Strategic Action Program and the biodiversity proposal), however, they have not been implemented because the states do not agree on how to proceed with environmental cooperation. When the signatory states of the

East Asian Action Plan attended the Thirteenth Meeting of COBSEA in November 1998, a discussion emerged on the wording of the Strategic Action Program. Referring to a section on regional cooperation, Indonesia objected to the use of the terms *convention, protocol, and legal framework,* since the Indonesian government "was not in favor of making legal/formal commitments" (COBSEA 1999:8). On the other side, Vietnam expressed support for the term *legal framework,* and China indicated that the area covered should be enlarged to all East Asian Seas—including the Philippine Sea, the East China Sea, and the Sea of Japan.

But although disagreements occur, the littorals seem to agree on central aspects of both the biodiversity proposal and the Strategic Action Program. The problem is that a lack of political will and funding prevent the initiatives from making practical progress. The scientists have not been successful in persuading governments to spend time and resources on cooperative arrangements to protect and manage common resources.

BARGAINING ON REGIME CREATION

Bargaining on regime creation is recognized by the advancement of proposals for international action through consensus building by one or more parties (Porter and Brown 1996: 70). In this context initiatives have come from both ASEAN and UNEP. Apparently, China has blocked both initiatives. Still, the lack of progress cannot be blamed on China alone. Generally speaking, there seems to be a lack of political will to implement suggested projects emerging from the various TWGs, not only from China but also from countries within ASEAN. This has slowed the progress of discussions within the workshops, as well as the implementation of project proposals worked out under the TWGs.

The Chinese are generally not eager to enter regional cooperative arrangements. Some say this is a result of the nature of the workshop process. The form of confidence-building diplomacy conducted in the workshops may not be the right way to engage China. According to some, it is too "pushy" (Chua 1999; Lai 1999). The workshop process resembles too much formal diplomacy, with the ASEAN countries trying repeatedly to lift the process to a formal level.[12] The Indonesian minister of foreign affairs, Ali Alatas, has on several occasions encouraged participants to make concessions and reach agreements on the South China Sea. As Lee Lai To (1999b: 167) has said: "The multilateral process is both difficult and fragile: the interest of many participants must be taken into consideration, and workshop recommendations could be easily ignored by the governments concerned. Efforts to formalize and institutionalize discussions have been rejected, so the workshop remains a talk-shop about such peripheral issues." China has been even more strongly opposed to all attempts to internationalize the issue. This was probably the reason China at first refused to take part in the UNEP initiative, fearing the involvement of UNEP—a UN agency—could entail internationalization of the entire South China Sea dispute (Talaue-McManus 1999). Chinese participating in the workshops have had a limited mandate; the Chinese government has been prepared only to discuss joint development projects that would not have implications for its sovereignty claims (Lee 1999a).

Several interviewees also mentioned a difference between Western and Asian ways of interacting through diplomacy (Chua 1999; Lai 1999; Sarne and Ortuoste 1999). The "Asian way" is presumably not dissimilar from what has been called "the ASEAN way." What some consider the ASEAN way of diplomacy has important bearings on the workshops and the UNEP initiative. The ASEAN way of diplomacy refers to a distinctive approach to dispute settlement and regional cooperation developed by members of ASEAN. This framework for interstate cooperation has a history that goes back to the establishment of ASEAN in 1967. Since that time ASEAN countries have faced a number of challenges: the end of the Konfrontasi between Indonesia and Malaysia; later the communist victory in Vietnam, Laos, and Cambodia; the Vietnamese occupation of Cambodia; Vietnam's alliance with the Soviet Union; the weakening of the U.S. military presence at the end of the 1990s; the surge of Chinese power; and the inclusion of four new members—Vietnam, Laos, Burma, and Cambodia.

In handling these challenges ASEAN developed a framework for interaction based on noninterference in the domestic affairs of others, nonuse of force, pacific settlement of disputes, and respect for the sovereignty and territorial integrity of member states. This is little different from other regional security arrangements around the world, but what is peculiar is the nature of interaction in the region. Interaction has been characterized by discreetness, informality, pragmatism, expediency, consensus building, and nonconfrontational bargaining styles totally different from Western ways of diplomacy (Acharya 1997: 328–329). One observer of economic cooperation within the Asia-Pacific Economic Cooperation forum says the Asian way is "to agree on principles first, and then let things evolve and grow gradually" (Hadi Soesastro, cited in Acharya 1997: 334):

> The ASEAN countries tried to follow their procedural norms when drafting the institutional designs of the various new forums. They saw the "ASEAN way" as a suitable blueprint for a future Asia-Pacific security architecture and wanted to maintain an atmosphere of informality and non-confrontation. The best example is the Indonesian Spratly Workshops. Although well into its seventh year now this conference series is still informal, with government officials only

attending "in their private capacities." The whole enterprise proceeds in the manner of an academic seminar; there are even scientists and other scholars participating. Since "sensible" and "confrontational" matters have been bracketed from the outset, the workshops spend more time talking about biodiversity and marine life than about conflicting claims and military activities in the islands. But this is part of the "ASEAN way": from this point of view, one should try to find common ground first and deal with contentious issues later. (Busse 1999: 52–53)

This is seen as different from the "American approach," where one "start[s] with legally binding commitments covering a wide range of issues, something that scares many people in Asia" (Suhadi Mankusuwondo, cited in Acharya 1997: 334).

According to some interviewees, the South China Sea Workshops contain too much of the "Western way of diplomacy." They turn Nikolas Busse's argument upside down. Two interviewees (Chua 1999; Lai 1999) seem to blame the Indonesians for these efforts. According to statements made at a workshop in Oslo in April 1998 (Leifer 1998), Hasjim Djalal, the workshop founder, was tired of repeatedly having workshop participants try to stall efforts to move forward with issues raised. Thus Indonesia is here the agent of a "Western way," whereas China seems to represent the ASEAN way. Indonesia, as the leading power within ASEAN and the initiator of the workshops, and the Canadian International Development Agency, which is funding the process, need some progression to legitimize the spending of millions of dollars and nine years on the process.

A discussion of the workshops has emerged in which the skeptics and the workshop conveners are debating the content and prospects of the process.[13] Skeptics say the workshops are merely a talking club and designate them as "the failure of Indonesian mediation" (Catley and Keliat 1997: 165–168). The workshop conveners, Djalal and Townsend-Gault, say skeptics are overly preoccupied with the Spratly Islands delimitation question that seems inextricable. It is important to keep in mind that the countries are talking to each other on a regular basis; that they have found some areas on which they are prepared to cooperate, especially marine scientific research; and that meetings continue to promote cooperation and understanding among the littoral states of the region (Hearns and Stormont 1996; Townsend-Gault 1998).

REGIME STRENGTHENING

Regime strengthening refers to further bargaining on an established regime that reflects shifts in understanding of the environmental problem, as well as in the domestic politics of some parties (Porter and Brown 1996: 69). According to Porter and Brown (1996), regime strengthening may proceed in three ways: (1) through the establishment of a protocol after earlier negotiations failed to establish binding commitments, as in the Helsinki Protocol; (2) by amendment of former established agreements through bans or other specific actions, as in the whaling moratorium in which harvesting of whales was banned on a global scale; or (3) through a separate agreement committing some of the parties to go further than the existing agreement, as in the acid rain regimes.

The closest the South China Sea region has gotten to regime strengthening is through the two initiatives discussed previously. The South China Sea Workshops were originally an attempt by the ASEAN states to prepare for the implementation of UNCLOS in the region. This was largely an outgrowth of the lengthy negotiations on the Law of the Sea throughout the 1970s in which the four ASEAN states—Indonesia, Thailand, Singapore, and Malaysia—actively participated. To prevent conflict and improve the standing of international maritime law in the region, Townsend-Gault and Djalal started the workshops in which different aspects of UNCLOS were discussed. Later, as mentioned earlier, other states of the region were included. To what extent the workshops have improved the standing of UNCLOS in the region is difficult to say, as contradictory trends are at work. In one respect all littorals in the region have agreed in principle to solve maritime conflicts in accordance with UNCLOS, but at the same time they are making decisions to occupy reefs and refrain from cooperation.

The UNEP initiative can be seen as an attempt to amend an existing agreement—the East Asian Seas Action Plan. The member countries of COBSEA have run the institution with few results since the beginning of the 1980s. But as COBSEA was enlarged to integrate all South China Sea littorals, it began to focus its work on that sea. The East Asian Seas Action Plan was seen as too general and theoretical in its approach to maritime environmental problems, so a separate action plan for the South China Sea would be a stronger contribution to ocean management. At the Twelfth COBSEA Meeting in 1996, most parties showed a willingness to modify the East Asian Seas Action Plan to redirect activities from scientific-based ones to a more comprehensive, holistic management and action-oriented approach.[14]

Has the regional scientific community been influential in the regime-strengthening process, in the establishment of the South China Sea Workshops, and in the decision to change the nature of activities within the East Asian Seas Action Plan? The South China Sea Workshops must be said to be a result of a global trend in maritime international law. UNCLOS brought a number of issues to the attention of governments, and one result was that the governments of ASEAN chose to move away from academic discussions of different aspects of UNCLOS to policy-oriented action. Djalal and other law of the sea experts within ASEAN saw that UNCLOS provided them with certain mechanisms that could guide the littoral states of the South China Sea region into peaceful cooperation, as had been experienced in the Malacca Strait agreement. But the workshops were not only a result of the UNCLOS process, they were also a result of effective entrepreneurial leadership on the part of individuals. According to Young (1994: 114–115) entrepreneurial leaders are:

> Neither representatives of hegemons who can impose their will on others nor ethically motivated actors who seek to fashion workable institutional arrangements as contributors to the common good or the supply of public goods in international society. Rather, international entrepreneurs are participants who are skilled in inventing new institutional arrangements and brokering the overlapping interests of parties concerned with a particular issue area.

Hasjim Djalal and his Canadian counterpart, Ian Townsend-Gault, began to discuss the situation in the South China Sea at the beginning of 1989 after the violent clashes between China and Vietnam in 1988. They agreed to seek money for a workshop that would include informal talks on avenues for cooperation based on the new directions of the law of the sea. Regardless of who should receive credit, the workshops were a positive accomplishment. Some have suggested that Indonesia, as the major power within ASEAN, had its own reasons for hosting meetings on the South China Sea. Geographic considerations, the desire to secure natural resources around the Natuna Islands, the initial success in mediating the Cambodia conflict, and the need to constrain China may all have been considered when Suharto and his foreign minister Ali Alatas gave Djalal the green light (Catley and Keliat 1997).

Regarding the UNEP initiative, one can say with more certainty that scientists have influenced governments to follow their advice on marine environment–related issues. Scientific projects and discussions have dominated COBSEA, and the inclusion of the Association of Southeast Asian Marine Scientists (ASEAMS) and senior scientists as national focal points of COBSEA has reserved an important role for marine scientists.[15] In 1996, when COBSEA expressed an aspiration to move from scientific to more action-oriented projects, that was largely a result of the influence of environmentalists. The formulation of the Transboundary Diagnostic Analysis and the Strategic Action Program for the South China Sea resulted largely from the contribution of senior scientists from the region.

CONCLUSION

In the South China Sea region an implicit maritime regime has emerged based on various agreements and arrangements between two or more

ASEAN states, such as in the Malacca Strait and the Gulf of Thailand. Through consensus building, consultation, self-restraint, sensitivity, and respect for neighboring countries, the ASEAN member states have succeeded in establishing a sort of "Asian multilateralism" quite different from "Western multilateralism," which is based more on the explicit regime type of arrangement. Since 1990 cooperation within ASEAN has occurred within the context of the South China Sea, also involving powers outside ASEAN (China and Taiwan). In some respects this regime-building process has been successful in that agreement has been reached on common areas of interest in which project proposals have been forwarded for implementation and talks are held annually under peaceful circumstances. Of the prioritized areas, the working group on marine scientific research is the most promising and is closest to seeing its project proposals implemented. Other projects will probably appear in the years to come if the workshops continue.

Based on these facts, one can say that the ASEAN way of regime building has succeeded in gathering former enemies and claimants for peaceful talks on common areas of interest. But as Amitav Acharya (1997: 342) stated, the ASEAN way has obvious shortcomings:

> Thus, whether the ASEAN model of subregionalism can perform successfully in the wider Asia-Pacific context is questionable. While ASEAN has developed a strong tradition of multilateralism in Southeast Asia, many Northeast Asian countries, notably China, lack any significant historical experience in multilateral security cooperation. ASEAN's relative unity and longevity owes much to specific historical circumstances, particularly to its members' common fear of communism and their shared security concerns arising from the decade-long Cambodia conflict. It is sustained by close inter-personal ties among ASEAN elites. Such commonalities and linkages are not present within the larger Asia-Pacific setting and are highly unlikely to develop in the future.

As both the UNEP initiative and the workshops show, China has been able to block virtually all attempts at moving forward in important areas because consensus is needed before any action can be taken.

I have emphasized the role of scientists and their knowledge in regime-building processes and have shown that scientists have been brought together for joint research and discussions. Networks created through these discussions may at some point lead to the establishment of a regional implicit or explicit regime for environmental management. The UNEP initiative, if successful, will be a significant step in that direction. So far, however, no such regime exists, and UNCLOS, although ratified by the important states around the South China Sea, has not been implemented. (Thailand's argument that it will not ratify UNCLOS before it is able to implement it has some virtue.)

Although governments and political leaders may have been made aware of the environmental challenges facing them, they have had to consider whether to prioritize environmental protection campaigns over spending on economic and social sectors. In developing countries the growth of the economy and the welfare of people are normally seen as more important than protecting the environment. This seems to be the case in the South China Sea region as well. In addition, some have feared that environmental cooperation could in some way infringe upon or impede actions to defend national security and sustain claims to sovereignty and maritime zones.

NOTES

1. The environmental security concept refers to a field of research in which the relationship between security issues and environmental issues is in focus. For a thorough discussion of the concept see Dokken (1997: 69–104).
2. According to Olav Schram Stokke and Øystein B. Thommessen, eds., *Yearbook of International Cooperation on Environment and Development 1998/99* (London: Earthscan, 1999), there are nine regional conventions within the Regional Sea Program of UNEP: the Black Sea, the wider Caribbean, the East African seaboard, the Persian Gulf, the Mediterranean, the Red Sea and the Gulf of Aden, the South Pacific, the Southeast Pacific, and the Atlantic coast of West and Central Africa. Action plans have been established for the East Asian seas, the northwest Pacific, and the South Asian seas.
3. Information on the workshops is taken from the website of the South China Sea Informal Working Group Project at the Centre for Asian Legal Studies, University of British Columbia, Canada <http://faculty.law.ubc.ca/scs>.
4. Hasjim Djalal is Indonesian ambassador at large and an expert on ocean affairs, and he was an active participant in the process leading up to UNCLOS. Djalal also receives support from the nongovernmental Centre for Southeast Asian Studies in Jakarta. He has been called the "Godfather" of the workshop project.
5. Ian Townsend-Gault is an expert on petroleum law and the law of the sea. He is associate professor and director of the Centre for Asian Legal Studies and a regional director (West Coast Office) of the Oceans Institute of Canada. His current responsibilities include coordinating the CIDA-funded projects Managing Potential Conflicts in the South China Sea and the Viet Nam–Canada Ocean and Coastal Cooperation Program.
6. Information on the workshops is taken from the website in note 3.
7. The situation described as the "Tragedy of the Commons" was first presented in an article by H. Scott Gordon (1954). Hardin's (1968) definition of the "Tragedy of the Commons" situation is built on that article, according to Young 1994: 6.
8. Part IX, Enclosed or Semi-enclosed Seas, Article 123: Cooperation of states bordering enclosed or semi-enclosed seas. States bordering an enclosed or

semi-enclosed sea should co-operate with each other (a) to coordinate the management, conservation, exploration and exploitation of the living resources of the sea; (b) to coordinate the implementation of their rights and duties with respect to the protection and preservation of the marine environment; (c) to coordinate their scientific research policies and undertake, where appropriate, joint programs of scientific research in the area; (d) to invite, as appropriate, other interested States or international organizations to cooperate with them in furtherance of the provisions of this article (UNCLOS 1999).

9. John Ruggie (1993: 13) defines multilateralism as "an institutional form which coordinates relations among three or more states on the basis of 'generalized' principles of conduct—that is, principles that specify appropriate conduct for a class of actions without regard to the particularistic interests of the parties or the strategic exigencies that may exist in any specific occurrence."

10. The Sixth Technical Working Group Meeting on Marine Scientific Research, Manila, Philippines, 25–28 November 1998.

11. Fifth Meeting of the Technical Working Group on Marine Scientific Research, Cebu, Philippines, 14–17 July 1996.

12. I refer here to Indonesian foreign minister Ali Alatas's address to the workshop in 1995, where he called on all participating countries to consider moving from informal to formal diplomacy on certain subjects. The move from track two to track one has not been made.

13. This refers to a debate that emerged in *Contemporary Southeast Asia* after the journal published an article by Ian Townsend-Gault (1998). The author suggests that there is a difference between the view of security analysts (proponents of realpolitik) and the view of law of the sea experts (adherents of international law) that somewhat resembles the debate between realists and liberalists/institutionalists in the international relations camp.

14. Opening address by Terttu Melvasalo, director of the Water Branch of UNEP, on behalf of the executive director of UNEP, to the Twelfth Meeting of the COBSEA in Manila, Philippines, 3–4 December 1996.

15. ASEAMS was established by UNEP and COBSEA to provide independent, expert scientific advice regarding programs implemented in the East Asian Seas region. ASEAMS is also designed to integrate the region's marine scientists with various national, regional, and international organizations (Chou Loke Ming and Hong Woo Khoo 1993).

REFERENCES

Acharya, Amitav. 1997. "Ideas, Identity, and Institution-Building: From the 'ASEAN Way' to the 'Asia-Pacific Way'?" *Pacific Review* 10, 2: 319–346.

Bleakley, Chris, and Sue Wells, eds. 1999. *Marine Region 13: East Asian Seas*. Report to the World Bank Environment Department <http://www.environment.gov.au/library/pubs/mpa/chap13.html>.

Brookfield, Harold, and Yvonne Byron, eds. 1993. *South-East Asia's Environmental Future: The Search for Sustainability*. Kuala Lumpur: Oxford University Press.

Busse, Nikolas. 1999. "Constructivism and Southeast Asian Security." *Pacific Review* 12, 1: 39–60.

Catley, Bob, and Makmur Keliat. 1997. *Spratlys: The Dispute in the South China Sea.* Singapore: Ashgate.

Chou Loke Ming and Hong Woo Khoo. 1993. "Marine Science Training, Networking and Information in the South China Sea Region." Paper presented at the First Working Group Meeting on Marine Scientific Research in the South China Sea, Manila, Philippines, 30 May–3 June.

Chua Thia-Engh. 1999. Interview, Manila, Philippines, 8 July.

Coordinating Body on the Seas of East Asia (COBSEA). 1999. *Report of the Thirteenth Meeting of the Coordinating Body on the Seas of East Asia (COBSEA) on the East Asian Seas Action Plan* <http://www.unep.org/unep/regoffs/roap/easrcu/publication/13cobsea>.

Coulter, Daniel Y. 1996. "South China Sea Fisheries: Countdown to Calamity." *Contemporary Southeast Asia* 17, 4: 371–388.

Dokken, Karin. 1997. *Environment and Security and Regional Integration in West Africa.* Oslo: University of Oslo, Department of Political Science.

Gomez, Edgardo. 1988. "Achievements of the Action Plan for the East Asian Seas." In UNEP, *Cooperation for Environmental Protection in the Pacific.* UNEP Regional Seas Reports and Studies, No. 97. Bangkok: UNEP.

Gordon, H. Scott. 1954. "The Economic Theory of a Common Property Resource: The Fishery." *Journal of Political Economy* 62: 124–142.

Hardin, Garrett. 1968. "The Tragedy of the Commons." *Science* 162: 1343–1348.

Hearns, G. S., and W. G. Stormont. 1996. "Managing Potential Conflicts in the South China Sea." *Marine Policy* 20, 2: 177–181.

Krasner, Stephen D., ed. 1983. *International Regimes.* Ithaca: Cornell University Press.

Lai, Francis. 1999. Interview, Bangkok, Thailand, 24 June.

Lee, Lai To. 1999a. *China and the South China Sea Dialogues.* Westport, CT: Praeger.

Lee, Lai To. 1999b. "The South China Sea: China and Multilateral Dialogues." *Security Dialogue* 30, 2: 165–178.

Leifer, Michael. 1998. Talk given at a workshop on the South China Sea at the Norwegian Institute of International Affairs, Oslo, Norway, 14 April.

Low, Jeffrey K.Y., Beverly P.L. Goh, and L. M. Chou. 1996. "Regional Cooperation in Prevention and Response to Marine Pollution in the South China Sea." Paper presented at the Second ASEAMS Scientific Symposium, UNEP, Bangkok, 30 August.

"Pollution Takes Its Toll on Halong Bay World Heritage Attractions." 1999. *South China Morning Post* [Hong Kong] (28 April).

Porter, Gareth, and Janet Brown. 1996. *Global Environmental Politics,* 2d ed. Boulder: Westview.

Ruggie, John Gerard. 1993. *Multilateralism Matters: The Theory and Praxis of an Institutional Form.* New York: Columbia University Press.

Sarne, Emma, and Maria Consuelo C. Ortuoste. 1999. Interview, Manila, Philippines, 5 July.

Southeast Asian Program in Ocean Law, Policy, and Management (SEAPOL). 2002. *The Southeast Asian Programme in Ocean Law, Policy and Management: SEAPOL Overview.* <http://www.seapol.org/ACTIVITIES.htm>.

Soegiarto, Aprilani. 1994. "Sustainable Fisheries, Environment and the Prospects of Regional Cooperation in Southeast Asia." Paper presented at the Monterey Institute of International Studies Workshop "Trade and Environment in Asia-Pacific: Prospects for Regional Cooperation," East West Centre, Honolulu, Hawaii, 23–25 September.

Stokke, Olav Schram, and Øystein B. Thommessen, eds. 1999. *Yearbook of International Cooperation on Environment and Development 1998/99.* London: Earthscan.

Talaue-McManus, Liana. 1999. Interview, Manila, Philippines, 9 July.

Thayer, Carlyle A. 1999. "Southeast Asia Borders: Maritime Issues" <.-ftp:// coombs.anu.edu.au/coombspapers/otherarchives/asian-studies-archives/ seasia-archives/politics/seasia-maritime-issues.txt>.

Townsend-Gault, Ian. 1998. "Preventive Diplomacy and Pro-activity in the South China Sea." *Contemporary Southeast Asia* 20, 2: 171–189.

United Nations Convention on the Law of the Sea (UNCLOS). 1999. 23 November <http://www.un.org/Depts/los/losconv1.htm>.

United Nations Environment Program (UNEP). 1999. Strategic Action Program for the South China Sea. Draft Version 3, February.

Young, Oran R. 1994. *International Governance.* Ithaca: Cornell University Press.

13

The Indonesian Forest Fires: Internationalizing a National Environmental Problem

ALLEN L. SPRINGER

States have, in accordance with the Charter of the United Nations and the principles of international law, the sovereign right to exploit their own resources pursuant to their own environmental policies, and the responsibility to ensure that activities within their jurisdiction or control do not cause damage to the environment of other States or of areas beyond the limits of national jurisdiction.
—*Stockholm Declaration on the Human Environment (1972), Principle 21*

During late 1997 and early 1998, fires spread through the brush, forests, and peat bogs of eastern Indonesia, destroying nearly 10 million hectares. A thick haze spread over much of Southeast Asia, affecting public health and devastating the tourist trade. The transboundary consequences of the fires transformed what was initially a national environmental problem into one of regional and global dimensions. The resulting damage, estimated as high as $8–$10 billion, made the Indonesian fires among the planet's most costly environmental catastrophes.

The fires' devastating impact focused international attention on developing practical measures to prevent or at least control a recurrence. The nature of the international response also raises important questions about the state of legal and institutional development of international environmental practice in which states seemingly acknowledged in the early 1970s their responsibility to control environmentally degrading activities under their jurisdiction. Despite the seriousness of the problem and the early recognition that this was a disaster to which the Indonesian government had directly contributed through its land-use policies and lax enforcement of existing law, remarkably little was said by Indonesia or other states about Indonesia's legal responsibility to control the fires and pay compensation to those beyond Indonesia's borders who were injured. As Simon Tay has put it, "The fires . . . challenge the adequacy of international environmental law, both in practice and in principle" (1999: 241).

This chapter examines the "internationalization" of the Indonesian forest fires. In a recent assessment of the development of Asian environmental law, Ben Boer used the term to denote a process whereby countries "are now looking externally to environmental conventions and agreements to guide their policies and laws, rather than remaining internally focused on developing their environmental management policies and regulatory systems" (1999: 1509). As used here, internationalization does not necessarily imply a process of conscious choice by the state whose policies and behavior might be affected by international norms. Moreover, the focus is as much on the role of outside states, organizations, and interest groups in pushing the process along as it is on the state itself. The objective is to understand better some of the factors shaping attitudes not just in Indonesia but throughout the international community as people were forced to confront a serious environmental challenge.

The chapter begins by reviewing briefly the fires and their presumed causes and effects, then looks at the steps taken at the national, regional, and global levels in response. Countries ranging from Malaysia and Singapore to Japan and the United States and international organizations—including the Association of Southeast Asian Nations (ASEAN) and the United Nations Environment Program (UNEP)—sought to assist Indonesia and, in so doing, transformed the fires into an international issue. The chapter then attempts to assess that response, to explain why more was not done—particularly by the states most directly affected—to focus attention on Indonesia's seeming obligation to act more decisively.

If a central observation emerges from this analysis, it is that a substantial gap remains between the language of the Stockholm Declaration and actual state practice, evident in the ways in which states reacted to the fires. Nonetheless, a process of internationalization has been under way that is acknowledging the legitimacy of the international community's interest in controlling the factors that led to the fires. It also offers hope that increased public awareness and organized pressure against governments, often too willing to hold back for fear of offending neighbors or upsetting "normal" relations, will encourage officials to accelerate this process and create a tougher legal framework to support environmental protection efforts.

THE FIRES

The fires of 1997–1998 were neither unprecedented nor unexpected, although the extent of the damage was both. Fires in Sumatra's Riau Province were discovered by satellite in January 1997, and the World Meteorological Organization reported "hot spots" on its maps of the region in May. By late

September the Worldwide Fund for Nature (WWF) was calling for a major international initiative to respond to the "planetary disaster" caused primarily by fires in Indonesian sections of Borneo (Kalimantan) and Sumatra (WWF 1997a). The El Niño effect contributed to the problem, as abnormally dry conditions helped the fires spread from the Indonesian scrublands into tropical rain forests not normally subject to such intense fire pressures. Rains in November and December brought temporary relief, but the fires picked up again in February, the result of an El Niño–shortened rainy season. By April the fires in East Kalimantan were even worse than those of the previous fall, although prevailing wind patterns reduced their transboundary impact. Fire-fighting efforts were complicated by the extreme drought. Heavy rains finally arrived in early May, returning in June and July and putting an end–for the time being–to the fire problem (Barber and Schweithelm 2000: 8).

Several studies have attempted to place an economic value on the damage caused by the fires, always a challenging undertaking but particularly so where the full extent of the injury to human health and regional ecosystems may not be known for decades. Early estimates focusing on just the 1997 fires suggested losses ranging from $2.4 billion to nearly $4.5 billion (see EEPSEA/WWF 1999). A more extensive analysis funded by the Asian Development Bank and covering the entire 1997–1998 period later reached what a World Resources Institute (WRI) study termed the "most reliable estimate to date" of economic costs between $8 billion and $10 billion (Barber and Schweithelm 2000: 15). One can debate the methodologies used by researchers, but the cost of the fires was undeniably very high, as the WRI study points out, substantially exceeding the assessed damages for the *Exxon Valdez* and Bhopal accidents combined.

Indonesia was most directly affected, with the most easily quantifiable impact felt in losses to agricultural and forestry production. The fires were best known, however, for a thick blanket of smoke that showed no respect for national boundaries and at times spread from Thailand to Singapore, Malaysia, and the Philippines—an area of 200 million people. Schools and factories were closed, and people were told to stay indoors as air pollution readings soared to dangerously high levels. Hospitals were flooded with patients seeking treatment for acute respiratory infections, asthma, and conjunctivitis; tens of thousands of people were directly affected. The smoke apparently contributed to several accidents, including the crash of an Indonesian airbus in which 234 died; one study placed the number of Indonesians killed by the fires at 527 (see generally Barber and Schweithelm 2000: 17–20). The fires received extensive publicity, and the effect on tourism throughout Southeast Asia was predictable and devastating—a particular concern given the importance of this $26 billion industry in attracting needed foreign exchange (Gallon 1997).

Beyond tourists driven away by the smoke, broader "extraregional" interests were also affected. Nongovernmental organizations (NGOs) led by the WWF publicized the threats to endangered species—most notably the orangutan—as the fires spread to "protected areas" (WWF 1997b). Less immediate but equally significant in impressing upon the public the global implications of the fires was their contribution to global climate change. Both the direct release of carbon dioxide, especially from the carbon-rich peat swamps, and the loss of the tropical forests—part of the carbon "sink" needed to absorb carbon dioxide—were significant. The World Bank later estimated that the 1997 fires alone "contributed about 30 percent of all man-made carbon emissions globally—more than the entire emissions from man-made sources from North America" (Barber and Schweithelm 2000: 17).

As the toll mounted and the range of affected parties increased, the question of blame took on at least political importance, both nationally and internationally. Government officials were tempted initially to depict the fires as a "natural" disaster for which El Niño was primarily responsible; the abnormally dry conditions clearly affected the fires' scope and duration. Fire has traditionally been seen in Indonesia as elsewhere, however, as a cost-effective way to clear land, leading to major uncontrolled fires in the past. These fires included the "Great Kalimantan Fire" of 1982–1983, in which approximately 3.2 million hectares had burned, and fires in 1991 and 1994 that had sent large volumes of smoke across international borders (Barber and Schweithelm 2000: 5–7). Once it became obvious that the overwhelming majority of the fires had been set deliberately, the debate shifted to identifying the culprits. Traditional government explanations for the recurrent fire problem had focused on small indigenous groups (Williams and Baker 1997), but the scale of the problem clearly implicated others. The timber industry quickly pointed to small farmers, timber smugglers, and palm oil and rubber plantations, arguing that foresters had a vested interest in protecting forest areas (Gopalakrishnan 1997). Aided by satellite photographs from the U.S. National Oceanic and Atmospheric Administration, however, the Indonesian government was able to identify 176 firms—including timber companies—believed to be engaged in deliberate burning. In April 1998 Indonesia's environment minister, Juwono Sudarsono, publicly accused the timber industry of responsibility for 65 percent of the damage done by the East Kalimantan fires ("Indonesian Fires No Accident" 1997).

Yet as Stephen Howard (1998) and Charles Barber and James Schweithelm (2000: 28–37) demonstrate, the Indonesian government contributed significantly to the context in which the fires occurred. It did so first through conscious government policies designed to develop the timber and palm oil industries and to shift populations from Java to frontier areas, like those in Borneo and Sumatra. The policies were developed within a governmental structure dominated by a centralized, unchecked, and unresponsive bureaucracy closely tied to the interests of a small number of business leaders personally connected to the Suharto family. The result, according to Barber and Schweithelm, is that the fires of 1997–1998 were ultimately "the logical and inevitable result of long-standing struggles over the control of forestlands and resources and a reflection of the imbalances and abuses of power that characterized [Suharto's] natural resources policies for three decades" (2000: 28).

THE RESPONSE: INTERNATIONALIZATION OF THE FIRES

Despite international concern about the fires' external effects, they were taking place on Indonesian soil—territory over which Indonesia had sovereign authority—and the process by which the fires were internationalized was neither simple nor direct.

INDONESIAN ACTIONS

Even as it faced an environmental and economic problem of tremendous domestic significance, the Indonesian government understood that it had to respond to the concerns of people beyond its borders, particularly since it had reassured its neighbors only two years earlier that the 1994 fires would not be repeated (Barber and Schweithelm 2000: 8). How to acknowledge the legitimate interests of others while not accepting legal responsibility for the fires and their consequences became a significant challenge for the Suharto regime.

An important step was taken on 15 September 1997 when President Suharto offered an apology to states "disturbed by the forest fires" (ASEAN 1997a). Suharto pointed to the extensive damage Indonesia itself was suffering and emphasized the challenges it faced in trying to control such vast areas of forest and tropical brush. The Worldwide Fund for Nature expressed appreciation for Suharto's "gesture" even as it pointedly termed the fires a "man-made natural disaster" (WWF 1997a). In October Indonesian cabinet ministers made the unusual move of answering questions about the fires at a public news conference where Transmigration Minister Siswono Yudohusodo acknowledged the "expensive lesson" that had been learned about the dangers of slash-and-burn techniques of land clearing (CNN 1997). When fires began again in February 1998, Environment Minister Sarwono Kusumaatmadja stated Indonesia's readiness to accept the blame for the resulting problems, although the operational significance of this proclamation was far from clear (BBC 1998b).

The strategy of accepting a kind of "moral" responsibility for the fires was coupled with repeated expressions of appreciation for the "understanding" shown by Indonesia's neighbors. What was presumably understood was not just that natural forces had helped cause the fires but that Indonesia's ability to respond effectively was constrained both by technical factors, such as a lack of fire-fighting capacity, and the economic situation plaguing Indonesia and the entire Southeast Asian region. Sarwono pointed out that Indonesia had only three planes capable of dropping water on the fires and called for increased financial assistance from the international community. Many Asian currencies had collapsed during the summer of 1997, with a resulting steep decline in demand for Indonesian timber and agricultural exports. The problem was only exacerbated by the effects of the fires (Dauvergne 2000). In April Sarwono's successor, Juwono Sudarsono, was even more blunt, suggesting that the Indonesian government did not perceive the fires as its top priority given the economic conditions: "These multiple crises have made it difficult [for my office] to introduce a sense of urgency" (BBC 1998c).

The Indonesian government also acknowledged the importance of taking steps both to punish those responsible for starting the fires and to prevent future disasters. In 1993 Indonesia had made it illegal to use fire as a means of clearing land, although the practice had continued with minimal government interference. After the 1997 fires began the government became tougher, starting with a list the Forestry Ministry published of companies believed to be responsible for fires on their lands. In October the forestry minister claimed the government had revoked the operating licenses of twenty-nine firms that were unable to disprove the allegations (Agence France-Presse 1997). Twenty farmers were arrested in East Kalimantan for continuing to burn in violation of Indonesian law (Disaster Relief 1997). At a December meeting of ASEAN environment ministers, Indonesia pledged to continue prosecuting those responsible for the fires, and Minister Sarwono said he would support a moratorium on developing new palm oil plantations (Head 1997).

REGIONAL REACTION

Indonesia's immediate neighbors were surprisingly restrained, given the level of damage the fires were inflicting. A 1999 study estimated that the 1997 fires alone did almost $670 million in damage to other countries, with Malaysia suffering $310 million in quantifiable loss and Singapore $74 million (EEPSEA/WWF 1999). When the fires reemerged as a serious threat in February 1998, a more critical reaction was evident. Still, the initial response was to send help, with Singapore providing satellite photos to identify "hot spots" and Malaysia offering firefighters and assistance in cloud seeding. The priority was clearly to stop the damage, and Singapore's environment minister publicly asked Indonesia to take more effective measures to control the burning, a request repeated by Malaysia in February (BBC 1998a).

Government actions did not reflect general public sentiment in the affected states. Anger was expressed by the public and the media, particularly in Malaysia, about a problem that seemed to many to require a more direct government response. Environmental organizations accused the Malaysian government of doing too little, and a rare public demonstration calling for more decisive action was held in Kuala Lumpur in late September (Mydans 1997a). The government, apparently sensitive to the criticism and worried about the impact of negative reporting on tourism, required academics commenting on the fires to clear their observations with the government (Kristoff 1997). Singapore's *Straits Times,* after publishing satellite photographs indicating the deliberate nature of the fires, editorialized that "the cost of the haze is getting unacceptably high and will get higher if not enough Indonesian officials act urgently, decisively" ("Indonesian Fires No Accident" 1997). The Bangkok *Post* went further: "If Indonesia refuses to address its deadly pollution seriously, its neighbors must force the issue" (quoted in Mydans 1997b: 3).

It was within ASEAN that the clearest regional response to the fires developed, although one very much in keeping with the cooperative, nonconfrontational approach evident bilaterally. ASEAN meetings provided a forum in which the Indonesian government apparently felt comfortable addressing its neighbors' concerns. ASEAN had been created in 1967 during a very difficult period for a region split between communist and noncommunist regimes and facing widespread military conflict. ASEAN's founders were preoccupied with the twin goals of encouraging political stability and promoting growth and economic development. They quickly developed what became known as the "ASEAN way," an approach to regionalism emphasizing dispute avoidance and cooperation in areas of mutual agreement. ASEAN's organizational role was deliberately kept low-key, as members emphasized the principles of sovereign equality and noninterference in their internal affairs and used a consensus-based decision-making process to prevent unwanted intrusions into domestic or controversial international issues. In the process ASEAN earned a reputation as a reactive rather than proactive body (Naidu 1998).

ASEAN's slow development of an environmental dimension should not come as a surprise. When it did expand its activities into the environmental sphere, it chose to focus less on issues of transboundary dispute than on areas of shared interest, like promoting the positions of developing states in global environmental negotiations on climate change and biodiversity. Particularly on issues such as deforestation, environmentalists have often perceived ASEAN states as obstacles rather than allies (Tay 1999: 256–257), consistently supporting the right of states to exploit their natural resources as a means of promoting economic development (Montes 1997). The environment is not mentioned in ASEAN's original charter, and the 1978 ASEAN Environment Program provides only a loosely structured and nonbinding framework. ASEAN environmental initiatives are more likely to involve "plans for cooperation between national institutions, rather than the creation or strengthening of any regional institutions as a central hub for policy-making or implementation" (Tay 1998: 204).

The 1985 ASEAN Agreement on Conservation of Nature and Natural Resources (ASEAN 1985) deserves mention, however. Should it ever come into force, the agreement would provide a stronger legal foundation for the organization's work; some provisions also have both general and specific relevance to the haze issue. Article 20 reaffirms the language of the Stockholm Declaration, acknowledging the parties' "responsibility of ensuring that activities under their jurisdiction or control do not cause damage to the environment or the natural resources of other Contracting Parties or of areas beyond the limits of national jurisdiction" and perhaps goes farther in stating the duty to "avoid to the maximum extent possible and reduce to the minimum extent possible adverse environmental effects." Article 6 requires parties to "endeavor to control clearance of vegetation and endeavor to prevent bush and forest fires." Yet as Boer (1999: 1533) points out, the agreement does not articulate clearly the nature of the liability regime should transboundary effects occur, nor does it provide any process through which affected states could try to receive compensation. Moreover, the language of Article 6 provides substantial room for arguing that a state has "endeavored" to prevent the problem and simply failed, perhaps because of inadequate resources. Still, it is worth noting that Indonesia is one of only three states to ratify the agreement, which requires six ratifications to come into effect.

ASEAN became involved in the haze issue after the 1994 fires. In June 1995 a Cooperation Plan on Transboundary Pollution (ASEAN 1995a) was developed that covered three transboundary issues: air pollution, movement of hazardous waste, and shipborne pollution. Although not binding, the plan was in part a response to the recurrent forest fires, referred to as "haze incidents." The agreement outlined a series of "strategies" to prevent and detect fires, both nationally and through enhanced regional cooperation. In September Indonesia organized visits by an ASEAN delegation to fire-prone areas, and the ASEAN environment ministers agreed to set up a Haze Technical Task Force, chaired by Indonesia, "to provide a more coordinated effort in combating the problem" through improved monitoring and information sharing (ASEAN 1995b).

Thus by the time of the 1997 fires the haze problem was on the ASEAN agenda, and at least a limited regional program—admittedly under Indonesian direction—was in place to respond. President Suharto used the September 1997 ASEAN Ministerial Meeting on the Environment held in Jakarta to offer the apology discussed earlier. No further regional action was taken at that meeting, however. It was not until December that the first of what became a series of ASEAN Ministerial Meetings on Haze was convened in Singapore. The ASEAN ministers emphasized that the "traditional spirit of ASEAN cooperation, solidarity and understanding . . . continued" and that their "joint effort to combat fires and smoke haze had in fact helped bind ASEAN countries even closer together" (ASEAN 1997b). Even as smoke was spreading over the region, the ministers still seemed ready to signal the priority attached to growth, noting that they would "continue to protect the environment in their pursuit of economic development" (ASEAN 1997b). Amid increasing public criticism of government inaction, however, they did agree on a Regional Haze Action Plan, which was trumpeted to the press as requiring "very specific measures and a specific timetable" (Head 1997). The plan acknowledged the seriousness of the problem and called for a number of actions to be taken to prevent and control future fires, including prohibiting open burning, enforcing existing laws more strictly, and establishing more effective fire response systems. The steps, however, were to be developed not at the regional level but through a series of National Plans to be finished by March 1998, with the Haze Technical Task Force meeting monthly to "review progress" and "provide guidance" on the plan's implementation.

With the return of the fires in February 1998, the issue took on new urgency. ASEAN environment ministers met in Sarawak on 22 February. The only concrete step taken was to "urge" Indonesia and Malaysia to implement a joint fire-fighting plan signed in 1997 (ASEAN 1998a). Meeting in Brunei in April, the ministers emphasized the link between the fires and broader environmental issues, such as global climate change and biodiversity. This was an important step, as it provided the basis for accepting a role for UNEP in coordinating international assistance efforts. The ministers also endorsed private initiatives to educate the public and raise funds, since "combating the fires was the responsibility of all sectors of the ASEAN community" (ASEAN 1998b). The Fourth Ministerial Meeting on Haze was held in June, after heavy rains had extinguished the Kalimantan fires. More emphasis was now placed on measures to prevent future fires, including a request that members consider legal reforms to put the burden of proof on landowners to show they were not responsible for fire occurring on land they nominally controlled (ASEAN 1998c).

THE GLOBAL RESPONSE

The broader international community responded to the fires with concern and offers of help. Sixteen non-ASEAN countries offered both direct fire-fighting assistance (e.g., water-bombing teams from Australia and the United States) and money (Tay 1998: 205). NGOs like the WWF played a particularly important role throughout the fires, monitoring developments in Indonesia and issuing periodic reports and comments to keep the issue alive in the global media. They made very effective use of the Internet to alert people outside the region to the threat the fires represented, particularly to endangered species and protected areas. Non-governmental actors have generally had more direct access to these "sovereign" resources than governments worried about appearing to intrude into the domestic affairs of other states. The presence of international NGOs was vital to keeping on the international agenda an issue some governments were tempted to ignore, and several ultimately earned a more formal place at the table when UNEP later began to coordinate international response efforts.

UNEP emerged as the focus of organized global efforts to assist Indonesia, although its involvement was clearly peripheral until the second round of fires began in 1998. In October 1997 UNEP had asked the World Conservation Monitoring Center to disseminate information about the fires, emphasizing the organization's concern for "internationally important" protected areas, including a World Heritage site in Java and a Ramsar Convention Wetland in Sumatra. UNEP stated its intention to "monitor developments in the region," but beyond that its role was unclear (UNEP 1997). UNEP's executive director, Klaus Töpfer, attended the February ASEAN ministerial meeting in Sarawak, but ASEAN did not mention UNEP directly until the April meeting.

On 20–21 April UNEP convened a conference in Geneva that included three separate sessions. The first was an Expert Workshop on fire fighting, which produced a "costed action plan" totaling just under $10 million to respond to the continuing fires in East Kalimantan. The second focused on "medium to long-term programs" to combat the fires, and representatives from UN and Specialized Agencies and other organizations reviewed their fire-related initiatives. NGO representatives pressed the conference to look beyond the immediate "symptoms" of the problem—the fires themselves—to examine their "underlying causes" and hold those responsible accountable for their actions. The third was a meeting of potential donors where the need to support preventive measures was also emphasized. The Indonesian government expressed particular gratitude for assistance designed to deal with the immediate situation in Kalimantan while reassuring donors that it did intend to address longer-terms issues, such as land-clearing practices. The conference concluded with a general acknowledgment that the Indonesian fires were a "regional, indeed a global issue and should be dealt with accordingly, at the various levels" (all quotations in this paragraph from UNEP/OCHA 1998), even if the operational implications of this recognition remained unclear.

UN Secretary-General Kofi Annan assigned responsibility for coordinating the UN response to UNEP's Töpfer. In Geneva Töpfer made clear his view that logging and plantation companies were the primary culprits and urged the Indonesian government to identify the responsible parties publicly (BBC 1998d). He also pressed donors to come up with the $10 million needed to fund the fire-fighting plan. Reflecting the difficult balancing act he faced, Töpfer told the G-8 foreign ministers in May, "While it is my hope that the international community will do more to assist Indonesia and the whole region, I am confident that the national authorities will also take appropriate steps with regard to land use policies if we are to prevent the situation from recurring again and again" (UNEP 1998).

The other major institutional players, indeed the organizations perhaps better positioned to push for the policy reforms advocated by Töpfer, were the UN's financial institutions—the World Bank, the Asian Development Bank, and the International Monetary Fund (IMF). Given Indonesia's financial crisis, IMF support was crucial to the Suharto regime, and the IMF's $43 billion bailout package—announced in January 1998—had provisions designed to bring significant changes to Indonesia's forestry policies. Similar pressures were placed on Indonesia in April by the World Bank (Barber and Schweithelm 2000: 39–41).

AN ASSESSMENT

The Indonesian fires were transformed from a national problem into an issue of regional and global significance. Yet despite serious public concern and pressure for action, the reactions of officials at all three levels seemed hesitant, slow, and largely ineffective. To understand better why this was the case and to assess prospects for the future, it is important to look more closely at some of the factors operating on each level.

INDONESIAN POLICY

Among the central questions is why, given the history of fires in both Sumatra and Kalimantan, the Indonesian government had not taken more effective steps to prevent a recurrence or at least to prepare a more adequate response. Observers have offered several lines of explanation.

Most prominent is the argument that the government simply lacked the desire to regulate the dealings of companies allied with the Suharto regime. Many have been critical of the close ties that existed between Suharto and people like Mohammad "Bob" Hasan, a leader in the timber industry and head of the Indonesia Forestry Society (Gopalakrishnan 1997). Rather than control their behavior, relevant government bureaucracies allowed them to stay "above the law for essentially three decades" (Barber and Schweithelm 2000: 1).

Beyond the problem of corruption, those government officials who wanted to enforce the rules that did exist were faced with a generally unresponsive population, the product of a limited environmental consciousness and a general disrespect for government agencies. Open burning remained a well-entrenched practice, and people largely ignored warnings by government officials as early as June 1997 about the fire danger. Even after the fires had spread, Environment Ministry officials complained that the companies identified as responsible for starting them showed little fear of governmental retaliation (Williams and Baker 1997). Limited budgets also hampered enforcement efforts. Although some licenses were revoked and prosecutions begun, few companies were punished (Barber and Schweithelm 2000: 8–9).

In their discussion of the "politics of fire," Barber and Schweithelm (2000: 12–14) point to the opportunity the crisis presented for people like Environment Minister Sarwono to challenge entrenched agricultural practices. His voice magnified by the media attention surrounding the fires, Sarwono was able to identify the large plantation owners, not the small farmers, as the responsible parties and to raise resource policy questions generally removed from public discussion. With NGOs and the media playing an unusually active role, groups not traditionally influential in resource policy decisions were brought into the policy-making process, although their significance faded when the rains arrived.

Another factor affecting the Indonesian government's behavior was the economic crisis that, on one level, constrained its ability to mobilize firefighting resources. Moreover, governmental attention was focused on the immediate plight of people suddenly faced with rapidly escalating costs of basic goods while real wages were falling by 30 percent. The traditional response was to try to grow out of such economic difficulties, and it was the palm oil plantations and other agribusiness sectors of the Indonesian economy—whose operations might have been curtailed for environmental reasons—that offered the chief "engine to help pull Indonesia out of economic downturn" (Dauvergne 2000).

To the extent that government attitudes and policies have been responsible for the continuing fire problem, the fall of the Suharto regime would seem to offer hope for the future. In May 1998 Suharto was replaced by a transitional government headed by B. J. Habibie, and in October 1999 Abdurrahman Wahid was elected president by the Peoples Consultative Assembly and promised significant reforms. Political changes brought about since, and to some extent because of, the 1997 fires helped bring new perspectives to bear on timber and other resource-use policies, as academics and NGO representatives found themselves increasingly included in the policy-making process (Barber and Schweithelm 2000: 39–40; Cotton 1999: 345–346).

Still, as a broad-based government of "national unity" that included people from Suharto's regime, the extent of Wahid's ability to deliver on reform measures was soon tested. In July 2000, when fumes from Sumatran fires again crossed into Malaysia and Singapore, the Wahid government pledged to stop the operations of twelve palm oil plantations and to impose heavy fines on them. Once again, however, officials were forced to admit that limited funds would hinder enforcement of the new policy (McCawley 2000). In July 2001 President Wahid was ousted by the legislature. The government has issued new guidelines intended to encourage more responsible timber management practices, but as regional climatic conditions suggest the return of El Niño, the prospects of avoiding a return of the regional haze are not encouraging (Easen 2002). There is also continuing concern that efforts to respond to separatist violence since the end of Suharto's reign have only undermined the ability and to some extent the incentive of subsequent governments to enforce an even more enlightened policy in rural areas (Richardson 1999).

One change that is probably not reversible is Indonesia's acknowledgment that the fires are an international issue and a legitimate focus of regional and global attention. The 1997 fires ended any sense that Indonesia need not respond to transboundary concerns, even if it attempted to keep the discussion within the relatively friendly confines of ASEAN and focused on "emergency relief" rather than more intrusive policy issues. The Indonesian government now routinely tries to reassure its neighbors that it will take action when the threat of widespread fire appears.

To say that the fires have been internationalized is not to suggest that there are no limits as to how the international community might effectively involve itself in Indonesia's resource-use policies. Nationalist sentiments still run deep, recently inflamed by what some see as the overly intrusive role of the international community in responding to the situation in East Timor. Thus the way international financial institutions use their considerable power to affect Indonesian policy remains an important and potentially volatile issue (Barber and Schweithelm 2000: 40).

REGIONAL RESTRAINT

Why did Indonesia's immediate neighbors, both in their bilateral relations and in ASEAN, not do more to challenge directly a state whose territory was so clearly being used to their detriment? How was it possible to maintain what appeared, at least on the surface, to be normal relationships even as the smoke from the Indonesian fires covered the region and threatened to undermine the legitimacy of ASEAN itself (Cotton 1999: 347–351)?

There are two fairly straightforward lines of explanation. First, the emphasis within ASEAN on cooperation over confrontation reflects a conscious effort to avoid precisely the kind of divisive behavior asserting legal rights could provoke. The ASEAN way does exist (Tay 1999: 282–292) and has been hard to criticize given the organization's apparent success in controlling unwanted political discord and, at least until recently, in promoting economic growth. Second, Indonesia's dominant, some would suggest hegemonic role within the region made it a particularly difficult neighbor to challenge.

A less obvious reason has to do with the nature of the issue itself. First, Indonesia was not alone in the practices that had triggered the fires. Fire had routinely been used elsewhere in the region as a means of clearing land, including in some of the states most victimized by the Indonesian fires. Second, the smoke from the fires was just one of the sources of the haze covering the region; local industry and automobile exhaust were also important contributors. Early in the crisis the head of the Malaysian Centre for Environment, Technology, and Development said, "The Government has shown it is not serious about taking steps to protect the environment. The haze is basically an internal problem. We can't just blame it on the Indonesians" (quoted in William and Baker 1997). Third, states in the region shared a fear of the effect of the smoke on tourism and were anxious to avoid bad publicity. To bring a formal legal claim against Indonesia relating to what was an ongoing problem would likely have required that state attempt to heighten the sense of danger posed by the fires. This risked doing more damage to the claimant in a context in which the problem was likely to continue. Although that would not prevent a state from making a claim after the crisis was over, ASEAN's conciliatory presence may have undercut the ability—at least politically—to do so. Indonesia carefully thanked its neighbors for their understanding, creating an even more difficult environment in which to bring later claims. Finally, as Tay (1999: 286) suggested, one of the difficulties encountered in responding to the forest fire issue, especially in clarifying rules of legal liability, has been its narrowness. Developing a broader legal framework, one that might include other transboundary problems of particular concern to Indonesia—as was done on a more informal level in the 1995 Cooperation Plan on Transboundary Pollution—would likely enhance the prospects for a "legal" approach in subsequent disputes.

Nonetheless, Indonesia's neighbors are becoming more assertive. In 1999 Brunei threatened to sue Indonesia if the latter failed to control fires that could disrupt the Southeast Asian games it was hosting (Barber and Schweithelm 2000: 40). Environmental activists argued that Malaysia and

Singapore should take Indonesia to the International Court of Justice (Kriner 1999). In an interesting indication of the direction regional politics could turn if a more confrontational approach were adopted, Indonesia's Forestry and Plantations minister suggested that Singapore and Malaysia should not just "make noises" about the fires: "Singapore has been receiving very expensive oxygen from us, hasn't it? . . . Imagine, if we were to calculate how much oxygen has been going there. . . . This concerns a common interest, so don't just make demands" ("Forest Fires" 1999: 21). On a more positive note, the statement also acknowledged the ecological interconnection of the region in a way that would undercut any claims of Indonesia's right to use its resources without regard to their transboundary impact.

Tougher measures have also been adopted within ASEAN. In June 1999 the environment ministers formally adopted a "zero-burn" policy and agreed to promote that policy among plantation owners (ASEAN 1999a). They also "committed themselves" to enforce the rules strictly and to use fires in central Sumatra as a test case of the new policy. Although the commitment was embodied only in a joint statement, a new level of seriousness was evident. Haryono Suyono, the Indonesian head of a disaster and relief team in Jakarta, said Indonesia had heard "the firm message" that it needed to control the fires (Richardson 1999). At the Eighth Ministerial Meeting on Haze in August (ASEAN 1999b), the ministers further agreed to develop an ASEAN Legal Framework on Transboundary Haze Pollution.

For all this new assertiveness, the ASEAN way is far from dead. In July 2000, amid another round of Sumatran fires and facing an impending ASEAN meeting, a representative of the Indonesian Foreign Ministry expressed confidence that its neighbors would not blame Indonesia for the fires even as he acknowledged that Indonesia did not have a plan to extinguish them (Chalmers 2000). His confidence was justified; the final communiqué spoke about the issue only in general terms (Chalmers 2000). Even an article in the *Financial Times,* which spoke of the "sharp pressure" exerted on Indonesia by its neighbors in the summer of 2000 to control new fires, also quoted Malaysia's prime minister as openly denying the existence of the haze: "What haze? I don't see any haze" (McNulty and McCawley 2000: 3).

BROADER PERSPECTIVES

It might be tempting to view the problems encountered in the response to the Indonesian fires as largely an ASEAN phenomenon. The experience, however, raises questions that go beyond the regional context in which this dispute was set. Many of the concerns became evident in the way the broader global community responded to the fires.

Perhaps because of the lack of a better alternative, UNEP was chosen to be the focus of the intergovernmental response. Formed after the 1972

Stockholm Conference on the Human Environment, UNEP was neither designed to be nor has it been the global "watchdog" environmentalists in the early 1970s had hoped to see created (Springer 1988b: 49–50). Developing countries, suspicious of an environmentalist agenda on which their needs might be secondary, insisted that the new organization take a more balanced approach to the relationship between environmental and developmental values. The result has been a relatively weak organization in terms of its institutional powers and budget, an organization playing a catalytic rather than a regulatory role in attempting to influence state behavior. UNEP has been important in helping to integrate developing countries into the broader process of international environmental policy making (Springer 1988a: 22–27). By the time of the Indonesian fires, however, UNEP was not prepared to play a strong advocacy role and instead moved more naturally into its assigned position of coordinating international assistance. Unfortunately, reviews of the international aid effort suggest that it fell far short of expectations (Barber and Schweithelm 2000: 13–14). According to Tay (1999: 260) it had only "some palliative effect . . . [and] has proven fickle and headline-driven."

Organizations like the IMF and the World Bank have played a more assertive role in trying to steer Indonesian resource-use policy in environmentally sensitive directions. This new activism by the UN financial institutions may be based in part on their own sense of "complicity" in past Indonesian policies, such as the World Bank's support of Indonesia's transmigration program until 1986 ("Asia's Forest Disaster" 1997). It is certainly a response to long-standing criticism by environmental NGOs of the pro-growth bias they have allegedly demonstrated. In addition to the conditions imposed on Indonesia as a price for loan support, the World Bank went so far as to suspend a $400 million loan payment in 1998 because of the Indonesian government's failure to make promised forestry reforms (Dauvergne 2000). Although the "incentives" given are generally to be welcomed and are undoubtedly an important acknowledgment of the concerns of major donors, there is a danger of triggering a backlash should the pressures become too obvious or heavy-handed (Tay 1999: 291–293).

The almost complete failure, until recently, of any of the participants in the forest fire issue to refer explicitly to legal norms to explain or justify their positions is among the most interesting and potentially troubling aspects of the dispute. Unlike the Bhopal accident and the *Exxon Valdez* oil spill, where civil remedies were available to pollution victims, to date there has been no serious talk that national courts might be in a position to offer compensation to those outside Indonesia injured by the smoke, much less discussion of a possible role for international adjudicative bodies. It would be a mistake, however, to attribute this lack to the "primitive" state of Asian international environmental law. Tay (1999: 284) reminds us that after the Chernobyl nuclear and Sandoz chemical accidents, no international claims were made by affected states. Even in the litigious world of North America, home of the famous Trail Smelter arbitral decision, Canada and the United States assiduously avoid reference to legal rights and duties in their extensive bilateral relationship (Springer 1997: 385).

Still, in Tay's view the Indonesian fires "demonstrate many of international environmental law's inadequacies" (1999: 242). Given what seems to be the general sense that Indonesia "should" have done more to prevent the fires, control their effects, and (perhaps) make amends to those who were injured, what aspects of the law might be inadequate?

THE LIMITS OF INTERNATIONAL LAW

One way of approaching the issue is to ask whether clear legal standards actually existed that could have been used to challenge Indonesia's behavior. Treaties provided little direction. The 1985 ASEAN Convention on Conservation of Nature and Natural Resources had never come into force, and the 1995 ASEAN program on transboundary pollution was simply a nonbinding plan of action—one that focused almost exclusively on the development of national strategies and voluntary cooperation. International law also includes customary state practice, but its use here raises serious questions.

First, declarations like the Stockholm Declaration on the Human Environment owe their legal value less to the fact of their utterance than to the actual behavior they are presumed to represent or at least promote. As suggested by the Chernobyl and Sandoz examples, state practice in the area of transboundary pollution may be far less consistently protective of environmental values than the words of Principle 21 imply.

Second, perhaps the standards of traditional customary international law, notoriously vague in their content, were not clearly violated by Indonesia. The Trail Smelter case, in which Canada was found liable for damage done in the United States by emissions from a smelter in British Columbia, is often seen as the quintessential statement of the normative responsibility of the state to control environmentally damaging activities within its jurisdiction (Springer 1988b: 47–48). Here there were multiple sources and types of sources of pollution, some located in the territory of "victim" states. Showing the "clear and convincing evidence" required by the Tribunal to link specific damages to the fires could be a challenge, particularly since some of the injury would become evident only over time and might not be easily quantified. Moreover, a serious argument can be made that the Trail Smelter case never suggested that a state was strictly liable for all activities taking place in its territory, just that it must exercise "due diligence" in attempting to control them (Zemanek and Springer 1991: 191–196, 199–200).

A third problem is determining who, if anyone, has the right to speak out in a legal sense on behalf of global interests such as curbing global climate change and preventing the loss of biodiversity. There has been much discussion of the need to develop in international law the concept of an "actio popularis" that would permit a state or some other international actor to represent shared environmental interests even if the claimant could not show specific damage being done to it (Springer 1983: 158–159). We are still far, however, from seeing such a principle firmly established in law, and states are well aware of the sensitive issues of sovereignty raised when "outsiders" challenge the way a state regulates resources in its territory.

A final challenge to the use of customary law to attack Indonesia is that concepts like "good neighborliness" were developed largely by European and North America states and are often less generally binding standards of law than expressions of the practice of like-minded, usually developed countries. As such, they are arguably replaceable in other contexts by the free choice of participating states—for instance, states more interested in promoting an alternative "ASEAN way" of conducting relations.

Put in these terms, one could see the reaction to the Indonesian fires as representing not a failure to apply or a refutation of existing international environmental law but as "practice" suggesting what the content of that law really is, at least from the perspective of the states most directly involved. Indonesia made clear its regret that the fires were happening and said it was doing all within its power (exercising "due diligence?") both to put them out and to prevent a recurrence. The reaction by Indonesia's neighbors suggests that they acknowledged Indonesia's limited ability to do more, especially given the trying economic conditions, and, if anything, that they shared a responsibility to respond to a common threat to the region. Collecting "damages" was less the issue than stopping existing and preventing future fires; the response was not reactive and punitive but reflected a determination to create a context for more effective preventive action. To the extent this includes developing new legal instruments, like the proposed ASEAN Legal Framework on Transboundary Haze Pollution, the approach may be similar to that taken in Europe after the Chernobyl accident, when emphasis was placed on negotiating new agreements governing transboundary warning and mutual assistance in case of future accidents.

More broadly, the Indonesian fires may reinforce a general shift, evident in other areas of international environmental law, away from using traditional concepts of state responsibility to punish states after the fact for violations of law. More emphasis has been placed on establishing rules governing what a state does before pollution occurs and the steps it subsequently takes to warn potential victims and mitigate the damage (Springer 1983: 141–152). Within this damage-prevention framework, where the focus is on processes to promote dialogue and cooperation, the content of state obligations is also undergoing serious rethinking. The concept of "common but differentiated responsibilities," which has been integrated into important agreements responding to ozone depletion and global climate change, challenges the traditional sense of states being bound to essentially equal standards. It provides substantial room, especially when applied as part of customary international law (rather than in a treaty-based regime where mechanisms may exist for interpreting and applying these differential standards fairly), for states to claim "special circumstances" that should be used either to define the content of the rules they are expected to follow or at least to reduce the impact of those rules on them. Many aspects of Indonesia's explanation of its behavior during the fires seem consistent with this approach. Had a formal claim for damages been made, one could imagine an Indonesian response that the extent of its liability should be determined with an eye to the burden compensation would impose or that the liability should be channeled to private parties.

The prevention approach may not lend itself easily to formal adjudication, but supporting its presumed wisdom are the many procedural challenges associated with actually bringing a more traditional international claim for after-the-fact damages (Springer 1983: 136–140, 156–161). In the Indonesian situation recourse to a body like the International Court of Justice would have been unlikely, and the ASEAN system does not encourage formal third-party dispute settlement.

This line of argument may to some extent take Indonesia and its neighbors off the hook for their reactions to the fires. It leaves unanswered (and unanswerable here), however, the crucial question of whether these new directions provide an appropriate legal foundation to regulate transboundary pollution. At least in the context of Southeast Asia, most observers would say it does not, a view seemingly acknowledged by current attempts to agree on a new legal framework for controlling haze. Although general agreement seems to exist on the need for legal reform, how this should be done is less clear. Whereas Tay questions the value of "strict legal liabilities and legalistic confrontation" (1999: 298–299), others argue that clearer normative standards and stronger institutional structures are needed (Boer 1999: 1534). In any case, the negotiations at least recognize that the legal framework in which the problem is placed does matter.

CONCLUSION

It is difficult not to be discouraged by the experience of the Indonesian fires, both the fact that they occurred and the nature of the response.

Indonesia allowed open burning to take place under very dangerous conditions after a history of damaging fires in the region, and the government's inability to get the fires under control resulted in catastrophic damage. Indonesia's neighbors, as well as regional and global institutions, responded cautiously and in ways suggesting little sense that legal issues were raised by Indonesia's behavior, that Indonesia was obligated to do more. No dramatic changes have been made since the fires; indeed, the fact that they have not recurred is probably more a result of global climate patterns than of any human or institutional intervention. Still, one can find some signs of hope even in this difficult experience and with them perhaps some lessons for the future.

First, the fires, in one sense an international issue from the moment significant levels of smoke crossed international borders, helped internationalize the Indonesian land-use policies that made them possible. Although not without qualifications and some resentment, Indonesia has effectively acknowledged the legitimacy of international concern about at least some elements of what would otherwise be the sovereign control the country exercises over resources located on its territory. ASEAN and its members have also felt pressure to take on a more assertive role. Although there is no evidence of major systemic transformation, the organization is talking more directly about potentially intrusive issues than it has in the past and is negotiating an agreement that could strengthen the legal context in which these issues are addressed. UNEP has moved from being a fairly distant observer of regional policies to a participant in those negotiations (UNEP 2001), and the IMF and World Bank stand poised potentially to provide both "carrots" and "sticks" that may be needed to cause Indonesia's practices to change. All of this is in keeping with a first lesson of the fires—namely, that governments and intergovernmental organizations, ASEAN in particular, gained very little by failing to confront Indonesia about its duty to take action to control the factors responsible for the fires. Early and direct acknowledgment of an environmental problem that has such clear transboundary implications is important if it is to be raised to the level of priority it deserves on crowded international agendas.

Second, the growing impact of the widely heralded "global civil society" seemed evident in this process. International NGOs, led by the WWF, were instrumental in informing people about the extent of the dangers posed by the fires and in putting pressure on governments on all levels to take the problem more seriously. Academics and local interest groups played an increasingly important part within Indonesia and neighboring states and moved closer to policy-making circles than they had been before, particularly in Indonesia. NGOs on all levels were more ready to talk in terms of legal duties than were governments, for which issues of reciprocity might arise in the future. In June 1998 Simon Tay, a professor at Singapore University, chaired an International Policy Dialogue on the Southeast Asian Fires, which attracted representatives from NGOs and academic institutions from across the region and beyond. Tay's report on the meeting put particular emphasis on the legal dimensions of the reform process participants would like to see undertaken (1999: 300–305). A second lesson is that more needs to be done, both in Indonesia and within ASEAN, to strengthen local NGOs and provide them with greater access to the arenas in which resource policy is made, given their critical role as a voice for environmental interests traditionally underrepresented in East Asia.

Third, the crisis suggested the increasing significance of private business, not just as the source of environmentally destructive behavior but also as a possible ally for environmentalists. Efforts to hide the haze problem were notably unsuccessful, and the tourism industry became an active force lobbying for more effective government action (TravelAsia 1997). Beyond this, claims by timber and palm oil plantation owners that they were among the fires' major victims are in fact true. As Barber and Schweithelm suggest (2000: 41), getting these corporate players behind reform efforts is a vital step. For them, sustainable development can and should be seen not as vague political rhetoric but as an operational and profitable policy goal. Here the lesson is that government has an important responsibility to devise means to encourage a constructive dialogue between environmentalists and businesses whose enlightened self-interest often seems to coincide with environmental goals.

Ultimately, preventing a recurrence of the Indonesian fires will require tough national measures, which internationalizing or "legalizing" the issue cannot guarantee. Indeed done in the wrong way, this could promote a defensive, confrontational struggle that would only delay needed reforms. To say this is not to say that international law has no place in the process or that legal reform cannot help encourage reluctant governments to confront unpleasant responsibilities. It simply means the challenge is to develop the right law and constructive means to invoke it.

Fortunately, forces are at work in Southeast Asia that may help promote that reform. A regional framework in which national land-use issues can be discussed without threatening state sovereignty, a growing and increasingly involved environmental community, and greater corporate awareness of the benefits of environmentally sensitive business practices all provide hope for the future development of international environmental law and cooperation in the region.

REFERENCES

Agence France-Presse. 1997. "Indonesia Counts the Cost of Forest Fires" (6 October) <http://www.forests.org/archive/indomalay/indfireb.htm>.

"Asia's Forest Disaster." 1997. *New York Times* (27 September) <http://www/forests.org/archive/indomalay/indfireb.htm>.

Association of Southeast Asian Nations (ASEAN). 1985. "ASEAN Agreement on Conservation of Nature and Natural Resources" (9 July) <http://sedac.ciesin.org/pidb/texts/asean.natural.resources.1985.html>.

————. 1995a. "ASEAN Cooperation Plan on Transboundary Pollution" (17 June) <http://www.asean.or.id/function/env/plan.htm>.

————. 1995b. Joint Press Release. Sixth Meeting of the ASEAN Senior Officials on the Environment, Bali, Indonesia (20–22 September) <http://www.asean.or.id/function/pr-env.htm>.

————. 1997a. Joint Press Statement. The Seventh ASEAN Ministerial Meeting on the Environment, Jakarta, Indonesia (16–18 September) <http://www/asean.or.id/function.prenv7.htm>.

————. 1997b. Joint Press Statement. ASEAN Ministerial Meeting on Haze, Singapore (22–23 December) <http://www/asean.or.id/function/prhaze1.htm>.

————. 1998a. Joint Press Statement. ASEAN Ministerial Meeting on Haze, Kutching, Sarawak (25 February) <http://www/asean.or.id/function/prhaze2.htm>.

————. 1998b. Joint Press Statement. Third ASEAN Ministerial Meeting on Haze, Brunei Darussalam (4 April) <http://www/asean.or.id/function/prhaze3.htm>.

————. 1998c. Joint Press Statement. Fourth ASEAN Ministerial Meeting on Haze, Singapore (19 June) <http://www/asean.or.id/function/prhaze4.htm>.

————. 1999a. Joint Press Statement. Sixth ASEAN Ministerial Meeting on Haze, Brunei Darussalem (16 April) <http://www.asean.or.id/function/prhaze6.htm>.

————. 1999b. Joint Press Statement. Eighth ASEAN Ministerial Meeting on Haze, Singapore (26 August) <http://www.asean.org.id/function/prhaze8.htm>.

Barber, Charles V., and James Schweithelm. 2000. "Trial by Fire: Forest Fires and Forestry Policy in Indonesia's Era of Crisis and Reform." Washington, DC: World Resources Institute <http:www.ruf.uni-freiburg.de/fireglobe/se_asia/projects/wri_1.htm>.

Boer, Ben. 1999. "The Rise of Environmental Law in the Asian Region." *University of Richmond Law Review* 32: 1503–1553.

British Broadcasting System (BBC). 1998a. "Malaysia Asks Indonesia to Stop Spread of Jungle Fires" (15 February) <http://news.1.this.bbc.co.uk/hi/english/world/asia-pacific/newsid_56000/56883.stm>.

————. 1998b. "Indonesia, Malaysia Urged to Tackle New Haze Threat." (25 February) <http://news1.this.bbc.co.uk/low/english/world/asia-pacific/newsid_59000/59907.stm>.

————. 1998c. "Fires 'Low Priority' for Indonesian Government" (20 April) <http://news1.this.bbc.co.uk/low/english/special_report/1998/04/98/hze_98/newsid_80000/80953.stm>.

————. 1998d. "UN Warns of Further Serious Indonesian Fires" (21 April) <http://news6.thdo.bbc.co.uk/hi/english/asia_pacific/newsid_81000/81540.stm>.

Cable News Network (CNN). 1997. "Indonesia Tries to Douse Political Fires as Smog Lingers" (7 October) <http://www.cnn.com/WORLD/9710/07/indonesia/>.

Chalmers, Patrick. 2000. "Sumatra Blazes Too Hot to Handle for ASEAN." *Reuters* (25 July) <http://www.enn.com/news/wire-stories/2000/07/07252000/reu_smog_15046.asp?site=mail>.

Cotton, James. 1999. "The >Haze' Over Southeast Asia: Challenging the Asean Mode of Regional Engagement." *Pacific Affairs* 72: 331–351.

Dauvergne, Peter. 2000. "Globalisation, Asia's 1997 Financial Crisis and Environmental Change." Paper presented at the Annual Meeting of the International Studies Association, Los Angeles, California, 14–18 March <https:wwwc.cc.columbia.edu/sec/dlc/ciao/isa/dap01/dap01.html>.

Disaster Relief. 1997. "Haze Predicted to Affect Asia for Years." *New Stories* (6 October) <http://www.disasterrelief.org/Disasters/971001haze/>.

Easen, N. 2002. "Playing With Fire: Indonesia's Age-Old Battle" (4 January) <http://www.cnn.com/2002/WORLD/aisapcf/southeast/01/04/indonesia.fires/index.html>.

Economy and Environment Program for Southeast Asia (EEPSEA) and Worldwide Fund for Nature (WWF). 1999. "The Indonesia Fires and Haze of 1997: The Economic Toll" <http://www.eepesea.org/publications/research1.ACF6s.html>.

"Forest Fires: Help, Don't Make Noise." 1999. *Straits Times* [Singapore] (25 August) <http://www.icsea.or.id/sea-span/0399/TPO902LL.htm>.

Gallon, Gary T. 1997. "Indonesian Fires One of the Worst Global Environmental Disasters." *Gallon Environmental Letter* 1, 14 (14 October) <http:csf.colorado.edu/bioregional/oct97/0048.html>.

Gopalankrishnan, Raju. 1997. "Indonesian Timber King Denies Responsibility for Fires." *Reuters* (3 October) <http://www.forests.org/archive/indomalay/indfireb.htm>.

Head, Jonathan. 1997. "Environment Ministers Agree Concerted Action to Prevent Forest Fires." BBC News (23 December) <http://news1.this.bbc.co.uk/hi/english/despatches/newsid_42000/42015.stm>.

Howard, Stephen. 1998. "The Burning Season." *World Today* (July) <https://wwwc.cc.columbia.edu/sec/dlc/ciao/olj/wt/wt_98howard.html>.

"Indonesian Fires No Accident, Singapore Paper Says." 1997. *Reuters* (2 October) <http://www.forests.org/archive/indomalay/indfireb.htm>.

Kriner, Stephanie. 1999. "Humans Turn Indonesian Fires Into Annual Disaster." *Disaster Relief* (23 August) <http://www.disasterrelief.org/Disasters/990810indonesiafires/>.

Kristoff, Nicholas D. 1997. "Asian Pollution Is Widening Its Deadly Reach." *New York Times* (29 November): A7.

McCawley, Tom. 2000. "Indonesia Gets Tough on Fires." *Financial Times* (27 July): 8.

McNulty, Sheila, and Tom McCawley. 2000. "Autonomy Cases Haze Over Indonesia's Fires." *Financial Times* (14 August): 3.

Montes, Manuel F. 1997. "Growing Pains: ASEAN's Economic and Political Challenges: The Economic Miracle in a Haze." *Asia Society* (December) <https:wwwc.cc.columbia.edu/sec/dlc/ciao/wps/mom03/mom03b.html>.

Mydans, Seth. 1997a. "Southeast Asia Chokes as Indonesian Forests Burn." *Mew York Times* (25 September): A14.

———. 1997b. "Its Mood Dark as the Haze, Southeast Asia Aches." *New York Times* (26 October): 3.

Naidu, G.V.C. 1998. "The Manila ASEAN Meetings and India." *Strategic Analysis* 22, 8 (November) <https:wwwc.cc.columbia.edu/sec/dlc/ciao/olj/sa/sa_98nag)1.html#txt10>.

Richardson, Michael. 1999. "Fear of Fires Rekindles as Jakarta Is Distracted: Asian Neighbors Doubt Indonesia Can Address Environmental Needs." *International Herald Tribune* (22 June) <http://forests.org/recent/1999/indosmog.htm>.

Springer, Allen L. 1983. *The International Law of Pollution: Protecting the Global Environment in a World of Sovereign States.* Westport, Conn.: Greenwood.

———. 1988a. "International Aspects of Pollution Control." In J. Kormondy, ed., *The International Handbook of Pollution Control.* Westport, Conn.: Greenwood.

———. 1988b. "United States Environmental Policy and International Law: Stockholm Principle 21 Revisited." In J. Carroll, ed., *International Environmental Diplomacy: The Management and Resolution of Transfrontier Environmental Problems.* Cambridge: Cambridge University Press.

———. 1997. "The Pacific Salmon Controversy: Law, Diplomacy, Equity and Fish." *American Review of Canadian Studies* 27: 385–409.

Tay, Simon S.C. 1998. "South East Asian Forest Fires: Haze Over ASEAN and International Environmental Law." *Review of European Community and International Environmental Law* 7: 202–205.

———. 1999. "Southeast Asian Fires: The Challenge for International Environmental Law and Sustainable Development." *Georgetown International Environmental Law Review* 11: 241–305.

TravelAsia. 1997. "Haze Is Poignant Reminder for Regional Environmental Action" (21 November) <http:/www/travel-asi.com/11_21_97/stories.feed.htm>.

United Nations Environment Program (UNEP). 1997. "New Internet Resource on Indonesia Forest Fires Available." *UNEP Information Note* [Nairobi] (28 October).

———. 1998. "Environmental Crisis in South East Asia Is Far From Over." *UNEP Information Note* [Nairobi] (14 May).

———. 2001. "Talks on South-East Asian Haze Open in Malaysia." UNEP News Release ROAP/01/02 (20 March) <http://www/enn.com/direct/display-release.asp?id=3743>.

UNEP and United Nations Office for the Coordination of Humanitarian Affairs (OCHA). 1998. "Meetings on the Indonesian Fires" (20–21 April). *Relief Web* <http://www.uni_freiburg.de/fireglobe/programmes/un/unep_ocha/unep_och_ri.htm>.

Williams, Louise, and Mark Baker. 1997. "The Threatened Planet—South Asia's Year of Reckoning." *Sydney Morning Herald* (6 October) <http://www.forests.org/archive/indomalay/indfireb.htm>.

World Wildlife Fund (WWF). 1997a. "Indonesian Fires: WWF Calls for Preventive Action." WWF Press Release (25 September) <http://www.panda.org/news/press/news_151.htm>.

———. 1997b. "Indonesia Fires: 30 Orangutans Dead, Other Species Threatened." WWF Press Release (3 October) <http:www.panda.org/news/press/news_155.htm>.

Zemanek, Karl, and Allen L. Springer. 1991. "State Responsibility and Liability." In H. P. Neuhold, W. Lang, and K. Zemanek, eds., *Environmental Protection and International Law.* Dordrecht: Martinus, Nijhoff.

About the Editor

Paul G. Harris is an associate professor of politics at Lingnan University, Hong Kong. He also holds an appointment as a senior lecturer in international relations at London Metropolitan University. He is director of the Project on Environmental Change and Foreign Policy; an associate fellow at the Oxford Centre for the Environment, Ethics and Society at Mansfield College, Oxford University; an honorary research fellow at the Centre of Urban Planning and Environmental Management at the University of Hong Kong; and a research fellow at the Centre for Asian Pacific Studies and the Centre for Public Policy Studies at Lingnan University. Dr. Harris's books include *International Equity and Global Environmental Politics* (Ashgate Press), *The Environment, International Relations, and U.S. Foreign Policy* (Georgetown University Press), and *Climate Change and American Foreign Policy* (St. Martin's Press). He has written numerous journal articles and papers on global environmental politics, American foreign policy, and international ethics.

OTHER BOOKS FROM THE PROJECT
ON ENVIRONMENTAL CHANGE AND FOREIGN POLICY

Confronting Environmental Change: Eco-Politics and Foreign Policy in East and Southeast Asia (Earthscan, forthcoming)

Global Warming and East Asia: The Domestic and International Politics of Climate Change (Routledge, forthcoming)

International Equity and Global Environmental Politics: Power and Principles in U.S. Foreign Policy (Ashgate Press, 2001)

The Environment, International Relations, and U.S. Foreign Policy (Georgetown University Press, 2001)

Climate Change and American Foreign Policy (St. Martin's Press, 2000)

Index